Thinking Security

Thinking Security
Stopping Next Year's Hackers

Steven M. Bellovin

✦Addison-Wesley

New York • Boston • Indiannopolis • San Francisco
Toronto • Montreal • London • Munich • Paris • Madrid
Capetown • Sydney • Tokyo • Singapore • Mexico City

Many of the designations used by manufacturers and sellers to distinguish their products are claimed as trademarks. Where those designations appear in this book, and the publisher was aware of a trademark claim, the designations have been printed with initial capital letters or in all capitals.

A complete list of sources and credits appears on pages 379–380.

The author and publisher have taken care in the preparation of this book, but make no expressed or implied warranty of any kind and assume no responsibility for errors or omissions. No liability is assumed for incidental or consequential damages in connection with or arising out of the use of the information or programs contained herein.

For information about buying this title in bulk quantities, or for special sales opportunities (which may include electronic versions; custom cover designs; and content particular to your business, training goals, marketing focus, or branding interests), please contact our corporate sales department at corpsales@pearsoned.com or (800) 382-3419.

For government sales inquiries, please contact governmentsales@pearsoned.com.

For questions about sales outside the United States, please contact international@pearsoned.com.

Visit us on the Web: informit.com/aw

Library of Congress Cataloging-in-Publication Data
Bellovin, Steven M., author.
 Thinking security : stopping next year's hackers / Steven M. Bellovin.
    pages   cm
Includes bibliographical references and index.
ISBN 978-0-13-427754-7 (hardcover : alk. paper)
1. Computer networks—Security measures. 2. Computer security. I. Title.
TK5105.59.B45154 2016
658.4'78—dc23
                                        2015030719

ISBN-13: 978-0-13-427754-7
ISBN-10: 0-13-427754-6

Text printed in the United States on recycled paper at RR Donnelley in Crawfordsville, Indiana.
First printing, November 2015

To Diane, for many reasons and then some,
and to Rebecca and Daniel who asked me not
to write another book but no longer live at
home and hence don't get a veto.

Contents

Preface

Most computer security books tell you what to do and what not to do. This one tells you why.

The list of security dos and don'ts is long: run antivirus software, get a firewall, lock everything down, follow extensive checklists, encrypt everything in sight, watch everything that goes on in your network, (especially) bring in over-priced consultants, and so on. The results are dismaying: companies are spending a great deal on security, but we read of massive computer-related attacks. Clearly, something is wrong.

The root of the problem is twofold: we're protecting (and spending money on protecting) the wrong things, and we're hurting productivity in the process. Unlike automobile locks, which increase a car's functionality by enabling you to park in bad neighborhoods, computer security tends to stop a user from doing something rather than enabling them to go into bad neighborhoods safely. People—read that as "employees"—*want* to be productive; when security measures get in their way, guess what's going to suffer? That's right: security.

The solution, though of course easier said than done, is similarly twofold: protect the right things, and make it easy for employees to do the right thing. That requires more than checklists; it requires thought about the actual threats and technology. That's what this book is about: how to think about security.

Protecting the Right Things

Security starts by knowing what you're protecting and against whom. A corollary to this is that any security advice that doesn't start with those two questions is wrong: you'll spend too much effort on the wrong things. If you're protecting national security secrets against foreign intelligence agencies, you probably need every defense ever invented and some that haven't been invented yet. You also need defenses against "the three Bs": burglary, bribery, and blackmail.

Many of us don't have spies as our enemies (though news reports suggest that that may be changing [Barrett 2015]). The typical attacker today is motivated by money; the question you have to ask yourself is how an attacker can monetize your computers and networks. If you work for a bank, the answer is pretty obvious; banks are, to quote the famous line, "where the money is." But any random computer can help the bad guys steal from the rest of us, so we can't let our guard down. These attacks, though, will be often opportunistic rather than targeted. Even then, there are different gradations of risk.

There's a corollary to this: defense is also about money. It makes no sense to spend more money to protect an asset than you have at risk. There's a saying that bears re-membering [Schiffman 2007]: "Amateurs worry about algorithms; pros worry about eco-nomics." Your goal is not to make a system penetration *impossible*; rather, it's to make it *too expensive* for your enemies, while not spending too much yourself.

Let's look at passwords as a typical example. We've been told for more than 30 years that weak passwords are a bad idea [Morris and Thompson 1979]. It's absolutely true; break-ins caused by poor password selection are very real. We're also told never to write down a password. However, the world has changed in many ways since 1979.

Suppose I pick a really strong password. Well, I'm not picking just one really strong password; I'm picking many different ones, for all the different web sites I have to log in to. There's no way I can remember all of them; I'm certain to forget a few, so I'll have to resort to a password recovery mechanism. And what is that? For many web sites, they'll just email me the password. The security of my account, then, depends on the security of my email, right? Not quite—there's more.

For many people, the real threat isn't a password guesser, it's a keystroke logger. That is, someone or something has surreptitiously installed some malware—some malicious software—on their computers; this software records all of their keystrokes, especially including passwords. Even if you have a very strong password that you have remembered, if you ever actually type it your account will be compromised [D. Florêncio, Herley, and Coskun 2007]. By contrast, if your password is emailed to you via a recovery mechanism and you use copy-and-paste to enter it, you never type it and you're *safer*. And your email account? Many people have their email passwords stored by their mailers; those are never typed, either. But if they are typed, all of the password-strength mechanisms for the original web site are useless, because this stolen email password will let the bad guys recover it.

Password security, then, is a far more complex problem than simplistic checklists would have us believe. You have to have good passwords, but you have to protect them in the right way against the right threats. There is no perfect answer. Making the best choice requires understanding the interactions, the trade-offs, and the threats. In other words, a checklist will not suffice; you have to understand *why* to do things.

Doing the Right Thing

Once upon a time, back in the days of dial-up access, there was a company in Silicon Valley that worried about security. They were worried about "war-dialers"—hackers who dial all of the phone numbers in an exchange, looking for a modem—and password-guessing attacks. So they did the obvious: they banned modems.

The problem with the ban was that it conflicted with the prevailing culture in Silicon Valley, where many of the best developers are fond of working at all hours while garbed in their pajamas or less. The developers did the obvious: they went to their local neighborhood computer store, bought a modem for $29.95, and hooked it to their office phone lines when they left for the day. Corporate security caught on soon enough, though, and countered by installing a digital phone system, one for which modems were not readily available. Getting a regular analog phone line required a signature from the vice president in charge of signatures. All looked good, but the security folks couldn't ban that other indispensable adjunct to modern corporate life: the fax machine. Suddenly, a lot of engineers needed fax lines in their offices; those requests, of course, were approved. To be sure, those $29.95 modems *could* send and receive faxes; it wasn't 100% bogus.

Everyone was happy—security was happy because they knew there were no dial-in lines, and the engineers were happy because they could log in from their hot tubs. All went well, until a disgruntled former employee started breaking in via these poorly protected, unofficial modems. And security was mystified, because they *knew* there were no modems.

Imagine, instead, if there were a centrally managed modem pool, with proper authentication and a login list linked to the personnel department's database. It would be secure enough and it would foster productivity without tempting people to evade the rules.

Security: Not Too Big, Not Too Small, Just Right

These two scenarios have a lot in common. Most importantly, they show that security decisions cannot be made in a vacuum. There's a large human element to worry about; security solutions that are not matched to people's behavior, good and bad, will fail.

Another point of similarity is that the defenses are often poorly matched to the actual threats. Strong passwords don't protect against keystroke loggers; nevertheless, countless users are annoyed by the necessity of complying with such rules. Worse yet, they have to comply with many sets of rules, all subtly different. Strong passwords are more easily forgotten, thus creating a reliance on password-recovery schemes; these are generally much weaker than the primary authentication scheme, as Sarah Palin learned when her email account was hacked [Zetter 2010]. The site she used went to great trouble to develop the recovery code, to collect and store the data, and to prompt for the questions. In a strong sense, they had to do that; people *will* forget passwords—but was the real flaw reliance on strong passwords in the first place?

Similarly, the ban on modems was intended to keep out war-dialers. They ignored the disgruntled insider attack, while at the same time they cost themselves productivity. They also suffered the more subtle problems of buying too many modems at retail prices, and they probably paid for too many extra phone lines.

Sometime in the next few years, your boss will read about the new Herkawat attack, and about how some Kushghab.com software will prevent it. Should you buy their product? How will you decide? Those, I hope, are the sorts of questions this book will help you answer, even for attacks and product names that don't come from a random password generator.[1]

A Guide to the Perplexed

This book is not an introductory security text. Think of it as a graduate course, one aimed especially at system administrators, IT managers, chief security officers, and system architects. I assume that you know what firewalls are, and what the difference is between symmetric and public key cryptography. You've probably seen the usual checklists, perhaps achieved a (checklist-based) security certification, and obeyed most (but not all) of their prescriptions. I won't tell you how to avoid buffer overflows, cross-site scripting, and SQL injection attacks; there are other books that do that. Rather, my goal is to teach you how to think about the implications of security decisions, and how to design an architecture that will deal with the consequences of failures. I don't know what the Internet will be like or what the popular services or devices will be 10 years hence; I'm quite certain that there will be some very surprising new ones, ones that haven't even reached the garage or dorm room tinkering stage yet. How will you protect yourself, from them or with them? Checklists are for when people know the right answers, but sometimes, none have been developed yet.

Part I of this book is about mindware: how to think about the subject. Of necessity, it includes a discussion of likely enemies. Part II discusses the basic technologies of interest, not just security technologies like firewalls, but also the special properties (or lack thereof) of wireless communications.

In Part III, I discuss putting it together. How do you build and operate real systems? We're living in an imperfect world; we need to solve our problems *now*.

Finally, in Part IV, I demonstrate these principles with a few case studies and offer some very vague thoughts about the future of the field.

---

1. "APG (Automated Password Generator)," http://www.adel.nursat.kz/apg/.

A Note on Link Rot

George R.R. Martin wrote [G. R. R. Martin 2000], "Valar morghulis... all men must die." The same seems to be true of links to web pages. I checked every URL in this book in August 2015—but by the time you read these words, some of the links will no longer work. Even the US Supreme Court suffers from this problem [Zittrain, Albert, and Lessig 2014]. Right now, there are no great solutions. The Wayback Machine (https://www.archive.org) is probably your best hope.

Acknowledgments

I obviously did not invent the science of computer security, nor am I self-taught. I owe a great debt to three giants from whom I learned a great deal: Fred Grampp of Bell Labs, Bob Morris of the Labs and the NSA's National Computer Security Center, and Fred Brooks of the University of North Carolina at Chapel Hill. Grampp's lessons on passwords, log files, and social engineering were very valuable. Morris taught me to think about utility when he asked someone presenting a design for a secure OS, "How do you do backup and restore?" The speaker had no answer; was his system too secure? Morris also taught me about the role of economics when evaluating security. Brooks taught me how to think about software *systems* and made me painfully aware of the problem of buggy code.

I owe many profound thanks to the many people I imposed upon when writing this book. In alphabetical order, they include (but of course are not limited to) Randy Bush, Bill Cheswick, Richard Clayton, Greg Conti, Simson Garfinkel, Levi Gundert, Paul Hoffman, Russ Housley, Maritza Johnson, Brian Kernighan, Angelos Keromytis, Brian Krebs, Bala Krishnamurthy, Susan Landau, Fabian Monrose, Kathleen Moriarty, Kevin Poulsen, Avi Rubin, Adam Shostack, Sal Stolfo, Rob Thomas, Win Treese, Paul van Oorschot, and of course all of the people from Addison-Wesley with whom I have worked on this book: John Fuller, Stephanie Geels, Julie Nahil, Melissa Panagos, Mark Taub, John Wait, and more. Errors, of course, are mine.

—Steve Bellovin
https://www.cs.columbia.edu/~smb

Part I
Defining the Problem

Chapter 1

Introduction

"Who are *you*?" said the Caterpillar.

This was not an encouraging opening for a conversation. Alice replied, rather shyly, "I hardly know, sir, just at present—at least I know who I *was* when I got up this morning, but I think I must have been changed several times since then."

"What do you mean by that?" said the Caterpillar sternly. "Explain yourself!"

"I can't explain *myself*, I'm afraid, sir," said Alice, "because I'm not myself, you see."

"I don't see," said the Caterpillar.

"I'm afraid I can't put it more clearly," Alice replied very politely, "for I can't understand it myself to begin with; and being so many different sizes in a day is very confusing."

"It isn't," said the Caterpillar.

"Well, perhaps you haven't found it so yet," said Alice....

> *Through the Looking-Glass, and What Alice Found There*
> —LEWIS CARROLL

1.1 Changes

One of the most visible aspects of the computer industry is how rapidly things change. Four aspects of the change rate are of interest here: performance improvements (obviously, today's computers are much faster); capability improvements (we can do things today that we couldn't do even a few years ago); price; and environment (because people and companies around us do more, we can interact with them electronically). All of these affect security.

Recently, I received a check in the mail and deposited it by taking a picture of it with my phone. Think of the technical security challenges the bank had to deal with to make that possible:

- They have to have very high confidence that the right person is connecting to the account.

- This server application has to be very robust against all sorts of attacks; it can, after all, touch live bank accounts. In particular, it can add money to an account, based on user input; quite conceivably, their previous online application *deliberately* couldn't do that, as a security measure.

- However—the deposit is conditional, based in part on the image of the check being examined, by a human or by software, to verify the amount. In other words, some sensitive part of their system has to process an enemy-supplied image file.

- They have to allow the upload of large image files, with the consequent need for bandwidth, disk space, and more.

- My phone's operating system has to be secure enough that rogue phone apps can't spy on or modify the banking transactions.

- All traffic has to be encrypted.

- The phone has to be assured of connecting to the proper destination.

- There needs to be a proper audit trail for all transactions.

- Everything must work seamlessly with the "traditional" web application (itself not more than 15 years old, and probably a lot less), human tellers, and the legacy back-end systems that may have originally been written in COBOL and entered on punch cards for some giant mainframe, but now probably runs on a mainframe emulator on the CTO's tablet.

- Given all of these other changes, the entire architecture's security characteristics should be revisited.

Obviously, my bank and many other banks have made the necessary changes; the application works. The system architects figured out what had to be done; the security folks, the programmers, the network engineers, and everyone else made the necessary changes.

The interesting question is what the internal debates looked like. Did a security person say, "No, you can't do that; our back-end process isn't robust enough to accept online deposits"? Did the user experience group have to fight with the security group about authentication for account setup? Did the lawyers want to know how well fraudulent transactions could be traced to a particular phone or physical location? Did the head of the security group still try to say, "No, you can't do it; it's just too risky"?

Sometimes, "no" is indeed the right answer. As noted, though, capabilities and environments change. The worst mistake one can make in the computer business is to blithely give yesterday's answer to today's question. The second worst mistake, of course, is rejecting yesterday's answer without thinking about it. The technical and economic constraints may be the same; alternately, the same answer may be correct for an entirely different reason. The challenge is performing the analysis correctly.

1.2 Adapting to Change

There are many ways to deal with change and its likelihood. You can leave enough hooks to handle all possible future contingencies; you can reject changes until you're dragged into the future, kicking and screaming (or go out of business); you can embrace all changes, willy-nilly—or you can stop to do the sober, careful analysis that the problem demands.

Planning for all contingencies is the simplest and most common option. After all, everyone who has been in the business more than a few years *knows* that change will come, and will come in unpredictable ways. There are a number of problems with this approach. For one thing, it's ugly and produces ugly systems. Jon Postel said it well [Comerford 1998]:

> It's perfectly appropriate to be upset. I thought of it in a slightly different way—like a space that we were exploring and, in the early days, we figured out this consistent path through the space: IP, TCP, and so on. What's been happening over the last few years is that the IETF is filling the rest of the space with every alternative approach, not necessarily any better. Every possible alternative is now being written down. And it's not useful.

Planning for everything also produces complex and bloated systems, and while memory and CPU are not critical resources these days, the engineering time to build, maintain, and

Hackers

Once in ancient days, the then King of England told Sir Christopher Wren, whose name is yet remembered, that the new Cathedral of St. Paul which he had designed was "awful, pompous and artificial." Kings have seldom been noted for perspicacity.

. . .

In the case of the King and Sir Christopher, however, a compliment was intended. A later era would have used the words "awe-inspiring, stately, and ingeniously conceived."

"A Tragedy of Errors"
—POUL ANDERSON

Words' meanings change over time. Once upon a time, "hacker" might indeed have meant "A person who enjoys exploring the details of programmable systems and how to stretch their capabilities, as opposed to most users, who prefer to learn only the minimum necessary."[a] That isn't the way it is commonly used today. In this book, I'll be using it to mean "A person who uses his skill with computers to try to gain unauthorized access to computer files or networks," per the OED; when writing about security, that is the commonly accepted definition. It is, perhaps, worth noting that the OED traces that usage to 1976, the same year as its first citation for "A person with an enthusiasm for programming or using computers as an end in itself." And if you prefer older meanings, we can go back to either 1481's "That which hacks; an implement for hacking, chopping wood, or breaking up earth; a chopper, cleaver; a hoe, mattock," or 1581's "A 'cutter', cut-throat, bully".

---

a. "The New Hacker's Dictionary," http://outpost9.com/reference/jargon/jargon_23.html#SEC30.

configure such systems is expensive and becoming more so. From a security perspective, though, complexity is fatal. *No one* understands a complex system, from the architects and programmers who design and build it to the engineers who have to configure it. A 1994 study showed that about 25% of security flaws were due to bugs in the specification, not the code [Landwehr et al. 1994]. In other words, it's not just a programming problem.

Let me give an example of how complexity—necessary complexity, in this case—can lead to a security problem. A web posting [Chan 2011] detailed how an Apple Smart Cover can be used to override the security lock on an Apple iPad 2 running iOS 5.0. (For those who are not initiates into the High Mysteries of the Cult of Apple, a Smart Cover is held to the iPad 2 via magnets. When the cover is peeled back, a sensor inside the iPad 2 notices the absence of the magnet, and wakes up the display. Also, to power off an iPad 2, you hold down the Power button for a few seconds until a confirmation request appears; at that point, you swipe across the designated area of the screen.)

The attack works as follows:

- Lock a passcode-enabled iPad 2.

- Hold down the Power button until it reaches the shutoff slider screen.

- Close the Smart Cover.

- Open the Smart Cover.

- Tap cancel.

What led someone to discover this attack?

If one simply presses the Home button on a blank-screen iPad 2, the lock screen illuminates; if nothing further is done, it blanks again after 10 seconds. On the other hand, if one opens a Smart Cover, the screen remains illuminated for 60 seconds, again reverting to a blank screen if nothing is done. On the gripping hand [Niven and Pournelle 1993], if one initiates the power-down sequence from a blank screen but does nothing, after 30 seconds the device switches to a very dim, non-interactive wallpaper screen. In other words, it goes through a very different sequence of states for each of these ways for waking up the display. The author of the aforementioned posting wrote, "I don't know how anyone would've figured that out but it definitely works."

Consider the state transition diagram shown in Figure 1.1. Two of the states, Covered and Lock screen, are parameterized: the transition from them depends on how they were entered. Arguably, they should be shown as separate nodes on the graph; however, the behavior suggests a single code path with memory. That is the key to the attack.

Someone who thinks like a security person (see Chapter 2) might wonder what would happen if an unexpected transition were to occur. In particular, consider the dotted arc

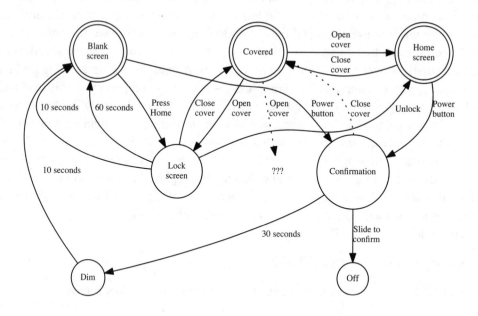

Figure 1.1: Simplified state transitions for unlocking or powering down an iPad 2. Activity can start from the Covered, Home, or Blank states. The dotted lines show the attack. Note that there are three possible destination states if the cover is opened, and two different ways to go from the lock screen to a blank screen.

from the Confirmation state to the Covered state. There is clearly memory in that state, since opening the cover can go to two different places. Is this memory always properly initialized? Clearly not—the actual transition in this case goes to the Home screen state, rather than the Lock screen state.

Change introduces complexity, but the risks of resisting all changes—the second common option—are sufficiently obvious that I won't belabor them, save to recall Ken Olsen's comment that "the personal computer will fall flat on its face in business" [Rifkin 2011]. Olsen was co-founder of the Digital Equipment Corporation, a computer company that no longer exists. Ignoring the world is not a security risk per se; nevertheless, the purpose of computer security is not security for its own sake, but to enable some other operation to function properly and (in some cases) profitably. Let me stress that: the purpose of an organization—a business, a school, a government agency, a hospital—is *not* to be secure; rather, security is an aid to carrying out its real purpose.

The third option for dealing with change is to embrace it. When a new device comes out, start using it. When there's a new service, install it. That way lies disaster; the risks are not always clear. Some years ago, Bruce Schneier wrote about the security risks of Unicode [Schneier 2000], the standard for handling all of the world's alphabets. At the time, I was skeptical, but he was quite correct. The first attack was fairly obvious—since the same glyph in different alphabets (such as the Cyrillic "a" versus the Latin "a") has different codepoints, the domain http://www.pаypal.com/ is different than the domain http://www.paypal.com, but the two look identical on screen [Schneier 2005]. A more subtle attack was discovered recently; it relies on the Unicode metacharacters to cause right-to-left rendering (necessary for languages like Hebrew and Arabic) to hide the `.exe` extension on some files [Krebs 2011b]. Handling cases like these requires not just good code, it requires a good understanding of people's behavior and of the salient characteristics of many different languages.

Note that Unicode or something like it is quite necessary, unless we want to exclude a large fraction of the world's population from the net. That is clearly unacceptable. Nor are the problems a matter of lack of forethought; there was no way, thousands of years ago when some of these languages grew up, that one scribe could say to another, "You know, in the far future, people are going to have these things called computers that will need to handle our alphabet and that of those uncivilized folk across the water, so let's all agree on a direction of writing and on a set of letters." We had to wait for a bit, until the new technology had been deployed and analyzed, for someone to realize that Unicode falls into a classic risk case: two different byte strings can produce the same visual display; the humans who rely on it cannot perceive the internal processing difference.

1.3 Security Analysis

The fourth and best approach to dealing with change is analysis. Naturally, everyone intends to do it, but it isn't easy. Doing it right requires approaching the problem de novo, rather than taking shortcuts. What are the components of the new system? What are their black-box properties? What else do we know or can we guess about them? What are their inputs and outputs? How are things combined? Is every input "secure"? If not, how can it be made secure?

Consider the problem of passwords (a subject that is discussed much more deeply in Chapter 7). Morris and Thompson demonstrated in 1979 that guessable passwords were a security risk [1979]; ever since, "pick strong passwords" has been an entry on every security checklist. However, they were writing about login passwords for a multi-user time-sharing system with remote access. The BIOS password for a server in a physically secure machine is in a very different environment. Do the same rules apply? How about my home desktop machine? I'm the only user, and while remote logins are possible I've configured the machine so that passwords are not accepted for such logins. Do I need a strong password? (If you're wondering, I have one, because I'm unconvinced that I'll always get the configuration right; if nothing else, a system update from Apple might change that file.)

It is tempting to say "ignore maxims from the past," but that is not quite correct, either. One should certainly examine the assumptions behind them, whether environmental (as in this case), based on the threat, or based on the assets being protected. (Teasing out these assumptions, especially the implicit ones, is one of the hardest things about security.) On the other hand, there is a lot of wisdom behind some of them; one cannot reject them all out of hand. Indeed, one of my touchstones—that complexity leads to insecurity— is nothing more than one of my personal checklist items, based on about 50 years of experience in the field and on a lot of research by many, many people.

Despite the vast and rapid changes in the computer business, the nature of threats hasn't changed much. Certainly, the technical details evolve over time; if nothing else, before there were web servers there was no need to know how to secure one. When web servers—or rifcaghy servers, whatever they are—do exist, though, you need to know those details. More importantly, you need to be able to answer several different questions:

- Do we need a rifcaghy server? More precisely, is there a *business* need for one, where "business" is shorthand for "the purpose of my organization"?

- What are the risks of rifcaghy servers? How can those risks be ameliorated?

- How much confidence do I have in that analysis?

- Are the residual risks more or less than the value to the business of running that service?

Security checklists are not going to give you the answer to any of those questions, until much of the world has been running rifcaghy for quite a while. At that point, you're behind the business curve; perhaps more seriously from a security perspective, your fellow employees may have been using external rifcaghy servers for quite some time, quite unaware of the risks. (Not convinced? Substitute "social media" for "rifcaghy." Substitute "smart phone." Substitute "cloud storage service.")

Furthermore, securing an organization or even a service is not something that's done once. As noted, technologies change, and software is updated. There are new devices, new connectivity, new threats, and new defenses. Even apart from that, designing a security solution is itself an iterative process. The corporate security group or even the security function in a smaller organization generally cannot design a meaningful protective architecture and simply toss it over the wall to the application programmers—and if they try to do so, the application programmers are likely to take the architecture and toss it themselves. I hesitate to say exactly where, but I do observe that it's very hard to fill up /dev/null.

The problem is that a security solution conceived of by only the security group is likely to pay too little attention to issues like cost and functionality. The problem is not just the cost of the security pieces itself or even the additional development cost; rather, it is the likely loss of functionality or market appeal of the actual product, and it is products that pay everyone's salaries. A perfectly secure service that no one will tolerate using is quite worthless; a security solution of that kind can, will, and should be rejected.

Given all that, the proper process looks like this:

while true **repeat**

1. Identify the assets at risk.

2. Ascertain the enemies interested in each asset, and assess their likely capabilities.

3. Select application technologies.

4. Evaluate the vulnerabilities for each piece.

5. Identify candidate defensive solutions.

6. Estimate the cost, including the cost in damage to the application if security is breached.

It's an iterative process; many solutions involve new assets that themselves need to be protected. Besides, even after you reach a stable answer, the outside world is not standing still; new implementations, new loads, new business requirements, and more mean that the security analysis group will never be out of a job.

But how can this be achieved? When a service is brand new, how is it possible to go through this sort of analysis? Since it would be redundant for me to say that by definition, that's the topic of this book, I'll give a better answer: absent a formal theory of secure system design (and I expect that such a theory will continue to be absent for many years to come), we need to learn from the past. More specifically, by looking at today's security technologies deductively, we can derive appropriate design principles; by applying these inductively, we can reason about tomorrow's rifcaghy services, and even the gushnewly and treltudy services of the day after.

Let's use firewalls as a brief example. (We'll revisit them in much more detail in Chapter 5.) When we look at why they worked in 1994, when Bill Cheswick and I wrote our book on them [1994], we see their basic assumptions: all traffic from the inside would reach the outside Internet via a very small number of chokepoints; only good guys lived on the inside; and the firewall was capable of filtering out inbound nastiness, operationally defined as anything that didn't match a security policy. How do those principles work today? By and large, they don't. Laptops and smart phones wander across the barrier to the outside, where they're unprotected; malware constitutes an enemy presence inside your organization; policies aren't—can't be—strong enough to describe things like PDF files infected with the latest 0-day exploits. It is tempting to conclude that firewalls are useless.

A deeper look at the principles, though, shows that we can still use firewalls, albeit rather differently. If we can find special circumstances where the principles hold—a server complex is a good example—we can still rely on firewalls as a strong defense. Furthermore, recognition of these principles as explicit guidelines teaches us administrative policies we need to enforce, such as not permitting any mobile devices into the server network, either directly or via a *virtual private network (VPN)*. That in turn says something about the resources we need to give the developers and administrators of that server complex.

This is how we have to proceed in the future. We shouldn't discard the past, nor should we let it straight-jacket us. Rather, we should use it as a guide.

1.4 A Few Words on Terminology

"You keep using that word. I do not think it means what you think it means."

Inigo in *The Princess Bride*
—WILLIAM GOLDMAN

I've already explained what I mean by "hacker" and why I use the word (page 6); no more needs to be said about that issue.

Several unusual terms—targetier, APT, Andromedan, and more—are explained in Chapter 3.

There are a number of technical terms I use freely, under the assumption that you know what I mean; these include RSA, MAC address, ARP spoofing, and more. As I noted in the preface, this book is not intended as an introductory text.

Finally, I will often use phrases like "business" or "business purpose." By no means do I intend to imply that this book is limited to the for-profit sector. Although I have indeed worked in industry, I'm now a professor and have served as Chief Technologist of the US Federal Trade Commission. All of these organizations have a goal, whether it's to make money, instruct students, perform research, protect the nation, or what have you. "Work"—and of course that includes computer work—done on behalf of any of these serves to further those goals. In the interests of clearer writing, I generally use the simpler form to include all of these. Please make mental substitutions as appropriate.

Chapter 2

Thinking About Security

> "Think, youth, *think!* For know, Lensman, that upon the clarity of your thought and upon the trueness of your perception depends the whole future of your Patrol and of your Civilization; more so now by far than at any time in the past."
>
> Mentor of Arisia in *Second Stage Lensman*
> —E. E. "DOC" SMITH

2.1 The Security Mindset

I've often remarked that the best thing about my job is that I get to think evil thoughts and still feel virtuous about it. Remarkably, it isn't easy. In fact, for most people it's remarkably hard to think like a bad guy. Nevertheless, the ability to do so is at the heart of what security people have to do.

Bruce Schneier explained it very well in an essay a few years back [Schneier 2008]:

> Uncle Milton Industries has been selling ant farms to children since 1956. Some years ago, I remember opening one up with a friend. There were no actual ants included in the box. Instead, there was a card that you filled in with your address, and the company would mail you some ants. My friend expressed surprise that you could get ants sent to you in the mail.
>
> I replied: "What's really interesting is that these people will send a tube of live ants to anyone you tell them to."

In other words, a security person will look at a mechanism and think, "What else can this do? What can it do that will serve my needs rather than the intended purpose?"

One way to "think sideways" is to consider every process as a series of steps. Each step, in turn, depends on a person or gadget accepting a series of inputs. Ask yourself this: what if one of those inputs was wrong or corrupted? Would something useful happen? Do I have the ability to cause that input to be wrong? Can the defender spot the error and do something about it?

Look again at Bruce's story. Someone at the company will read the card and send a tube of ants somewhere. However, one of the inputs—the address to which to send the bugs—is under the control of the person who filled out the card, and thus can trivially be forged.

There's another input here, though, one Bruce didn't address. Can you spot it? I'll wait...

✷   ✷   ✷

Most of you got it; that's great. For the rest: how does the company validate that the *card* is legitimate? That is, how do they ensure that they only send the ants to people who have actually purchased the product?

Once, that would have been easy; the card was undoubtedly a printed form, very easily distinguished from something produced by even the best typewriters. Forging a printed document would require the connivance of a print shop; that's too much trouble for the rather trivial benefit. Today, though, just about everyone has very easy access to word processors, lots of fonts, high-quality printers, and so on. If you put in a very modest amount of effort, you can reproduce the form pretty easily. For that matter, a decent scanner can do the job. (Note that easy forgery is a problem for other important pieces of paper, too; airplane boarding passes have been forged [Soghoian 2007].)

The next barrier is probably the cardboard the card is printed on. This isn't as trivial, but something close enough is not very hard to obtain.

To a computer pro, the fixes are obvious: put a serial number on each card and look it up in a database of valid, unused ant requests. Add some sort of security seal, such as a hologram, on the card [Simske et al. 2008]. Ask for a copy of the purchase receipt, and perhaps the UPC bar code from the box. For that matter, creating hard-to-forge pieces of paper is an old problem: we call it paper money. Problem solved?

Not quite—we don't even know if there was a problem. The defensive technologies cost money and time; are they worth it? What is the rate of forged requests for ants? Is the population of immature forgers—who else would be motivated to send fake ant delivery requests?—large enough to matter? More precisely, is the cost of the defense more or less than the losses from this attack? This is a crucial point that every security person should memorize and repeat daily: the purpose of security is *not* to increase security; rather, its purpose is to prevent losses. Any unnecessary expenditure on security is itself a net loss.

There's one more lesson to take from this example: was the old security measure—the difficulty of forgery—rendered obsolete by improvements in technology? The computer field isn't static; giving yesterday's answers to today's questions is often a recipe for disaster.

2.2 Know Your Goals

What are you trying to do? What are your security goals? The questions may seem trite, but they're not. Answering them incorrectly will lead you to spend too much, and on the wrong things. (Spending too little generally results from being in denial about the threat.)

All too often, insecurity is treated as the equivalent of being in a state of sin. Being hacked is not perceived as the result of a misjudgment or of being outsmarted by an adversary; rather, it's seen as divine punishment for a grievous moral failing. The people responsible didn't just err; they're fallen souls to be pitied and/or ostracized. And of course that sort of thing can't happen to us, because we're fine, upstanding folk who have the blessing of the computer deity—$DEITY, in the old Unix-style joke—of our choice.

Needless to say, I don't buy any of that. First and foremost, security is an economic decision. You are trying to protect certain assets, tangible or not; these have a certain monetary value. Your goal is to spend less protecting them than they're worth. If you're uncomfortable trying to attach a cost to things like national honor or human lives, look at it this way: what is the best protection you can get for those by spending a given amount of money? Can you save more lives by spending the money on, say, antivirus software or by increasing the rate of automotive seat belt use? A hack may be a more spectacular failure (and you're entitled to take bad publicity into account in calculating your damages), but it's not a sin, and you are not condemned to eternal damnation for getting it wrong.

What should you protect? Not only is there no one answer, if you're reading this book you're probably not the right person to answer it, though you can and should contribute. The proper answer for any given system revolves around the worst possible damage that can occur if your worst enemy had control of that computer. That, in turn, is very rarely limited to the street price of a replacement computer. Consider what supposedly happened in 1982: the "most massive non-nuclear explosion ever recorded," because a Soviet pipeline was controlled by software the CIA had sabotaged before it was stolen from a Canadian company [R. A. Clarke and Knake 2010; Hollis 2011; Reed 2004]. That's an extreme case, of course, but it doesn't take a Hollywood scriptwriter's imagination to come up with equally crazy scenarios. (This story may also be the result of someone's imagina-

A Word About Serious Adversaries

Although most of this book is about ordinary sorts of attacks, at times I will talk about serious adversaries, the kind of people who can create something like Stuxnet or infiltrate defense contractors. We all know who they are. If you're American, you probably blame China's People's Liberation Army Unit 61398 [Mandiant 2013] and Russia [NCIX 2011]. If you're Chinese, you probably blame the NSA [Sanger, Barboza, and Perlroth 2013; Tatlow 2013; Whitney 2013]. France and other European countries may feel the same way [Gallagher 2012; MacAskill 2013], especially in the wake of the Snowden revelations. Iran blames Israel's Unit 8200 [UPI 2012]; Israel probably blames some shadowy Palestinian group that has Iranian backing. In some countries, you may blame your own government, but governments in such countries probably don't want you saying so.

I'm not taking sides. In the interests of euphony and informality, I want to avoid clumsy phrases like "nation-state"—last time I looked, there were very few city-states left, and as far as I know none of them have "cyberwarfare" units—and pick a simple proper noun. I've chosen "Andromeda," as in the nearby galaxy, and the crack Andromedan hacker unit MI-31. You may, of course, choose to mentally substitute Ruritania or Warhoon or Andorra[a] or whatever country (or city-state) you think might attack you. (In fact, I cheat—in the LaTeX source file for this book, I use \Enemy, \Enemyan, and \Unit, so I can change it whenever I want. . . .)

For lesser threats, I'll use the phrases *joy hack*, *opportunistic attack*, and *targeted attack*; see the next chapter for an explanation.

---

a. "Andorra," http://people.wku.edu/charles.smith/MALVINA/mr005.htm.

---

tion. Most published reports seem to derive from Reed's original published report [2004]. Reed was an insider and may have had access to the full story, but it's hard to understand why anything was declassified unless it was deliberately leaked—or fabricated—to warn potential enemies about the US government's prowess in cyberweaponry. The details and quote given here are from [R. A. Clarke and Knake 2010, pp. 92–93]. Zetter, who has done a lot of research on the topic, doubts that it happened [Zetter 2014].) Malware designed to steal confidential business documents, to aid a rival? It's happened [Harper 2013; B. Sullivan 2005]. A worm that blocks electronic funds transfers, so that your company appears to be a deadbeat that doesn't pay its bills? Why not? (If you think it sounds far-fetched, see [Markoff and Shanker 2009]: the United States seriously contemplated hacking the Iraqi banking system to deny Hussein funds to pay his troops, buy munitions, and so on.

"'We knew we could pull it off—we had the tools,' said one senior official who worked at the Pentagon when the highly classified plan was developed.") All of these could happen. However...

The roof of your factory is almost certainly not armored to resist a meteor strike. When selecting the site for your office building, you probably didn't worry about the proximity of a natural gas pipeline that a backhoe might happen to puncture. Most likely, you're not even expecting spies to hide in the false ceiling above the reception area, so they can sneak past a locked door in the dead of night. All of these threats, cyber and otherwise, are possible; in general, though, they're so improbable that they're not worth worrying about—which is precisely my point.

In most situations, the proper defense posture is an economic question. There are no passages in Leviticus prescribing exile from your family because your system was hacked. You are not a lesser human being if your laptop suffers a virus infestation. You may, however, be a bad system administrator if you don't have good backups of that laptop. Not using encryption when connecting from a public hotspot is negligent. Ignoring critical vendor patches is foolish. And of course, you should know how to recover from the loss of any computer system, whether due to hackers or because a wandering cosmic ray has fried its disk drive controller.

In general, one should eschew paranoia and embrace professionalism. If you run the network for an X-ray laser battery used for anti-UFO defense, perhaps you should worry about Andromedan-instigated meteor strikes aimed at your router complex. On the other hand, if the network you're trying to protect controls the cash registers for a large chain of jewelry stores, MI-31 isn't a big concern, but high-end cyberthieves might be. Regardless, you need to decide: what are you trying to protect, what are you leaving to insurance, and what is too improbable to care about? You cannot deploy proper defenses without going through this exercise. Brainstorming to come up with possible threats is the easy part; deciding which ones are realistic requires expertise.

Here are two rules of thumb: first, distinguish between menaces and nuisances; second, realize the scope of some protection efforts. Let's consider some concrete examples.

Imagine a piece of sophisticated malware that increases the salary reported to the tax authorities for top executives, while leaving intact the amounts printed on their paystubs. When the executives file their tax returns, the numbers they report will be significantly lower, triggering an audit. What will happen? Ultimately, it will likely be a non-event. A passel of lawyers and accountants will spend some time explaining the situation; ultimately, there will be too much other evidence—contracts, annual reports, bank records, other computer systems, minutes of the Board of Directors' compensation committee, perhaps discussions with an outside consulting firm that knows the competitive landscape —to make any charges stick. In other words, this is a nuisance attack. By contrast, malware that damages expensive, hard-to-replace equipment—think Stuxnet or the "Aurora" test [Meserve 2007; Zetter 2014] that destroyed an electrical generator—is a serious threat.

A more plausible scenario is malware that tries to steal important corporate secrets. There are enough apparent cases of this occurring that it's a plausible threat, with attackers ranging from random virus writers to national intelligence services and victims ranging from paint manufacturers to defense contractors [NCIX 2011]. Protecting important secrets is *hard*, though; they're rarely in a single (and hence easy to isolate) location. Nevertheless, it's often worth the effort. Even here, some analysis is necessary: can your enemies actually use your secrets? Unless your enemy has at least the tacit support of a foreign government or a very large company, efforts that require a large capital outlay may be beyond them—and support from competitors isn't always forthcoming, much to the dismay of some bad guys [Domin 2007].

There is no substitute here for careful analysis. You need to evaluate your assets, estimate what it will take to protect them, guess at the likelihood and cost of a penetration, and allocate your resources accordingly.

One special subcase of the protection question deserves a more careful look: should you protect the network or the hosts? We are often misled when we call the field "network security"; more often, saying that network security is about protecting the network is like saying that highway robbery means that a piece of pavement has been stolen. The network, like the highway, is simply the conduit the attackers use.

With a couple of exceptions, attackers are uninterested in the network itself. Connectivity is ubiquitous today; few attackers need more per se. They often want hosts with good connectivity, especially for spamming and launching DDoS attacks, but the pipe itself doesn't need special protection; protect the hosts and the pipe will be fine.

There are some important special cases. The most obvious is an ISP: its purpose is to provide connectivity, so attacks on its network cut at the heart of its business. The main threat is DDoS attacks; note carefully that an ISP has to mitigate attacks coming from hosts it has no control over and which may not even be directly connected to its own network.

There are two other special cases worth mentioning; both affect ISPs and customers. The first is access networks, those used to connect a site to an ISP; the second is networks that have some unusual characteristic, such as very low bandwidth where every extra byte can cause pain. In these situations, even modest attacks on the infrastructure can lead to a complete denial of service. As before, the network operator will have little or no direct control over the hosts that are causing trouble; consequently, its responses (and its response plans) have to be in terms of network operations.

Don't confuse the question of what to protect with where the defenses should be. Protecting hosts might best be done with network firewalls or network-resident intrusion prevention systems; conversely, the best way to deal with insecure networks is often to install encryption software on the hosts.

There's an important special case that's almost a hybrid: the "cloud." What special precautions should you take to protect your cloud resources? The issue is discussed in more detail in Chapter 10; for now, I'll note that "Is the cloud secure?" is the wrong question; more precisely, it's a question that has a trivial but useless answer: "No, of course not." A better question is whether the cloud is secure *enough*, whether using the cloud is better or worse than doing it yourself.

2.3 Security as a Systems Problem

Changing one physical law is like trying to eat one peanut.

"The Theory and Practice of Teleportation"
—LARRY NIVEN

Here's a quick security quiz. Suppose you want to steal some information from a particular laptop computer belonging to the CEO of a competitor. Would you:

(a) Find a new 0-day bug in JPG processing and mail an infected picture to the CEO?

(b) Find an old bug in JPG processing and mail a picture with it to the CEO?

(c) Lure the user to a virus-infected web site that you control (a so-called "watering hole" attack)?

(d) Visit the person's office on some pretext, and slip a boobytrapped USB stick into the machine?

(e) Wait until her laptop is brought across a national border, and bribe or otherwise induce the customs officer to "inspect" it for you?

(f) Bribe her secretary to the do same thing without waiting for an international trip?

(g) Bribe the janitor?

(h) Wait till she takes it home, and attack it via her less-protected home network? The NSA considers that a threat to its own employees.[1]

(i) Penetrate the file server from which the systems administrator distributes patches and antivirus updates to the corporation, and plant your malware there?

(j) Install a rogue DHCP server or do ARP-spoofing to divert traffic from that machine through one of yours, so you can tamper with downloaded content?

(k) Follow her to the airport, and create a rogue access point to capture her traffic?

(l) Cryptanalyze the encrypted connection to the corporate VPN from her hotel?

(m) Infect someone else in the company with a tailored virus, and hope that it spreads to the executive offices?

(n) Send her a spear-phishing email to lure her to a bogus corporate web site; under the assumption that she uses the same password for it and for her laptop, connect to its file-sharing service?

(o) Wait until she's giving a talk, complete with slides, and when she's distracted talking to attendees after the talk steal the laptop?

Obviously, some of these are far-fetched. Equally obviously, all of them can work under certain circumstances. (That last one appears to have happened to the CEO of Qualcomm.[2]) In fact, I've omitted some attacks that have worked in practice. How should you prepare your defenses?

The point is that you can't have blinders on, even when you're only trying to protect a single asset. There are many avenues for attack; you have to watch them all. Furthermore, when you have a complex system, the real risk can come from a sequence of failures. We told one such story in *Firewalls* [Cheswick and Bellovin 1994, pp. 8–9]: the production gateway had failed during a holiday weekend, the operator added a guest account to facilitate diagnosis by a backup expert, the account was neither protected nor deleted—and a joy hacker found it before the weekend was over. In another incident, I was part of a security audit for a product when we learned that one of the developers had been arrested for hacking. We wondered whether a back door had been inserted into the code base; when we looked, we found two holes. One, I learned, was an error by another developer

---

1. "Best Practices for Keeping Your Home Network Secure," https://www.nsa.gov/ia/_files/factsheets/ I43V_Slick_Sheets/Slicksheet_BestPracticesForKeepingYourHomeNetworkSecure.pdf.

2. "Qualcomm Secrets Vanish with Laptop," http://www.infosyssec.com/securitynews/0009/2776.html.

(ironically, she was part of the audit team). The other, though, gave us pause: it took a common configuration error and two independent bugs—for one of which the comments didn't agree with the code—to create the problem. To this day, I do not know whether we spotted deliberate sabotage; on odd-numbered days, I think so, but I wrote this on an even-numbered day.

Complex systems fail in complex ways! More or less by definition, it isn't possible to be aware of all of the possible interactions. Worse yet, the problem is dynamic; a change in software or configurations in one part of a network can lead to a security problem elsewhere. Consider the case of an ordinary, simple-minded firewall, of the type that may have existed around 1995 or thereabouts. It may have been secure, but two unrelated technological developments, each harmless by itself, combined to cause a problem [D. M. Martin, Rajagopalan, and Rubin 1997].

The first was the development of a transparent proxy for the *File Transfer Protocol (FTP)* [Postel and Reynolds 1985]. By default, FTP requires an inbound call from the server to the client to transmit the actual data; normally, the host and port to be contacted are sent by the client to the FTP server. Normally, of course, a firewall won't permit inbound calls, even though they're harmless (or as harmless as sending or receiving data ever is). The solution was a smarter firewall, one that examined the command stream, learned which port was to be used for the FTP transfer, and temporarily created a rule to permit it. This solved the functionality problem without creating any security holes.

The second technological development was the deployment of Java in web browsers [Arnold and Gosling 1996; Lindholm and Yellin 1996]. This was also supposed to be safe; a variety of restrictions were imposed to protect users [McGraw and Felten 1999]. One such restriction was on networking: a Java applet could do network I/O, but only back to the host from which it was downloaded. Of course, that included networking using FTP. The problem is now clear: a malicious applet could speak FTP but cause the firewall to allow connections to random ports on random protected hosts.

The philosophical failure that gave rise to this situation requires deeper thought. First, FTP handling in the firewall was based on the assumption, common to all firewall schemes, that only good guys are on the inside; thus, malicious FTP requests could not occur. A hostile applet, however, was a malicious non-human actor, a scenario unanticipated by the firewall designers. Conversely, the designers of the Java security model wanted to permit as much functionality as they could without endangering users; firewalls were not common in 1995, let alone ones that handled FTP that way, so it's not surprising that Java didn't handle this scenario.

Amusingly enough, the problem may now be moot. The rise of the web has made FTP servers far less common; disabling support for it on a firewall is often reasonable.

Figure 2.1: SQL injection attacks.

Furthermore, if users encrypt their FTP command channels [Ford-Hutchinson 2005], the firewall won't be able to see the port numbers and hence won't be able to open ports, even for benign reasons. Four separate developments—the creation of smarter firewalls, the deployment of Java, the rise of the web and the decline of FTP, and the standardization of encrypted FTP—combined to first cause and then defang a security threat.

Although protecting an enterprise network is complicated, there's a very important special case that is itself almost as complicated: protecting a "single" function that is actually implemented as many interconnected computers. Consider a typical e-commerce web site. To the customer, it appears to be a single machine; those who've worked for such companies are already laughing at that notion. At a minimum, the web server is just the front end for a large, back-end database; more commonly, there are multiple back-end databases (inventory, customer profiles, order status, sales tax rates, gift cards, and more), links to customer care (itself a complex setup, especially if it's outsourced), the network operations group, external content providers, developer sites, system administration links, and more. Any one of these can be the conduit for a break-in. SQL injection attacks (Figure 2.1) occur when the web server is incautious about what it passes to a database. Customer care personnel have—and must have—vast powers to correct apparently erroneous entries in assorted databases; penetration of their machines can have very serious consequences. System administrators can do more or less anything; it doesn't take much imagination to see the threats there. Note carefully that firewalls are of minimal benefit in such a setup; the biggest risks are often from protocols that the firewall has to allow. SQL injection attacks are a good example; they're passed to the web server via HTTP, and thence on to the database as part of a standard, apparently normal query.

2.4 Thinking Like the Enemy

One of the hardest things about practicing security is that you have to discard all of your childhood training. You were, most likely, taught to flee from evil thoughts; there's no point to planning how to do something wrong unless you're actually intending to do it, and of course you wouldn't ever want to do something you shouldn't.

Being a security professional turns that around. I noted at the start of this chapter that my job entails thinking evil thoughts, albeit in the service of good; however, it's not an easy thing to do. It is, nevertheless, essential. How does a bad guy think?

I've already discussed the obvious starting point: identifying your assets. Identifying weak points, beyond the checklist that every security book gives—buffer overflows, SQL injection and other unchecked inputs, password guessing, and more—is harder. How can you spot a new flaw in a new setup? If you're developing a completely different kind of Internet behavior (Peer of the Realm to Peer of the Realm bilesharing?), how can you figure out where the risks are?

By definition, there's no cookbook recipe. To a first approximation, though, the process is straightforward: attackers violate boundaries and therefore defenses have to. For example, suppose that a particular module requires that its input messages contain only the letters A, D, F, G, V, and X. It's easy to guess that trouble could result if different characters appeared; the question is how to prevent that. The two obvious fixes are input filtering in one module or output filtering in another. The right answer, though, is both, plus logging. Output filtering, of course, ensures that the upstream module is doing the right thing. Indeed, it may be a natural code path: call the communications routine, and let it encode the message using the six appropriate permissible characters. Nothing can go wrong—except that the bad guy will look at other ways to send Q, Z, and even nastier letters like J and þ. Can a random Internet node send a message to the picky module? What about a subverted node on your Intranet? Another module in the same system? Can the attacker get access to some LAN that can reach the right point? Is there some minor, non-sensitive module that can be subverted and tricked into sending garbage? None of these things should happen, of course, but a defensive analyst has to spot them all—and since spotting them all may be impossible, you want input filtering, plus logging to let you know that somewhere, your other protections have fallen short.

There's another lesson we can learn from that scenario: the more moving parts a system has, the harder it is to analyze. Quite simply, if code doesn't exist, it can't be subverted. As always, complexity is your enemy. This applies within modules, too, of course; a web server is vastly more complex, and hence more likely to contain security holes, than a simple authentication server. Thus, even though an authentication server contains more sensitive data, it is less likely to be the weak point in your architecture.

When trying to emulate the enemy, the most important single question is what the weak points are. That is, what system components are more likely to be penetrated. There is no absolute way to measure this, but there are a few rules of thumb:

- A module that processes input from the outside is more vulnerable.

- A privileged module is more likely to be targeted.

- All other things being equal, a more complex module or system is more likely to have security flaws.

- The richer the input language a module accepts, the more likely it is that there are parsing problems.

The question is addressed more fully in Chapter 11.

Don't neglect the human element. True, only MI-31 is likely to suborn an employee, but someone with a grudge, real or imagined, can do a lot of harm. What would you do if your boss came to you and said, "We're about to fire Chris," when Chris is a system administrator who knows all of the passwords and vulnerabilities? How about "The union is about to go on strike; can we prevent them from creating an electronic picket line?" "There's going to be a large layoff announced tomorrow; can we protect our systems?" All of these are real questions (I've been asked all three). Distrusting everyone you work with is a sure route to low morale (yours and theirs); trusting everyone is an equally sure route to trouble, especially when the stakes are high or when people are stressed. Put yourself in a given role—again, you're emulating a role, not a person—and ask what damage you can do and how you can prevent it. The answer, by the way, may be procedural rather than technical. For example, if your analysis indicates that bad things could happen if a fake user were added to the system, have a separate group audit the new user list against, say, a database of new employees.

Conti and Caroland have another good pedagogical idea [2011]: teach students to cheat. They gave a deliberately unfair exam, which elicited the predictable (and justifiable) complaints. They told the students they were allowed to cheat, but the usual penalty—failing—would apply if and only if they were caught. The response was magnificently creative, which is what they wanted. Breaking security *is* a matter of not following the rules; people who don't know how to do that can't anticipate the enemy properly. Their conclusion is quite correct:

> Teach yourself and your students to cheat. We've always been taught to color inside the lines, stick to the rules, and never, ever, cheat. In seeking cyber security, we must drop that mindset. It is difficult to defeat a creative and

determined adversary who must find only a single flaw among myriad defensive measures to be successful. We must not tie our hands, and our intellects, at the same time. If we truly wish to create the best possible information security professionals, being able to think like an adversary is an essential skill. Cheating exercises provide long term remembrance, teach students how to effectively evaluate a system, and motivate them to think imaginatively. Cheating will challenge students' assumptions about security and the trust models they envision. Some will find the process uncomfortable. That is OK and by design. For it is only by learning the thought processes of our adversaries that we can hope to unleash the creative thinking needed to build the best secure systems, become effective at red teaming and penetration testing, defend against attacks, and conduct ethical hacking activities.

It pays to keep up with reporting on what the bad guys are doing. The trade press is useful but tends to be later to the game; you want to be ahead of the curve. Focus first on the specific things bad guys want. If you think you'd be targeted by the Andromedans, you should probably talk to your country's counterintelligence service. (Don't skip this step because you're a defense contractor and you know what MI-31 wants; their methods—and those include compromise of intermediate targets—are of interest as well; the counterintelligence folks want to know what's going on.)

The changes in target selection over the years have been quite striking. In general, the hackers have been ahead of the bulk of the security community, spotting opportunities well before most defenders realized there was a problem. Mind you, the possibility of these attacks was always acknowledged, and there were always some people warning of them, but too many experts assumed a static threat model.

The first notable shift from pure joy hacking happened in late 1993; advisories described it as "ongoing network monitoring attacks" on plaintext passwords.[3] What was more interesting, if less reported, was that a number of ISPs had workstations directly connected to backbone links. Given the LAN technology of the time—unswitched Ethernet—any such machine, if penetrated, could be turned into an eavesdropping station. It remains unclear how the attackers knew of the opportunity; the existence of such well-located machines was not widely known. The essence of the incident, though, is that the good guys did not understand the security implications of the placement of those machines; the bad guys did.

Attackers' target selection improved over the years, notably in the attention paid to DNS servers, but the next big change happened around 2003. Suddenly, splashy worms that clogged the Internet for no particular reason more or less stopped happening; instead,

---

3. "CERT Advisory CA-1994-01 Ongoing Network Monitoring Attacks,"
http://www.cert.org/advisories/CA-1994-01.html.

starting with the Sobig virus [Roberts 2003], the malware acquired a pecuniary motive: sending spam. The virus writers had formed an alliance with the spammers; the latter paid the former for an enhanced ability to clog our inboxes with their lovely missives. It took quite a while for the good guys to understand what had happened, that infecting random PCs was no longer just to allow the perpetrators to cut another notch into their monitors. Again, the bad guys "thought differently." This was followed by the widespread appearance of phishing web sites and keystroke loggers. Financial gain had become the overwhelming driver for attacks on the Internet.

The next change occurred shortly afterwards, with the Titan Rain [Thornburgh 2005] attacks. Widely attributed to China, these attacks appeared to be targeted industrial espionage attacks against US government sites. The concept of cyberespionage isn't new—indeed, a real attempt goes back to the early days of the Internet [Stoll 1988; Stoll 1989]—but use on a large scale was still a surprise. Today, we may have moved into another era, of high-quality, militarized malware (Stuxnet, Duqu, and Flame) generally attributed to major governments' cyberwarfare units [Goodin 2012b; Markoff 2011b; Sanger 2012; Zetter 2014].

What happened? What is the common thread in all of these incidents? With the exception of the cryptanalytic element in Flame [Fillinger 2013; Goodin 2012b; Zetter 2014], there was nothing particularly original or brilliant about the attacks; they're more the product of hard work. Their import is that the attackers realized the significance of changes in what was on the Internet. It wasn't possible to attack, say, the US military in 1990, because except for a very few research labs, it wasn't online. When it was online, the hackers struck.

The essence of these incidents was better thinking about targets and opportunities by the attackers than by the defenders. In some sense, that's understandable—it's hard to get management buy-in (and funding) to defend against attacks that have never before been a real threat—but that doesn't forgive it. There's an old Navy saying that there are two types of ships, submarines and targets. The same can be said of cyberspace: there are two types of software, malware and targets, and the good guys are blithely building more targets. Will the next unexpected step be cyberwarfare? That's a very complex topic, well beyond the scope of this book, and while I don't think that the worst scenarios one sees in the press are credible I do think there's significantly more potential risk than some would have you believe. The important point here comes from the title of this section: one has to think "outside the box" about next year's targets. If you deploy a brand new service, what are the *non-obvious* ways to pervert it?

Beyond target selection, defenders have to think about how their systems are exploited. At the architectural stage, pay more attention to longer-term trends than to the bug du jour. Eavesdropping, SQL injection attacks, buffer overflows, and the like have

---

Cyberwar?

I set out my ideas on cyberwarfare in [Bellovin 2013], but here I'll give my beliefs in a nutshell. First, there's no such thing as "cyberwarfare" per se; there are wars that employ weapons, which may or may not be cyberweapons. Second, wars don't start simply because someone has a new weapon, whether it's malware, a nuclear-tipped ICBM, or a better crossbow. Weaponry can enable a war, but one will start for other reasons. Even during the height of the Cold War, few strategists expected a *Bolt out of the Blue (BOOB)* attack; the same is likely true today. Furthermore, the characteristics of cyberattacks make them more suitable as tactical weapons, not strategic weapons. For more on this last point, see [Libicki 2009].

All that said, it doesn't mean that any malign interaction between countries constitutes a war, or even a casus belli. A DDoS attack is not in the same category as an air strike, nor is state-sponsored electronic espionage the same as a commando raid. Here's a simple metric: if the same action—I'm including spying here—were done by a satellite, how would it be categorized? By a drone? Special forces? An intelligence agent? A locally recruited but foreign-controlled spy or saboteur? A local group with funding or other ties to another country? Intelligence activities clearly do not make the cut, nor do disinformation campaigns. Actions that cause physical damage may or may not qualify; certainly, they generally do not lead to full-scale war unless done repeatedly.

---

been with us for decades; they'll always need to be guarded against. A specific vulnerability in version $e^{\pi i}$ of some module may be of interest operationally, but dealing with it poses a complex problem; there's often little you can do save to monitor more intensively until you get a patch from your vendor. Is availability of your service important enough that you should take the risk of leaving it up? Only you can answer that question—but be sure you know there's a question that needs answering.

Consider it from the bad guy's perspective, though. Suppose you're a hacker, and you've obtained or written some code to exploit a new vulnerability. What do you do with it? Attack one target? Many targets? Wait a while and see if it really works for others? Some attackers want instant gratification: what can I steal *now*? Others, especially the more sophisticated ones, take a longer-range view: they'll use their new code to make initial penetrations of interesting targets, even if they can't do anything useful immediately, and plant a back door so they can return later.

Chapter 3

Threat Models

"And by the way, we are belittling our opponents and building up a disastrous overconfidence in ourselves by calling them pirates. They are not—they can't be. Boskonia must be more than a race or a system—it is very probably a galaxy-wide culture. It is an absolute despotism, holding its authority by means of a rigid system of rewards and punishments. In our eyes it is fundamentally wrong, but it works—*how* it works! It is organized just as we are, and is apparently as strong in bases, vessels, and personnel."

Kimball Kinnison in *Galactic Patrol*
—E. E. "Doc" Smith

3.1 Who's Your Enemy?

The correct answer to most simple security questions is "it depends." Security isn't a matter of absolutes; it's a matter of picking the best set of strategies given assorted constraints and objectives.

Suppose you're a security consultant. You visit some client and are asked whether you can secure their systems. The first question you should ask is always the same: "What are you trying to protect, and against whom?" The defenses that suffice against the CEO's third grader's best frenemy will likely be insufficient against a spammer; the defenses that suffice against a spammer won't keep out the Andromedans.

A *threat* is defined as "an adversary that is motivated and capable of exploiting a vulnerability" [Schneider 1999]. Defining a threat model involves figuring out what you have that someone might want, and then identifying the capabilities of those potential attackers. That, in turn, will tell you how strong your defenses have to be, and which classes of vulnerabilities you have to close. If you run the academic computing center for a university, you probably don't have to deal with extraordinary threats (though login credentials for university libraries are eagerly sought); on the other hand, if your company's products are so highly classified that even the company doesn't know what it makes, things like physical security and extortion against employees become major concerns. An accurate understanding of your risk is essential to picking the right security posture—and hence expense profile—for your site.

In the 1990s, most hackers were so-called *joy hackers*, typically teenage or 20-something males (and they were almost all male) who wanted to prove their cleverness by showing how many supposedly tough systems they could break into. It's not that there weren't intruders motivated by espionage—there were, as Cliff Stoll demonstrated [Stoll 1988; Stoll 1989]—and Donn Parker noted the existence of financially motivated computer crimes as long ago as 1976 [Parker 1976], but the large majority of the early Internet break-ins were done for no better motive than "because it's there."

The world has changed, though, and today most of the problems are caused by people pursuing specific goals. There are some *hacktivists*—people who attack systems to pursue ideological goals—but the large majority of problems are caused by criminals who, when not maturing other felonious little plans, are breaking into computer systems for the money they can make that way. They use a variety of different schemes, most notably spamming and credential-stealing. In fact, most of the spam you receive is sent from hacked personal computers. This has an important consequence: *any Internet-connected computer—that is to say, most of them—is of value to many attackers*. Maybe your computer doesn't have defense secrets and maybe you never log on to your bank from it, but if it can send email, it's useful to the bad guys and thus has to be protected.

We thus have a floor on the threat model; it extends all the way up to Andromedan attacks on national security systems. There is, though, a large middle ground. The rough metric of how much risk your systems are subject to is simple: how much money can a criminal make by subverting it? For example, computers used for banking by small businesses are major targets—large companies use much more complex payment schemes and consumers typically don't have that much money in their bank accounts—but small businesses will typically have a fair amount. It's thus worth an attacker's while to take over such machines and either use them directly or install keystroke loggers to collect login credentials.

One thing they don't seem to go after very often is credit card numbers entered on individual computers—they're not worth the trouble. Stolen credit card numbers are in sufficiently large supply that their market value is low, only a few dollars apiece [Krebs 2008; Riley 2011], so collecting them one or two at a time isn't very cost-effective. (Enough information for easy identity theft is even cheaper: $.25/person for small volumes; $.16/person in bulk [Krebs 2011a].) A large database of card numbers is a much more interesting target, though, and some very large ones have been penetrated. Alberto Gonzalez is probably the most successful such criminal. As *The New York Times Magazine* put it [Verini 2010],

> Over the course of several years, during much of which he worked for the government, Gonzalez and his crew of hackers and other affiliates gained access to roughly 180 million payment-card accounts from the customer databases of some of the most well known corporations in America: OfficeMax, BJ's Wholesale Club, Dave & Buster's restaurants, the T. J. Maxx and Marshalls clothing chains. They hacked into Target, Barnes & Noble, JCPenney, Sports Authority, Boston Market, and 7-Eleven's bank-machine network. In the words of the chief prosecutor in Gonzalez's case, "The sheer extent of the human victimization caused by Gonzalez and his organization is unparalleled."

The cost to the victims was put in excess of $400 million; Gonzalez himself made millions [Meyers 2009].

The most interesting corporation Gonzalez hit was Heartland Payment Systems, one of the biggest payment-card processors in the country. *The Times* noted that "by the time Heartland realized something was wrong, the heist was too immense to be believed: data from 130 million transactions had been exposed," probably affecting more than 250,000 businesses. What's especially interesting is his target selection: most people are unaware that such a role exists; Gonzalez researched the payment systems enough to learn of it and to hack one of the major players.

Most computers, of course, don't store or process 180 million card numbers; obviously, very few do, but these systems merit extremely strong protection. Somewhat less obviously, there are a fair number of systems that connect to the large database machines—administrators, individual stores in a chain, even the point-of-sale systems. All of these need to be added to the threat model—control of these computers can and will be monetized by attackers, and money is the root of most Internet evil.

There is, in fact, a burgeoning "Underground Economy" centered on the Internet. It includes the hackers, the spammers who pay them, the DDoS extortionists, the folks who run the phishing scams and the advance fee (AKA "419") frauds, and more. Someone in one part of the world will order something via a stolen credit card and have it delivered to a vacant house. Someone else will pick it up and reship it, or return it for cash that is then wired to the perpetrator. Hardware-oriented folks build ATM skimmers, complete with cameras that catch the PIN as it is entered.

A lot of these folk are engaged in other sorts of criminal activity as well. To them, the Internet is just one more place to make money illegally. A 2012 takedown of an international Internet crime ring included seizure of a web site that featured "financial data, hacking tips, malware, spyware and access to stolen goods, like iPads and iPhones"; some of those arrested allegedly "offered to ship stolen merchandise and arrange drop services so items like sunglasses, air purifiers and synthetic marijuana could be picked up" [N. D. Schwartz 2012]. Information may want to be free, but sunglasses?

It is also worth remembering that employees are not always trustworthy, even if they are employed by major companies. One of Gonzalez' accomplices, Stephen Watt, worked for Morgan Stanley at the time of the hacks [Zetter 2009c], though as far as is known he never engaged in criminal activity connected with his employment. Insider fraud is a very serious problem, one that is rarely discussed in public.

3.2   Classes of Attackers

The easiest way to visualize threats is to consider two axes: the skill of the attacker, and whether the attacker is trying to get *you* in particular or someone at random. It's shown in *threat matrix* (Figure 3.1).

What I dub the *joy hacker* is close to the Hollywood stereotype: the teenage or 20-something nerdy male who lives in his parents' basement, surrounded by crumpled soft drink cans and empty pizza boxes, and whose only contact with the outside world is via his computer, with nary a "girl" in sight [M. J. Schwartz 2012]. He'll have a certain amount of cleverness and can do some damage, but the effect is random and limited because his hacking is pointless; there's no goal but the hack itself, and perhaps the knowledge gained. It's youthful experimentation, minus any sense of morals.

The joy hacker exists, though much of the stereotypical picture is (and was) wrong. From a security perspective, though, gender and the presence or absence of parents, base-

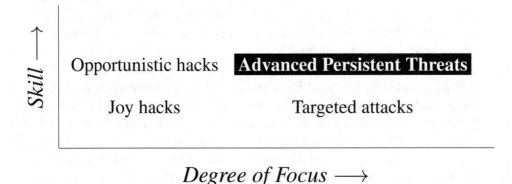

Figure 3.1: The threat matrix.

ments, pizza, and romantic interests are irrelevant. What matters is the unfocused nature of the threat—and the potential danger if you're careless. Make no mistake; joy hackers can hurt you. However, ordinary care will suffice; if you're too hard a target, they'll move on to someone simpler to attack. After all, by definition they're not very good.

A related (but lesser) threat is the *script kiddie*. Script kiddies have little real understanding of what they're doing. They may try more different attacks, but they're limited to using canned exploits created and packaged by others.

As joy hackers progress (I hesitate to use the phrase "grow up"), they can move along either axis. If they simply develop more skills, the attacks are still random but more sophisticated. They don't want your machine in particular; they want *someone's*. They may care about the type of machine (perhaps their exploits only work against a certain version of Windows) or its bandwidth, but exactly whose machine they attack is irrelevant. Most worms are like this, as are many types of malware—they spread, and if they happen to catch something useful, the hacker behind it will benefit and probably profit.

Opportunistic hackers are considerably more dangerous than joy hackers, precisely because they're more skilled. They'll know of many different vulnerabilities and attack techniques; they'll likely have a large and varied arsenal. They may even have some 0-days to bring to bear. Still, their attacks are random and opportunistic; again, they're not after you in particular. They may briefly switch their attention to you if you annoy them (see the box on page 172 for one such incident) or if they're paid to harass you, but on the whole they don't engage in much target selection.

Their lack of selectivity doesn't make them harmless. It is likely that this class of malefactor is responsible for many of the botnets that infest the Internet today; these botnets, in turn, send out spam, launch DDoS attacks, and so on. For many sites, the opportunistic hacker is *the* threat to defend against.

Targetiers aim specifically at a particular person or organization. Here, to reverse the old joke, it's not enough to outrun the other guy; you have to outrun the bear. Depending on how good the bear—the attacker—is, this might be quite a struggle. Targetiers will perform various sorts of reconnaissance and may engage in physical world activities like dumpster-diving.

These people are quite dangerous. Even an unskilled attacker can easily buy DDoS attacks; more skilled ones can purchase 0-days. If they're good enough, they can ascend to the upper right of our chart and be labeled *advanced persistent threats (APTs)*.

One particularly pernicious breed of targetier is the insider who has turned to the Dark Side. They may have been paid, or they may be seeking revenge; regardless, they're inside most of your defensive mechanisms and they know your systems. Worse yet, human nature is such that we're reluctant to suspect one of our own; this was one factor that hindered the FBI in the investigation that eventually snagged Robert Hanssen [Fine 2003; Wise 2002].

Targetier?

For lack of a better noun, I've chosen to use "targetier," by analogy with "bombardier," to denote someone who launches a targeted attack. However, that is probably etymologically incorrect.

Targetier—the word is listed in the OED, along with many other variants (targeteer, targettier, targatier, targatyer, targuattier, targueteere, targuetier, and targuettier)—is defined as "A foot-soldier armed with a target; a peltast." But that meaning of "target" isn't the one we generally think of; it's a "A light round shield or buckler," that is, a defensive mechanism, not a goal. "Targeter," the obvious noun for me to use, is even further from the meaning we want; the OED defines it as "A shield-maker, or a shield-bearer."

3.3   Advanced Persistent Threats

> **Apt**: An Arctic monster. A huge, white-furred creature with six limbs, four of which, short and heavy, carry it over the snow and ice; the other two, which grow forward from its shoulders on either side of its long, powerful neck, terminate in white, hairless hands with which it seizes and holds its prey. Its head and mouth are similar in appearance to those of a hippopotamus, except that from the sides of the lower jawbone two mighty horns curve slightly downward toward the front. Its two huge eyes extend in two vast oval patches from the centre of the top of the cranium down either side of the head to below the roots of the horns, so that these weapons really grow out from the lower part of the eyes, which are composed of several thousand ocelli each. Each ocellus is furnished with its own lid, and the apt can, at will, close as many of the facets of his huge eyes as he chooses.
>
> *Thuvia, Maid of Mars*
> —EDGAR RICE BURROUGHS

APTs are, of course, the big enchilada of threat models, the kind of attack we typically attribute to the Andromedans. There's no one definition of APT; generally speaking, though, an APT involves good target intelligence and a technical attack that isn't easily deflected. Also note that there are levels of APT; Gonzalez et al. are arguably in that quadrant, but they did not have the capabilities of a major country's intelligence service.

The best-documented example of a real APT attack is Stuxnet [Falliere, Murchu, and Chien 2011; Zetter 2014], a piece of malware apparently aimed at the Iranian uranium centrifuge enrichment plant. The source is unclear, though press reports have blamed (credited?) Israel and the United States [Broad, Markoff, and Sanger 2011; Williams 2011]. Stuxnet meets anyone's definition of an APT.

The actual penetration code used four different 0-days, vulnerabilities that were unknown to the vendors or the community. (Actually, two of them had been reported, but the reports were either unnoticed or ignored by the community—but perhaps not by the people behind Stuxnet; it is unknown whether they read of these exploits or rediscovered them.) Stuxnet did not use the Internet or Iranian intranets to spread; rather, it traveled over LANs or moved from site to site via USB flash disks. The attackers apparently charted its spread [Markoff 2011a], possibly to learn a good path to the target [Falliere, Murchu, and Chien 2011; Zetter 2014]. Once it got there, special modules infected the *programmable logic controllers (PLCs)* that control the centrifuge motors. The motor speeds were varied in a pattern that would cause maximum damage, the monitoring displays showed what the plant operators expected to see, and the emergency stop button did nothing.

There were other interesting things about Stuxnet. It would only attack specific models of PLC, the ones used in the centrifuge plant. It installed device drivers signed with public keys belonging to legitimate Taiwanese companies; somehow, these keys were compromised, too. It also used *rootkits*—software to conceal its existence—on both Windows and the PLCs. We can deduce several things about Stuxnet. First, whoever launched it believed they were aiming at a high-value target: 0-days, while hardly unknown, are rather rare. Perhaps significantly, APTs appear to be the primary user of 0-days [Batchelder et al. 2013, p. 9]. Furthermore, once they've been detected, they're useless; vendors will patch the holes and anti-malware software will recognize the exploits. That someone was willing to spend four of them in a single attack strongly suggests that they *really* wanted to take out the target.

The next really interesting thing is how much intelligence the attackers had about their target. Not only did they know a set of organizational links by which a flash drive attack might spread, they also knew precisely what type of PLCs were in use and what motor speeds would do the most damage. Did they learn this from on-site spies? Other traditional forms of intelligence? Another worm designed to learn such things and exfiltrate the information? A Stuxnet variant intended for the latter has been spotted [Markoff

2011b]; some sources think that that was the goal of Flame [Nakashima, G. Miller, and Tate 2012; Zetter 2014], too. The first two options strongly suggest an intelligence agency working with something like the Andromedans' MI-31 (or, if the press reports are accurate, the NSA and/or Unit 8200).

The last really interesting thing about Stuxnet is the resources it took to create it. Symantec estimates that it took at least five to ten "core developers" half a year to create it, plus additional resources for testing, management, intelligence-gathering, etc. Again, this points to a high-end adversary willing to spend a lot on the attack. Stuxnet was indeed, as I noted in my blog, "weaponized software" [Bellovin 2010].

Stuxnet is a classic example of an APT attack, but there have been others. The penetration of Google in late 2009, allegedly by attackers from China [Jacobs and Helft 2010], is often described as one; another well-known example is the attack on RSA [Markoff 2011c], though that claim has been challenged [Richmond 2011].

What makes an attack an APT? Uri Rivner, the author of RSA's blog posting on what happened to them, has it right [Rivner 2011]:

> The first thing actors like those behind the APT do is seek publicly available information about specific employees—social media sites are always a favorite. With that in hand they then send that user a Spear Phishing email. Often the email uses target-relevant content; for instance, if you're in the finance department, it may talk about some advice on regulatory controls.

He goes on to talk about how a 0-day exploit was used, but often that's less important; no one will spend more on an attack than they have to, be it in 0-days or dollars. All attackers are limited; people who can carry out these attacks are the scarcest resource of all, even for the Andromedans.

It's an interesting question why so many companies seem proud to announce that they've been the victim of an advanced persistent threat (APT). Are they saying that their internal security is so good that nothing less could have penetrated it? Or are they bragging that they're important enough to warrant that sort of attention?

Recall the definition of threat: "an adversary that is *motivated* and capable of exploiting a vulnerability." Capabilities are often the easiest part; plenty of garden-variety opportunistic hackers can find 0-days, and even script kiddies can send phishing emails. What's really important is the motivation: *who* wants to get you? Someone who's interested in something ordinary, like a corporate bank account, may come after you with a 0-day, but probably not. If they fail at getting you, though, they'll probably move on; there are plenty of other targets. However, if you manufacture anti-Andromedan weaponry, MI-31 may try something newer or more clever, because they *really* want what you've got. The most important question, then, when determining whether you may be the target of an APT is whether you have something that an enemy of that caliber might want.

It is important to remember that not all advanced attackers will want the same things. Weaponry might be of interest to the Andromedan military, but that isn't all that's at risk. Some countries' intelligence agencies may work on behalf of national economic interests; as long ago as 1991, first-class seats on Air France were reportedly bugged to pick up conversations by business executives [Rawnsley 2013]. Enterprises that might be military targets in the event of a shooting war may be penetrated to "prepare the battlefield" [National Research Council 2010].

An APT attacker won't be stopped by the strongest cryptography, either. There are probably other weaknesses in the victim's defenses; why bother going through a strong defense when you can go around it? It's easier to plant some malware on the endpoint; such code can read the plaintext before it's encrypted or after it's decrypted. Better yet, the malware can include a keystroke logger, which can capture the passwords used to encrypt files.[1]

Andromeda's MI-31 won't restrict itself to online means. Finding a clever hole in software is a great academic game; pros, though, are interested in results. If the easiest way to break in to an important computer is via surreptitious entry into someone's house, they'll do that. As Robert Morris once noted when talking about a supposedly secure cryptosystem: "You can still get the message, but maybe not by cryptanalysis. If you're in this business, you go after a reasonably cheap, reliable method. It may be one of the three Bs: burglary, bribery or blackmail. Those are right up there along with cryptanalysis in their importance" [Kolata 2001].

What should you do if you think you are a potential target for an APT? While you should certainly take all of the usual technical precautions, more or less by definition they alone will not suffice. Two more things are essential: *good* user training (see Chapter 14) and proper processes (Chapter 16). Finally, you should talk to your own country's counterintelligence service—but at this point, they may already have contacted you.

A caveat: There's a piece of advice given to every beginning medical student: when you hear galloping hoofbeats, don't think of zebras. Yes, zebras exist, but most likely, you're hearing horses. The same is true of attacks. Many things that look like attacks are just normal errors or misconfigurations; many attacks that appear to be advanced and targeted are ordinary, opportunistic, garden-variety malware. If you are hit by an APT, don't assume you know who did it.

---

1. See *United States v. Scarfo*, Criminal No. 00-404 (D.N.J.) (2001), http://epic.org/crypto/scarfo.html, for an example of a keystroke logger planted by law enforcement. Governments do indeed do that sort of thing [Paul 2011].

In fact, don't even assume it was really an APT. When JPMorgan Chase was hacked in 2014, news reports suggested foreign government involvement [Perlroth and Goldstein 2014]:

> Given the level of sophistication of the attack, investigators say they believe it was planned for months and may have involved some coordination or assistance from a foreign government. The working theory is that the hackers most likely live in Russia, the people briefed said.
>
> They said the fact that no money was taken did not necessarily mean it was a case of state-sponsored espionage, only that the bank was able to stop the hackers before they could siphon customer accounts.

Further investigation told a different story [Goldstein 2015]: "Soon after the hacking was discovered at JPMorgan, agents with the Federal Bureau of Investigation determined the attack was not particularly sophisticated even though the bank's security people had argued otherwise. The hacking succeeded largely because the bank failed to properly put updates on a remote server that was part of its vast digital network."

Attribution is one of the toughest parts of the business. A National Academies report quoted a former Justice Department official as saying, "I have seen too many situations where government officials claimed a high degree of confidence as to the source, intent, and scope of an attack, and it turned out they were wrong on every aspect of it. That is, they were often wrong, but never in doubt" [Owens, Dam, and Lin 2009, p. 142].

3.4   What's at Risk?

What do you have that's worthwhile? A better way to ask that question is to wonder, "What do I have that an attacker—any attacker—might want?"

Generically speaking, every computer has certain things: an identity, bandwidth, and credentials. All of these are valuable to some attackers, though of course which attackers will value a particular computer will depend on just what access that machine grants them. An old, slow computer that is nevertheless used for online banking would indeed be attractive to some people. Furthermore, the more or less random pattern of non-APT attacks means that it may indeed be hit. To a first approximation, *every* computer is at risk; the excuse that "there's nothing interesting on this machine" is exactly that: an excuse. This fact is the base level from which all risk assessments must start.

For generic machines, the next level up depends on particular characteristics of the machine. Computers with good bandwidth and static IP addresses can be used to host illicit servers of various types: bogus web servers for phishing scams, archives of stolen data, and so on. They're also more valuable as DDoS *botnet* nodes because their fast links let them fire more garbage at the victim. (Aside: some sources say that in the Underground Economy bots are called *boats*, because they can carry anything—their payload modules are easily updatable and are quite flexible. The same machine that is a DDoS engine today might host a "warez" archive tomorrow and a phishing site the day after.)

The more interesting—and higher-risk—category involves those computers that have specific, monetizable assets. A large password file? That's salable. A customer database? Salable; the price will depend on what fields are included. Credit card numbers in bulk are lucrative, especially if they're linked to names, addresses, expiration dates, *card verification values (CVV2s)*, etc. Lists of email addresses? Spammers like them, both for their own use and for resale to other spammers. Real web servers can be converted into malware dispensers.

Particular organizations often have data useful to people in that field. A school's administrative computers are valuable to people who want to sell improved grades. Business executives have been accused of hacking in to rivals' systems [Harper 2013; B. Sullivan 2005]. Corporations have been accused of hacking into environmental groups' computers [Jolly 2011].

A closely related set of at-risk machines are client machines that connect to actual target machines. Login credentials can be stolen or the entire machine hijacked to get at the data of interest.

If you work for a large company, you have a special problem: you almost certainly do not know of everything that's valuable. Indeed, some of the most valuable data may be very closely held; you may never have heard of the unit that has it. The attackers might know, either through blind chance or because they have other useful intelligence. For example, major corporate hires are sometimes mentioned in the trade press or in business publications. If a new executive is hired with a particular specialty not related to what your company is currently doing, it's news—but it's news that you, as a computer security specialist, may not have seen. Someone tracking that technology or your company might spot it, though, and target this new business unit.

The solution—and it's easier said than done—is, of course, cooperation within the company. Every business unit with valuable data needs to tell the corporate security group that it exists. They don't have to say just what it is; they do need to know and report its value and to what class of rival. Another company? A company with a reputation for lax corporate ethics? A company headquartered in a country that doesn't respect intellectual property rights? A minor foreign intelligence agency? The Andromedans themselves? The hard part is not just the intracompany cooperation, though that can be challenging enough; rather, it's getting non-security people to understand the nature of the threat. There's a lot of hype out there and noise about threats that aren't real; consequently, there are a lot of skeptics. (Tell them they need to buy their own copy of this book. . .) Again: the issue of what defenses to deploy is a separate question from ascertaining which assets are at risk.

3.5   The Legacy Problem

When identifying what's at risk, don't neglect legacy systems. Greenfield development is very rare; virtually all non-trivial software development projects are based on ancient code and/or have to talk to ancient database systems running on obsolete hardware with an obsolete OS. It's probably economically infeasible to do anything about it, either. The application may be tied to a particular release and patch level of its OS [Chen et al. 2005]; fixing that would cost a significant amount of money that isn't in the budget because the code currently (mostly) works. Besides, organizationally it's someone else's system, and you haven't the remit to do anything about it. But if a penetration happens because your new application opened up a channel to someone else's ancient, crufty code, you *know* whose problem that is.

All that said, the asset still exists; protection of it still needs to be part of your analysis. The solutions won't be as elegant, as complete, or in most cases as cheap as it would be had things been designed properly; as noted, perfect foresight is impossible. I return to this issue in Section 11.5.

Part II

Technologies

Chapter 4

Antivirus Software

"Let me put it another way. You have a computer with an auto-dial phone link. You put the VIRUS program into it and it starts dialing phone numbers at random until it connects to another computer with an auto-dial. The VIRUS program then *injects* itself into the new computer. Or rather, it reprograms the new computer with a VIRUS program of its own and erases itself from the first computer. The second machine then begins to dial phone numbers at random until it connects with a third machine. You get the picture?
…

"It's fun to think about, but it was hell to get out of the system. The guy who wrote it had a few little extra goodies tacked onto it—well, I won't go into any detail. I'll just tell you that he also wrote a second program, only this one would cost you—it was called VACCINE."

Don Handley in *When Harlie Was One*
—DAVID GERROLD

4.1   Characteristics

Antivirus software is one of those things that drives traditional security people crazy. It shouldn't be necessary, it shouldn't work, and it should never be listed as a security essential. However, it is needed, it often works, and sometimes—though not always—it really is important.

Viruses were once seen as an artifact and a consequence of the "primitive" operational and security environment of personal computers. After all, in the early Apple and Microsoft worlds, programs ran with full hardware permission; the operating system was more a program loader and a set of utility routines than a full-fledged OS. A real OS had protected mode and access controls on files; people said that viruses simply couldn't happen in such a world.

To some extent, of course, that was true. Boot sector viruses "couldn't" exist because no virus would have access rights to the boot sector of any drive. Similarly, no virus could infect any system file because those were all write-protected against any ordinary users' programs.

Two things shook that belief. First, the Internet ("Morris") worm of 1988 [Eichin and Rochlis 1989; Spafford 1989] spread almost entirely without privileges; instead, it exploited buggy code and user-specified patterns of trust. Second, Tom Duff showed that it was possible to write viruses for Unix systems, even viruses that could infect shell scripts [Duff 1989a; Duff 1989b]. To understand why these could happen, we need to take a deeper look at the environment in which viruses exist.

It is a truism in the operating system community that an OS presents user programs with a *virtual instruction set*, an instruction set that consists of the unprivileged subset of the underlying hardware's op codes combined with OS-specific *"virtual instructions"*; these latter (better known as *system calls*) do things like create sockets, write to files, change permissions, and so on. This virtual machine (not to be confused with virtualization of the underlying hardware à la VMware) does not have things like Ethernet adapters or hard drives; instead, it has TCP/IP and file systems. Early DOS and Mac OS programs had full access to the underlying hardware (hence the ability to overwrite the boot sector) as well as to the virtual instructions provided by the operating systems of the day. Morris and Duff (and of course Fred Cohen in his dissertation [1986], which—aside from being the first academic document to use the term "virus"—presented a theoretical model of their existence and spread) showed that access to the privileged instructions was unnecessary, that the OS's virtualized instruction set was sufficient. We can take that two steps further.

First (and this is graphically illustrated by Duff, and formally modeled by Cohen), the *effective target environment* of a virus is limited to those files (or other resources) writable by the user context in which it executes. The effect of file permissions, then, is to limit the size of the effective target environment, rather than eliminating it; as such, file permissions slow virus propagation but do not prevent it. In other words, this virtual instruction set is just as capable of hosting viruses as the real+virtual instruction set; it's just that these viruses won't multiply as quickly.

Other than effective target environment, the main parameter in modeling virus propagation is the *spread rate*, i.e., the rate at which the virus is invoked with a different target

Why Were Early Operating Systems So Primitive?

One oft-puzzling aspect of computer history is why it took so long for "real" operating systems—that is, ones with some sort of protection and access control—to appear in the personal computer space. The answers are, not surprisingly, rooted in economics, but not in the obvious way.

It pays to look back at the early Unix systems. In their classic paper on Unix, Ritchie and Thompson [1974] described a machine (which ran on hardware "costing as little as $40,000") that had 144K bytes of RAM and about 50M bytes of disk. This was admittedly a large computer of its kind, and a smaller system would have sufficed.

Let's consider the Apple Macintosh SE, introduced in 1987.[a] Its minimum configuration was 256K of RAM, far more than Ritchie and Thompson had had. Similarly, the IBM PC XT shipped with at least 128K in 1983 [Morse 1982]. Again, that was clearly enough memory. Furthermore, by 1986 IBM was shipping a machine based on the Intel 80286 chip, which supported memory management and protected mode [Intel 1983]. What was the issue?

One constraint was disk: early machines didn't necessarily have a hard drive, and floppies were too slow. Still, even early models of IBM System/360s could run in tape-only configurations (I used one—TOS/360, the Tape Operating System—in 1968); the notion of a real OS without a hard drive is not preposterous. The real problem was software compatibility.

DOS—the Disk Operating System that was at the heart of Microsoft's early relationship with IBM—existed before a lot of the hardware was capable of running a real OS. Windows 3.1 was just a thin gloss on DOS; it had to be able to support older applications that assumed that they could do BIOS calls to get at the disk, load their own graphics card driver, etc. That in turn meant that when Windows 95 came along—the first version of Windows that really was an operating system, one that provided its own device drivers for everything—compatibility with older applications meant that DOS mode still had to be supported. Windows XP finally had file access control, but many of the Windows applications that had been developed since 1995 assumed that they were running with full OS privileges, and hence wouldn't work on ordinary user accounts. It wasn't until Windows Vista, in 2007, that there was finally a version of Windows that had full protections and an unprivileged user environment that was actually functional. Until then, PC users were paying for decisions made in 1981, when the original IBM PC was shipped.[b] To quote Melinda Shore, "hardware brevis, software longa."

---

a. "Macintosh SE: Technical Specifications," http://support.apple.com/kb/SP191.
b. "IBM Archives: The Birth of the IBM PC,"
   http://www-03.ibm.com/ibm/history/exhibits/pc25/pc25_birth.html.

environment. While that latter could mean the creation of new, infectable files, more likely it means being executed by a different user, who would have a different set of write permissions and hence a very different effective target environment. (For a more detailed and formal model of propagation, see [Staniford, Paxson, and Weaver 2002].)

The second generalization of a suitable virus environment is even more important than the role of file permissions: *any* sufficiently powerful execution environment can host a virus; it does not have to be an operating system, let alone bare hardware. It is easy to define "sufficient power": all it has to be able to do is to copy itself to some other location from which it can execute with a different effective target environment. That might be a different user on the same computer, or it might be a different computer; for the latter, the transport can be automatic (as is the case for worms) or aided by a human transmitting the file. Going back to our virtual instruction set model, any programmable environment will suffice, if the I/O capabilities are powerful enough. Microsoft Office documents, with their access to *Visual Basic for Applications (VBA)*, are the classic example, but many others exist. LaTeX—the system with which this book was written—comes very close; it has the ability to write files, but many years ago a restriction was imposed that only let documents write to files in the current directory. This effectively froze the effective target environment, since very few directories contain more than one LaTeX document. PostScript is another example, though I'll leave the design (and limitations) of a PostScript virus as an exercise for the reader. Even LISP viruses have appeared in the wild [Zwienenberg 2012].

There's one more aspect of the virtual instruction set that bears mentioning: what matters is the *actual* instruction set, not just the one intended by the system designers. Just as on the IBM 7090 computer a STORE ZERO instruction existed by accident [Koenig 2008], a virus writer can and will exploit bugs in the underlying platform to gain abilities beyond those anticipated by the programmers. Bugs are not necessary—the IBM "Christmas Card" virus[1] spread because of the credulity of users—but they do complicate life for the defender.

Collectively, these points explain why the classic protection model of operating systems does not prevent viruses: they can thrive within a single protection domain and spread by ordinary collaborative work. Duff's experiments relied on the prevalence of world-writable files and directories, but such are not necessary. His design, involving an infected Unix executable, would not work well without such artifacts of a loosely administered system, since Unix users rarely shared executable files, but higher-level environments—Word, PostScript, etc.—could and did host their own forms of malware.

A corollary to this is that the classic operating system protection model—an isolated *trusted computing base (TCB)*—does not protect the users of the system from themselves.

---

1. "The Christmas Card Caper, (hopefully) concluded," http://catless.ncl.ac.uk/Risks/5.81.html#subj1.

It also explains why, say, the Orange Book [DoD 1985a], the US Department of Defense's 1980s-vintage specification for secure computer systems, is quite inadequate as a defense against viruses: they do not violate its security model and hence are not impeded by it.

In short, classic operating system design paradigms do not and cannot stop viruses. That is why antivirus programs have been needed.

To understand why virus checkers "shouldn't" work, it is necessary to understand how they function. It would be nice, of course, if they could analyze a file and *know* a priori that that file is or isn't evil [Bellovin 2003]. Even apart from the difficulty of defining "evil," the problem can't be solved; it runs afoul of Turing and the Halting Problem [Cohen 1987]. Accordingly, a heuristic solution is necessary.

Today's virus checkers rely primarily on *signatures*: they match files against a database of code snippets of known viruses. The code matched can be part of the virus' replication mechanism or its payload.

The disadvantages of this sort of pattern-matching are obvious. One, of course, is that its success is crucially dependent on having a complete, up-to-date signature database. The antivirus companies love that, since it means that customers have to buy subscriptions rather than make a one-time purchase, but it's entirely legitimate; by definition a new virus won't be matched by anything in an older database.

Virus writers have used the obvious counter to signature databases; they've employed various forms of obfuscation and transformation of the actual virus. Some viruses encrypt most of the body, in which case the antivirus software has to recognize the decryptor. Other viruses do things like inserting NOPs, rearranging code fragments, replacing instruction sequences with equivalent ones, and so on.

Naturally, the antivirus vendors haven't stayed idle. The obvious defense is to look for the the invariant code, such as the aforementioned decryptor; other techniques include looking for multiple sequences of short patterns, deleting NOPs, and so on. Ultimately, though, there seems to be a limit on how good a job a static signature analyzer can do; in fact, experiments have shown that "the challenge of modeling self-modifying shellcode by signature-based methods, and certain classes of statistical models, is likely an intractable problem" [Song et al. 2010]. Fundamentally different approaches are needed.

One, widely used today by antivirus programs, employs *sandboxed* or otherwise controlled execution. It is based on two premises: first, virus code is generally executed at or very near the start of a program to make sure it does get control; second, the behavior of a virus is fundamentally different than that of a normal, benign program. Normal programs do not try to open the boot block, nor do they scan for other executable files and try to modify them. If such behavior patterns are detected—and there are behavior patterns (see, e.g., [Hofmeyr, Somayaji, and Forrest 1998]) as well as byte patterns in a signature database—the program is probably malware.

Note, though, the word "probably." Antivirus programs are not guaranteed to produce the correct results; not only can they miss viruses (*false negatives*), as discussed above, they can also produce *false positives* and claim that perfectly innocent files are in fact malicious.

A second approach, used somewhat today but likely to be a mainstay in the future, relies on anomaly detection. Anomaly detection relies on statistics: the properties of normal programs and documents are different than those of malware; the trick is avoiding false positives.

One challenge is how to identify useful features that distinguish malware from normal files. Data mining is the approach of choice [Lee and Stolfo 1998] in many of today's products, but it's not the only one. Another study attempted to detect *shellcode*—actually, machine code, especially machine code intended to invoke a shell—in Word documents by looking at *n*-gram frequencies [W.-J. Li et al. 2007]. While in theory more or less anything can appear in a Microsoft Office document—"modern document formats are essentially object-containers...of any executable object"—some sections of legitimate documents are much less likely than others to contain shellcode. Li and company found that by counting the frequency of various *n*-grams, they could detect infected documents quite successfully.

Anomaly detectors require *training*; that is, they need to "know" what is normal. Training is commonly done by feeding large quantities of uninfected files to an analyzer; the analyzer builds some sort of statistical profile based on them. This is then used to catch new malware.

Naturally, what is "normal" changes over time and by location. A site that tends to include pictures in its Word documents will look quite different than a site that does not. Similarly, as new features are added, statistical values will change. Thus, even anomaly detection requires frequently updated databases.

The problem with anomaly detection is, as noted, false positives. While signature schemes can have such issues, the rate is very much higher with anomaly schemes. Users doing different things, either on their own or because the applications that they use have changed, can appear just as anomalous as malware. A partial solution is to correlate anomaly information from different sites [Debar and Wespi 2001; Valdes and Skinner 2001]. If a file seems somewhat odd but not quite odd enough to flag it definitively, it can be uploaded to your antivirus vendor and matched against similar files from other sites.

The final piece of the puzzle is how to find new malware. Sometimes, machines or files believed to be infected are sent to the antivirus companies; indeed, that is how Stuxnet and Flame were found [Falliere, Murchu, and Chien 2011; Zetter 2012; Zetter 2014]. More often, the vendors go looking for infections. They deploy machines that aren't patched, get on spam mailing lists and open—execute—the attachments, etc. They also haunt locales known to be infested. "Adult" sites are notorious for hosting malware; before suitable scripting technologies were developed, some vendors had employees whose job responsibilities were to spend all day viewing porn. (Anecdotal evidence suggests that yes, it is possible to get bored with such a job, even in the demographics believed to be most interested in such material.)

4.2   The Care and Feeding of Antivirus Software

Antivirus software is not fire-and-forget technology. It needs constant attention, both because of the changing threat environment and the changing computing environment. Other operational considerations include handling false negatives, handling false positives, efficiency, where and when scanning should happen, and user training.

The need for up-to-date signature and anomaly databases is quite clear. What is less obvious is how the operational environment interacts with virus scanning. To pick a trivial example, if you don't run Microsoft Office you don't need a scanner that can cope with Word documents; if the former changes, you do.

Sometimes, the environmental influences can be more subtle and serious. Once, three separate versions of a program's installer were falsely flagged as viruses by a particular scanner.[2] It seems likely that the installer had an unusual code sequence that happened to match a virus's signature.

Several of the other factors interact as well. Consider the false-negative problem, often due to an inadequate or antiquated database. Many people suggest running two different brands of antivirus software to take advantage of different collections of viruses. That's reasonable enough, if you didn't have to worry about (of course) cost, performance, and increasing your rate of false positives. Assuming that the false positive rate is low enough (it generally is), one solution is to use one technology at network entry points—mail gateways, web proxies, and perhaps file servers—while using a different technology on end systems. That also helps deal with the cost issue; you don't have to buy two different packages for each of your many desktops and laptops.

That strategy has its own flaw, though: network-based scanners can't cope with encrypted content. Encrypted email is rare today; encrypted web traffic is common, and web proxies pass HTTPS through unexamined. Furthermore, there is one form of encryption that has been used by malware: encrypted .zip files, with the password given in the body of the message.

In most situations, the proper response to the encryption problem is to ignore it. If you have antivirus software on your end systems, it will probably catch the malware. Most of what's missed by major scanners is the rarer viruses; they all handle the common ones.

---

2. "Pegasus Mail v4.5x Released," http://www.pmail.com/v45x.htm.

You might be inclined to worry more if you're being targeted by the Andromedans; after all, they can find 0-days to use against you. However, by definition 0-days aren't known and hence won't be in anyone's signature files; besides, MI-31 can run their code through many different scanners and make sure it gets through unmolested. However, you might find, after someone else has noticed and analyzed the malware, that signatures are developed (as has happened with Stuxnet); in that case, your end system scanners will pick up any previous infections. Anomaly detectors are another solution. (There's an interesting duality here. As mentioned earlier, anomaly detectors need to be trained on uninfected files. An exploit for a 0-day by definition won't be in the training data and is therefore more likely to be caught later on. By contrast, the lack of prior instances of the 0-day means that it won't be in a signature file. The world is thus neatly bifurcated; the two different technologies match the two different time spans. One caveat: just because something hasn't been noticed doesn't mean it doesn't exist. Sophisticated attacks, especially by our friends the Andromedans, may not be noticed for quite a while. Again, this happened with both Stuxnet and Flame.)

Using multiple antivirus scanners is a classic example of when one should not treat insecurity as a sin. It's an economic issue; gaining this small extra measure of protection isn't worth it if it costs you too much. If your end systems are well managed—that is, if they're up to date on patches and have current antivirus software—infrastructure-based scanning is an extra layer. It's a useful extra layer and shouldn't be neglected if feasible; the question is what it costs, not in dollars but in lost functionality and perhaps user miseducation. Consider: if you're in an environment where sending around .zip files is common, barring them costs productivity. Users rapidly learn to evade this, by changing the extension—and teaching users to evade security mechanisms is never a good idea.

Don't neglect the opportunity to detect viruses after they've infected a machine. For the most part, today's viruses aren't designed for random malicious mischief; rather, they have very specific goals. Catching that sort of behavior is a good way to find infected machines.

The form of detection to use, of course, depends on the goal of the virus; since you can't know that you'll have to employ several. One form is extrusion detection, as discussed in Section 5.5: looking at outbound traffic for theft of data. This is especially useful if you're the victim of a targeted attack (especially an Andromedan attack), since exfiltration of proprietary data is a frequent goal of such attackers. Another good approach is to look for command and control traffic; infected machines are frequently part of a botnet managed via a peer-to-peer network. This isn't easy to spot, though there are some fruitful approaches. Traffic flow visualization [D. Best et al. 2011; T. Taylor et al. 2009] is one approach. If you know your machine population well, you can look for client-to-client traffic; such behavior is uncommon except in peer-to-peer networks.

4.3   Is Antivirus Always Needed?

One of the most controversial issues surrounding antivirus software is on which machines it should be used. Some people say it needs to be used everywhere; others say it should never be used. Since absolute statements are always wrong, let's approach the question analytically.

An antivirus package is another layer of defense. Per the analysis above, it protects against threats that an OS cannot catch; it's also capable of blocking attacks that somehow managed to get through some other layer. On occasion, this is a matter of timing; a new security hole may be difficult to fix. Or it might be that the vendor quite rightly wants— needs, actually—to put the fix through testing and quality assurance before shipping it. Antivirus firms can ship signature updates much more quickly, because they're *advisory*. In a very strong sense, the division of responsibilities between the antivirus package and the OS is like the split between the C compiler and lint [S. C. Johnson 1978]:

> In conclusion, it appears that the general notion of having two programs is a good one. The compiler concentrates on quickly and accurately turning the program text into bits which can be run; *lint* concentrates on issues of portability, style, and efficiency. *Lint* can afford to be wrong, since incorrectness and over-conservatism are merely annoying, not fatal. The compiler can be fast since it knows that *lint* will cover its flanks.

Just so. There is, however, one extremely crucial difference: unlike a programmer deciding to ignore a lint warning, deciding to turn off virus-checking is a very difficult decision, and well beyond the pay grade of most users. It's tempting to say that people know when they're doing dangerous things, such as downloading programs from random Internet sites, and when they're doing something that should be safe, such as installing software from a major vendor's official distribution page. Indeed, many very legitimate packages caution you to turn off your virus scanner prior to running the installer. It's not that simple. Even apart from timing coincidences and malware that waits for a software installation to fire up, out-of-the-box products have been infected with viruses, including Microsoft software CDs [Barnett 2009], IBM desktops [Weil 1999], Dell server motherboards [Oates 2010], and even digital picture frames [Gage 2008].

One consideration that often leads people to omit antivirus technology is a system's usage and/or connectivity. An ordinary end-user's desktop machine is the environment for which, it would seem, antivirus packages were developed; users, after all, are constantly visiting sketchy web sites, downloading dubious files, and receiving all manner of enticing (albeit utterly fraudulent) email. But what about servers? Embedded systems? Systems behind an airgap? Embedded systems behind an airgap? All of these can be vulnerable, but in different ways.

Servers can be infected precisely because they're *servers*: they're listening for certain requests, and if the serving applications are buggy they can be vulnerable to malware. This is, after all, what leaves them very vulnerable to many of the usual attacks: stack-smashing, SQL injections, and more. It is important to realize that nowhere in the operational definition of an antivirus program is any requirement that the signatures only match self-replicating programs. Anything can be matched, including garden-variety persistent malware. In fact, the word "antivirus" is a misnomer; it is, rather, *antifile* software, and can flag any file that matches certain patterns, as long as the file is of a type that it knows to scan.

Embedded devices—the small computers that run our cars, printers, toasters, DVD players, televisions, and more—are often quite vulnerable [Cui and Stolfo 2010]. Perhaps surprisingly, they're frequently controlled by general-purpose operating systems (often, though not always, Windows), and they're very rarely patched. An address space-scanning virus isn't particular; it doesn't know if it's probing your colleague's desktop or the office thermostat; if it answers in the right way, it can be infected. Furthermore, since the software powering such devices is very rarely updated, they're generally susceptible to very old hacks. Unfortunately, they also never have antivirus software, and if they did the signature database would be out of date. (What release of what OS is your car's tire pressure monitor running? It might be vulnerable [Rouf et al. 2010]. Note, too, that although there is local wireless connectivity to your wheels, there is no Internet connectivity and hence no way to automatically download signature updates. Perhaps your mechanic is regularly updating the base software—but perhaps not.) Even nuclear power plants have been infected [Poulsen 2003; Wuokko 2003].

How was the Davis-Besse nuclear power plant infected? There was a firewall that was properly configured to block the attack, but it only protected the direct link to the Internet. The Slammer worm, though, infected a machine at a contractor's facility, and that contractor had a direct link to the operator of the plant. This link was not protected by the firewall, which permitted the worm to attack an unpatched server within the nuclear plant operator's network. In other words, there were several different ways the problem could have been prevented—but it wasn't.

Airgapped systems—ones with no network connections, direct or indirect, to the outside world—are sometimes seen as the ultimate in secure, protected machines. Grampp and Morris wrote [1984], "It is easy to run a secure computer system. You merely have to disconnect all dial-up connections and permit only direct-wired terminals, put the machine and its terminals in a shielded room, and post a guard at the door." Unfortunately, in many ways such systems are *less* secure.

How can attacks enter? The easiest way is via USB flash disk. Indeed, Stuxnet is believed to have been introduced into the Iranian centrifuge plant in exactly that fashion, since one of the 0-days it used caused autoexecution of code on a flash disk [Falliere, Murchu, and Chien 2011]. For a while, the US military banned such devices because of a very serious network penetration via that mechanism [Lynn III 2010]. Who provided the infected flash disks in these cases? It isn't known (at least not publicly), but it could have been a legitimate user who found it in a parking lot; in at least one test, most users fell for that trick [Kenyon 2011]. Alternately, a machine legitimately intended to communicate across the airgap, perhaps to provide new software for it or to receive outbound reports, might have been infected; when the communications flash drive was inserted into it, the drive (or the legitimate files on it) could have been infected, to the detriment of its communicants beyond the airgap. Add to that the difficulty of installing patches and signature file updates on machines that can't talk to the Internet and you see the problem: the administrators were lulled into a false sense of security by the topological separation, and they didn't do the hard work of otherwise protecting the machines.

Is the xkcd cartoon (Figure 4.1) wrong? Is it necessary and proper to have antivirus software on voting machines? As in so many other situations, it depends. There can be false positives; indeed, antivirus software was (incorrectly, it turned out) blamed for problems with a voting system [Flaherty 2008]. But voting systems are supposed to be carefully controlled, running only certified software [Flaherty 2008]:

> Unlike other software, the problem acknowledged by Premier cannot be fixed by sending out a coding fix to its customers because of federal rules for certifying election systems, Rigall said. Changes to systems must go through the Election Assistance Commission, he said, and take two years on average for certification and approval—and that is apart from whatever approvals and reviews would be needed by each elections board throughout the country.

If the machine is only running certified software, and if proper procedures are followed, there should be no chance of any attacks, and hence no need for protective add-ons.

Note, though, that second "if" (and remember the Davis-Besse nuclear power plant). In practice, voting machines are often not properly protected. Ed Felten, a prominent computer science professor at Princeton, has made a habit of touring his town and photographing unguarded machines [2009]. Nor are the systems secure against someone who has physical access; reports on this are legion, but the summary Red Team report in the California "Top to Bottom" review makes it clear just how bad the situation can be [Bishop 2007]. Similarly, the protective seals are not effective defenses against tampering [Appel 2011]. In short, though in theory antivirus software isn't needed, in practice it might help—except that the vulnerabilities are so pervasive the attackers could disable any protective mechanisms at the same time as they replaced all of the other software on the machine. Besides, how, when, and by whom would the signature databases be updated?

Figure 4.1: Voting machines with antivirus software.

(The larger question of electronic voting machine security and accuracy is quite interesting. Fortunately, however, most of it is well outside the scope of this book. Let it suffice to say that most computer scientists are very uneasy about *direct recording electronic (DRE)* systems. For further details, see [Rubin 2006] or [D. W. Jones and Simons 2012].)

There's one more situation where antivirus software isn't needed: when the incidence of viruses is so low as to render the protection questionable. In that case, you pay the price—the cost of the software, hits to system efficiency, possible false positives—without reaping much benefit. Mac OS X currently (September 2015) falls into that category, though with the growing popularity of the platform that probably won't be true for very much longer. Again, antivirus software is not an abstract technology; it can only protect against real, past threats. If there are no threats, there's nothing to put into the signature database. The most serious attacks on Macs have involved either social engineering or a Java hole; the former can be avoided with education (but see Chapter 14) and the latter by upgrading to the latest release of Mac OS X, which does not include Java. (Microsoft Office macro viruses could, in theory, affect Macs as well, but they seemed extinct because of long-ago fixes by Microsoft. Some people say they're starting to come back [Ducklin 2015].) This might, though, be a great time to start collecting Mac OS X files for baseline data for anomaly detectors. After all, given the extremely low rate of infection, you're virtually guaranteed that you won't inadvertently train your model on unsuspected malware.

One last word of warning: just because your attention is focused on the Andromedans, don't neglect antivirus protection. Sure, it won't stop 0-days, but MI-31 will happily use older vulnerabilities if they'll suffice. Why use an expensive weapon when a cheap one will do the job?

4.4 Analysis

Antivirus—more properly, antimalware—software is a mainstay of today's security environment. Unfortunately, it is losing its efficacy. One recent article [Krebs 2012] noted that of a recent sample of nasty malware—programs aimed at stealing banking credentials from small businesses—run through multiple scanners via https://www.virustotal.com/, most were not detected. A mean of just 24.47% and a median of 19% of scanners caught these files. This means that the most relied-upon defense usually fails. If people blithely click on attachments under the assumption that they're protected, they're in for a very rude shock. The other defenses here—getting people to stop clicking on phishing messages, and either bug-free or quickly patched software—seem even more dubious. Will there be technical changes that can help?

The two areas most likely to change are the efficacies of signature-based detection and anomaly-based detection. A decline in the former would spur greater reliance on the latter; however, it is unclear whether its false positive rate is good enough at this point.

The death of signature-based scanning has been bruited about for quite some time; thus far, it has not quite come to pass. The virus writers may improve their technology, but the antivirus companies have been around for a long time and have invested a lot in their technology; its death will most likely manifest itself as a long decline rather than as a sudden cessation. To be sure, many of the rapid updates are possible only because anomaly detectors have flagged something as suspicious enough to merit analysis by humans.

Anomaly detection is at its best on systems that do the same sort of thing. An embedded device is a better setting for it than, say, a shared computer in a library or Internet cafe. Variations in usage patterns can trigger an upsurge in false positives; this is not a current technological limit but an issue inherent to the technology: by definition, anomaly detectors look for behavior that doesn't match what has been happening. (Normal variations do happen. Consider the previous paragraph, where I quite unintentionally used the words "bruited" and "cessation." Searching my system reveals that I virtually never use either of those words in my writing, but they both showed up here. An anomaly detector might conclude—incorrectly!—that I did not write those sentences. No, I didn't do it consciously, either; those words just happened to jump out of my brain at the right time.)

Another technology that is coming into use is digitally signed files. Just how this is implemented matters a lot; thus far, performance has been mixed.

The basic notion is that an executable file can be digitally signed; this is intended to give the user assurance that it hasn't been tampered with by a virus. Issues include who signs it, protection of the private signing keys (see Chapter 8 for more discussion of this), and when and how checking is done. Note that the limitations I describe are properties of the concepts themselves, not of their implementation.

In what I will call the "Microsoft device driver model," many different developers have keys and certificates signed by Microsoft. (Apple's *Gatekeeper* system for Mac OS X uses the same model.) Such a design offers some protection against low-end virus authors, but not against the Andromedans; there are too many trusted parties, and experience has shown that at least a few will fail to take adequate care. For that matter, MI-31 is quite capable of setting up a fake development shop and acquiring its own, very legitimate certificate. (The CIA has run its own covert airlines [M. Best 2011]; software development shops are much cheaper.)

The iOS signing model, used for iPhones, iPads, and other iToys, is very different: Apple is the sole signing party, and it nominally scrutinizes programs before approving them. There is only one private key to guard—but of course, if it's ever compromised a tremendous amount of damage can be done. There is thus less risk from low-end attackers but more risk from the very high end. One can also question just how good a job Apple or anyone else can do at finding cleverly hidden nastiness.

Android has an interesting variant: applications have public keys; these are used to verify updates to those applications. Thus, whoever has obtained the private key for, say, Furious Avians could create fake, malicious updates to it, but not to the Nerds with Fiends game; users who had only the latter and not the former would not be at risk.

When the signature is checked matters a great deal. If it's checked each time the file is loaded (e.g., on iOS you are protected against on-disk modification by some currently running nastyware; the risk, though, is that the checking code itself might be subverted. You are still protected if the malware has achieved penetration with user privileges rather than root privileges; a variant scheme would have signature checking done at a lower layer still, perhaps by the hypervisor or what a Multics aficionado would call "Ring 0" [Organick 1972].

There is an interaction here with the different signing paradigms. In the iOS model (and assuming that the One True Key hasn't been stolen), the attacker must either disable all checking or install a substitute verification key and resign all executables on the machine, a task that is quite expensive and probably prohibitively so. With the device driver model, the virus can include a signing key and use it to revalidate only those files it modifies.

Some systems check signatures at installation time. This provides no protection against changes to already-installed programs. It does ensure that what the vendor shipped is what you get and protects you from infection en route. That happened with some copies of the SiN game, where some secondary download servers were apparently infected [Lemos 1998] by the CIH virus; quite possibly, it was also the root cause of the infected CDs that Microsoft shipped [Barnett 2009]. Perhaps more importantly, you're protected against drive-by downloads, though there a great deal does depend on the implementation.

The ultimate utility of signed code as an antivirus defense remains to be seen. Furthermore, the benefits need to be weighed against the social costs of giving too much power to a very few—two or three—major vendors.

The other technical trend in this space is the increased use of sandboxing, running applications with fewer privileges. The notion has been around in the research community for many years. Long ago, Multics supported multiple protection rings even for user programs [Organick 1972], though few if any made effective use of it. Other, more recent work includes my own design for "sub-operating systems" [S. Ioannidis and Bellovin 2001; S. Ioannidis, Bellovin, and J. Smith 2002], a design that permitted any user to create a very large number of subusers with fewer permissions. In the commercial world, both Windows and Mac OS X use sandboxing for web browsers and some risky applications. Quite notably, Adobe has modified its popular but troubled PDF viewer to run in a sandbox on Windows Vista and later.

The benefit of a sandbox, though, is crucially dependent on two things: how much the isolated application needs to interact with the outside world, and how effectively those interactions can be policed. Consider, for example, an email message with an attached file, handled by a sandboxed mailer. If the file contains a virus, at best I might be barred from opening it—the mail sandbox should disallow execution—but at the least, should the file be executed, it would run with fewer permissions than even the mailer itself. On the other hand, if the attachment is a document I'm expected to edit I want to be able to open it normally; then, however, I take the risk that that document wasn't really sent by my colleague but was in fact generated by a virus on her machine.

The ultimate in sandboxing is the *virtual machine (VM)* (Section 10.2). As I've noted elsewhere [Bellovin 2006b], assuming that you're safe because the malware is running in its own VM is like letting your enemy put a 1U-height server into racks in your data center. Would you trust such a machine on your LAN? Even without the intended and expected interactions, you would probably (and rightly) consider that to be a serious risk. A VM is no better—and applications generally do need to interact with other parts of your system.

In essence, a sandbox can do two things: it can reduce both the effective instruction set and the effective target environment of programs executed within it. Taken together, these properties can drastically reduce or even stop the spread of viruses and worms.

Should you run antivirus software? For generic desktop systems, the answer is probably yes. It's relatively cheap protection and is usually trouble free. Similarly, server or firewall-resident scanners can block malicious inbound malware before it reaches your users. Be sure, though, that your environment and policies are such that definitions are regularly updated. As a corollary, it's wasteful on most embedded systems, simply because of the lack of any regular update mechanism. If an attacker can persuade such a device to download and run some file, you probably have bigger architectural problems.

Chapter 5

Firewalls and Intrusion Detection Systems

Summoning grids—pentacles with attitude—have a number of uses. Unsurprisingly, summoning spirits from the vasty deeps of Hilbert space is one of them. They can also be used, by the foolhardy or terminally reckless, to open gateways to other spaces (most of which are utterly inhospitable to human-like life). Finally, they can be used to create a firewall, like a science fictional force-field only buggier and prone to hacking attacks by extra-dimensional script kiddies with pseudopods. Which is why nobody with any sense uses them casually.

The Apocalypse Codex
—CHARLES STROSS

5.1 What Firewalls Don't Do

Since the dawn of the commercial Internet, firewalls have been a mainstay of the defense. Many books have been written about them, including two I co-authored [Cheswick and Bellovin 1994; Cheswick, Bellovin, and Rubin 2003]. That said, their utility, and in particular the protection they provide, has diminished markedly over the years. The time has come to ask whether the general-purpose firewall—the one protecting an enterprise—is still worth its capital, operational, and productivity cost.

When the world was young and Bill Cheswick and I wrote the first edition of *Firewalls and Internet Security*, laptops were rare, Wi-Fi and hotel broadband were non-existent, and smart phones weren't even dreamed of. External users logged in to time-sharing machines via the firewall to read their email; companies had very few Internet links to other companies. Even the web was new; the section on it was one of the last things we added to the book before it went to press, and we declined the suggestion that something called a "URL" be employed to state the location of useful resources.

None of that is true today. There is a massive amount of connectivity through and around a typical large firewall, hundreds or even thousands of links. We noted quite some years ago that AT&T had at least 200 links to business partners [Cheswick, Bellovin, and Rubin 2003, p. xiii]; anecdotally, that sort of interconnection has grown greatly in the intervening time. Employees telecommute and travel, staying in touch all the while from a variety of devices including personally owned ones. Attempts to restrict what employees do from their own machines are generally futile (see Chapter 14). Furthermore, much of the important employee traffic to the company, especially email retrieval, is easily encrypted; adding a customs stop at the firewall can *weaken* security, since the encryption is no longer end to end. Whence, then, the traditional firewall? Does it actually do any good? Note carefully that I'm not saying that firewalls *were* wrong; I do not believe that at all. Rather, I'm saying that the world has changed and that the decision to rely on them should be reexamined and perhaps abandoned.

It helps to go back to what we wrote in *Firewalls*. The real problem, we noted, was buggy code; the purpose of the firewall was to keep the bad guys away from the bugs. Today's firewalls demonstrably cannot do that. Web browsers on $\aleph_0$ different devices are exposed to malware daily, and you can't even start to use a hotel network until you turn off all proxying and VPNs. Similarly, all sorts of nastiness is emailed to people every day, often on their unofficial, unapproved, personally owned, external email accounts, accounts that they check from their employee laptops. (Yes, I know that many security policies prohibit such behavior. They also prohibit employees from copying data to flash drives so that they can get work done at home or while they're on the road. Again, see Chapter 14.)

Beyond that, modern computers—though not (yet?) most tablets or smart phones—all have built-in firewalls; if those are properly configured (see Section 15.3), you may get more security at less cost by scrapping your customs booth. If we enhanced these devices still further to use cryptographically based distributed firewall technology [Bellovin 1999], we'd be in better shape still.

5.2   A Theory of Firewalls

Fundamentally, a traditional firewall is a security policy enforcement device that takes advantage of a topological chokepoint. Let's look at it analytically. There are three properties necessary for a firewall to be effective:

1. There must exist a topological chokepoint at which to place a firewall. Formally, we can regard the network as a graph and the firewall as a cutpoint that partitions the graph into two or more disjoint components.

2. The nodes on the "inside" of the firewall share the same security policy. (See Section 16.2 for more discussion about creation of security policies.)

3. All nodes on the "inside" must be "good"; all nodes on the outside are, if not actually "bad," untrusted.

When one or more of these conditions does not hold, a firewall cannot succeed. Today, none are true for the typical enterprise.

Property 1 fails because of the number of links a typical company has, links that do not go through "the" firewall. These links may be to suppliers, customers, joint venture partners, outsourcees, what have you.

Property 2 fails because of the number of computers used today. With so many nodes, the policies have to differ drastically. When firewalls first became popular, only a small subset of employees needed Internet connectivity. For all practical purposes, there was no web. Email was not the way business was done. Documents were faxed rather than scanned and attached. If, by some chance, your company needed connectivity to another company, you leased a circuit from the phone company, but that wasn't a gross exposure because most companies didn't have very much connectivity even internally. (Bear in mind that *Firewalls* came out $1\frac{1}{2}$ years before the release of Windows 95, the first Microsoft operating system with TCP/IP support. You could get TCP/IP, but it was an add-on product from some outside vendor. Most machines were not upgraded in that fashion.)

Property 3 fails, too, partly because of the large population on the inside, and partly because of mobile nodes: if they get infected when they're on the outside, they're effectively bad guys when inside the firewall.

There's a corollary to this: firewalls can work in environments where these conditions still hold. To take a neglected but important case, most residences are protectable by firewalls. (Admittedly, parents and teenagers often disagree on the proper security policy or even on what constitutes "good" behavior. Besides, consumers have smart phones and laptops, too. Computer-savvy parents will sometimes set up a separate "teen-net," isolated from "parent-net.")

It is worth noting that these three properties, with the possible exception of Property 3, are not absolute; tolerating minor deviations is feasible. You can have two or possibly three firewalls—with more than that, coordinating policy is hard, and there's too much chance of return traffic going through a different firewall—you can have a small number of different policies for machines like the mail server, etc.

Given this model, we can construct scenarios where firewalls are effective. A degenerate case is a single machine. If we regard the firewall as residing between the network interface and the TCP/IP stack (and this is, in fact, how it is often implemented), all three conditions are obviously satisfied. What makes this interesting is where policy comes from. All current operating systems permit the machine's administrator to set the policy for that machine. Some packages permit a central administrator to ship policy to many endpoints. Finally, if we use cryptographically verified identity to accomplish our partition (and thus use a virtual network topology rather than a physical one), we achieve the distributed firewall described in [Bellovin 1999].

A more interesting case is a departmental print server. The policy is simple: anyone within the department is allowed to print; no one outside is allowed to print at all. Property 2 is therefore satisfied. Departments typically don't have rich connectivity, thus satisfying Property 1. Finally, since by policy anyone on the inside has permission to use the printers, everyone is by definition good, satisfying the final property.

There's one wrinkle. If the department has an external link, perhaps to a supplier, systems on the far side of that link should be barred from reaching the printer. That could be accomplished by a packet filter on the router handling that connection; alternately (and per the discussion below on threat models), it can be ignored.

It is fair to ask what other choices there might be. Any network connected device needs some sort of access control; many do not provide it, or do not do a good job of it. Your typical printer, for example, does not support TLS or logins and passwords; if it did, many computers would have trouble talking to it. However, some sort of access control is necessary; I do *not* want some bored teenager launching a denial of service attack on my paper budget or on my printers' hardware [Cui and Stolfo 2011]. (I recently bought a new home printer with IPv6 support—which I promptly turned off because there was no access control option; anyone who knew its name or IP address could have reached it.)

There are other services that are commonly used within a department or other small group; file servers are the obvious example. These often do have their own authentication; nevertheless, the service provided is sufficiently sensitive (and the underlying code has been sufficiently buggy, at least in the past) that an extra layer of protection is useful.

The solution is a *point firewall*, a simple firewall in front of a limited set of resources. Point firewalls work because of their scope: they are not trying to protect arbitrarily many devices, they are not enforcing complex rules, they are not dealing with thousands of exceptions. There is also a more subtle philosophical difference: their primary function is not just bug deflection; rather, they are add-on access control mechanisms. Nevertheless, since they are enforcing a policy they qualify as firewalls.

If we add the threat environment to our model, we can generalize still further. In particular, we will assess the properties separately for different threat levels. When we do, we see that enterprise firewalls do provide a modicum of protection against low-skill hackers. Specifically, let's consider joy hackers.

Property 2 is effectively true; typically, everyone has the same policy against the sorts of attacks launched by joy hackers. A simple "no inbound calls" policy, plus rules to force all mail and perhaps web traffic through specific virus scanner-equipped gateways will likely handle all of the usual attacks from that grade of bad guy.

Property 1 is more subtle. If we temporarily ignore links to other companies, we're left with the usual handful of connections to ISPs; these are the traditional locations for firewalls. This property is thus satisfied.

It is Property 3 that is the most interesting for this scenario. I will assert that at the joy hacker level, to a first approximation all employees are honest good guys. Yes, there is embezzlement, insider trading, and the usual rate of petty thefts from the stockroom or the paper cabinet (Bell Labs used to use four ring loose leaf binders, apparently to discourage people from bringing these home as school supplies). However, what little low-grade technical malfeasance there is tends to be locally targeted; employees will attack what they know, and by definition unskilled attackers do not have the tools or knowledge to learn the extended network topology, especially to other companies. We thus satisfy Property 3 and Property 1.

The risk from mobile devices remains, but today's dangerous viruses are not the work of script kiddies. We can thus conclude that traditional enterprise firewalls do provide some protection.

Our protection breaks down if we consider opportunistic hackers, and of course all bets are off when dealing with MI-31. An opportunistic hacker is capable of launching sophisticated viruses and worms, working out (or stumbling on) a path through inter-connected companies (or using a worm that does the same thing), and so on. We thus lose Property 1. Property 2 also fails, because a sophisticated attacker can find and exploit weaker policies. Still, the biggest risks can be deflected, at least partially, if we can protect the external links (Chapter 11).

Targetiers don't have much technical skill, but they are targeting you. If nothing else, it means that we lose Property 3 because such people will resort to physical presence in their attacks. Depending on just how much skill they have, they may also be able to exploit links between companies, which violates Property 1. In other words, enterprise firewalls do not protect against higher grades of attackers.

It is important to realize that the three properties were applicable all along; however, in the mid-1990s the threat profile was very different. There were few targetiers or Andromedans, with the arguable exception of Cliff Stoll's Stasi-controlled East Germans [1988; 1989]. There were opportunistic attackers, including some very good ones, but with no interconnected companies and few mobile devices their scope of operation was limited.

✳ ✳ ✳

Another way to think about firewalls is to realize that no firewall can provide protection at any layer other than the one at which it operates. A typical packet filter, for example, works at layer 3 and a bit of layer 4 (the port numbers); as such, it can filter by IP address and service. It can't look at MAC addresses (especially from more than one hop away because it never sees them!), nor can it look inside email messages. The trouble is that a good firewall needs to operate at multiple layers. It may need to do TCP normalization, to deal with attackers who are playing games with the subtle semantics of TCP [Handley, Kreibich, and Paxson 2001]; it definitely needs to scan email for viruses, block nasty web sites, and more. Furthermore, the trend in recent years has been to layer more and more non-web protocols on top of HTTP or HTTPS, rather than directly on TCP or TCP+TLS; simple port number filtering or circuit relaying will no longer do the job. (HTTP is sometimes referred to as the "universal solvent for firewalls.") Indeed, even in *Firewalls* we described the need for FTP and X11 application proxies; the need has gotten much more urgent since then.

One result of the increased attention to higher-level protocols has been the rise of *Deep Packet Inspection (DPI)* [N. Anderson 2007]. A DPI firewall has rules and policies that look at more or less arbitrary parts of packets. This is difficult, and not just because of performance issues; in general TCP implementations will split up messages as they see fit, forcing a DPI system to reassemble packets and keep extra state. Furthermore, the ability to express policies in terms of the contents of packets has led to evermore complex policies; these themselves are a significant source of trouble.

The result of this shift is that firewalls have gotten far more complex. There are many more different application that are of interest; each of them requires custom code on the firewall to enforce policies and to delete or otherwise defang sketchy stuff. This is bad for security. It pays to look back at what Cheswick and I wrote in *Firewalls*:

> **Axiom 1 (Murphy)** *All programs are buggy.*

> **Theorem 1 (Law of Large Programs)** *Large programs are even buggier than their size would indicate.*

Are Network Address Translators Firewalls?

Network address translators (NAT boxes) [Srisuresh and Egevang 2001] are a source of controversy in the networking community. Some people denounce them as the spawn of Satan, excrescences on the body technic that interfere with end to end communication. Others point to their necessity—we've long since run out of IPv4 addresses—and tout the interference as a security virtue: NATs are firewalls, they say. Are they right? If so, do their benefits outweigh their disadvantages?

By definition, NATs operate at the network layer, with a slight excursion up to the transport layer to inspect and modify port numbers. As a consequence, they provide no protection against things like emailed malware and nasty web sites. The answer to the first question is therefore obvious: NATs are not firewalls per se; however, they do provide protection more or less equivalent to that of a packet filter. Combined with protections common to many consumer ISPs or large enterprises—a central mail server with virus detection, and web filtering done by a proxy or by the features built in to many browsers—there is a tolerably complete level of protection, more than one would have without the NAT. Alternate schemes based on host resident filtering generally require configuration, ruling them out for most home use.

The issue of balance, though, is rather more complicated and subjective. Some of the cost is already borne by everyone, in the form of excess protocol complexity or in the need for auxiliary helper servers. There are other features that don't work very well through NATs. As end systems become more and more hardened against direct attacks, the benefits of NATs decrease and the costs become higher. On balance, I'd say they're not worth it—and I've enjoyed having direct IPv6 access to my house without interference from a NAT. Of course, until IPv6 becomes ubiquitous, most home users have no real choice.

Proof: By inspection.   ∎

Corollary 1.1 *A security-relevant program has security bugs.*

Theorem 2 *If you do not run a program, it does not matter whether or not it is buggy.*

Proof: As in all logical systems, (**false** $\Rightarrow$ **true**) = **true**.   ∎

Corollary 2.1 *If you do not run a program, it does not matter if it has security holes.*

Theorem 3 *Exposed machines should run as few programs as possible; the ones that are run should be as small as possible.*

Proof: Follows directly from Corollary 1.1 and Corollary 2.1.   ■

Corollary 3.1 (Fundamental Theorem of Firewalls) *Most hosts cannot meet our requirements: they run too many programs that are too large. Therefore, the only solution is to isolate them behind a firewall if you wish to run any programs at all.*

In other words, the reason that firewalls were secure is that they ran many fewer programs, and hence didn't have as much vulnerable code. Given the hundreds of applications that a modern firewall has to support, and given the complexity of some of those applications (e.g., SIP), it is far from clear that less code is involved. In fact, an enterprise firewall today, supporting very many users, endpoints, and policies, is arguably running *more* Internet-facing code than a typical host. Perhaps the code is higher quality, and perhaps the firewalls are better administered than end user machines—but perhaps not.

The code complexity issue is another driver for smaller, more specialized firewalls. The XML-scanning firewall protecting some database machine may be just as buggy as the same code on an apatosaurus-sized firewall for the enterprise, but if it fails it exposes one database machine, not an entire company.

✷   ✷   ✷

We can therefore draw some conclusions about the role of firewalls in today's net.

- Small-scale firewalls, protecting a network about the size run by a single system administrator, still serve a useful function. Generally speaking, these will be packet filters and hence not require extra hardware.

- Complex server applications are rarely amenable to firewall protection, unless the firewall has some very, very good (and very, very well-written) sanitizing technology.

- An enterprise firewall retains value against low-skill attackers but is actually a point of risk, not protection, when trying to filter complex protocols against sophisticated adversaries. If you have such services that must be accessible from the outside, use packet filtering on the enterprise firewall and a separate protection layer near the server itself. This is discussed in more detail in Section 11.3.

Planning for Failure

Given the complexity of some application firewall modules, it is not unreasonable to suspect that they might fail. What is the proper course of action? The proper design *assumes* that a failure can happen and tries to mitigate the consequences. Here are two approaches.

The first approach is to abandon the notion of an application-specific firewall for that system. Unless the firewall can do filtering or blocking that the host itself can't do, it doesn't add any value over a high-quality host application. Web servers are a good example; the danger comes from the HTTP itself and the scripts that are run in response; what can the firewall add? What a simple firewall, such as a packet filter, *can* do is block access to other ports on the server and prevent illicit outgoing calls. So—the server is hacked, but the attacker can't go anywhere else in the company and may not even be able to steal the data. This is a cheap design, in that all it needs is a router port with the appropriate access control rules; only the dodgy server is behind that port.

The second approach uses a properly designed application firewall; again, all that's behind it is the server you want to protect. By "properly designed" I mean one that implements the same type of dual protection: a packet filter followed by an application-specific module. There are two utterly crucial internal architectural details. For one thing, the application proxy must be "behind" the packet filter, that is, between the packet filter and the port facing the server, so that any outward-bound traffic from the proxy to the rest of the company must pass through the packet filter.

Furthermore, the internal structure of the firewall must be such that if the proxy module itself is penetrated, the attacker cannot reprogram the packet filter. Unfortunately, it's very hard to learn that sort of internal detail about the design.

- Arguably, mobile devices—laptops, tablets, smart phones—should never be fully trusted, not because they use wireless connections, but because they're much more likely to carry malware (see Property 3). This suggests that your wireless LAN should be outside the firewall, with a VPN+filter for access by iToys and the like. The suggestion is analyzed in greater detail in Chapter 9.

5.3   Intrusion Detection Systems

"Do you mean to admit that *you* may have been invaded and searched—tracelessly?" Alcon fairly shrieked the thought.

"Certainly," the psychologist replied, coldly. "While I do not believe that it has been done, the possibility must be conceded. What we could do, we have done; but what science can do, science can circumvent."

Second Stage Lensman
—E. E. "Doc" Smith

An *intrusion detection system (IDS)* is a backup security mechanism. It assumes that your other defenses—firewalls, hardened hosts, goat entrails (tofu entrails for vegetarian security professionals) offered up in the dark of the moon—have failed. The task then is to notice the successful attack as soon as possible, which permits minimization of the damage, either via automated systems or their backup humans.

Most of what I've said about antivirus technology is true of IDSs as well. An IDS can be signature or anomaly based; the same advantages and disadvantages apply. The key difference is deployment scenarios and hence inputs; antivirus programs operate on files, whereas IDSs are more multifarious.

IDSs are generally classified as network or host intrusion detection systems; for the latter, they can operate on network or host behavior or content. Each of these approaches has benefits and limitations.

The big attraction of anything network based is the same as the big attraction of a firewall: it's scalable, in that there are typically many fewer networks to instrument than hosts. In fact, the firewall is one very common location to install a network IDS, since by definition all traffic from the outside is supposed to pass through that chokepoint.

Doing intrusion detection in the network, by grabbing packets in flight, is difficult. The obvious problem is dealing with encrypted traffic; more seriously, it's all too easy to miss packets. There are also theoretical issues with enemies who try to exploit odd corner cases in the network protocol specs [Handley, Kreibich, and Paxson 2001], though such behavior seems to be rare or unknown in the wild. (If the Andromedans are doing this, perhaps they haven't yet been caught at it?)

The simplest form of network IDS relies on IP addresses and port numbers: if the packets are going to destinations that some parties shouldn't try to reach, you know there's a problem. The technique is analogous to the "network telescope" concept [Cheswick 2010; C. Shannon and Moore 2004]: if some IP addresses are deliberately left empty, packets sent to them (or from them!) are a priori suspicious. The same can be true of certain ports on sensitive hosts, especially if you have good information on just who can legitimately send to them.

If that's all you want to do, though, don't bother trying to look at packets. Your routers are already doing that; some places have built IDSs based on routers' NetFlow data.[1]

More sophisticated network monitoring can be done as well. There are comparatively simple systems that look for simple patterns of data, such as Bro [Paxson 1998; Paxson 1999] or Snort [Roesch 1999]. DPI systems [N. Anderson 2007] are more sophisticated; they look at higher layers of the stack and are often used for various sorts of governmental monitoring [Poe 2006].

The fundamental problem with any form of network IDS is that it lacks context. Yes, DPI and other forms of network monitoring can detect suspicious packets, but it's difficult for even the best network scanners to reassemble every file in transit and then scan it for malware. That sort of thing is much easier to do on hosts. Hosts can also look at log files; more importantly—and all but impossible to do on the wire—they can scan their own file systems for unexpected changes [G. Kim and Spafford 1994a; G. Kim and Spafford 1994b; G. Kim and Spafford 1994c]. Finally, host based IDSs are network independent; they can detect problems no matter how they arrive, whether via the Internet or carried in on an infected USB flash disk.

Host-based IDSs can do one more thing more easily than their network partners: they can emulate network protocols, above the level of any encryption. Depending on their purpose, they can be part of or intermediaries for the real network daemons; alternatively, they can be pure fakes, doing nothing but detecting things that you hope will never happen. This is an ancient technique [Bellovin 1992], but it is useful nevertheless.

5.4 Intrusion Prevention Systems

> We have a VPN, and firewalls, and you do not want to mess with them because the design spec for the Laundry's firewall software is not to keep intruders out, but to make them undergo spontaneous combustion when they get in: as Bob puts it, it's the only way to be sure.
>
> *The Annihilation Score*
> —Charles Stross

Suppose a network IDS does detect something unpleasant. Then what? An *intrusion prevention system (IPS)* can best be described as an IDS with an attitude. Rather than simply detecting something bad, they try to do something about it. The trick is avoiding collateral damage, or at any rate collateral damage that's worse than what the attack would

---

1. "PaIRS: Point of contact and Incident Response System," http://goo.gl/xhroc.

have caused if left unmolested. The worst situation is a successful attack whose goal was to induce you to perform harmful actions.

Consider, for example, the Slammer worm [Moore et al. 2003]. Slammer spread via a single UDP packet to port 1434, used by a Microsoft SQL server. Because UDP does not require a 3-way handshake the way TCP does, the worm spread extremely quickly; its growth rate was limited by the outbound bandwidth of infected hosts. One can postulate an IPS that noticed links being clogged, saw a tremendous spike in traffic to a rarely seen port, and automatically set up a filter rule blocking such packets. It makes perfect sense, and that is in fact what was done by many ISPs. Now imagine a variant of Slammer that emitted three packets to UDP port 53 for every one it sent to 1434. The packets to 53— DNS—would, for this example, be harmless, but would a network based IPS know that? All that it can see are three facts: links are being clogged by an unprecedented flood of traffic; many of the unusual packets are to port 1434; even more of them are to port 53. Would it try to shut down both ports? If so, the IPS would effectively turn off the Internet. (N.B. I've slightly simplified the details of this enhanced attack; correcting it is left as an exercise for the reader.)

An IPS can do many things. As with an IDS it can be host or network resident; both sitings have advantages and disadvantages. Depending on where it is located, it can block connections, quarantine files, modify packets, and more [Scarfone and Mell 2007]. Forrest and Somayaji described one that slowed down suspect processes, rather than killing them [2000]; this scheme doesn't do irrevocable harm if it's guessed incorrectly.

Ultimately, the IPS problem rests on three pillars: very good detection, selection of countermeasures, and matching the countermeasures to confidence in identification of the root cause of the problem. This last issue is much less studied than the second, which in turn is much less studied than the first.

5.5 Extrusion Detection

Extrusion detection is a specialized form of IDS. It's aimed at one particular form of harm: someone trying to steal your data and export it. The trick is picking up the outbound data transfer. There are two challenges: picking out the right data, amidst all of the legitimate (or at least normal) traffic, and distinguishing authorized from unauthorized transfers. This latter isn't trivial; uploading a chip design to a foundry can be the normal way of doing business, while sending it to the Andromedans' web server most likely is not. Extrusion detection has one principal advantage over many other types of security systems: it can cope with rogue insiders.

There are a number of ways to perform extrusion detection. One of the simplest is the *honeypot*: create fake files that will attract the attention of a spy, commercial or govern-

The WikiLeaks Cables

The case of the classified US diplomatic cables given to WikiLeaks and then published provides an interesting case study in extrusion detection. The factual basis for this analysis is mostly taken from [Capehart 2012a; Capehart 2012b; Capehart 2012c; Capehart 2012d; Capehart 2012e], a series worth reading for the discussion of procedural issues (even though I feel that some of Capehart's conclusions are debatable); also see [Zetter 2011] and [BBC 2014].

What happened is that Chelsea Manning (at the time of the actions and the trial, male and known as "Bradley"), an apparently untrustworthy individual who nevertheless had access to systems holding classified documents, developed scripts to do bulk downloads. The downloaded documents were burned onto a CD labeled "Lady Gaga"; the contents of the CD were then shared with WikiLeaks.

There has been a lot of criticism of the US State Department for having such sensitive data available with very weak controls. While the issue is indeed debatable, it was the result of a deliberate decision to increase availability of data, even highly classified data, to individuals with suitable clearances; lack of information sharing had been seen as one of the problems leading up to the 9/11 terrorist attacks.

However, what could and should have been done was to log accesses, and *look for unusual patterns*. Apparently, more than 250,000 cables were downloaded. Are there any legitimate uses for that sort of bulk download by a single individual? Proper log files, and proper analysis of them, would have shown that something unusual was happening. At the least, security personnel could have investigated.

Manning herself apparently understood the problem. She wrote, "Weak servers, weak logging, weak physical security, weak counter-intelligence, inattentive signal analysis. . . a perfect storm" [Poulsen and Zetter 2010].

Marcus Ranum has summed it up nicely [Field 2010]:

> Then the other piece of the puzzle that I find is really interesting is the apparent inability of the people who lost the data, the original data holders, to tell what data was stolen and while it was being stolen *[sic]*. And this is an important message for anyone who is a CISO [Chief Information Security Officer] because it shows what can happen when your data leaks if you don't have auditing and logging in place so that you can go back and say, "Well, OK if we do believe this guy leaked a bunch of information, what information did he actually access and when?" Of course, ideally you would get in front of that process and maybe detect the fact that somebody who really didn't have a need to access this particular information was downloading [this information] in one fell swoop. That is kind of a red flag, I would think.

Precisely.

mental, and wait for someone to grab one. This has been done a number of times, most famously by Stoll [1988; 1989] in the "Wily Hacker" incident. (Bill Cheswick and I subtitled *Firewalls* "Repelling the Wily Hacker" in homage to Cliff, and we used that phrase with his permission.) Briefly, he discovered intruders in a University of California computer system and traced them to Germany. To allow enough time for technicians to trace the attackers' phone calls—this was in the days of dial-up modems—he created fake documents about the Strategic Defense Initiative, a missile defense system, and waited for someone to look at them. His trap was successful; the attackers' response included sufficient indicia of espionage that he notified the FBI.

In the more usual scenario, you don't know whether you've been penetrated. Accordingly, the proper honeypot strategy requires a wide range of believable-seeming decoys. Exactly what decoys you should create depends on your system; you want something that resembles normal items on that system. Bowen at al. [Bowen 2011; Bowen et al. 2009] describe a number of types of decoys—"honey documents"—including fake logins for banking web sites; they also define criteria for decoy generation. One notable aspect to their work was the use of *web bugs*, normally used by advertisers to track consumers on the web. With a web bug, opening the document causes an attempt to fetch a file (typically a 1×1–pixel transparent GIF) from a monitored HTTP server.

Naturally, a sufficiently knowledgeable attacker can dodge many decoys. Someone who suspects web bugs, for example, would simply read exfiltrated documents on an offline computer. Indeed, intelligence agencies' classified networks are generally disconnected from the outside world [R. A. Clarke and Knake 2010], so no strategy that relies on active documents can succeed. A different approach is needed, one based on IDS technology.

The big advantage of honey documents is that they're transport independent. That is, no matter how the files are exfiltrated, the trap can be sprung on any network connected machine used to view them. Even printing them out first doesn't help; the monitors will detect the documents being opened inside the enterprise.

You may be able to detect network based exfiltration while the documents are being transported if your network is configured in a firewall-friendly manner, that is, if Property 1 holds. An extrusion detection module can be installed at the firewall; it can then attempt to detect misbehavior from amidst the noise of routine Internet traffic. As with IDSs, one can approach this from a signature or anomaly detection perspective. Signature detection can look for certain documents or perhaps markings—should the strings "Company Confidential" or "Top Secret UMBRA" appear in outbound mail?—or anomaly detection. Anomaly detection might be as simple as volume—does this person or IP address normally send so much data? Does someone in that organization normally send so much?—or it may be based on the statistical characteristics of the outbound data.

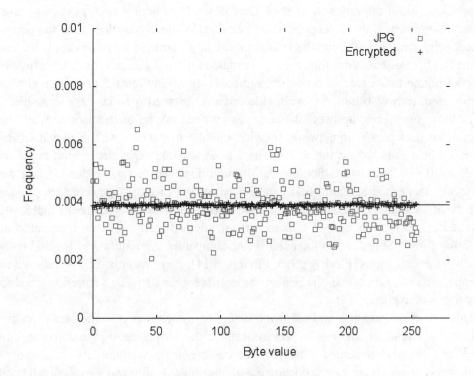

Figure 5.1: A byte frequency plot for a JPG file and an encrypted version of the same file. (The $x = 0$ value was omitted, since the frequency of 0 in the JPG file was so high that it obscured the other differences.) The horizontal line is $y = \frac{1}{256}$, what a perfectly even distribution would be. Note that JPG and other highly compressed formats like MP3 are harder to distinguish from random data; encrypted files in general do (and should) look very random. In a test of 1024-byte blocks, Oprea et al. found that less than 2% had an entropy that appeared close to that of random data [2005].

There are some interesting wrinkles here that makes extrusion detection harder in some ways than firewalls or intrusion detection. For one thing, someone exporting information is freer to use encryption because he or she can control both ends of the channel. By contrast, an attacker breaking in to an organization can only encrypt traffic if the vulnerability being exploited uses encryption. Of course, once the penetration is complete, the attacker can install any sort of back door desired, including encrypted ones. Even if encryption is used, the defenders aren't helpless. While crypto does hide the precise content being sent, it can't hide the volume; more importantly, encrypted data has a very unique flat byte distribution; this, too, is anomalous if from a source or to a destination that does not normally receive such. An example is shown in Figure 5.1, which compares the byte frequency distribution of a JPG file and an encrypted version of the same file.

In some situations, the firewall-like topology need not be of the user network, but rather of the data-providing network. Imagine a data center with a web front end serving thousands of clients around the world. There is no feasible perimeter around the users; however, all sensitive data is flowing out through that web server. Proper log files and analysis of them (see Section 16.3) can also be a form of extrusion detection. Indeed, the lack of such analysis has been claimed to be at fault in the WikiLeaks diplomatic cables case; see the box on p. 73. Some organizations already track all outbound traffic. In the United States, some financial sector companies are required to log and retain certain communications [FINRA 2010; FINRA 2011]; these records can be analyzed for improper exports. Of course, the rest of the perimeter needs to be secured to preclude other forms of export.

One can view intrusion and extrusion detection systems as in some sense the dual of firewalls. The latter attempts to prevent trouble; the former attempt to detect it. Firewalls are primarily concerned with what the communications endpoints and protocols are; detection systems are more concerned with the contents. Firewalls are generally centralized; detection systems function better if decentralized. Both yield benefits; both have their limitations.

5.6 Analysis

It is very clear that the trend towards decentralization is going to continue. Ever-cheaper processing power makes it possible to put CPUs more or less everywhere; increasingly, these CPUs have communications capabilities. Today, interacting with some of these varied computers is optional; more and more, it will become a necessity. A generation ago, an airplane flight required a paper ticket that you exchanged for a cardstock boarding pass at the airport. Today, tickets are electronic and you're encouraged to print your own boarding pass, but if you want you can often display it as a 2-D barcode on your smart phone. In not very many years, smart phones will become the normal way to fly, with temperamental barcode scanners replaced by network communication with the passenger's phone. Will corporate security policies permit installation of the necessary app on employees' iToys? They'll have to.

There are also considerations of physical laws. If you're in Tokyo and trying to download some local content, routing your request via the corporate firewall in Rio de Janeiro *will* slow you down; neither DARPA nor the ITU can increase the speed of light, and bandwidth is intimately linked to latency. It's not just that security policies that ignore reality will be ignored (though that will happen, too); rather, it's that they'll start to interfere very seriously with productivity. People derive inner satisfaction (and better merit reviews) if they're more productive; they derive neither from obeying security policies they generally don't understand. Only if there is a problem will there be consequences, but 99% of the time ignoring policy results in no harm whatsoever. It's the last 1% that gets them—and their employers—in very big trouble.

Things might change. We're currently at a point where there are three plausible, currently visible directions in which technology can move. First, it might move to a purely decentralized model, where there is no perimeter and any device can be used for anything. The rise of the "gig economy" [Editorial Board, New York Times 2015] will push in that direction. Second, a cloud plus random device solution may dominate. In that case, although today's perimeter-and-firewall solution will vanish, the cloud-based servers can become a locus for logging, intrusion and extrusion detection, and other forms of protection against large-scale attacks. Finally, things can stay about the way they are today. I say "about" because there are too many advantages to the other two paths for the status quo to hold completely, but the extent to and rate at which it will erode remain unclear.

There's a potential variant on the "lots of devices" model that might arise: the local ad hoc network scenario. In it, a user's device (somehow) associates itself with other devices in the neighborhood. The obvious and probably non-threatening examples are things like hotel room displays, keyboards, and the like; perhaps more interestingly, one can imagine a laptop taking over some sort of mobile Wi-Fi hotspot or connecting to a local disk or neighboring laptop to share content. In scenarios like this one, the perimeter is fuzzier still.

The conclusion is that we have to figure out how to push our security policies towards the edges. This is not the simplistic "I don't believe in firewalls" chant of 20 years ago; the need for good security policies—generally, organizational security policies—and mechanisms is stronger than ever; we just have to change how and where we enforce them. This may be the real conundrum of the "bring your own device" movement; it's not that consumer devices are necessarily less secure than corporate-issued ones as it is the difficulty of an IT department installing its own policies on an employee's widget. Quite likely, they have neither the authorization nor the knowledge to do so, especially for newer or rarer widgets.

Better virtualization and policy languages will help. If the work environment can be properly isolated from the play environment, and if a system-independent policy language can be devised (and of course implemented by consumer gadgetry purveyors), this issue can be avoided. It's not an easy task, since it will be necessary to implement this functionality in such a way that malware can't disable it.

∗   ∗   ∗

Intrusion detection and its counterpart intrusion prevention are widely seen as the most promising avenues to pursue, given that purely defensive measures have not succeeded despite more than forty years of effort [Wulf and A. K. Jones 2009]. The challenge, though, is considerable; not only must an IDS cope with a change in people's legitimate activities, it must cope with changing software and changing technology. A new release of a web browser might sandbox each tab or window, which would produce different patterns of system calls than the older versions did; similarly, the rise of mobile devices to, say, read email via a cellular network will reduce the contribution of LAN-based mailers to the total traffic mix and thus change its overall characteristics. These sorts of changes are legitimate and probably inevitable, but the same package that has to adapt to these changes must also detect the very subtle changes of a new "low and slow" attack.

Extrusion detection is even more challenging than policy enforcement. Generally speaking, physical access wins; it is very hard to prevent the owner of a device from getting at any or all of its contents. One thing that will help is if vendors implement a distributed logging system. Even in, say, a peer-to-peer distributed corporate file system, a request for a file should generate a log message back to some central correlator. I would argue that for security purposes, logging is even more important than delivering the data; a user will retry the download but won't be similarly motivated to resend missed log messages.

It is hard to predict what other trends will take root even in the next five years, let alone ten or twenty. The human and organizational need for collaborative work will not change, but the mechanisms will. A generation ago, people swapped floppy disks. (Two generations ago, it was decks of punch cards.) We moved from there to central repositories and/or emailing files back and forth. Today, collaboration is moving towards the cloud. How long will that continue? Will peer-to-peer mechanisms take over instead? If I'm on a train or plane, I'd rather not have to deal with an intermediary when I'm working with someone a few rows back; I'd rather use a mobile network. That part looks feasible—but how will it be done securely, and how will transactions be logged?

What is really needed is a way for packets or messages of security interest to be flagged reliably, thus simplifying policy enforcement [Bellovin 2003]. Until that happens, all of these mechanisms will be imperfect.

Chapter 6

Cryptography and VPNs

He unlocked his desk, opened the drawer-safe, and withdrew the Executive's Code Book, restricted to the executive heads of the firms listed quadruple A-1-* by Lloyds.

The Demolished Man
—ALFRED BESTER

6.1 Cryptography, the Wonder Drug

Some years ago, shortly after *Firewalls and Internet Security* [1994] was first published, a friend who wasn't fond of firewalls remarked that someday, he was going to write a book on how to do Internet security "correctly." I asked him what that entailed; he replied, "Use Kerberos or other forms of cryptography." Now, Kerberos [Bryant 1988; S. P. Miller et al. 1987; Neuman et al. 2005; Steiner, Neuman, and Schiller 1988] is a perfectly fine system; in *Firewalls*, we called it "extremely useful." But to call it or any form of cryptography the "correct" way to do Internet security is to misunderstand both the security problem and what cryptography can and cannot do for you.

Although theoreticians have come up with many interesting cryptographic tricks (and some are even in commercial use), the two most common uses of cryptography are to prove identity and to hide data from prying eyes. It can do these things very well, but at a price. The most obvious is that keys have to be protected. To quote another friend of mine, "Insecurity is like entropy: it can't be destroyed, but it can be moved around.

With cryptography, we substitute the insecurity of the key for the insecurity of the data, because we think we can protect the keys better."

A second major price is the difficulty of devising proper cryptographic mechanisms. Cryptography is a very difficult and subtle branch of applied mathematics; remarkably few people are qualified to practice it. *Never* use a proprietary encryption algorithm, especially if you're told that it's more secure because it's secret. The same applies to cryptographic protocols; they're also quite hard to get right. I'll give just one example. SSL 3.0 was devised for Netscape in 1996. It was devised by one world-famous cryptographer, analyzed by two others [Wagner and Schneier 1996], and served as the basis for the *Internet Engineering Task Force's (IETF) Transport Layer Security (TLS)* protocol [Dierks

---

Crypto Exploits

In the military world, sophisticated attacks on cryptography are not at all unknown. During World War II, for example, the Americans sent a message in the clear, in order to learn the Japanese code group for the island of Midway [Kahn 1967]. Peter Wright tells the story of planting microphones to hear the number of clicks as rotor settings were changed [Wright 1987].

Things like that are very rare or unknown in the civilian sector. The most sophisticated exploit was against a code-signing key for Texas Instrument calculators [Goodin 2009]. Firmware updates for their calculators have to be digitally signed; TI, though, used 512-bit keys. That's much too short; some hobbyists factored the public keys, which let them determine the private key and sign their own code.

A more serious problem with 512-bit keys has turned up, too. As best as can be determined—at this writing, not all the facts are in—a number of code-signing certificates with 512-bit keys exist, and these keys have been factored as well [Bijl 2011]. Signed code will often be accepted silently by Windows systems; if malware is signed— and it has been—it can easily be installed without the user noticing anything.

Gonzalez et al. appear to have used WEP-cracking. While the public record is not entirely clear, the Canadian report on the incident says that TJX used WEP [Privacy Commissioner 2007], and some of the counts in the information against one of Gonzalez' confederates states that he connected to TJX's wireless network.[a]

(Continued)

---

a. "Information, United States v. Christopher Scott, (D. Mass. August 5, 2008), ¶3.d ," http://i.cdn.turner.com/cnn/2008/images/08/05/scott.information.pdf.

One spectacular exploit was found in the Flame malware [Zetter 2012; Zetter 2014]. Even early analyses concluded that it was developed by a major government, though quite unaccountably Andromeda was never named as a suspect in news reports. One of the many interesting things Flame did was to use fake certificates (Chapter 8) to sign modules. That in itself isn't new; Stuxnet did it, too. But Flame had two new wrinkles. First, it exploited a Microsoft design error, rather than a stolen key. Second, and far more interesting, it relied on a cryptanalytic attack unknown to the civilian sector to generate forged certificates [Fillinger 2013; Goodin 2012b; Zetter 2014]. One can argue that a large criminal enterprise could have built a large piece of malware, but only a major government's SIGINT agency could have done the cryptanalysis. The attack had a complexity of at least $2^{46.6}$ and probably more, because it was apparently optimized for a massively parallel architecture. In other words, this was not a commercial threat, this was a government.

The oddest known case of a cryptanalytic attack involved an individual who just wanted revenge against his neighbors [Kravets 2011]. He cracked their WEP password, hacked their computers, and used his stolen access to plant child pornography and send threatening emails. There's another lesson in this incident, though: the neighbor's defenses were set up assuming that the risk was an opportunistic attack; instead, they were targeted. Threat models are not always obvious.

The news from crypto-cracking isn't all bad. I know of at least one case where the good guys read botnet traffic because the bad guys were using bad crypto [Anonymous 2011].

and Rescorla 2008], which itself received a lot of scrutiny from members of the IETF's TLS working group. In 2011, a new flaw was found [Rescorla 2011], present in the most commonly deployed versions of TLS; other new problems have been found since then. [Sheffer, Holz, and Saint-Andre 2015] lists attacks known through February, 2015, but at least one more has been found since then [Adrian et al. 2015]. Don't try it at home, kids; even trained professionals have trouble getting protocols right.

The third issue to be aware of is the difficulty of retrofitting cryptography to existing systems, especially if there are complex communication patterns or requirements. A simple reliable transport channel between two nodes that know and trust each other can easily be secured with TLS. Multiparty communications with complex trust patterns are considerably more difficult and may require the inclusion of additional, mutually trusted parties. Ideally, the cryptographic mechanisms should be designed together with the system. Unfortunately, "green field" architectures are very rare; most of the time, we have to deal with legacy requirements, legacy systems, and legacy code, and aspects that are not just difficult to encrypt but downright hostile to encryption. You might very well need a custom protocol—which, of course, is a bad idea for other reasons.

What happens if you get the cryptography wrong? Is there a real threat? Thus far, the many cryptographic weaknesses that have been found in deployed systems have only rarely been exploited, at least as far as the public knows. None of the more complex protocol attacks have been reported in the wild, with the arguable exception of Flame [Goodin 2012b; Zetter 2014]. Those exploits do take a fair amount of skill and often need specific types of access. More to the point, such attacks haven't been necessary; there always seem to be easier ways in. However...

Flaws of this type are very hard to fix. The problem is in the protocol itself, not a particular piece of code; very likely, *all* implementations will be vulnerable. (Implementing cryptography correctly is itself a Herculean task; it's even harder to get right than ordinary code.) It's often impossible to fix just one end at a time; both ends (or all endpoints) may need to be upgraded simultaneously. (Think how many hundreds of millions of endpoints need patching to upgrade to TLS 1.2, which is immune to the known flaws!) And even though designers try to build in negotiation mechanisms to allow for an orderly transition, they don't always get it right [Bellovin and Rescorla 2006].

Finally, there's one class of attacker—the advanced persistent threat—where cryptographic weaknesses are a very real problem. MI-31 knows a lot about the subject, and if that's the easiest way in they'll use it.

6.2   Key Distribution

Where do long-term keys come from? How does one party know the other's keys or enough about them to trust them? These questions are at the heart of the key distribution problem.

For a small number of nodes, especially if they're in reasonable geographic proximity, manual distribution can work. The problem, though, lies in the word "small": it's an $O(n^2)$ process. The usual solutions are key distribution centers and public key cryptography, often in the form of certificates.

A *key distribution center (KDC)* is a special computer, trusted by all parties, that hands out keys. Every other computer shares a key with it; this key is used to protect and authenticate traffic between it and the KDC. When some computer wants to talk to another, it asks the KDC for a *session key* to the other machine. Somehow—I'll omit the details; see any good cryptography text or the Kerberos documentation [Bryant 1988; S. P. Miller et al. 1987; Neuman et al. 2005; Steiner, Neuman, and Schiller 1988] for how to do it—the other computer learns the session key, too, in a message protected by its long-term key.

There are three crucial points to notice. First, the key provisioning problem is reduced to $O(n)$; for even modest-sized n, this is important. Second, the KDC plays a crucial security role, and hence is an important target for any sophisticated adversary. Suppose, for example, that MI-31 has intercepted traffic between computers A and B. This traffic is protected by some random session key $K_{A,B}$ generated by the KDC and distributed to those nodes. But that distribution takes place under long-term keys $K_{A,KDC}$ and $K_{B,KDC}$, which are both known to the KDC. An attacker who breaks into the KDC, even very much later, can obtain those keys and read all recorded traffic; the only caveat is that the key set-up messages must be recorded, too. Finally, although the provisioning problem is now $O(n)$, it must be done via a secure process that preserves both confidentiality and authenticity; there is by definition no existing key to protect the traffic between a new machine and the KDC.

The latter two problems are frequently handled by use of public key technology. A new node can generate its own key pair and send only the public key to the KDC; this changes a confidentiality and authenticity problem into just an authenticity problem, which is often much easier to solve. Furthermore, the KDC no longer shares any long-term secrets with individual nodes; it knows only public keys. When it generates a session key, it encrypts it with the two computers' public keys; it never sees the corresponding private keys, and thus cannot read what it itself has written. There is thus no threat to past traffic if a public key-based KDC is compromised, though there is of course a threat to keys handed out before a compromise is detected and remediated.

The final step is for the KDC or some other mutually trusted party to sign each computer's $\langle name, publickey \rangle$ pair. This is known as a certificate; certificates are discussed in great and gory detail in Chapter 8.

6.3 Transport Encryption

There are two primary ways encryption is employed: for *transport encryption*, where a real-time connection is being protected, and for *object encryption*, where a sequence of bytes must be protected across an arbitrary number of hops amongst arbitrary parties. We'll deal with each of them in turn.

Transport encryption is the easiest (not *easy*, merely *easiest*) cryptographic problem to solve. Fundamentally, two parties wish to talk. At least one, and often both, have keying material. How do you set up a "secure" connection?

The first phase is *key setup*, during which the two parties somehow agree on a common session key. (Resist the temptation to preprovision static keys to use as session keys [Bellovin and Housley 2005]; at best, you lose certain abilities, and at worst it's a complete security disaster, where the enemy can read, modify, create, etc., all traffic.) Some key setup schemes include authentication—often, bilateral authentication—whereas in others, the application must do it itself if necessary. Beyond that, there are three requirements for key setup: that the two parties agree on the same key, that no one else can obtain those keys, and that the keys be *fresh*, that is, new for this session and not old keys being reused. This last requirement helps protect against the various sorts of nastiness that an enemy can engage in by replaying old traffic into the current session.

An optional key setup property is *forward secrecy*. Forward secrecy means that if an endpoint is compromised after the session is over, the keys for that session cannot be recovered. The more competent your attackers, the more important this is. In particular, if you're worried about the Andromedans, you should use it; they're just the sort of folks who will record your traffic and later, when they find they can't cryptanalyze it, they will hack in to try to get the keys another way.

The second phase, of course, is the actual data transport. It, too, has certain important properties. You should always use authentication with encryption; there are too many nasty games an attacker can play if you don't, by judiciously modifying or combining various pieces of ciphertext [Bellovin 1996]. Some textbooks will say that you only need to use authentication when using stream ciphers. They're wrong. Authentication is vital with stream ciphers, but it's almost always extremely important. (There are a few—a very few—situations where one can omit it. As usual when dealing with materia cryptographica, that's a call that should only be made by qualified experts, and many of them will get it wrong. In 1978, in the very first paper on key distribution protocols, Needham and Schroeder said it very well [1978]:

> Finally, protocols such as those developed here are prone to extremely subtle errors that are unlikely to be detected in normal operation. The need for techniques to verify the correctness of such protocols is great, and we encourage those interested in such problems to consider this area.

They were remarkably prescient; indeed, their own designs had several flaws [Denning and Sacco 1981; Lowe 1996; Needham and Schroeder 1987].) There are some newer modes of operation that combine encryption with authentication in a single pass; this is the preferred way to proceed.

Another important property of the transport phase is replay protection. Just as keys must be fresh, so, too, must messages. Don't make the mistake of assuming that just because the IP and UDP service models permit reordering, duplication, damage, replay, etc., that they're benign when done by a clever attacker. Again, there are rare exceptions, but this decision should be left to qualified experts.

Different sorts of encryption need to be used for UDP and TCP. The former is a datagram protocol; accordingly, use of a stream cipher is almost certain to be disastrous. (That is one of the flaws in WEP; see the box on page 177.)

The last phase is tear-down. It seems trivial, but you want to ensure that your conversation hasn't been truncated. Accordingly, the "goodbye" signaling should be cryptographically protected, too. One last thing: when you're done, destroy the session key; even if you're not using forward secrecy, there's no point to making life too easy for the attackers.

Transport encryption can be applied at different layers of the stack. What protection is obtained depends on the choice; all have their uses.

Link-layer protection, such as assorted Wi-Fi encryption schemes (Chapter 9), has two primary uses: it limits access to a LAN to authorized users, and it protects against eavesdropping and traffic analysis, especially on particularly vulnerable links. Wi-Fi nets are the most obvious choice, but it is used as well on things like international satellite links: a satellite has a large signal footprint, and many unauthorized recipients can pick up transmissions [Goodin 2015b]. In the past, when there was a lot less undersea fiber, many companies used link encryptors for all international connections, even fiber or copper, because they might be rerouted to a satellite circuit in case of an outage. In some cases, there was suspicion that outages were not accidental—some countries seemed to have a very large number of very clumsy fishing trawlers. But that's the sort of attack frequently launched by the Andromedans, which means that link encryption can't be your only layer of defense if you're the actual target: a typical connection traverses many hops and hence many links.

On certain kinds of connection and against certain enemies, link encryption has a very powerful property: an eavesdropper can't even tell that a message has been sent. The NSA realized this more than fifty years ago [Farley and Schorreck 1982]:

> Mostly we were aiming for online equipment and, in fact, eventually generated the notion that we had a circuit and there was something going on the circuit twenty-four hours a day. If you had a message to send you just cut in and sent your message. But an enemy intercepting that link would simply see a continuous stream of off/on signals which when you examine them all looked random and you can't tell when or where a message was inserted along in there. That was the aim, the goal.

Network-layer encryption can be end to end, end to gateway, or gateway to gateway; it is most commonly used for virtual private networks (VPNs), discussed below (Section 6.5). The chief advantages of network encryption is that it can protect multiple hops and all traffic. A crucial limitation is that the granularity of protection is typically per machine (or per destination pair), which may not be what is desired, especially for servers or other multiuser computers. (The IPsec standards do permit finer-grained keying; this is difficult to do and rarely implemented.)

Transport-level cryptographic protocols have been defined (see, for example, [Bittau et al. 2010]), but are rarely used in practice. They require kernel modifications, which makes them hard to deploy, and they offer limited advantages compared with application-level encryption. Unlike network-layer encryption, it's easy to do fine-grained keying; in addition, transport encryptors can protect the TCP header [Postel 1981] against malicious modifications. Users are thus protected against session-hijacking attacks [Joncheray 1995]. However, network-layer has often been good enough; the utility of fine-grained keying for typical VPN scenarios is not obvious.

The most common layer at which encryption is done is the application layer; in particular, TLS and its older sibling SSL are heavily used for web transmission security. TLS has two tremendous advantages: it's relatively easy to add it to more or less any two-party, TCP-based application, on more or less any operating system; in addition, configuration is quite straightforward compared to, say, IPsec. There's even a UDP version of it now, DTLS [Rescorla and Modadugu 2006]. TLS doesn't do everything; that's probably one of the secrets to its success. All that said, there are caveats—important ones—that implementers and system administrators should heed; see Chapter 8.

At what layer should you encrypt? Not surprisingly, there's no one answer; it depends on what your goals are. There have been times when I have used four layered encryption mechanisms, each of which serves a different purpose:

- WPA2, to limit access to the LAN to authorized users (Unknown to me at the time, there may also have been cryptographic protection of some of the telephony links; see [Malis and Simpson 1999] for a definition of a point-to-point link-layer encryption protocol.)

- A VPN, to protect my traffic from the local network operator

- SSH [Ylönen 1996] to a remote site I control, used to tunnel my web traffic to my HTTP proxy, to protect my traffic from the remote network—my VPN is to a university network that has experienced serious attacks (page 172)

- HTTPS to a remote web site, for end-to-end protection of credit card or login information

The combination of SSH and the VPN is unusual (and arguably unnecessary), but one of those two is quite important and neither is redundant with WPA2 or HTTPS.

I've spoken here about two-party conversations. Multiparty secure communications are possible, too, but the actual mechanisms are considerably more complex and are well beyond the scope of this book. That said, if you're trying to protect all traffic between a pair of computers, or you're trying to protect all traffic between two groups of machines (including the case where one group is just a single machine), you should consider using a VPN instead (Section 6.5).

6.4 Object Encryption

Object encryption is much harder than transport encryption because by definition you're not talking to the other party when you encrypt something. Accordingly, you can't negotiate things like cipher algorithms; you have to know in advance what the other party supports. You don't know whether your key setup has succeeded; you have to encrypt and pray. With long-lived objects (such as email messages), you may want to read or verify them long after you've lost or deleted the relevant keys. In a multihop protocol, you may not know what portions of the data are deemed modifiable by some hop or other. Worse yet, you might know and find yourself unable to do anything about it, especially if you're trying to bolt the crypto on to an existing design—secure email and DNSSEC come to mind. Replay detection is harder; detection of message deletion is much harder because each object is effectively a datagram.

Here, too, there are phases: key acquisition, message canonicalization, encryption and/or signing, and transport encoding, though in some situations some of these steps may be omitted.

Key acquisition is exactly what it sounds like: getting the keys for the other parties. As with transport encryption, it can be preprovisioned, though in the more common case you'll be using certificates (see Chapter 8). If you're only trying to authenticate the object, rather than encrypt it—a scenario that is possible for transport, too, though rather less common—you need to ensure that the receivers have your key as well. If you're using certificates, you can just include the certificate in the message. If you're not using certificates, the recipients either know your key or have the difficult problem of verifying the authenticity of any included keys, so there's no point to putting them in the message.

One special case of key acquisition is when it's your own key; more accurately, it's the key you're going to want to use at some arbitrary time in the future to decrypt the object. This is especially serious for things like encrypted archival backups, since you may not ever need them, but if you do you'll need the key as well. The issue, then, is not acquiring the key per se but rather figuring out how you're going to preserve it while still keeping it safe from prying eyes.

Message canonicalization is a problem that applies to signed, unencrypted objects. When objects are moved from system to system, transformations such as adding or deleting white space, expanding tabs, and changes in the end-of-line character—a simple line feed on Unix-derived systems; a carriage return/line feed sequence on Windows—are

Disk or File System Encryption?

There are two ways to encrypt a drive: *disk encryption* and *file system encryption*encryption!file system. The two are quite different; each has its strengths and weaknesses. (Note that I'm not talking about manually encrypting individual files—generally speaking, that's an error-prone nuisance.)

Disk encryption (sometimes referred to as *full disk encryption (FDE)*) protects individual disk blocks. Each block, typically 512 or 2,048 bytes, is encrypted separately, probably in CBC mode with some function of the block number used as the *initialization vector (IV)*; this includes blocks on the free list. It's a good choice for hardware vendors, since the encryption is agnostic to operating system file formats. The most important advantage, though, is that you don't have to think about what's protected: everything on the disk is.

Disk encryption can be done either by the OS or by the disk hardware. The latter generally offers better performance, but of course not all drives offer it. And you still need OS and perhaps BIOS support; the key, after all, has to come from somewhere.

File system encryption, on the other hand, protects individual files. Metadata are exposed, including things like file size, access patterns, and more; these may represent a serious security leak. That said, it's still the most useful technique for remote file systems; they are, per their name, *file systems*. The interface presented is that of a directed graph, not a remote disk volume. A good summary of the issues in encrypting file system design is presented in [Blaze 1993].

It is tempting to mount an encrypted remote disk image, for example, a .dmg file on Mac OS X or a .vhd file on Windows, and decrypt it on the client. That can work for single-client access. However, unless the underlying OS's file system code was written to deal with shared disk drives, you're likely to experience ghastly failure modes due to lack of locking of, say, the free list. There's another issue as well: to do this, you often have to specify—and allocate—space for the entire virtual disk at creation time; free space on that disk is thus not available for use by the parent disk. By contrast, an encrypted file system has just one free list, that of the underlying OS.

There's one more important distinguishing issue: granularity of keying. With disk encryption, the entire volume is protected by a single key. With file system encryption, different subtrees can be protected by different keys, held by different users.

commonplace. XML objects can be embedded in other objects, which in turn might induce a change in indentation. A digital signature verification will not survive such changes. Accordingly, a canonical representation is often defined; the signature and verification calculations are performed over it, rather than over any given real instantiation.

Transport encoding is an optional phase. It is necessary if some channels over which the object is likely to be transported cannot handle arbitrary byte sequences. Arguably, one could say that this isn't really part of the encryption process—one can represent any byte sequence as a series of hexadecimal digits—but if some channel is especially likely to be used its properties should be taken into account. The S/MIME standards (partially based on the earlier PEM design) for signed and/or encrypted email are one case in point; many email systems can't handle binary values, so a base-64 encoding [Josefsson 2006; Linn 1989] was specified. Another interesting case is DNSSEC, the extension to the DNS for digitally signed records [Arends et al. 2005a; Arends et al. 2005b; Arends et al. 2005c]: DNS packets over UDP were limited to 512 bytes by [Mockapetris 1987], which is not enough to accommodate both the actual response and a digital signature. Accordingly, the DNSSEC standards had to mandate the use of the EDNS0 extension [Vixie 1999]. (DNSSEC is actually a case study in the difficulty of retrofitting object security to an existing protocol. The advanced student of such matters would be well advised to compare today's standards with the predecessor [Eastlake 1999]: many of the changes were needed because of subtle protocol and operational aspects.)

The temporal aspects of object security raise some interesting philosophical issues. Certificates expire; they can also be revoked if the private key is compromised or if there's reason to fear that the certificate might be fraudulent (Chapter 8). What does it mean to check the signature on signed email, if the certificate was revoked? Can you still read an encrypted email message, if your certificate has expired since then? What if you have a digitally signed program? Can you install it after the expiration date? Should you run it after certificate revocation? There may be a timestamp in the file saying when it was signed, but of course an enemy can change the system clock before signing some malware. Should software vendors re-sign their software when the certificates roll over? What about copies on CDs? How do you validate the code if you're installing something such as a network device driver on an offline machine? This is discussed at great length in Section 8.4.

Storage encryption raises other issues, especially because the popular mythology often conflates the notions of "encrypted disk" and "information security." To put it briefly, encryption is useful if and only if your threat model includes attacks that do not go through the operating system; most notably, this includes someone with physical access. Good places to use storage encryption are USB flash drives (they're regularly lost), laptops (judging from how many of them seem to walk away, one can only conclude that laptops have feet), off-site backup media, and the like. Bad places for it are most desktops and virtually all servers, unless your threat model includes targeted burglaries aimed at the information on your drives rather than the hardware's resale value, or perhaps seizures by the police. (Of course, you can't count on drive encryption defeating the police, since they now have technology to keep your machine powered up while they cart it away to their lab.[1]) There's one more physical security threat that many people overlook: what happens to the disk drive when you discard your computer? Most people do *not* remember to wipe their disk first [S. L. Garfinkel and Shelat 2003].

Why not encrypt other disks? The main reason is that it generally doesn't do any good. Suppose the enemy doesn't have root or Administrator privileges on the machine? In that case, ordinary file permissions will keep the data safe. On the other hand, if the attacker has gained elevated privileges, he or she can impersonate the legitimate users, replace software, steal keys, and so on. In other words, it doesn't do much good; it just increases system overhead, though that's often quite low these days. You might, of course, want to encrypt your drives to protect yourself against random burglaries and the discarded drive problem. That's not bad reasoning, but remember that it won't protect against electronic intrusions that are more likely to target your information. The threats are very different, and a single defense does not address both.

Supplying keys for encrypted storage objects poses another problem. For interactive use—inserting a flash drive, booting a laptop, etc.—it's not a big deal; the user can just type in the passphrase at the right time. But what about server keys? Most servers run in lights-out computer rooms; there's no one present to type in the key at boot time.

6.5 VPNs

"What do you think happens if you open a gateway for an ancient evil to infest our departmental LAN?"

Bob Howard in *The Jennifer Morgue*
—CHARLES STROSS

Virtual private networks (VPNs) are intended to provide seamless, secure communications between a host and a network or two or more networks. While there are many types in use, we'll focus on encrypted ones—this is, after all, the cryptography chapter in a security book. The big advantage of VPNs is that they provide fire-and-forget crypto: once you turn one on, all of your traffic is protected.

---

1. "HotPlug: Transport a live computer without shutting it down,"
   http://www.wiebetech.com/products/HotPlug.php.

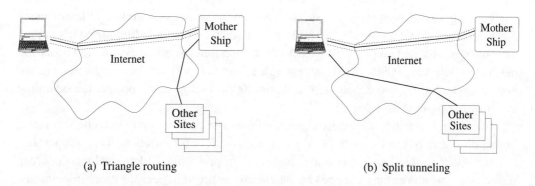

(a) Triangle routing   (b) Split tunneling

Figure 6.1: VPN routing configurations. The dotted lines show the encrypted link back to the home organization.

Although many VPN topologies are possible, only two are common: connecting multiple locations of a single organization, and connecting road warriors' laptops (and often other toys) back to the mothership. For the most part, they use similar technologies. Let's look at the road warrior case first.

A virtual private network is intended to seem and operate like a real network, with one crucial difference: some of the "wires" are in fact encrypted network connections that may pass through many other networks and routers. These links—*tunnels*—are often treated like any other network links. This has several implications for VPN configuration. First, packets are routed to the virtual interface, including using the usual longest prefix match [Fuller and T. Li 2006]. This makes *triangle routing*—sending all traffic through the VPN gateway—straightforward, by pointing the default route at the tunnel interface; typically, it also permits direct connection to resources on directly connected LANs, since they have a longer prefix than 0/0. This is often necessary—how else will packets reach the real network's default gateway?—but carries certain risks; in particular, you are sometimes not shielded from attacks originating on-LAN. This is a particular concern when on untrusted networks, such as coffee shop hotspots. The alternative, adding prefixes only for the organizational LAN to the tunnel link, is known as *split tunneling*; see Figure 6.1.

It's important to remember that a road warrior VPN is connecting some machine to your network and giving it essentially unfettered access. Is that machine trustworthy? More or less by definition, it lives outside your firewall some of the time—has it been infected? Perhaps more to the point, it is often used outside of the social milieu of an office; what are euphemistically termed "adult sites" are notorious malware purveyors [Wondracek et al. 2010]. Such sites sometimes label themselves *not safe for work (NSFW)*. Their concern is what your coworkers or boss might see, but there's a security aspect as well. Has that laptop connecting via the VPN been infected?

Viewing virtual network links strictly like any other network link, and hence using them in accordance with the routing table, has another, more subtle limitation: it's impossible to pass only certain ports over the VPN, as opposed to certain destination hosts and networks [Bellovin 2009a]. While in principle routing by port number can be done [Zhao and Bellovin 2009; Zhao, Chau, and Bellovin 2008], I know of no production operating systems that support it.

The use of triangle routing raises some complex issues. It certainly hurts performance, in that all traffic has to be routed to the home network before heading to its proper destination. On the other hand, it provides two types of protection: it lets road warriors reap the benefits (whatever they may be) of the enterprise firewall; perhaps more importantly, it ensures that plaintext traffic to assorted web sites is shielded from others on the same, untrusted LAN. (A lot of the plaintext traffic, and in particular much web traffic, is unencrypted; this in turn can expose people to *sidejacking* attacks [Krebs 2007], where web authentication cookies are stolen from unencrypted sessions after login.)

From a security perspective, then, it would seem that triangle routing should always be used, with the VPN activated immediately at boot time. Unfortunately, there are some complications. First, many hotspots use boxes that intercept the first web request and pop up a box with the usual login, advertising, terms of service, liability waiver, and so on. If even initial web traffic is routed towards the VPN, the interception can't occur, in which case the user can't log in and the network path isn't unblocked for use. The fact that the VPN can't be set up is a minor inconvenience compared with not being able to talk at all. Perhaps users could take advantage of the local net exception to the VPN's routing and try to connect to some hypothetical on-LAN web server; however, most normal people neither know nor care what IP address their laptop has at any given time. Besides, some of the resources necessary to complete some of these web logins are off-LAN and hence would be caught by the VPN.

The second issue is a little odder. On some systems—Macs are notorious for this—some applications wake up and try to transmit as soon as a network connection appears. Depending on timing and VPN design, they may start sending as soon as the network is unblocked, before the VPN can finish its setup.

On top of that, of course, there are performance issues: the possible overloading of the official gateway's link (fixable by spending more money on a faster link), and the latency from the user to that gateway, which is often a matter of geography and hence is fixable only by finding applied physicists who don't think that the speed of light is really that stringent an upper bound on signal propagation times.

Picking what VPN technology to use is harder than deciding that you need one; VPNs are the poster child for the saying that the nice thing about standards is that there are so many to choose from.[2] There are at least five obvious choices: IPsec [S. T. Kent and Seo 2005]; Microsoft's *Point-to-Point Tunneling Protocol (PPTP)* [Hamzeh et al. 1999]; the *Layer 2 Tunneling Protocol (L2TP)* [Townsley et al. 1999], the IETFication of PPTP which needs to run over IPsec to be secure; OpenVPN [Feilner 2006]; and a plethora of so-called "TLS VPN" products [Frankel et al. 2008].

IPsec probably has the cleanest architectural vision. It is available on virtually all platforms, supports a wide range of authentication methods, and can secure more or less anything layered on top of it. Unfortunately, its adoption has been hindered by too much complexity in the base specification (e.g., per-user keying of port-specific IPsec connections), plus about $\aleph_0$ different options [Srivatsan, M. Johnson, and Bellovin 2010]. The key management protocol, *Internet Key Exchange (IKE)* [Kaufman 2005], has even more options than that. IPsec also has trouble with NATs [Srisuresh and Egevang 2001]; it seems it does too good a job of protecting the IP and TCP headers [Aboba and Dixon 2004]. There is a mechanism in IKE to negotiate NAT traversal [Kivinen et al. 2005]; naturally, this involves another option, rather than it being standard for all IPsec configurations. Worse yet, according to various reports, different implementations don't interoperate very well; they're a fine choice for single-vendor shops but can often be problematic otherwise.

PPTP is a Microsoft invention. It's basically a LAN extension protocol—remote machines appear to be on the same LAN, and things like broadcast messages are supposed to work—with its own built-in encryption mechanisms. In some environments, the LAN orientation can cause trouble because remote machines have different timing characteristics, especially if they're reached by slow links; talking to them is not cheap, and broadcast messages carry a notable cost. Still, the ubiquity of Windows means that almost any machine you have will support PPTP. There are two significant limitations, though, that should be considered. First, PPTP uses *Generic Routing Encapsulation (GRE)* [Hanks et al. 1994] for transport. GRE is blocked by many packet filters; reconfiguration may be necessary to support it. Second, the authentication protocol has serious flaws [Marlinspike and Hulton 2012; Schneier and Mudge 1999].

L2TP is, as noted, the IETF's version of PPTP. Because the security comes from IPsec, if you want to use it you have to deal with both the LAN orientation of PPTP *and* the configuration complexity of IPsec. It does exist, it is supported, and it is used, but it's hard to identify a compelling unique niche for it unless you're already running IPsec for other reasons. L2TP uses UDP for transport, which means that it passes easily through most rational NAT boxes. Unfortunately, "rational NAT box" is often an oxymoron.

OpenVPN is the open source community's response to the problems people have experienced with IPsec, PPTP, and L2TP. OpenVPN runs on most platforms of interest,

---

2. "How Standards Proliferate," http://xkcd.com/927/.

can communicate through NATs, and supports both triangle routing and direct routing. The disadvantage is that it's virtually always add-on software, no matter what OS you're using.

The last option is the TLS (or SSL) VPN. The key differentiator here is the use of TLS to provide the protected transport; it in turn builds on the many years of easy inter-operability of web browsers and servers. In fact, they do more than build on TLS, they actually use web browsers. This is both the benefit and the limitation of the technology.

In *TLS portal VPNs*, the server is just a glorified web server: after the usual process, the user is presented with a web page customized to show links to the resources he or she is allowed to access. Crucially, though, when the links are clicked on, the browser itself does not contact another machine directly; instead, the TLS VPN server acts as a proxy, contacting the internal server on the client's behalf and forwarding data in both directions. This in turn exposes the two crucial limitations of portal VPNs. First and most obviously, only specific services can be reached. Second, the encryption from the browser is not end to end. Apart from the fact that the VPN gateway itself becomes a very tempting target, since a lot of traffic will be in the clear on it, it also rules out authentication methods like client-side certificates (Section 7.8).

TLS tunnel VPNs support other applications, but in a curious way: the browser down-loads some active content (Java, JavaScript, ActiveX, what have you) that acts as a more conventional VPN. That is, the active content *is* the VPN endpoint for an IPsec-like VPN, but only for connections from that machine.

Although TLS VPNs are relatively simple to configure and operate, they have some unique limitations. First, because there are no standards there is little interoperability. This is not a serious issue for portal VPNs; it is very serious for tunnel VPNs. A related issue is that the necessary active content modules may not exist for all client platforms of interest.

There's a more subtle limitation as well: more than any other type of VPN, TLS VPNs rely on the user to do the right thing. Any way to trick the user into disclosing login credentials (e.g., phishing) will work against a TLS VPN, since the client is, after all, a browser. Furthermore, portal VPNs require the user to consent to the installation of some active content. This an extremely dangerous habit to teach people. (Aside: there was once a web-based corporate expense vouchering system written in Java. Employees who used it—more precisely, who were required to use it—would visit this page, at which point the Java applet would be downloaded. This applet required more access rights than the standard Java sandbox permitted; accordingly, there was a pop-up box asking user permission to do this. The real security experts complained that this was teaching bad habits; the answer that came back from On High said that the vendor had been thoroughly checked by the corporate security group and that the applet was safe. That response, of course, missed the point completely, which if nothing else shows that even corporate security groups are very fallible.)

6.6 Protocol, Algorithm, and Key Size Recommendations

Given all this, what protocols, algorithms, etc., should you use? For standard situations, this is generally a relatively easy question to answer. With cryptography, though, in addition to the usual questions about threat model, there are two more things to think about: work factor and time.

Unlike most security situations, in cryptography we often have a quantitative upper bound on the effort an adversary must expend. When using a symmetric cipher with an n-bit key, the enemy's work factor is bounded at 2^n: that number of trial decryptions is guaranteed to find the key. (I'm ignoring the question of how they can recognize when they've gotten the right answer. It's generally not too hard; see [Bellovin 1997] and its references for some discussion of the topic.) If we can estimate the enemy's resources, we can determine whether that upper bound is sufficient.

That's the good news. The bad news is the time dimension: encrypted data often must be protected for a long time, and it's quite imponderable how much cryptanalysis will improve over the years. There's an NSA saying that Bruce Schneier is fond of quoting: "attacks always get better; they never get worse." We can calculate a lower bound on the attacker's economic improvement by assuming that Moore's Law will continue to hold. Assume that you've determined that an m-bit key is adequate today, given your estimate of your enemy's resources. The data you're encrypting must remain secret for 30 years. By Moore's Law, we know that there will be approximately 20 halvings of the price-performance of a given amount of CPU power. Accordingly, you should use a cipher with a keylength of at least $n + 20$ bits.

We can approach the question from another angle: the attacker's maximum possible resource commitment. Assume that the enemy has 10^7 processors, each of which can try 10^9 keys per second. (10^7 nodes is a large but not preposterously large botnet. 10^9 decryptions/second is too high by a factor of at least 10 and probably 100 for a general-purpose processor or GPU core.) There are about $3.15 \cdot 10^7$ seconds in a year, which yields $3.15 \cdot 10^{23}$ guesses per year, which in turn corresponds to a keylength of about 78 bits. Adding 20 bits for a 30-year margin and another 20 bits to reduce the odds of a lucky guess early in the effort gives a keylength of 118 bits. In other words, using a standard 128-bit key is more than ample. (It's also worth noting that even a very powerful enemy who can manage 10^{16} trial decryptions per second is unlikely to devote all that to one single problem, such as your data, for 30 years. A few years ago, I told a friend with spooky connections about a new paper on cryptanalytic hardware. The design would cost

Physical Limits

Can we bound the effort an attacker can launch by physical science? Let's restrict our attention to the solar system, since the speed of light is an effective barrier to programming other stars.

The sun contains most of the matter in the solar system; its mass is approximately $2 \cdot 10^{30}$ kg. A proton masses about $2 \cdot 10^{-27}$ kg; assuming that the sun is entirely composed of protons (a reasonable assumption, since neutrons have about the same mass and electrons are three orders of magnitude less massive), we see that the solar system has about 10^{57} protons. Call every one of these a computer, and assume it can do 10^{15} decryptions per second. In a full year, then, this solar system-sized computer could manage 2^{254} decryptions, so a 256-bit key is safe, even against super-powered villains...

We can take this a step further: why limit our proton computers to 10^{15} decryptions/second? It's unclear whether time is quantized in the same way that energy is. On the other hand, according to some interpretations of physical theory, times shorter than 10^{-44} seconds aren't meaningful [Baez, Unruh, and Tifft 1999]. This bounds the speed of our solar system computer to 10^{101} operations per second, or $3.8 \cdot 10^{108}$ operations per year. This translates to a keylength of about 361 bits.

many millions to build and would take a year for each solution. He laughed, thinking of the political fights that would ensue: which intercepts would be worth solving on such slow, expensive hardware?)

There's one more aspect to take into account: advances in cryptanalysis. Can someone, such as the Andromedans, crack a modern cipher? While this can't be ruled out—though no one ever knowingly uses a cipher that their enemies can break, the history books are full of examples of world-changing cryptanalytic feats—it's important to realize what a solution would look like. Ciphers today don't shatter; it is all but impossible to imagine a solution where one plugs in some ciphertext, presses a button, and an answer pops out immediately. Rather, there's a work factor associated with a solution, often a considerable work factor. Consider the *Data Encryption Standard (DES)*, a now-obsolete 56-bit cipher endorsed at the time by the NSA. The best attack on it ever published, linear cryptanalysis [Matsui 1994], requires 2^{43} known plaintexts. As it turns out, for completely different reasons, encrypting more than 2^{32} DES blocks with the same key is a bad idea; no one will encrypt 2,048 times more data. In other words, the attacker almost certainly cannot collect enough ciphertext, let alone the corresponding plaintext, to launch the attack. If a modern 128-bit cipher is cracked, it's likely that the work factor is reduced to something that is still preposterously large, but not up to the nominal 2^{128} standard. There's still plenty of safety margin.

An interesting statement appeared in the press recently. James Bamford, probably the foremost NSA watcher, wrote: [2012]:

> According to another top official also involved with the program, the NSA made an enormous breakthrough several years ago in its ability to cryptanalyze, or break, unfathomably complex encryption systems employed by not only governments around the world but also many average computer users in the United States. The upshot, according to this official: 'Everybody's a target; everybody with communication is a target.'

Is that statement accurate? If so, what work factor is still needed? The context of the statement was a description of a massive new NSA datacenter.

It is worth stressing that this analysis has primarily focused on the upper bound, the one given by key size. A cipher can be much weaker than that! A monoalphabetic substitution cipher on the 26-letter English alphabet has 26! possible keys, or a key size of about 88 bits. It is nevertheless simple enough to solve that there are puzzles based on it in daily newspapers. However, the amount of cryptanalytic review that today's public ciphers undergo is a reasonable guarantee that they're nowhere near that weak.

There's one more way to look at the problem: an appeal to authority. In 2009, the NSA published a remarkable document, their so-called *Suite B Cryptography* specifications.[3] In it, they state that 128-bit *Advanced Encryption Standard (AES)* encryption is strong enough for Secret data, and 256-bit AES is good enough for Top Secret data. Assuming that this isn't disinformation (and I don't think that it is), the NSA is saying that a 128-bit cipher is good enough for most national security data. (Of course, given Bamford's statement, perhaps it is disinformation.)

Should you go to 256 bits? After all, that's what they recommend for Top Secret data. Your cryptography is rarely the weakest point. The NSA itself says, "Creating secure cryptographic components, products and solutions involves much more than simply implementing a specific cryptographic protocol or suite of cryptographic algorithms." Unless your computers and practices are in line with NSA's own habits—and they're almost certainly not—your algorithms and key sizes are not your weak link. And the NSA itself? From what I've heard, they want 256-bit keys to guard against the possibility of massively parallel quantum computers being developed; such a computer could crack a 128-bit key in $O(2^{64})$ time. Their enemies may not be your enemies, though, and their requirements are stringent; I've seen redactions they ordered in a document more than 65

---

3. "NSA Suite B Cryptography," http://www.nsa.gov/ia/programs/suiteb_cryptography/.

years old. That said, newer versions of their Suite B document do suggest planning for quantum-resistant algorithms and key lengths.

I conclude that 128-bit keys are adequate for almost all purposes and against all enemies short of MI-31. You can use longer keys if it doesn't cost you anything (256-bit RC4 runs at the same speed as 128-bit RC4), but it rarely makes much security sense.

Stream ciphers are harder to employ properly than are block ciphers, but they do have their uses. RC4 has been the most popular choice, and it is extremely fast; that said, it has a number of serious cryptanalytic weaknesses [Golić 1997; Knudsen et al. 1998; Vanhoef and Piessens 2015]. Don't use it for new applications; instead, use AES in counter mode. In fact, do your best to eliminate all uses of RC4 within your infrastructure. (The history of RC4 is too tangled to explain here; the Wikipedia article is a good starting point. The best source for a description of the algorithm itself is an expired Internet draft.[4])

If we're going to use 128-bit keys for our symmetric ciphers, what size modulus should be used for RSA or Diffie-Hellman moduli for equivalent strength? There have been analytic efforts based on how many operations are required to factor large numbers; two of the best-known analyses are by the *National Institute of Standards and Technology (NIST)* [Barker et al. 2012] and the IETF [Orman and Hoffman 2004]; a comprehensive survey of recommendations can be found at http://www.keylength.com/. The calculations are complex and I won't repeat them here, but they don't completely agree. That said, both agree that a 3,072-bit modulus is adequate for 128-bit ciphers, and 2,048-bit moduli are sufficient for 112-bit ciphers. Although the 3,072-bit size is probably more mathematically accurate, it is considerably more expensive in CPU time, especially on low-end devices. Unless you feel that you really need 128 bits of *security* (as opposed to key size, since AES doesn't support 112-bit keys), 2,048-bit moduli are adequate. Again, if the Andromedans are after you, a more conservative choice may be indicated; even the NSA says so. 1,024-bit moduli are too small; research results suggest that MI-31 or its competitors can break them [Adrian et al. 2015].

The situation for elliptic curve algorithms is more complex, since deployment has been hindered by confusion about their patent status (but see [McGrew, Igoe, and Salter 2011]). That said, most of the analyses, including the NSA's, concur that a 256-bit modulus is suitable for 128-bit ciphers. The problem is that using elliptic curve cryptography requires picking a curve; it's not entirely clear which are the safest.

One choice is the set of curves standardized by NIST [NIST 2013]. In years gone by, that would have been uncontroversial; NIST standards have generally been seen as strong. However, one of the Snowden revelations was that the NSA tampered with the design of a NIST standard random number generator used for cryptography [Checkoway

---

4. "A Stream Cipher Encryption Algorithm 'Arcfour',"
   http://tools.ietf.org/id/draft-kaukonen-cipher-arcfour-03.txt.

Table 6.1: Size Recommendations for Cryptographic Primitives

Purpose	Size (bits)
Symmetric cipher key length	128
RSA or DH modulus	2,048
Elliptic curve modulus	256
Hash function (output)	256

et al. 2014; Green 2013; Perlroth, Larson, and Shane 2013]; since then, many people have come to distrust *all* NIST standards. The NIST curves do include some mysterious constants; might they have been selected to produce a curve that the NSA can break? Some people prefer the Brainpool curves [Lochter and Merkle 2010], but there is concern that those curves could have been manipulated, too [Bernstein et al. 2014]. Others have opted for Bernstein's Curve25519 [2006], which is very fast; however, there are some technical issues with its point representation that pose some compatibility issues. If you don't trust NIST and the NSA, the latter two choices are arguably safer, but which of the two is best is not yet completely obvious.

By contrast, the proper hash function output size is very strongly and clearly related to cipher key length: it should be double to avoid birthday paradox attacks. In other words, if you're using a 128-bit cipher, use a hash function with 256-bit output.

My size recommendations are summarized in Table 6.1.

For protocols, the IETF made a series of recommendations in 2003 that have held up pretty well [Bellovin, Schiller, and Kaufman 2003]. Some of the protocols described there (e.g., IPsec and TLS) have newer versions, but in general the advice given there is worth following. Table 6.3 summarizes it and adds some newer items.

Recommendations for the cryptographic algorithms themselves (Table 6.2) are a bit more problematic. RSA, Diffie-Hellman, and elliptic curve are all considered secure when used with proper modulus sizes, per Table 6.1. Elliptic curve is often preferred because it requires less CPU and produces smaller output; however (and especially in the wake of the Snowden revelations), there is concern over which curves to use.

Considerations of cryptanalytic strength and output size both rule out the MD5 and SHA-1 algorithms as hash functions. The 256-, 384-, and 512-bit variations of SHA-2 [Eastlake and T. Hansen 2011; NIST 2015b] all look quite strong. NIST has selected an algorithm known as Keccak as SHA-3 [NIST 2015a], but a NIST cryptographer has recently stated that "cryptanalysis since 2005 has actually eased our concerns about SHA-2."[5] The

---

5. "IETF 83 Proceedings, Security Area Open Meeting,"
   http://www.ietf.org/proceedings/83/slides/slides-83-saag-0.pdf.

Threat Modeling: A Case History

A friend recently posed the following question:

> Given an 80-bit random key, whitened with SHA-2-256 and used as an AES key, what is your estimate of the probability that a national actor can recover the original key using brute force techniques in the next five years? The only crib is that the plaintext is in ASCII, with the top bit cleared.

Further questioning revealed that he wanted to protect a password hint file on a smart phone that might be lost; he assumed that he would notice the loss, and would be able to change his passwords within a week. In other words, there is no long-term confidentiality threat to the data. Let's crunch the numbers.

DES, a 56-bit cipher, was solved by brute force in 1997 for $250K [Electronic Frontier Foundation 1998]. My friend wants to be safe in 2017, about 13 Moore's Law doublings since 1997. On the other hand, he's planning on using an 80-bit key rather than 56, so the net increase in difficulty is 11 bits, or a work factor increase of 2^{11}. The cost, then, is about $2^{11} \cdot \$250,000$, or $500 million. Can a nation spend that much on a cryptanalysis box? Assuredly, though few private companies could. Thus far, there would seem to be a real threat. However...

The suggested algorithm involved "whitening" the key: using SHA-2-256 to spread the random bits uniformly around the 256-bit AES key. This avoids any possible short-cut attacks based on the assumption that the high-order 176 bits of the key are all 0s. This is a non-standard way of doing things: a brute force attack would require connecting an 80-bit counter to a hash function, and then feeding that in as the key to a cipher. (It would also slow down the attack; at least in software, AES is much faster than SHA-2-256.) If my friend is the only one doing this, the question is rather different: is it worth spending that much money on a special-purpose machine good only for cracking one particular individual's passwords? Unless his passwords are *really* important, one would have to be skeptical. However, if the CEOs of much of the Fortune 500 were to adopt this scheme, the scales might tilt back.

There's one more point to consider: is the threat model correct? Is he really a target of the Andromedans? Would he really know if MI-31 had taken his phone, and hence be able to change his passwords? Might they sneak into his hotel room and copy its memory while he's at the pool? Would they resort to a cyberattack instead, and insert some malware that would wait for him to unlock the file? For that matter, what they'd really be interested in is the data protected by those passwords. Are those systems hackable? Are their sysadmins bribable? His 80-bit key may not be the weakest link.

significance of SHA-3 is that it is based on fundamentally different design principles than MD5, SHA-1, and SHA-2; a new cryptanalytic attack on one is unlikely to affect the other. At this point, both seem like excellent choices.

A somewhat troublesome part is the block cipher algorithm. AES is standardized, endorsed by the NSA, and has been the subject of a lot of academic study. That said, and even discounting Bamford's comments because he didn't say what algorithms are vulnerable (and for all we know was himself the victim of disinformation), there is a modest amount of uneasiness about it; it doesn't seem to have the safety margins one would like. There have been attacks on weakened versions of AES with 256-bit keys [Biryukov, Dunkelman, et al. 2010], and attacks only marginally better than brute force [Bogdanov, Khovratovich, and Rechberger 2011], but some cryptographers feel that these attacks are still stronger than one would like. Others feel that there's no problem [Landau 2004]. Thus far, there are no results that pose any credible threat—the attacks on 256-bit AES were related-key attacks, which shouldn't be an issue for properly designed protocols—but it bears watching. It's even harder to decide what to recommend in its place. One obvious thing to do is to increase the number of rounds in AES (at a modest cost in performance) and/or improve the key scheduling algorithm, especially for the 192- and 256-bit variants; those algorithms were criticized while the algorithm was still being considered for standardization. Ferguson et al. [2000] wrote, "Compared to the cipher itself, the Rijndael key schedule appears to be more of an ad hoc design. It has a much slower diffusion structure than the cipher, and contains relatively few non-linear elements." Of course, doing that means that you have a non-standard cipher, with all that that implies for compatibility. Camellia [Matsui, Nakajima, and Moriai 2004], a Japanese standard, has gained some adherents and should be a drop-in replacement for AES. Still, it has not received as much analysis because AES is the 800-kilogram gorilla in the crypto world.

On the other hand, is AES really weak? Some years ago, Biham et al. found a marginally more efficient attack than brute force on a slightly weakened version of the NSA-

Table 6.2: Recommended Cryptographic Algorithms

Algorithm	Function
AES	Block cipher; generally speaking, new applications should use Galois Counter Mode
Counter mode AES	Stream cipher
SHA-2-256/384/512 SHA-3-256/384/512	Hash function
RSA or EC	Public key algorithm

Table 6.3: Recommended IETF Cryptographic Protocols

Protocol	Uses
IPsec	General network-layer encryption [S. T. Kent and Seo 2005]
TLS	Simple encrypted circuits [Dierks and Rescorla 2008]; use Version 1.2 or newer
HMAC/SHA-2	Message authentication [NIST 2015b; Weinrib and Postel 1996]
Security/Multipart	Secure email and similarly formatted text [Ramsdell and Turner 2010]
XMLDSIG	Signed XML [Eastlake, Reagle, and Solo 2002]
CMS	Secure objects [Housley 2009]

designed algorithm Skipjack [Biham, Biryukov, and Shamir 1999]. I marveled aloud about it to a very knowledgeable friend, noting that taking away just one round made such a difference. His reply: "You call it a weakness; I call it good engineering." Maybe the NSA really has that deep an understanding of cipher design—or maybe the safety margin is low. We'll know for sure in a few decades; for now, I do recommend AES's use.

6.7 Analysis

As long as we stay with today's standard models of interaction—client/server, for simple transmission or object security—I don't expect significant changes in protocols. The important cases are handled reasonably well; the difficult problems, such as preserving access to the key used to encrypt a backup tape, are inherent in the problem statement. One can't rule out breakthroughs, of course—prior to Diffie and Hellman's work [1976], no one in the civilian world had even conceived of the concept of public key cryptography— but such insights occur once in a generation at most.

An interesting question is what will happen with different interaction models, such as inherently 3-way or 4-way sessions with no one universally trusted party. (No, I don't know what sort of really popular application would require that; if I did, I might find myself a venture capitalist.) The key management protocol might be a bit tricky, but lots of other things get complicated with more than two parties.

My very strong statement that people should stick with well-understood, standardized protocols is extremely likely to stand. Remember the quote from Needham and Schroeder discussed earlier. It goes down as one of the more prescient statements in a technical paper; indeed, it took 18 years for what in retrospect was an obvious flaw in one of their own schemes to be discovered [Lowe 1996].

A place I hope we'll see improvements is the usability of cryptographic technology. A certain amount of over-the-wire flexibility is mandatory, if only to permit migration to different algorithms over time. Unfortunately, this protocol flexibility generally manifests itself as more buttons, knobs, and sliders for the poor, benighted users, who neither know nor care about, say, the rationale for using what is essentially SHA-2-256 truncated to 224-bit output [Housley 2004] to better match triple-DES; all they know is that they're presented with yet another incomprehensible option. Couple that with the inherent issues of trust management—who *really* owns a given key?—and you end up with applications that very few people can actually use successfully [Clark et al. 2011; S. L. Garfinkel and R. C. Miller 2005; Whitten and Tygar 1999]. Thus far, cryptography has succeeded where users weren't given any decisions to make; if it's all hidden away under the hood, people accept it and feel better for having used it.

Given the concerns I expressed in the last section, do I think that the algorithm recommendations in the previous section will change soon? It's important to note the assumptions behind my suggestions. First, I'm assuming no drastic improvements in the price/performance of hardware. Even if I'm off by a factor of 100—about 7 bits of keylength—it probably doesn't matter. If Moore's Law runs into a brick wall within the desired secrecy lifetime (it will at some point; it seems extremely unlikely that we can produce gates smaller than an atom), the situation is better yet for the defender. I'm also assuming no unforeseen cryptanalytic results. The algorithms and protocols discussed are all well studied, but breakthroughs happen. Again, it is unlikely that a modern algorithm will suddenly shatter, so there will still most likely be a large work factor required—but that's a prediction, not a promise.

Large-scale quantum computers, should they ever become real, will change things significantly. In particular, there are efficient quantum factoring algorithms [Shor 1994]; that will probably rule out all of today's public key algorithms. However, it's still unclear whether such computers are possible.

Finally, remember Shamir's advice in 1995: "Don't use cryptographic overkill. Even bad crypto is usually the strong part of the system."[6]

Given all that, where should cryptography be used? The security advantages of universal encryption are clear enough that I won't bother reviewing them; the disadvantages are not always obvious beyond the problem of "what do I do if lose my key?" That latter is especially serious (albeit obvious) for object encryption, enough so to merit a blanket statement: do not encrypt stored objects unless the risk is *very* great; if you do, take

---

6. "Notes on 'Cryptography—Myths and Realities,' a talk by Adi Shamir, CRYPTO '95," http://www.ieee-security.org/Cipher/ConfReports/conf-rep-Crypto95.html.

adequate precautions to preserve keys at least as carefully. If you're encrypting backup media, stage regular practice drills in retrieving files (a good idea in any event, if only to test the quality of the backups and your operational procedures for using them) and keys.

There are other disadvantages as well. The difficulty in network operations has long been recognized: it's impossible to see the contents of an encrypted message, even if you need to understand why it's causing trouble. This can also cause problems for security folk; network intrusion detection systems can't peer inside, either. It would be nice if we had some sort of magic cryptanalysis box that could only look at packets with the evil bit set [Bellovin 2003]; thus far, no one has developed a suitable one.

There's a more subtle issue, though. Obviously, protecting cryptographic keys is extremely vital. A key that doesn't exist on a machine can't be stolen from it; a key that is there but itself strongly encrypted is likewise effectively immune to compromise. This poses a dilemma: the best way to keep a key safe is to avoid using it. Of course, if we never use it, it's rather pointless to have it. Nevertheless, we can draw an important conclusion: high-value keys should be employed as sparingly as possible and removed from machines when they're no longer necessary. Given the rate of host compromise, a long-term key in constant use—say, for routinely signing all outbound email—is at great risk; a recipient should therefore attach a lot less value to the signature than one produced by a key that is rarely used and well protected at other times. In the absence of strong key storage (and general-purpose hosts rarely have such facilities), strong overall security therefore requires different keys for different sensitivity levels, suitable (and suitably usable) software to let users manage such complexity, plus a lot of user education and training on how to behave.

Chapter 7

Passwords and Authentication

"I haven't told him about you, but I have told him to trust absolutely whoever has the key word. You remember?"

"Yes, of course. *Meshuggah*. What does it mean?"

"Never mind." Abrams grinned.

Ensign Flandry
—POUL ANDERSON

7.1 Authentication Principles

Authentication is generally considered to be one of the most basic security principles. Absent bugs—admittedly a very large assumption—authentication effectively controls what system objects someone can use. In other words, it's important to get authentication right.

Most discussions of authentication start by describing the three basic forms: something you know (e.g., a password); something you have, such as a token or a particular mobile phone; and something you are, that is, some form of biometric. While this categorization is indeed useful, it understates the *systems* nature of authentication. The total environment—who will use it, how you deal with lost credentials, what the consequences are of lack of access or access by the wrong person, and more—is at least as important. The most important question of all is how people will actually use the authentication technology in the real world.

Another important thing to remember: we authenticate in many more situations today than we did in the not very distant past. Once upon a time, we would log in to a work machine or two. Now, we log in to many different web sites, mail systems, devices, doors, and even cars. The challenges, and hence the solutions, can differ.

7.2 Passwords

This book is about demythologizing security. Few areas are in sorer need of that than passwords. The trouble started with a classic—and still correct—paper by Morris and Thompson [1979], which among other things showed why guessable passwords were bad. However, that result is often misapplied today; in particular, insufficient attention is paid to the threat model (what assets you are protecting, and against whom) and to the tension between security and usability. ([Singer, W. Anderson, and Farrow 2013] gives a good presentation of the history of how we got to where we are and of the many mistakes and unjustified assumptions made along the way.)

The problem of password strength is easy to explain. Simple experiments using the classic Unix password-hashing algorithm show that given a hashed password, an early 2009 laptop—by no means a state-of-the-art computer—can try more than 150,000 password guesses per second. If the enemy has 1,000 such computers—trivial for any self-respecting botnet owner—all possible passwords of up to eight lowercase letters can be tried in less than half an hour. Even if digits are included in the mix, the guessing time is still only about 5¼ hours. The attacker's problem is often even simpler than that; people don't pick truly random strings like "gisegpoc" or "A*9kV#2jeCKQ"; they prefer words or names, or simple variants of these. A recent study based on the RockYou dataset, a list of passwords posted by some hackers, showed that 19 of the top 20 passwords found fit this model [Weir et al. 2010]; the list of most frequent choices included "abc123", "princess", and the ever-popular "password" (#4 on the list, preceded only by "123456", "12345", and "123456789").

It seems simple enough to solve—just choose strong passwords!—but it's very problematic in practice. Users today don't have just one or two passwords to remember, they have many dozen passwords—at the moment, I personally have well over 100—with importance ranging from online financial accounts down to stores, for-pay news sites, social networking sites, and assorted random places that simply want you to register. I cannot possibly remember that many different passwords, let alone that many strong ones. Besides, each site has different rules for what a password should be like. Some sites insist on punctuation; others ban it. Some want long passwords; others have length limits. Some insist on mixed case; others don't check that, but are case sensitive; still others are case insensitive. The most restrictive set of rules I've seen comes from a US Customs and Border Protection site used by the public.

This is the actual text, copied and pasted from their web site:

- Minimum Length : 8

- Maximum Length : 12

- Maximum Repeated Characters : 2

- Minimum Alphabetic Characters Required : 1

- Minimum Numeric Characters Required : 1

- Starts with a Numeric Character

- No User Name

- No past passwords

- At least one character must be ˜ ! @ # $ % ˆ & ∗ ( ) −_+ ! += { } [ ] \ | ; : / ? . , < > " ′ ' !

Good luck remembering your password for it, especially since you'll use that account about once a year.

Suppose you do forget your password. What then? *Every* real-world system has to have some provision for password recovery or reset. This is very much a trade-off between cost and security; except for high-value sites (banks, employers, etc.), there are rarely secure solutions. This issue is discussed in more detail in Section 7.5.

Another important issue is the change in threat model. When Morris and Thompson wrote their paper, the primary danger was theft of the password file, followed by an offline guessing attack. Remember that in those days, /etc/passwd was world readable; anyone with unprivileged access to the machine could grab a copy. They certainly realized that the host or its login command could be subverted, in which case it was game over, but that wasn't the threat model their solution was intended to deal with. Unfortunately, today that is one of the most serious problems. The attackers aren't stupid; phishing attacks, compromising servers, and compromising client hosts are the easiest ways to grab passwords. But if the attacker has accomplished any of these, a strong password is no defense at all; a keystroke logger doesn't care about the number of special characters you've chosen. Is password strength obsolete [D. Florêncio, Herley, and Coskun 2007]?

Well, not necessarily. As is frequently the case, the correct answer is "it depends." In this case, it depends on the kinds of attacks you're trying to defend against and on your total system design:

1. What types of guessing attacks are you trying to guard against, online (where the attacker actually tries to log in) or offline, based on a stolen hashed password file?

2. Are the passwords in question employee passwords or user passwords? If the latter, are some users especially likely to be targeted? For example, do you have (or expect to have) celebrity users? There are unscrupulous tabloid papers and web sites that will pay handsomely for dirt about the famous; that in turn can attract more focused attacks.

3. More generally, are you concerned with opportunistic or targeted attacks?

4. What do you assume the enemy can do? Subvert client machines? Subvert your

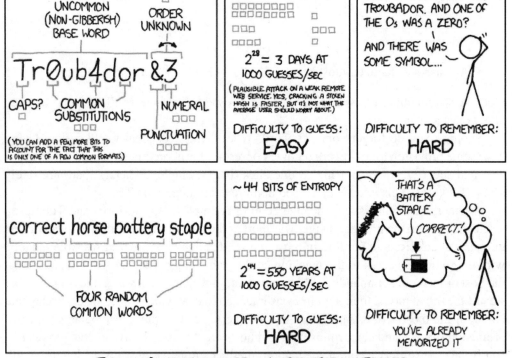

Figure 7.1: Picking a good password.

servers? Steal your password file? Launch phishing attacks? Bribe employees? Eavesdrop on communications?

I'll discuss the questions in order, though (of course) the answers interact.

Offline attacks against hashed passwords is the threat model against which strong passwords were suggested as a defense. If that's the risk, password strength is still relevant.

Online guessing is another matter. While password strength may be an issue, the attacker's problem is the effective guessing rate: How many tries per second does the system allow? Is there an upper bound, after which the account is locked for some period of time?

It's relatively straightforward to design a system to respond relatively slowly; indeed, Morris and Thompson designed their scheme to be inherently slow, to frustrate offline guessers as well. An obvious and frequently implemented variant is to slow things down more for each incorrect guess. That gets tricky, though. Is the slowdown per session? The attacker can counter by creating many sessions, perhaps even simultaneously. The defender's obvious counter is to tie the guess rate to a login name, but that creates interesting synchronization and locking issues, especially on large-scale distributed systems. If there's too much contention for a per-user lock, simply trying incorrect guesses can constitute a denial-of-service attack against the legitimate user.

Taken to the limit, the notion of slowing down the response to an incorrect login attempt is to lock the account for some substantial period of time, on the order of hours. Again, an attacker can abuse this to lock out legitimate users. Some financial sites require human intervention to unlock accounts, but you can afford that only if you make a considerable profit for each user. By contrast, companies that make very little per user, such as social networking sites, can't afford people for that sort of event; they have to rely on automated processes. The question you have to ask yourself here is pretty obvious: What is the expected rate of loss from password-guessing attacks, compared with the cost of reset and the loss of annoyed legitimate users? That is, you're balancing the cost of an account breach against the cost of a forgotten password or locked-out account. Picking strong passwords cuts the cost of the former while increasing the cost of the latter. (If you're planning to turn this question into a spreadsheet, remember to include generous error bars; there are considerable uncertainties in many of the input parameters. "Never let your precision exceed your accuracy.")

Handling online password-guessing attacks is hard enough when the passwords belong to your customers. The question may be completely different when dealing with employee passwords (item 2). The risk of lockout can be quite serious if the locked-out accounts belong to your system administrators or security response team, especially if

What Makes a Password Strong?

Suppose you do want to pick a strong password. Will compliance with, say, the rules mentioned on page 109 do it? Perhaps surprisingly, the answer is "not necessarily."

The essence of the problem is how to increase the attacker's work, ideally to the point that it is statistically extremely improbable for any guess to be right. Let's look at that list.

The first character must be numeric, so there are only ten choices. Only one digit is required; since switching between letters and numbers is inconvenient, most people will use a consecutive string of digits followed by a consecutive string of letters. A punctuation character is needed, but the easy, natural choice is to put a period at the end. A common choice, then, will be one or more digits, one or more letters, and a period, where the total number of digits and letters will be seven. There are 10 digits and 26 letters, and six choices for how many digits versus letters. The total number of combinations, then, is

$$\sum_{i=1}^{6} 10^i \cdot 26^{7-i}$$

which comes to 5,003,631,360. (It's actually a bit less than that because of the rule about repeated characters.) Using the assumptions from page 108—1,000 computers each doing 150,000 guesses per second—it will take about 30 seconds to try them all. Not everyone following those rules will have a guessable password, but the rules themselves don't guarantee it.

[D. Florêncio and Herley 2010] argue persuasively that password strength policy is determined more by whether or not users have a choice about using the site, rather than by security needs. Thus, monopoly providers—employers, government agencies, and so on—impose strong restrictions because they can. Shopping and advertising sites, which fear losing users—that is, opportunities for profit—impose weaker requirements: "We conclude that the sites with the most restrictive password policies do not have greater security concerns, they are simply better insulated from the consequences of poor usability."

The essence of a good password is given in Figure 7.1: unpredictability. The specific scheme it suggests—four random, common words—is decent; the trouble, though, is that most people won't pick random words nor will they put them in random order. (Besides, four words is probably too short, given today's attackers.) I suspect that it works well only if the system assigns passwords.

Are there other rules? Sure; the trick is simple: create a large-enough search space. But it can't be any large search space; it's got to be one from which people will actually choose (more or less) uniformly. Even picking eight random lowercase letters gives about 209 billion choices, more than 40 times as many as that convoluted set of rules might yield, but as we've seen that's insufficient; 209 billion isn't that large a number these days. The problem is that people's choices from the space prescribed by those rules are decidedly nonuniform. Password choice is a *people* problem.

the denial of service is just one part of a larger, more serious attack [Grampp and Morris 1984]. In other words, detecting guessing attacks is easy; deciding how to respond is hard.

Employee passwords can be a simpler problem. The easiest solution is to avoid using passwords entirely, especially for external access. You can afford other forms of authentication, and you can invest in training. You can apply different policies if the login attempts are coming from the employee's usual haunts (perhaps a given IP address or LAN) rather than external logins. You can try to ensure that employees use different passwords for different services; in particular, if your employees are also users of your publicly available services, you want them to use different passwords. This is hard, though; people are aggressively uncooperative when dealing with policies that seem arbitrary. If external passwords like "plugh" and "xyzzy" are acceptable but your system insists on special characters in internal passwords, you'll undoubtedly find that the same people who picked "plugh" and "xyzzy" will use "plugh." and "xyzzy!" internally.

The issue of targeted versus opportunistic attacks (item 3) interacts strongly with item 2. If your organization is being targeted, cracking a single employee account can lead to profound damage. This may even be true for external service passwords, if they have privileged access to the service. Note carefully that often, a disgruntled employee or ex-employee is the most likely person to launch such an attack—and such a person might know things that an outsider doesn't know, such as the names of spouses or pets.

For user accounts, there is *always* some risk of targeted attacks. Some users will have to contend with a disgruntled spouse, a suspicious partner, a mischievous friend, or the like.

The last issue (item 4) is the easiest to understand: if the attacker can eavesdrop on communications or can subvert machines at either end, password strength is irrelevant. If the attacker can steal the password file, the issue is whether you store passwords in the clear or hashed. (Stealing a password file may not involve subverting a machine. How good is the physical security of your off-site backup media? You do store copies off-site, right? No? You have another serious problem.) If you store them in the clear, the attacker has won. (Do you store them in the clear? See Section 7.3 and Section 7.5.) A skilled attacker will almost certainly be able to compromise some client machines, at the very least, and will quite possibly be able to compromise the server. An Andromedan will be able to compromise the server and/or steal the password file.

Several conclusions can be drawn from all this. First, employee passwords, if used, should be very strong. However, you're better off using better authentication for employees. Second, while rate-limiting guesses is a good idea, you can't carry that too far except for high-value systems. Third, given the rate of compromise of random client systems, the stress on strong passwords is misguided for many, many systems; the cost of password loss (including the risks of secondary authentication; see below) is higher.

A closely related issue is enforced password changes, especially at frequent intervals. Conventional wisdom says that this is a good idea; often, though, it is counterproductive. Again, a thorough analysis of the threat model is necessary.

The original rationale for frequent password changes came from the US Department of Defense in 1985 [DoD 1985b]. They gave an equation to calculate the proper frequency. Unfortunately—and even apart from the gross uncertainties in some of the input values—the analysis ignores modern threats like keystroke loggers. (It was rather hard to plant a keystroke logger on a 1985-vintage terminal. Many were electromechanical, hardcopy devices that didn't even have CPUs; the few that did were mostly programmed in ROM and were largely immune to attack. Only a very few were "smart.") More seriously, it ignores user behavior.

Gene Spafford did a thorough analysis of the threats some years ago [Spafford 2006].

> ... [P]eriodic password changing really only reduces the threats posed by guessing, and by weak cracking attempts. If any of the other attack methods succeed, the password needs to be changed immediately to be protected—a periodic change is likely to be too late to effectively protect the target system. Furthermore, the other attacks are not really blunted by periodic password changes. Guessing can be countered by enforcing good password selection, but this then increases the likelihood of loss by users forgetting the passwords. The only remaining threat is that periodic changes can negate cracking attempts, on average. However, that assumes that the passwords choices [*sic*] are appropriately random, the algorithms used to obfuscate them (e.g., encryption) are appropriately strong, and that the attackers do not have adequate computing/algorithmic resources to break the passwords during the period of use. This is not a sound assumption given the availability of large-scale bot nets [*sic*], vector computers, grid computing, and so on—at least over any reasonable period of time.

User response to password change requests makes matters even worse. Grampp and Morris observed many years ago [Grampp and Morris 1984] that people tended to use patterns when rotating passwords: a suffix of "03" for March, "04" for April, and so forth. A large-scale study by Zhang, Monrose, and Reiter [Zhang, Monrose, and Reiter 2010] confirmed this: they developed an algorithm that could guess about 41% of new passwords from seeing the old ones. Their scheme often succeeded even with online guesses; 17% of passwords could be found in five or fewer tries using just one of their algorithms. Again, their conclusion is unambiguous: "We believe our study calls into question the continued use of expiration and, in the longer term, provides one more piece of evidence to facilitate a move away from passwords altogether."

7.3   Storing Passwords: Users

Passwords present a conundrum. They should be (at the least) reasonably strong. People have far too many passwords; it simply isn't possible to remember that many random-looking strings—but the conventional wisdom is that writing down passwords is dangerous. The alternative, used by just about everyone, is to reuse the same password or one of a small set of passwords, for multiple purposes; this means that a single compromise can expose all of your resources. What's to be done, if you have to use passwords but you can't memorize them and you can't write them down and you can't reuse them?

As always, let's go back to our threat model. It turns out that writing down passwords (or some approximation thereof) isn't always a bad idea. If you're worried about joy hackers, in fact, it's probably a good idea; they're not likely to abandon their pizza box lair to steal your wallet. Sure, MI-31 might do something like that—indeed, the FBI has done similar things when pursuing foreign spies [Williams 2010]—but unless you're being targeted for attack by the Andromedans, there are easier ways for a skilled attacker to collect passwords, such as keystroke loggers. The only caveat is that passwords should not be stored "near" the resource being protected since that might expose them to the same attack.

There's a simple analogy here. People are regularly warned not to write down the PINs for their ATM cards. This is correct, as far as it goes, since you don't want someone who has stolen your wallet or purse to be able to loot your bank account. However, an *obfuscated* PIN—say, the last four digits of what appears to be a phone number in your address book—is probably OK, as long as it's not obvious what you've done. The Andromedans might trace every contact number you're carrying; the average pickpocket won't, and the cleverer thieves will resort to things like mag stripe skimmers and hidden cameras [Kormanik 2011].

In a computer context, "near" is a trickier concept. A strong sense of "not near" might be "on a different device"; thus, you could store your computer's passwords on your phone. That may be an ideal, but good luck seeing the tiny special characters (your passwords are strong ones, right?) and copying them to your browser. Besides, if you sync your phone to your computer, the distance is less than you thought, and if you have a smart phone you'll probably want the passwords usable on it, too, so you don't really have as much separation as you thought you did.

A more usable notion of distance is "not in the same application." That is, store your web passwords in some program other than your browser; if your browser is compromised (and for most users, browsers are their most vulnerable applications), the rest of your password stash is safe. You still have the ability to copy and paste passwords from the dedicated application. That won't protect you if your computer's OS is compromised, but neither will anything else. Of course, there are trade-offs here, too—if you copy and paste a password, it's going to be on the clipboard, where other malware (or simple user carelessness) can paste it to the wrong place. A browser-based password manager has another advantage: it can protect you against phishing attacks. If you never type your web site passwords, but instead rely on the manager, you're safe: it won't send a password to your bank unless *it* believes you're talking to the bank, and not to some site that merely looks like it. (A really good design would look at the certificate name, rather than just the URL, but that helps only if the login prompt is itself on an HTTPS-protected page. Too many are not.)

There are two more things to take into account: the confidentiality and availability of your password stash. Availability seems obvious; it's not, because different people have different usage patterns.

The Security of Password Managers

There are a number of password managers available. How safe are they? I'm going to use a few real-world examples, not as reviews or recommendations of products— those would be silly to put in a book, in a field as fast moving as this—but to illustrate security design trade-offs. I'm ignoring usability, except for how it affects security; I'm also paying no attention to price or platforms supported. All of these are, of course, very important considerations when actually buying something.

Encryption Most password managers encrypt the passwords, though the one built in to Firefox makes the existence of a master password—the encryption key—optional. Some managers encrypt the URLs, too; others do not, which poses privacy risks for people who visit sketchy web sites.

Synchronization Synchronization between gadgets is crucial for people who use more than one device, especially if the stored passwords are strong, that is, random. LastPass uses its own cloud server; if it is penetrated, an attacker could mount a guessing attack on the encrypted password store. 1Password can use Dropbox or iCloud for synchronization, including on their mobile apps (and the same caveats about the potential vulnerability of a cloud storage service apply). It can also sync over a LAN; is the protocol secure?

(Continued)

Given that password repositories are, after all, just files or collections of files, most password managers will work with more or less any synchronization system, up to and including flash drives and sneakernet.

Some products (e.g., LastPass) provide web access to your password collection, specifically to permit access from public machines. While undoubtedly convenient, encouraging use of sensitive passwords—including your master encryption password—from potentially insecure machines is dangerous.

Web authentication Many password managers (1Password, LastPass, Robo-Form, and more) will automatically fill in login forms in a browser window. Although a tremendous convenience, from a security perspective it's both good and bad: bad, because it fails the "nearness" test (page 115); good, because it helps prevent phishing attacks. Pass Safe instead makes it very easy to copy a password to the clipboard for easy pasting into a web form; significantly, it clears the clipboard when you close the application, thus preventing you from accidentally pasting the password elsewhere.

External hardware IronKey and CHIPDRIVE use external USB devices. That's great, since your passwords can't be stolen when the device isn't inserted, but human nature suggests that most people will leave their devices plugged in most of the time.

Finally, password managers are not easy to get right [Z. Li et al. 2014]. See Section 11.7 for some discussion on how to evaluate software packages.

If you use only one computer—more precisely, if you use a disjoint set of computers for different sets of accounts—this isn't a big concern; you simply store a (suitably protected) password stash on that computer. If you use two or more computers, though, you need something available to each of them. There are two basic answers: a portable device, such as a USB flash drive, or some form of cloud storage. Portable devices seem more secure, but if you encrypt the files that's not really an issue. They're also more subject to loss or simply being left in the wrong place. (Have you ever wanted to `grep` your house for your keys? You know—the keys on the key ring that have your flash drive attached? The ones your teenager borrowed, along with your car?) For that matter, it's too easy to leave a flash drive plugged in for too long.

There's another obvious form of portable storage: a piece of paper. Apart from failing the availability test (What's your backup for a piece of paper? How well does that piece of paper stand up to repeated folding?) it fails the confidentiality test, in that you probably have to write down the site name next to the username and password. This means that anyone who steals that paper will have (apart from the rest of your wallet's contents) your credentials for, say, the Bank of Zork.[1] You may be able to obscure that one by listing the site as "J. Pierpont Flathead" or by writing "Hippolyta" for Amazon.com, but that's not a solution that is generically useful.

Confidentiality is usually achieved by encrypting the stored passwords; this is generally a good idea, *if* it is done correctly. Some cloud storage providers do offer encryption; their solutions are acceptable if and only if the decryption is done on your machine and they never see a decryption key. (Read the service description *very* carefully; some providers encrypt files only for transmission, or encrypt the stored files with a key that they themselves possess.) If your service provider doesn't do the right thing (or if you don't trust them or can't decrypt their service description), use an encrypted file or disk image. All modern operating systems provide such a facility, either in the base system or as an easy add-on.

A dedicated password storage application may be better, since it will automatically encrypt the storage and will generally do the right thing about caching recently used passwords. There are many from which to choose; make sure that the one you select will let you store the encrypted passwords in the proper spot for use with multiple devices (a cloud drive, a flash disk, etc.). Also pay attention to cross-platform compatibility, including with devices like phones and tablets. Think hard about the frequency and circumstances under which you reenter your master password; there's a trade-off here between ease of use and protection of the data.

The password with which you encrypt the stored passwords is extremely sensitive. If someone gains access to the encrypted store (by stealing your flash drive, hacking the cloud provider, seizing your computer via a search warrant, or what have you), this password is all that stands between the attacker and all of your accounts. It is worth considering whether you want to have different encryption passwords for sites of different sensitivity, but that's easier said than done. What's important is the probability of malware on your machine being able to get at the plaintext of the passwords. You may think that an online banking password deserves very strong protection (and it does), but if the computer in question is part of the accounts payable office of a medium-sized business, you'll need to get at that password more or less continuously anyway, so the encryption matters rather less than one might think. For that scenario, you're better off using a dedicated computer, one used for *no* other functions. (Brian Krebs has long advocated using a "Live" CD for banking, especially for small businesses [Krebs 2009]. It's not that Linux is inherently

---

1. "Bank of Zork," http://www.thezorklibrary.com/history/bank_of_zork.html.

more secure—I don't think that it is—but it's less targeted, and using a Live CD means that infections won't be persistent; rebooting restores you to a clean state. And if you don't have a CD drive on your computer? Get a USB flash disk with a physical read-only switch. They're a bit hard to find, but they do exist.)

There is one more variant that should be considered. There are password managers that generate per-site passwords from the domain name and a user-specified master password (see, for example, [Halderman, Waters, and Felten 2005; Ross et al. 2005], but there are many others). The good thing is the inherent protection that design provides against both phishing and password reuse. The bad thing is that any site that legitimately receives its own password can launch a guessing attack on the master password; if found, it lets them generate *all* per-site passwords for that user. There's another problem: you can't change just one password. If a site makes you change your password (perhaps because they've been compromised), you can only do this by changing your master password, which in turn means that you have to change *all* of your passwords.

7.4   Password Compromise

Someday, your password or passwords or password file may be compromised. Now what?

If you're an individual, you need to do three things. First, change your password on the affected site. Second, change your password everywhere else you used that same one. That should be easy, since of course you don't reuse your own passwords, but you probably know people who do. Pass this advice on to them.... Finally, and most seriously, assess what information or resources are associated with that password. A financial account? Check your statements *very* carefully, preferably on paper; there's malware in the wild that can tamper with online statements [Zetter 2009a]. Physical address information? Data that can be used for identity theft? Access to your own computers or files? In case of mass compromise, by skilled attackers who aren't targeting you, you're probably safe— they likely have information on far more people than they can profitably steal from—but if it's part of a targeted attack, you're in trouble.

If you run a large, public-facing site, you have a very different problem. The hardest part is figuring out exactly what information was compromised; that in turn is heavily dependent on the details of your system architecture. What machine was the target of the initial compromise? (Note that this may or may not be the same as the machine whose compromise you detected.) From there, what can an attacker do that cannot easily be done from the outside? Is there data that can be retrieved? If you have an ordinary database system that is exposed to random queries from the trusted—but not *trustworthy*—web server, everything in that database has to be considered exposed. You then have an ethical—and in many cases, legal—obligation to notify all affected users. Depending on the precise circumstances and applicable laws, you may also need to notify assorted credit card companies, government regulators, and so on.

How serious a problem this is depends heavily on your system architecture and database design. If you've stored *personally identifiable information (PII)*, you have considerably more liability under the laws of the European Union, Canada, and other civilized jurisdictions, but perhaps not under US law. Planning ahead can save you a great deal of grief. It is worth reading the report of the Office of the Privacy Commissioner of Canada [Privacy Commissioner 2007] on the TJX hack; briefly, if they had stored the hash of driver's license numbers rather than the numbers themselves, they'd have been able to achieve their business goals while neither exposing the information to compromise nor violating Canadian privacy law. (System design is discussed in more detail in Chapter 11; intrusion response is in Chapter 16.)

Notifying users is a separate problem. Many public sites have very little in the way of contact information for their users; often, it's at most an email address, and those tend to suffer from bitrot. You can and should use those email addresses for breach notification, but you shouldn't be surprised if many of your messages bounce or get caught by spam filters. Depending on the severity of the problem and what information you have, you may need to resort to paper mail; again, you will likely see a nontrivial number of undeliverable letters. There may also be legal constraints: some jurisdictions, such as New York state, require paper mail notification for PII breaches unless the user has consented in advance to email notification.

In many situations, the best approach is to modify what happens after login for those users: they're diverted to a special sequence that tells them what happened and goes through secondary authentication procedures to authorize a password change sequence. With luck—or good system design—the secondary authentication data is on a separate machine, one that wasn't compromised at the same time as the computer used to hold passwords. How difficult it is to present a different set of screens to the user after login depends heavily on your system design. You may find you need this capability anyway to handle multiple languages, changes in terms of service, and so forth. Again, planning ahead will be a big help.

If the compromise is severe enough, it's possible you'll have to shut down your online presence. This has happened to some very big companies, such as Sony [Schreier 2011]; needless to say, pulling the plug can result in a serious hit to your bottom line.

You have more difficult decisions to make if passwords are compromised on an enterprise system. On one hand, those passwords are considerably more valuable than are those to, say, a newspaper's web site. On the other hand, if you lock people out of their work accounts you lose their productivity. Sometimes, that's the right trade-off. I've seen situations where employees were handed their new passwords when they walked into the building the next morning. That, however, works poorly if many people telecommute or are traveling. The good thing here is that you have much more in the way of secondary authentication and contact information. As before, of course, advance planning—including consultations with your corporate counsel—is a good idea.

7.5   Forgotten Passwords

It's a fact of life: users (including employees) *will* forget their passwords. What do you do about it? Traditionally, there are two approaches: send the password to them or create a new password and send that to them. Sometimes, a supplementary authentication procedure is employed for extra protection.

Users tend to like receiving their original password. After all, it's probably one they use elsewhere, possibly trivially modified to accommodate your strength rules; seeing it will remind them what they did: "Oh, yeah, I replaced the 'o' in 'password' with a '0.' "

The fact that it's popular doesn't make it a good idea. The problem isn't so much that you've emailed it to them (that may or may not be safe, as I discuss below) as it is that you can only do this if you store cleartext passwords. If your login program can read that list, so can many other programs, including attackers' malware and your own corrupt employees. That in itself can be bad enough; what makes it really bad is that people reuse passwords. The same magic string that lets people into their favorite porn sites will quite likely be used to let them into their bank's or their employer's systems.

Generating a new password is a much better idea. True, people will probably change it to something they find more memorable, but they can do that anyway. Many sites that send out passwords insist on this, for no good reason. If strong random numbers [Eastlake, Schiller, and Crocker 2005] are used to generate the password, why not let it persist? What is the incremental risk? There seems to be some notion that "the system knows your password, and that's bad." The system will know your password as soon as you type it in; what's bad is if the system stores it. The other issue is where the user stores the notification of the new password; if that is likely to be insecure relative to the value of the resource being protected, a mandatory change may be in order.

To be sure, generating passwords isn't trivial. At a minimum, you need a good supply of random numbers [Eastlake, Schiller, and Crocker 2005]. There's a standard published algorithm for generating pronounceable passwords (such as [NIST 1993]), but that algorithm has problems [Ganesan and Davies 1994]. More seriously, the notion of generating pronounceable passwords is based on a false premise: not just that such a password is easier to remember, but that someone is going to want to remember it. As I've already mentioned, in the real world most people have far too many passwords and they can't even dream of remembering most of them. Typability—on whatever platforms are of interest, including smart phones—is far more important.

As noted, some sites use supplementary authentication mechanisms to validate lost password requests. In principle, this is a good idea; in practice, it's often insecure or unworkable. The challenge is fearsome and difficult: What sorts of questions can you ask a user that that person will *always* remember, but that cannot easily be discovered by an attacker? Your childhood pet? It might be on your Facebook page. Where you went to school? You may be listed on the school's page. That old standby, mother's maiden name? It's a venerable choice, having been used at least as early as 1882 [Bellovin 2011b; F. Miller 1882], but it doesn't work very well. Apart from the complexities of modern society compared with 1882's conventions [Newman 1989] or the fact that many women do not change their names when they marry, marriage records are public documents; an attacker can easily look up the data. You might think that this would happen only in a serious, targeted attack, perhaps by MI-31, but in fact the attack has been automated [Griffith and Jakobsson 2005] since many of these records have been put online.

Secondary authentication is more challenging for public figures, since there is frequently a lot of information available about such people. The Sarah Palin email account incident is a good case in point [Zetter 2008]; all the attacker needed to know was Palin's birthday, zip code, and the answer to a simple security question: where did she meet her spouse? It might be challenging to learn that about a random person, but for someone who is the subject of as much media attention as she was, it's pretty easy.

This illustrates another issue: those very close to a person know the answers to these questions. Divorce cases are particularly thorny, since soon-to-be-ex-spouses are often on their worst behavior. Snooping on email has happened in such circumstances [Springer 2010]; technical measures are likely to be inadequate. It is interesting to speculate what will happen in the future with online banking passwords.

The challenge is to ensure that the password, old or new, reaches the right individual and only the right individual. In an employment situation, the employee's supervisor might be the best person to handle it, since he or she presumably knows the employee. That doesn't work as well with today's distributed companies, where solitary employees can be in any part of the globe. Similarly, in university environments students are sometimes told to show up with their ID card to get their passwords reset; again, this is problematic with the rise of distance learning.

To address this, some have suggested "social authentication"—letting your friends authenticate you. In one scheme, designed to deal with the loss of a token, another legitimate (but preconfigured) user can use his or her own credentials to obtain a temporary authentication code for a colleague [Brainard et al. 2006]. This is combined with the user's PIN for a single login session. The big risk here is that lots of people can now grant access; if they're careless about security or dishonest, you have a problem. A related notion relies on users' abilities to recognize their friends; unfortunately, that seems to be very susceptible to targeted attacks [H. Kim, Tang, and R. Anderson 2012].

The most common way to hand out reset passwords is by email. This can be perfectly appropriate; some resources are of little enough value that the risks of email being intercepted are acceptably low. For more valuable passwords, some form of out-of-band authentication is a better idea. Banks will generally send paper mail with new credentials; SMS messages are another good way, though the malware artists have started building phone apps that do nasty things when phones are used for authentication [Crossman 2013; Pauli 2014].

If you use email, the message will be in the user's inbox. How well protected is that, both immediately and over the long term for people who don't delete their email? For passwords of modest value, you're probably safe; for something like an employee password being sent to a free mail account, it's rather more dicey. (This is one of the rare instances where people have to use outside servers for work-related matters: more or less by definition, if they've forgotten their employee password they can't get at their internal email.) There are two good choices here: require an immediate password change, or send a URL for a password reset page. A lot depends on your overall system design—how hard is it to have special case handling of successful logins, versus how much access does your (externally facing) web server have to the password database. If you do send a URL, it should have two crucial properties: it should be usable only once, and it should only be usable for a limited amount of time.

Ultimately, the risk is that many secondary authentication systems are weaker than the primary one, especially against certain threats. The more you're the subject of a targeted attack, the more risk you're facing. A random 419 scammer halfway around the world won't steal an envelope from your mailbox; an Andromedan agent might.

7.6 Biometrics

"We need something that will identify any representative of Civilization, positively and unmistakably, wherever he may be. It must be impossible of duplication, or even of imitation, to which end it must kill any unauthorized entity who attempts imposture."

Dr. Nels Bergenholm in *First Lensman*
—E. E. "Doc" Smith

There's a saying in the security business: if you think that biometrics are the answer, you're asking the wrong question. That's exaggerated, of course, but so are many of the claims made for biometrics. More than any other form of authentication, biometrics must be looked at from a systems perspective.

Although many biometrics have been proposed over the years, including speech, typing rhythms, and hand geometry, three are of major importance: fingerprints (100+ years of criminology have given us reasonable assurance of their uniqueness; besides, scanners have become very cheap); iris scans, widely regarded as the most secure [Daugman 2006]; and facial recognition, due to the ubiquity of cameras and the potential in physical security situations for walk-through authentication. Acceptors generally don't store the actual image of any of these; rather, they store a *template*—more or less the equivalent of a hashed password—against which they match a submitted biometric. (As with many aspects of biometric, reality is often more complex. Some schemes, e.g., [Ballard, Kamara, and Reiter 2008] and [Pauli 2015], do store images; in others, the templates are effectively reversible.)

A biometric authentication system consists of a number of components: a human (or parts thereof), a sensor, a transmission mechanism, a biometric template database, and an algorithm are the minimum. An attack can target any of these, which means that they must all be protected.

Let's start with the human. The premise of biometric authentication is that it always Does the Right Thing. It can't be forged, it can't be forgotten, and it will always work. None of these are true. Researchers have successfully spoofed fingerprint readers with gelatin casts made from molds created from latent fingerprints [Matsumoto et al. 2002]. Facial recognition has been spoofed by photographs [Boehret 2011]. Thieves have chopped off people's fingers to fool cars' fingerprint readers [J. Kent 2005] and compromised biometric scanners [Whittaker 2015]. A non-trivial percentage of the population has fingerprints that cannot be read by common scanners [S. T. Kent and Millett 2003, p. 123]. And there's the obvious: someone who injures or loses a body part may not be able to use systems enrolled in before the incident.

Sensors are sometimes designed to compensate for some of the spoofing attacks. Many contain "liveness detectors": pulse detectors, thermal devices, and so on, that try to verify that the body part being monitored really is a live body part attached to a real, living person. Determined adversaries have been able to work around many of these defenses. For example, [Matsumoto et al. 2002] notes that capacitive detectors were intended to resist attacks that had been launched successfully against optical scanners, but their techniques worked against both kinds of sensors.

Suppose your laptop has an iris scanner. Can you use that to log in to some remote web site? Recall that the remote web site doesn't see a finger or a fingerprint; rather, it sees a stream of bits. An enemy who can eavesdrop on the transmission line can easily replay the bit stream, thus spoofing the "absolutely secure" biometric authenticator. At a minimum, the transmission link needs to be encrypted; depending on the operational environment, the sensor and encryptor may need to be inside a tamper-resistant enclosure.

The most misunderstood part of biometric authentication systems is the actual algorithm used to do the match. Processing, say, a retinal image is not the same as checking a password. The latter will always yield a definite answer of "right" or "wrong." By contrast, the former is a probabilistic process; sometimes, the correct body part will be rejected, while at other times someone else's will be accepted. Worse yet, there is a trade-off between the *true accept rate (TAR)* and the *false accept rate (FAR)*: the more you tune a system to reject impostors, the more likely it is that it will reject the real user. A 2004 report from NIST [Wilson et al. 2004] makes this clear. If the best available fingerprint scanner was tuned for a 1% FAR when trying to pick out an individual from a large collection, the TAR was 99.9%. But cutting the FAR to .01% cut the TAR to 99.4%. (Facial recognition was much worse; for the same FAR rates, the TAR was 90.3% and 71.5%.)

While the technology has improved since then,[2] the trade-off issue remains. There are several implications for systems design. The first is what the consequences are of a true accept failure (sometimes known as the *insult rate*). That is, if a legitimate user is rejected by the system, what happens? Can that person try again, perhaps repeatedly? As discussed earlier, locking someone out for too many password failures is often a good idea; do we do the same with biometrics? Do we resort to secondary authentication, with all of its costs and risks? There is no one answer to this question; a lot depends on your application and system design.

The FAR raises its own issues. One can be understood by simple mathematics: for any given FAR rate, with enough different biometric templates, the probability of a false match becomes quite acceptable. Suppose that our system is tuned for a FAR of .01%. If there are n entries in our database of acceptable biometrics (i.e., n faces or iris scans from $n/2$ users or full fingerprints from $n/10$ users), the odds of a successful attack are $.9999^n$. At $n = 6,932$, the odds tip in the attacker's favor. The countermeasure is obvious: require an assertion of identity before the scan, and match the input biometric against a single user's templates, rather than against your entire database. (The fingerprint scanners built in to many laptops generally don't do this, because n isn't high enough to matter. Undoubtedly, though, they're tuned for a relatively high FAR, in order to keep the TAR acceptable.)

The cost of a trial to the attacker also interacts with the FAR. If the cost is high enough—say, what will happen if Pat Terrorist tries to cross a border with Chris Clean-record's biometrically enabled passport—the attackers can't easily launch an impersonation attack. Conversely, if trials are cheap—a self-service visa kiosk?—the attack is feasible if there is a large enough supply of cooperative people with passports and clean records.

The last element of our abstract biometric authentication system is the template database. Given a template, can an attacker easily construct a fake biometric that matches it? If so, the legitimate users have a very serious problem if the database is ever compromised: most people have a very limited supply of fingerprints and irises to use, and even fewer faces. It's *much* easier to change your password than to change your eyeball. Templates are supposed to be irreversible, much like the hash of a password, but some researchers have managed to attack them successfully [Galbally et al. 2013]. Beyond that, possession of the database allows for low-cost trials to exploit the FAR. The database compromise issue, which is a conceptual one rather than an artifact of today's technological failings, may be the ultimate limit on the growth of biometrics.

There are other difficult issues. What resources, precisely, are accessible via by biometric authentication? On a local system—say, a laptop that is unlocked by a fingerprint

---

2. "NIST: Performance of Facial Recognition Software Continues to Improve,"
   http://www.nist.gov/itl/iad/face-060314.cfm.

swipe—part of the answer is access to a local database of cryptographic keys, such as Apple's keychain. When passwords are used to authenticate access to the laptop, that password is converted to a key that is in turn used to decrypt the database. Converting a password to a key is straightforward; there are even standards saying how to do it properly, such as [Kaliski 2000]. Not so with biometrics; by their nature, they're inexact. Here's an experiment to try. Mount your camera on a tripod and take two indoor pictures of the exact same scene. Strip out the metadata (such as timestamps) and see whether the resulting files are identical. If they differ in even a single bit, they can't be used as keys.

The solution is a technology known as *fuzzy extractors* [Dodis, Reyzin, and A. Smith 2007]. Without going into the details, a fuzzy extractor generates a uniformly random string from noisy input; this string is suitable for use as a cryptographic key. Unfortunately, in practice biometrics tend to be too noisy to work well in such situations. It might be possible, but there are very few, if any, such products available today.

There's one more important reason to avoid biometrics: privacy. A biometric identifier is more or less the ultimate in PII; using one unnecessarily not only brings you into the ambit of various privacy laws, it exposes you to serious public relations problems should your database be stolen. Furthermore, because biometrics can't be changed, in some cases the consequences are serious and long-lasting [Volz 2015]:

> Part of the worry, cybersecurity experts say, is that fingerprints are part of an exploding field of biometric data, which the government is increasingly getting in the business of collecting and storing. Fingerprints today are used to run background checks, verify identities at borders, and unlock smart phones, but the technology is expected to boom in the coming decades in both the public and private sectors.
>
> "There's a big concern [with the OPM hack] not because of how much we're using fingerprints currently, but how we're going to expand using the technology in the next 5-10 years," said Robert Lee, cofounder of Dragos Security, which develops cybersecurity software.
>
> . . .
>
> One nightmare scenario envisioned by Ramesh Kesanupalli, an expert in biometrics, is that agents traveling across borders under aliases could be spotted for their true identities when their prints are scanned. Kesanupalli also warned that the fingerprints could end up somewhere on the black market, making biometrics a novel good to be trafficked on the Internet that could be useful to a buyer for decades.

Where does this leave us? The risk of compromise of large template files seems high, given the rate of compromise of conventional password files. That, combined with the fact that a remote server sees only a bit stream, suggests that biometrics cannot and should not be used for general Internet authentication. On the other hand, use of a biometric when the submitter is under observation—a border checkpoint or a bank teller's station are good examples—is rather safer, since the ability of an attacker to spoof the input is considerably reduced. Even here, the insult rate issue has to be considered in the total system design: a biometric match failure does not always indicate enemy action, and hauling people off to the hoosegow because they've had cataract surgery (which will sometimes but not always affect the scan [Roizenblatt et al. 2004]) or have aged since the template was captured [Fenker and Bowyer 2011] does not seem like a good idea. (The privacy concerns apply to governments, too, even in the United States.)

Biometrics are also a reasonable authentication mechanism for local resources, such as an encrypted flash drive, an authentication token, or a phone. In such cases, the use of tamper-resistant enclosures is strongly suggested to forestall attempts at bypassing the authentication. There is still some risk from targeted attacks—MI-31 probably has your fingerprints and iris scans from the last time you crossed the border into Andromeda—so good sensors, liveness detectors, etc., are still a good idea. The insult rate problem can be dealt with by replacing the device (you always need to plan for lost authentication tokens; see below) and/or by storing a backup access key in a physically secure location. (Newer Apple iOS devices can be unlocked by a fingerprint. However, a PIN is required for the first unlock after each reboot, since the key used to encrypt sensitive portions of the devices' memory is derived in part from the PIN [Apple 2015]. The fingerprint template itself is stored in a secure part of the CPU.)

7.7   One-Time Passwords

The phrase *one-time password (OTP)* is often misused. It does not refer to a single technology; rather, it refers to any scheme that appears to accept a simple password that is never reused. That is, instead of being some static concept—a conventional password, or even a fingerprint or other biometric—what is sent is a dynamic value, one that depends implicitly or explicitly on time or past history.

Often, the notion of an OTP is conflated with a particular technology, such as RSA's popular SecurID token (Figure 7.2). Not so; there are many other types of OTP.

An OTP scheme has two crucial properties. First, its output must be effectively non-repeating. By "effectively" I mean that the odds of a repetition should be no greater than would occur by chance. Thus, if a single-use password P_i is drawn from the closed interval $[0, n-1]$, the probability that $P_i \in \{P_0, P_1, \ldots, P_{n-1}\}$ should be approximately $1/n$. Second, seeing some set of values should not allow an adversary to predict future values. That is, no matter how many P_x the adversary has seen, the odds of a successful guess at

P_i should remain no better than $1/n$. Note that this property rules out the use of a secret permutation of $[0, n-1]$ as the sequence of OTPs, though we could do it if we relax our condition to say that the probability of a successful guess must merely be less than some suitably small ε and $i \ll n$.

In practice, OTP schemes generally depend on a strong cryptographic function and a secret. Thus, the SecurID tokens display $F(K, T)$ where T is the time. (The scheme is actually rather more complicated than that; for my purposes, this simplification will suffice.) An adversary who could invert F—today, AES is used—could recover K and thus generate responses. There are two obstacles. First, if F is strong (and AES is believed to be) the attacker won't be able to invert it, especially with the limited number of samples available compared with encrypted traffic. Second, for purely pragmatic reasons the output of F is often truncated. Thus, the display of a SecurID is generally capped at six digits, or about 20 bits, leaving 108 bits of the output of the AES encryption unknown. Even if you could find K for one particular value of those bits, you don't know that that value is actually the one that the actual token's calculation produced; there are, after all, $2^{108} - 1$ other possibilities. Did you find the right K for the next T?

Figure 7.2: An RSA SecurID authentication token.

The same analysis holds true for typical challenge/response OTPs. In those, the server sends the client some random value N; the client (who is assumed to have a secure computing device) responds with $F(K, N)$. As before, F is hard to invert and only a truncated form of its output is transmitted.

There are OTP schemes that don't require the client to have anything more sophisticated than a piece of paper. Lamport's scheme [Lamport 1981] uses a noninvertible function F and a secret seed value x; he defines password i to be $F^{k-i}(x)$ where k is the maximum number of passwords that can be derived from x. Thus, if $k = 1,000$, the first user password is $P_0 = F^{1,000}(x)$, the next are $P_2 = F^{999}(x)$, $P_3 = F^{998}(x)$, …. A user going on a trip could simply print out some number of passwords on a sheet of paper, and cross out each one as it is used. As before, the security of the scheme depends on the secrecy of some value (in this case, x rather than a key K) and the non-invertibility of F. There is one salient difference in the usual implementations [Haller 1995]: the output of F cannot be truncated, since a server expecting password i will have stored password $i - 1$—the last password successfully sent—and will verify it by calculating $F(P_i)$ to see whether it matches what it just received. (Clearly, one could define F to be the truncation of some F' that has a longer output; while this saves typing, it is the output of F—the truncated version—that is iterated. Consequently, there is no ambiguity resulting from the attacker's lack of knowledge of many bits of the output.)

One can carry this further: why bother with a public algorithm to generate P_i to print on a piece of paper; why not just give the user a printout of the next several of random passwords generated and stored by the server? Lamport rejected that idea because of the storage costs, but storage is much cheaper today. More seriously, if the server is storing many passwords, an attacker can steal that list, which isn't possible if just the last one used is stored. A second reason—that if the user has local computing capacity, he or she could simply type a password for x—is arguably a disadvantage today, since there may be a keystroke logger collecting x. In addition, if x can be a password, it is possible to run a password guesser on the F^i.

In fact, some banks do send such papers to their users, often with the password sequence protected by a scratch-off overlay. There's a variant that is used: a two-dimensional grid, where the bank will ask for, say, $\langle x_1, y_1 \rangle$ and $\langle x_2, y_2 \rangle$. Fundamentally, this is just a challenge/response scheme, where K is the user's grid and F is "look up two values in the table."

OTP schemes solve a lot of problems, but they all have certain limitations. For one thing, most rely on the user having something: the token, the key, perhaps the seed for Lamport's algorithm if a password isn't used, or some such. From a systems perspective, they're at least as challenging to manage as passwords. If a SecurID or challenge/response token is lost, it has to be replaced; this may involve an overnight express shipment for telecommuters or road warriors. The alternative—some form of manual single-use password set by a help desk—is effectively a reliance on secondary authentication techniques; as we have seen, those are often far weaker than ordinary passwords, let alone one-time passwords. This is the worst of all possible worlds: higher cost *and* less security.

Because physical objects are subject to theft as well as accidental loss, most sites using OTPs supplement them with a PIN. Of course, PINs can be forgotten just as easily as can passwords, thus taking us back to the world and costs of secondary authentication.

Apart from question of secondary authentication, how secure are OTPs? The answer is rather more mixed than appears at first glance.

There are two major benefits from the use of OTP schemes. First and foremost, the problem of password guessing is eliminated. (I'm assuming, of course, that the seed for Lamport's scheme is not a typed password.) Against many forms of targeted attack, this is a very significant advantage indeed. However, as we have seen, this is often a small part of the password problem. A second benefit is that a token can't easily be shared. Or rather, it can be lent, but when it is the authorized user no longer has possession of the token and hence can no longer log in. (Using "soft tokens" on phones is one way to limit this risk. While the phone isn't as tamper resistant as a dedicated hardware token, few people want to be without their toys.)

I'm sure many of you are now thinking, "But what about the one-time use property??!!" This is certainly a strength, but it's not nearly as significant as it once was. For one thing, the risk of over-the-air eavesdropping today is much less than it was even ten years ago. Many forms of cryptography are in widespread use, including VPNs. Anyone who logs in to a remote system without using encryption is vulnerable to many other forms of attack. Even with encryption, though, an attacker who has compromised one end of the connection or the other can steal a credential. True, a password stolen that way can be reused. If the attacker has compromised the server, it doesn't matter much; he or she is already in a position to do anything to any account. And if the client is compromised? Against modestly clever malware, it doesn't matter much.

Suppose you're sitting at your computer, typing one character at a time from your OTP device or paper. The malware is watching and waiting for you to type the next-to-last digit. It then sets up ten new connections to the server, replays the digits you've already typed, and then tries a separate guess at the last digit on each of the connections. One will succeed. For that matter, if your machine is compromised you don't even know that you've set up a single connection; you may be talking to the malware all along. Of course, when the malware collects the entire password, it simply says "connection dropped" or "password incorrect" or some such. Obviously you mistyped the password, right?

There are similar attacks at the server end. Suppose you fall for a phishing attack and enter a single-use password into a fake web site. The attacker can collect it and log in in your stead.

Clearly, the same stunts could be pulled with conventional passwords. OTPs do have an advantage—the stolen session or credentials can be used only once (and for time-based tokens, only for a limited time). But reduced harm is not the same as no harm.

There have also been phishing attacks on banks' paper-based OTP systems. In fact, I've heard of one scheme that told victims that they needed to revalidate their online access by entering the next three numbers in the sequence.

There's more to consider, starting with the server-side infrastructure. What happens if your servers are compromised? With several of the schemes I've just described—time-based authentication, challenge/response, and probably the two paper-based schemes—

the server knows the clients' secrets. Someone who hacked that database could then impersonate those clients indefinitely. Given the number of high-profile password databases that have been hacked, there is no reason to think that the OTP equivalents are immune.

In fact, the entire back-end infrastructure has to be seen as part of the security perimeter. An attacker who can modify account data, perhaps by using the administrative interface to record that a new token with a new (and known) K has been assigned to a given user, can take over that user's account. Don't underestimate this problem—SecurID succeeded so well in the marketplace precisely because they didn't sell just tokens or just cryptographic routines; they sold an entire *system*, of authentication software, servers, administrative code to add and delete users, databases, and so on. That was quite good, both as marketing strategy and because such code is definitely needed, but all of it and the machines it runs on are security sensitive. Can you protect them well enough? Note that any authentication system needs at least some of those components; engineering a secure system requires understanding which components you have and figuring out how to protect them.

Finally, there is the question of where the authentication secrets come from. Who picks K or x? Is that a secure process? If they're supplied by a vendor, does the vendor protect them properly? This is not an idle question; Lockheed was penetrated using data on the SecurID system stolen from RSA [Drew 2011]. Exactly what was stolen has never been disclosed, but one guess is information on the Ks used by Lockheed. The attacker had to have had more data than that—users generally connect via a login name, but the tokens' keys are indexed by serial number—so either a penetration attempt needed the mapping between logins and serial numbers, or the attackers had to try an entire set of serial numbers (and hence keys) for some selected set of users.

7.8 Cryptographic Authentication

Cryptographic authentication is generally considered the strongest type. It can be, though sometimes implementation flaws vitiate the protection. As always, it is vital to look at the entire system, rather than just the 0s and 1s of the algorithm.

While there is no precise definition of *cryptographic authentication*, intuitively I mean a protocol where both parties are using cryptography and cryptographic secrets (i.e., keys) to do the authentication. In particular, it is a scheme in which the user's authentication isn't forwardable to another site, thus preventing *monkey-in-the-middle (MitM)* attacks. Furthermore, the process includes negotiating keying material for session encryption. Often, though not always, such mechanisms provide *bilateral authentication*. If users are to employ keys and cryptography, though, it implies that (a) they have sufficient, secure local computing capacity to do the necessary calculations, and (b) they have secure, long-term storage for keys. Sufficient local computing capacity is easy; *secure* capacity and *secure* key storage are another matter entirely.

Why, though, is cryptographic authentication so strong? Is that actually true? Or is it all perception? Some of the strength comes from the properties outlined above, but some of it may indeed be perception.

The biggest theoretical advantage of cryptographic authentication is that it is, in principle, based on random keys rather than on a weak password. Saying that, though, begs the question of key storage and protection. As I noted earlier, insecurity can't be destroyed, only moved around. If the cryptographic key is derived from a password, or a password is used to protect it, the inherent strength of the scheme isn't necessarily stronger than passwords. Consider, for example, a system that uses cryptographic authentication but uses PKCS #5 [Kaliski 2000] on the user's side to derive a cryptographic key from a password. The server doesn't need the password itself; it does need its copy of the key. But this value is in effect a hashed password, against which a guessing attack can still be launched.

Am I saying, then, that such a system is no stronger than ordinary passwords? Not quite; there's still a difference, but it's a bit more subtle: the user's password is not sent to the server, and hence can't be captured that way. This in turn gives rise to the anti-MitM property: the server does not receive anything that it can forward to another site. Phishing attacks are rendered harmless; no stealable, let alone reusable, credentials are transmitted.

The optional bilateral authentication property is even more useful, since a clever attacker may still try to trick a user into revealing sensitive information even if there's no authentic server on the other end of the connection. If the two parties can use cryptographic mechanisms to negotiate a session key, this key can be used for challenge/response authentication in both directions. We can turn that around. If we have a shared key, the bilateral authentication property can guarantee that there is no MitM; an attacker won't have the necessary long-term key to perform its part of the authentication dance. Do not, however, rely on users to notice failure of bidirectional authentication; make sure your systems will not operate in such cases.

The keying material can, of course, be used to encrypt the entire session. This provides the usual protections; that is particularly important in this context because the encryption protects against someone hijacking an authenticated session after it's fully set up. Even without that, though, cryptographic authentication is indeed very strong—*if* you can store and protect the private key.

There are three principal mechanisms that can be used for private key storage: password derivation, external devices, and locally encrypted storage. None is perfect; all have their disadvantages.

I've already described the issues with deriving a key from a password; per the analysis, though, it's still a better choice than sending the password directly. The most common way this is used, though, is with single-sign-on systems (Section 7.10) such as Kerberos. A word of warning: a keystroke logger is just as effective against this use of a password as against the more common use.

External device storage of keys is the most secure option. However, as discussed in Section 7.9, there are still significant concerns. They're mostly cost and convenience issues, but there is one security concern: if there's malware on your machine, it can use the key, or sit in the middle of an authentication session you intend to initiate and use your key to initiate its own session instead.

The third option is probably the most common. Passwords can be used to encrypt .ssh private keys or private keys associated with certificates, especially with TLS. The problems with the other two schemes are present (I expect that keystroke loggers will be upgraded to steal the encrypted key file as well as the password used to protect it); the bigger issue, in most situations, is availability of the file containing the key. If your users frequently use more than one machine (and for many people, that's the norm, not the exception), the key file—often the same key file—has to be present on all of the machines. This can be addressed by using cloud storage or USB flash drives to hold the key; many see this as ideal, since it makes it possible to use such authentication on public kiosk machines or in Internet cafés. That's actually a disadvantage; such machines are notorious lairs of all sorts of malware. Using cryptographic authentication from an infected machine is just as insecure as any other way of using such a machine.

One final pessimistic note: a cryptographic authentication scheme is, ultimately, a cryptographic protocol; all of the warnings, caveats, and cautions that apply to cryptographic protocols in general apply here, too. *Don't* invent your own.

7.9 Tokens and Mobile Phones

Tokens—something you have—are a popular authentication mechanism for security-sensitive organizations. Often, this is a good idea: Using tokens avoids all of the weaknesses of passwords: their secrets can't be guessed, the authentication sequence is (almost always) not repeated, one can't share a token without losing use of it oneself, and so on. All that said, the risks and limits of tokens must be considered as well. As always, we must look at the problem from a systems perspective.

One obvious issue is the cost: tokens cost money and at first blush are more expensive than passwords. While there is certainly an initial cost, the total expense for authentication is rather more complex to assess. Passwords carry hidden costs, both in the form of complex secondary authentication mechanisms and in the much greater costs of recovering from password-related compromises. There is also the question of whether all relevant applications can adapt to tokens. The biggest incompatibility is the semantic mismatch between applications that instantiate many sessions over time and the single-use property of most token-based systems. The obvious example is anything web based. HTTP is stateless; in general, any new request or even any element on a single page can entail a separate TCP connection and hence separate authentication. That is clearly unacceptable. The usual answer, of course, is to use token-based authentication to create some other, longer-lived authentication scheme, such as a web cookie. This, though, creates a different secret, one that is not stored in the token and hence one that may be more vulnerable to abuse. Cross-site scripting attacks to steal cookies are the classic example.[3]

It is important to realize that the flaw is not in token-based authentication per se; cross-site scripting attacks are based on the properties of web browsers, regardless of how the initial authentication was done. From a systems perspective, though, the site is not getting the security it sought by deploying tokens.

A similar weakness can occur if some malware waits for the token-supplied authentication string to appear. This string is captured by the malware and used for its own login, rather than the user's; the desired site gets some random garbage, which of course produces a failed authentication. No one will particularly notice this, though; it will likely be interpreted as a random failure or a typographical error. (Thought experiment: how often have you had a web interaction fail, only to succeed when you resubmitted the same information? Did your security antennae twitch? Should they have?) Again, the problem is not in the concept of tokens; however, the benefits of tokens are not realized.

Apart from security risks, the question of application compatibility is sometimes a deal breaker. For common tokens and popular applications on mainstream platforms, there may not be a problem; the vendor may have provided a suitable interface. Alternately, the platform may use generic authentication interfaces that any application can use. As noted in Section 7.7, the software support for a token should comprise far more than just the token itself or a simple "Is this authentication valid?" routine.

Earlier, I spoke of the problem of forgotten passwords. Tokens, of course, can be forgotten, lost, or stolen. If authentication must be done by a token and the token is left at home, the user has no way to authenticate, and hence no way to work. What do you do? Lose a day's productivity? Fall back to secondary authentication? Employ some temporary authentication scheme? The answer, of course, depends on how you balance security and cost: a high-security site will pay the price and not use an insecure secondary authentication scheme. At the least, it will require in-person vouching by someone who knows the careless employee. Other sites, of course, will make other choices. An oft-suggested solution to some issues surrounding tokens is the so-called *soft token*: software that em-

---

3. "Cross-site Scripting (XSS)," https://www.owasp.org/index.php/Cross-site_Scripting_(XSS).

ulates a dedicated token running on some computer. A popular choice is a smart phone, since many people are more likely to forget their clothing than their phones (Figure 7.3). There is a serious danger lurking here, though: ordinary computing devices are not at all resistant to reverse engineering; it's relatively easy to build malware that extracts secrets from other applications.

We don't have to posit the creation of phone-based malware that targets authentication systems; examples already exist. One popular one [M. J. Schwartz 2011] targets a different way in which phones are used as tokens: the server sends a random string to the user via an SMS ("text") message. Theoretically, only the user has that phone, and hence is the only one who will see the challenge; consequently, this seems to be a simple way to implement challenge/response authentication via a token. It's simple—but it may not be secure.

It may also pose a privacy issue. Most people have only one mobile phone number, which they may keep for life. This in turn makes it a persistent, unique identifier, bound to one individual. This is exactly the sort of thing that marketers love for matching profiles. If you sign up for a bunch of cloud services that use text messages as part of the login process—at this point, Google, Paypal, Dropbox, Apple's iCloud, and more all support this—you may be opening the privacy door very wide. It may be a good trade-off, since the privacy harm from having these accounts hacked is also very great, but it is a trade-off.

Figure 7.3: Is she reading text messages before getting dressed? Taking a selfie? Not really; the sculpture is Erastus Dow Palmer's *Indian Girl, or the Dawn of Christianity*, and dates to 1856.

Phones, especially smart phones, are popular targets for thieves. Fortunately, the average street thief is unlikely to extract secrets or otherwise exploit the authentication properties of a phone; the same, of course, cannot be said for MI-31. If a phone used for authentication to sensitive data is stolen, is it clear what the motive is [Allen 2012]?

For reasons like this, tokens should *always* be used together with some other form of authentication, such as a password, PIN, or biometric. Great care has to be taken in the design of any such two-factor authentication scheme, especially if the second factor is sent directly to the token rather than to the server: MI-31 can quite likely bypass authentication done by the token itself, unless the token was specifically (and competently) designed to resist just this threat. Soft tokens are especially vulnerable to this threat; absent strong evidence for the security of the underlying platform, their use should be eschewed in high-risk scenarios.

One more point must be made about tokens: you should always have some plan for invalidating lost tokens and switching authentication to new ones. Tokens *will* need replacement, whether because of loss, theft, fire, accident, or simple hardware failure. A corollary is that if any data is accessible solely through a secret resident on the device, you'd better have a backup copy of that secret. Encrypting your files with a key stored only on a user's smart card is a recipe for disaster; keep another copy safe somewhere else.

7.10   Single-Sign-On and Federated Authentication

Single-sign-on (SSO) schemes use a two-phase authentication scheme: the user somehow authenticates to a central server; the fact of this authentication is then communicated to any other systems the user wishes to communicate with. A federated authentication scheme is essentially the same thing, save that the central server is an outside party that can vouch for identities to many other outside sites. There are three primary issues for an internal SSO system: the initial authentication, how the additional authentications are done, and the user interface to the latter. There are additional issues when external parties are involved; those will be discussed later.

The first question is relatively easily disposed of: in theory, any standard authentication system can be used, and the usual strengths and weaknesses apply. There is one very important caveat, though: an SSO is a very tempting target for attackers, especially the more skilled ones, and hence requires more than the usual protection. By extension, since a login to such a server gives a lot of access, stronger forms of user authentication are probably a good idea. At a minimum, the authentication used for an SSO server should be at least as strong as you would want for any given system that will trust that authentication.

There is another issue: the form of SSO authentication used interacts with the later authentications. In particular, these later authentications sometimes rely on some sensitive material passed to the user's computer by the SSO server. This transmission needs to be protected, which implies some sort of cryptography; that in turn favors cryptographic schemes that permit easy setup of an encrypted channel. The alternative, used for web-based SSO schemes, relies on the use of a TLS-protected session to the SSO server.

A web-based authentication system will probably rely on *cookies* [Barth 2011] to maintain the logged-in state. However, cookies can be returned only to the site that set them, so some other mechanism must be used to pass the login information to other web sites. Generally, this is done by out-of-band communication between such web sites and the SSO site.

It helps to consider the one possible (and oversimplified) sequence of operations. Assume that some user Chris first contacts www.ReallyAwesomeSSO.com and logs in. That site sends Chris's browser a cookie. (If Chris is really lucky, that cookie will have appropriate cryptographic protections, but that's another matter.) She then contacts the site she really wants to visit: FeralAmoebae.com. The page from FeralAmoebae.com contains a URL—an IFRAME, an image, some JavaScript, or what have you—pointing to www.ReallyAwesomeSSO.com and containing some per-session unique string. Chris's browser therefore contacts www.ReallyAwesomeSSO.com and sends back the identifying cookie. When www.ReallyAwesomeSSO.com sees it, it uses its out-of-band channel to tell FeralAmoebae.com which user has connected using that unique string. (More accurately, FeralAmoebae.com will ask www.ReallyAwesomeSSO.com what user corresponds to that string.)

The best-known web-based SSO service at the moment is *Facebook Connect*.[4] Its operation (based on the IETF's OAuth 2.0 design [Hardt 2012]) is rather more complex than my outline, partly because it's a real system and not a toy example and partly for a more substantive reason: it requests *authorization* from the user for what information it will send FeralAmoebae.com (or whomever). This is part of the third question: How easy is it for the user to control what is sent to whom? In this case, the big issue is user privacy; Facebook knows a lot about people, and not all of them want all of that to be sent to every random web site they visit that happens to have a contract with Facebook.

There is an additional privacy issue: in schemes like this, the SSO knows every affiliated site you visit. Is this acceptable? It may be fine for public-facing web sites, though not necessarily to their users. For employers, though, this is rarely a good choice.

There are more general SSO schemes than the web-based one I've just outlined. Imagine a world of multiple identity providers. A user could have accounts with several of these. After logging in to one, the SSO server returns some sort of cryptographically sealed object. To log in to some other systems, the user designates which of the cached identities—that is, which of the several cryptographically protected identities she has available—should be forwarded to the desired site. That site, in turn, is told the identity provider involved and Chris's identity as known to that provider.

---

4. "Authentication—Facebook Developers," http://developers.facebook.com/docs/authentication/.

Again, the user interface is crucial. If nothing else, Chris wants to make sure that her employer doesn't receive her credentials from HiTechEmploymentAgencySSO.com, since it would be rather embarrassing to Chris. From the employer's perspective, it has to decide which identity providers it trusts. Only its own? Facebook's? The local government's? The one it knows is run by a front organization for MI-31? In a federated system, what can matter the most is the tuple ⟨provider, identity⟩. This is, of course, the crucial distinction between authentication and authorization: which tuples will you authorize?

There are a number of systems based on this paradigm. Microsoft's is one of the best known,[5] but there are many others, including at least one open-source system. The concept of federated identities is at the heart of the *National Strategy for Trusted Identities in Cyberspace (NSTIC)*, the White House's scheme for identification on the net [White House 2011].

There are other products intended for SSO within an organization. Kerberos, described earlier, is one such. In such cases, issues of reliability and privacy don't arise as much. However, the user interface question is still crucial: if a user has nice, transparent access to everything within a company, any malware that user is running has the same access.

7.11   Storing Passwords: Servers

How should sites store password databases? What about other sorts of authentication data? Let's look at passwords first. Note well: I assume that there *will* be some sort of security failure at your server complex; if there isn't, there's no reason to do anything fancy. But if you assume perfect security and you're wrong, the results can be disastrous.

Back when the world was young, passwords were stored in cleartext in a read-protected file. They weren't encrypted because pre-DES, there were no suitable encryption algorithms. Besides, operating system file protections were thought to be good enough. The classic Morris and Thompson paper [1979] showed why that was a bad idea, so people switched to hashed passwords but in readable files. Password-guessing attacks remained an issue, so most vendors eventually switched to hashed passwords in read-protected files.

That's all well and good for single machines. It doesn't work nearly as well for networked complexes of machines or for large server complexes with vast numbers of users who have no traditional login access to most machines. They might be users of your ISP, or subscribers to your mail service, or customers of your web site, but they all have logins and passwords. And you're probably operating at a scale not seen on single hosts; you'll

---

5. "A Guide to Claims-Based Identity and Access Control (2nd Edition),"
   https://msdn.microsoft.com/en-us/library/ff423674.aspx.

have somewhere between tens of thousands and possibly tens of millions of accounts. (Facebook claims more than 1.4 billion active users, more than 18% of the world's population.[6] And they all have passwords.)

Clearly, many enterprises need a password or authentication server of some type. How should it be protected? The analysis has to start with two questions: what are the operational needs for this server, and what are the consequences of a breach? Initially, let's look at the second question.

The type of authentication you require plays a large role in answering this question. If your users are employing public key authentication, the database is relatively benign; a leak exposes only public keys. Public keys are, by definition, allowed to be public; seeing one doesn't permit an attacker to learn the corresponding private keys. In that case, there is little reason to take special precautions with the data. (Under certain circumstances, it is possible for a private key and hence the corresponding public key to be derived from a password; a colleague and I proposed such a scheme many years ago [Bellovin and Merritt 1993]. This opens the risk of password-guessing attacks; see below.)

One step down is the case in which stolen data allows illicit entry to your own services, but to no others. A Kerberos database or other collections of symmetric keys fall into this category. This is clearly a disaster for you, but not for your users (except, of course, the damage they suffer from abuse of their login on your system).

The worst situation is if plaintext passwords are compromised. As I noted earlier, people reuse logins and passwords; a compromise on your site is likely to lead to a compromise of many accounts on many other sites. Quite apart from any moral blame you might incur, it is quite conceivable that you're running a risk of legal liability. Since the only reason to store a plaintext password is for password recovery, the answer is simple: don't do that.

Some people will claim that there's another reason: using a password as a key for a symmetric cipher requires both sides to have the password. That's not quite correct. What both sides need is the same shared secret; rather than the password itself, it should be some value deterministically and irreversibly derived from the password. The simplest solution is to store, say, the MD5 hash of the password; that value, though, is useful when attacking other sites that use the same scheme. Instead, hash (or better yet, HMAC [Bellare, Canetti, and Krawczyk 1996; Krawczyk, Bellare, and Canetti 1997]) the password with your service name. This value—HMAC(PW, https://www.example.com)—is useful when talking to you and only when talking to you.

Guessing attacks are a risk against any storage of data derived from passwords. The problem and its solution go back to Morris and Thompson [Morris and Thompson 1979]: add a salt and iterate the hash. More details on modern versions are given in [Kaliski

---

6. "Company Info," https://newsroom.fb.com/company-info/.

2000]. Unfortunately, that isn't straightforward in a distributed environment, where both sides may need to calculate the shared secret before any communication takes place. (*Encrypted Key Exchange (EKE)* [Bellovin and Merritt 1992] is such a protocol.) Instead, calculate a different hash:

$$H'(\text{username, site, password})$$

and use the high-order 64 bits as the salt and the low-order 18–24 bits as the iteration count. Why 18–24 bits? The purpose of the iterated hashing is to slow down dictionary attacks; if every password is hashed 100,000 times, an attacker processing a series of guesses is slowed down to $1/100,000$ the previous rate. Unfortunately, the good guys are slowed down, too, so we have to pick a suitable compromise. Informal experiments show that about 300,000 iterations of MD5 are about right for slower smart phones. Salting is vital, since it guards against precomputation attacks.

Server-side considerations for iteration count are a bit more complex. You need to know the peak period login rate u (users per second); c, the number of CPUs you can dedicate to iterated hashes; and t, the CPU time per hash. The maximum iteration count is then $h \cdot u/c$. If it's too low—that is, if it makes guessing attackers easier—you need more CPUs.

The challenge/response, time-based, and paper-based OTP schemes generally do not suffer from password-guessing vulnerabilities, so other sites are safe. However, the data is useful for attacking your own site's accounts and hence must be carefully protected. Lamport's scheme is quite nice in this regard; the stored data cannot be used for new authentication, on your site or elsewhere, and it inherently uses iteration. If the maximum count is set high enough, there will always be a substantial base number of iterations that an attacker will have to do even if the seed secret is derived from a password. (However, if you're relying on the limited-number-of-logins property of his scheme, you should iterate many times before using that value to seed the algorithm.)

A summary of the risks to different types of authentication data storage is given in Table 7.1.

It is tempting to suggest that usernames also be hashed before storage. After all, knowing that user smb has password 123456 is rather different from knowing that user 79e0f325804dafbdaef73b3b17c0fd8d has that password or even password e10adc3949b-a59abbe56e057f20f883e. Unfortunately, it's probably fruitless; the attacker can quite likely figure out a large portion of the usernames from other data lying around the system, and it's rather easy to do the necessary hashes.

Let's turn our attention to the other question I posed near the start of this section: What are the operational needs? A site that stores passwords also has to store secondary authentication information. Most public-facing sites and many internal sites have such

Table 7.1: Risks from Compromise of Stored Authentication Data, in Approximate Order of Decreasing Risk

	Scheme	*Potential Damage*
1	Plaintext passwords	Immediate login to your site and others
2	Simple hashed shared secrets	Immediate login to at least your site; easy guessing attacks against your site and others
3	Paper schemes	Immediate login to your site only
4	Time-based and challenge/response	Immediate login to your site only
5	Password-based Lamport	Guessing attacks against your site and others
6	Non-password Lamport; public key	None

information; it's quite critical and much harder to protect by hashing because there are so few choices for so many of the common fields. Place of birth? There are fewer than 20,000 incorporated places in the United States.[7] Favorite color? Most people don't know that many color names.[8] Mother's maiden name? More than 90% of American surnames can be found in fewer than 100,000 guesses.[9] One can even find lists of common pet names online. I suspect that the numbers are comparable for other countries, though the data may be harder to obtain for some. In other words, typical secondary authentication data is almost as risky to store as plaintext passwords.

Other important operational needs, beyond secondary authentication, include adding users, deleting users, changing or resetting the password, and (of course) verifying a login attempt. Don't neglect the fact that an authentication server is, among other things, a computer, which means that it has all of the usual computer needs: software maintenance, disk backup and recovery, database synchronization with the other replicas of the authentication files, sysadmin login for routine troubleshooting, and more.

There is another, more subtle concern: database consistency. It's never a good idea to store the same data in two different places; the two instances *will* get out of sync. Sites typically store other, non-sensitive profile information on their users, whether for direct operational needs (Which mail server holds this person's email?), revenue related (Which type of targeted ads are believed to be most effective?), or simply user preferences such

---

7. "Population Estimates," http://www.census.gov/popest/data/intercensal/cities/cities2010.html.
8. "Color Survey Results," http://blog.xkcd.com/2010/05/03/color-survey-results/.
9. "Demographic Aspects of Surnames from Census 2000,"
    http://www2.census.gov/topics/genealogy/2000surnames/surnames.pdf.

as preferred language. If you store that sort of information with the authentication data, you increase the attack surface; if you store it separately, you have more consistency problems. Worse yet, things like credit card numbers are sensitive in a different way and may merit their own secure storage.

Table 7.1 makes it clear that if you are using safe authentication technologies (i.e., the last row in the table), it doesn't much matter where you store the data; the most convenient server will suffice. Conversely, the risks from at least the first two rows and probably the first four are sufficiently great that extra care is needed. Such authentication data should be stored on a separate server, with a lot of attention paid to the protocols and operational environment. (Design issues are discussed in Chapter 11.) Only the fifth row, password-based Lamport, presents a difficult choice; keeping the data in the general user profile database is a defensible choice, but if you need secure authentication storage anyway (e.g., for secondary authentication data) you may as well put the primary data there as well (but see Chapter 11 for other considerations).

7.12 Analysis

Figure 7.4 summarizes the properties of a number of different authentication mechanisms, when dealing with different issues: threats, forgetting or losing something, and so on.

	Guessing	Forgetting	Device loss	Server file stolen	Temp access	External trust	Phishing/ logging
Passwords	✗	✗	✓	✗	✓	✓	✗✗
Lamport's	?	✗	✗	✗	?	✓	?
Chall/resp	✓	✓	✗	✗✗	✗	✓	✓
SMS	✓	✓	?	✓	✗	?	✓
Time-based	✓	✓	✗	✗✗	?	✗	✓
Crypto	✓	✓	?	✗,✓	?	✓	✓
Biometric	✓	✓	?	✗	✗	✓	✗✗
Federated	?	?	✓	✓	?	✗	?

✓	No particular problem; strength of this mechanism
?	Some trouble or implementation-dependent
✗	Significant risk
✗✗	Very serious risk

Figure 7.4: Properties of different authentication mechanisms.

What's striking is that none of the analyzed mechanisms are good under all circumstances. Password authentication, that much-maligned mechanism, is better than most when it comes to granting temporary access or the need to trust external parties. Most alternatives concentrate on the most glaring issues with passwords, users forgetting their passwords, attackers guessing them, or capture of a password by phishing sites or keystroke loggers. Almost all are weaker under other circumstances. In fact, most pairs of mechanisms fall short, too, though the combination of a password sent to a site and some form of federated authentication not relying on passwords comes close. The real benefit from avoiding passwords is that you're not vulnerable if some other password-using site is compromised.

There are no perfect solutions here. Even read requests from /dev/brain run afoul of the bilateral authentication. issue. (While that could, presumably, be solved by writes to /dev/brain by the verifying computer, the mind boggles at what could happen if that pro-

---

Picking a Strong Password?

There are two strategies for picking a good password, practical and theoretical.

The practical approach is simple: use anything that won't be found by the attackers' patterns. Thus, if attackers are generating passwords based on lowercase letters, you'd be safe if your simple password used only uppercase. The problem, of course, is that you don't know what the attackers do, and they could change it easily enough. In other words, a practical approach won't work very well. (However, if you want to do it, the best thing to do is to use a multiword phrase; so few people do that that most attackers won't bother trying.)

Looking at it theoretically, you want a password space so large that it can't be searched. If you have s symbols in your "alphabet" and n letters, then the size of the guess space g is, quite obviously, $g = s^n$. Thus, in the example shown in Figure 7.1, $s = 2^{11} = 2,048$ and $n = 4$, giving $g = 2^{44}$ or about $1.8 \cdot 10^{13}$. What is crucial is that your password be chosen uniformly from that space.

The next question is how large g should be. That depends on the attacker's computing resources and how long you want your password to resist attack. To futureproof ourselves, increase the numbers from p. 108 to grant the attacker 1,000,000 machines that can do 10,000,000 guesses per second: 10^{13}. At that rate, the space covered by that algorithm will be exhausted in a couple of seconds. Clearly, that's not good enough against an enemy with those resources.

(Continued)

We can compensate by either using five words or choosing our words from a list that's twice as long. The former gives us $3.6 \cdot 10^{17}$ possibilities; the latter $2.8 \cdot 10^{14}$, and may be harder to remember because the words are less common. Choosing six words takes us to $7.3 \cdot 10^{20}$; guessing time comes to about 116 days, which is probably good enough.

Any other algorithm can be evaluated this way. Suppose you're restricted to eight characters, digits, or mixed case letters only. (Yes, there are such sites, even today.) How well do you fare? If you choose randomly, you get $n = 8$, $s = 62$, and hence $g = 2.1 \cdot 10^{14}$. That's clearly not good enough, but under those silly rules it's the best you can do. Simply using 10 characters instead of eight takes us to $8.3 \cdot 10^{18}$, which is probably adequate. Beware of simple "fixes" like adding punctuation, since many people will just append a period or comma. Suppose you did that instead of the eighth alphameric character. That *cuts* the search space to $62^7 \cdot 3$, for seven characters, those seven followed by a period, or those seven followed by a comma, giving just $1.0 \cdot 10^{13}$ choices.

I could go through more arithmetic, but it's really just a simple exercise in combinatorics. Pick your own algorithm—but remember, if you don't choose randomly from the space, the calculations are very different. Early password guessers succeeded, despite much slower computers than we have today, because people tended to pick *words*, and English words have only about 2.3 bits/letter [C. E. Shannon 1948; C. E. Shannon 1951], giving an effective $g = 3.5 \cdot 10^6$.

The algorithm from Figure 7.1? If you let a generator pick a few random words from a list, you're fine. However, if you ask the generator for ten sequences and pick the "easiest to memorize," you've cut the search space dramatically—except for the very practical point I mentioned at the top of this box.

cess were hacked. . . .) That said, sites need to pick *some* authentication solution, despite all of the limitations of usability, human frailty, and so on. A few points stand out:

- Passwords are not suitable for high-security needs. This includes most logins for medium and large enterprises. Even smaller enterprises should move away from passwords if the threat model so indicates.

- That said, passwords will not go away, even in sensitive environments; converting all applications to use stronger authentication is at best time consuming. It will be a very long time before web sites convert to any other authentication mechanism. Accordingly, technical means, such as password managers, should be used to cope with the password reuse problem. This will also help with the password strength problem, though as noted this isn't as big a threat as is commonly trumpeted.

- Implement bilateral authentication; it's strong protection against phishing. Some password managers do this automatically: they'll send a password only if they recognize the site, and they're not fooled by clever email messages.

- Master passwords—those used with password managers or SSO systems, those used to decrypt private keys, and so forth—are especially crucial and need the best protection. These should indeed be "strong."

- Like much of security, authentication is a systems issue. Special care must be taken with secondary authentication mechanisms and password reset schemes.

- Plan for exceptions. Know in advance how to handle lost or stolen passwords, compromised servers, and more.

Finally, there are many fads in authentication. As discussed above, *all* schemes have their limitations and weaknesses. Decide based on the threat model and your operational environment.

A more interesting question is what would cause me to change these recommendations. The strengths and weaknesses of passwords are likely to remain pretty stable for the foreseeable future. On the attacking side, the basic techniques have been known since 1979; while there have been performance improvements and storage capacity changes, these are not revolutionary. We are even less likely to see changes in how humans cope with passwords, since *homo sapiens 2.0* isn't even in beta yet.

Improvements in tokens, and in particular in their cost and usability, are more likely. Many different versions have shown up over the years; with the notable exception of the SecurID, none have really caught on. It is worth restating why SecurID succeeded: they sold a complete *system*, not just tokens and basic support software. A competitor would have to match that and more; it would have to support logins to more devices of interest (smart phones? cars?) and be some combination of cheaper, more secure, or more usable. The latter is probably the greatest technological barrier, but the other issues are non-trivial. The best chance for a change is if a major vendor (probably Microsoft or Apple) were switch to tokens as the preferred login scheme, with suitable support and (most likely) subsidized tokens.

I doubt that biometrics will displace passwords in the next 10–20 years. While we will certainly see improvements in correctness and in sensor design, some of the other issues—dealing with database compromise, changing biometrics after compromise, remote authentication—are inherent in the problem statement and will not go away.

The variable most likely to change is how people authenticate. If some other style catches on, such as federated authentication, the role of passwords will indeed diminish.

Given the many variables here—cost, privacy, trust, compatibility, security, and more—it is difficult to make any concrete predictions. All that said, it does seem to be the scenario to watch most closely.

Chapter 8

PKI: Public Key Infrastructures

"I see a complex netting of obligations, but within it there is a pyramid of power. No one is truly independent, but as you near the top of the pyramid power increases enormously; however, it is seldom used to its fullest. There are lines of obligation that reach in all directions, upwards, downwards, sideways in a totally alien manner."

Charlie in *The Mote in God's Eye*
—LARRY NIVEN AND JERRY POURNELLE

8.1   What's a Certificate?

Public key cryptography, as originally described by Diffie and Hellman [1976], seemed simple. Someone uses your public key to encrypt a message to you; you use your private key to decrypt it. However, Diffie and Hellman paid little attention to how communicants acquire each others' public keys, saying only:

> The enciphering key E can be made public by placing it in a public directory along with the user's name and address. Anyone can then encrypt messages and send them to the user, but no one else can decipher messages intended for him.

> Public key cryptosystems can thus be regarded as multiple access ciphers. It is crucial that the public file of enciphering keys be protected from unauthorized modification. This task is made easier by the public nature of the file.

Read protection is unnecessary and, since the file is modified infrequently, elaborate write protection mechanisms can be economically employed.

They do not say where this public directory is, who runs it, how the other party gets access to it, or just what these "elaborate write protection mechanisms" might be. More seriously, they do not conduct a threat analysis. How does everyone agree on or find the proper public directory? Who runs it? Can you trust that party with the "crucial" responsibility of write-protecting the file? How does that party distinguish "unauthorized" from authorized modification? In other words, there are profound systems questions.

Part of the answer was devised by an MIT undergraduate, Loren Kohnfelder, who invented *certificates* [1978]. In the simplest form, a certificate is a digitally signed message containing a user's name and his or her public key. Reality, of course, is more complex; at a minimum, real-world certificates need things like algorithm identifiers.

Today, certificates are generally embedded in a framework known as *public key infrastructure (PKI)*. The Internet Security Glossary [Shirey 2007] defines PKI as "The set of hardware, software, people, policies, and procedures needed to create, manage, store, distribute, and revoke digital certificates based on asymmetric cryptography." Note carefully that the definition includes "people, policies, and procedures," and not just code. Because of the wide variety of uses of PKI, the semantics of many of these operations are quite complicated; I'll only skim the surface. (For more information on the details of PKI, see [Housley and Polk 2001].)

Complex semantics tends to breed complex syntax; certificates are no exception. Most certificates you will encounter use the X.509 standard [ITU-T 2012], and in particular the Internet's "PKIX" profile [Cooper et al. 2008]. X.509 has complexity in full measure, including highly structured names, highly structured addresses, serial numbers, usage flags, and even corporate logos [Santesson, Housley, Bajaj, et al. 2011; Santesson, Housley, and Freeman 2004], among many other fields. (Actually, originally X.509 wasn't even intended to define general-purpose certificates, but that's another story.)

A more interesting addition to the basic concept are *attribute* fields. An attribute is some characteristic about the certificate holder, attested to by the signer. For people, it might be something like their age. Attributes can be used with or without names. As we shall see, pure attribute certificates are quite useful.

The fundamental questions about certificates are about security: who signs the certificates? Do you trust them? Are they honest? Are they competent, both at procedures (e.g., verifying the holder's identity) and technically (e.g., preventing unauthorized access to their signing key)? Questions like these are at the heart of this chapter.

8.2   PKI: Whom Do You Trust?

When you use a certificate in any way, you are utterly relying on the trustworthiness of its issuer. Understanding the exact mechanisms used today isn't easy, though; the total certificate system architecture is quite complex. Let's look at the pieces of the traditional X.509 setup.

The heart of the certificate system is the *certificate authority (CA)*. A CA does just what its name implies: it issues—signs—certificates. These certificates may be for end users, or they may be for sub-CAs. For end-user certificates, they also indicate (up to a point) the permitted uses for the certificate: encryption, digital signatures, etc. If a sub-CA issues a certificate, the trust question becomes more complex: you have to trust not just the immediate issuer but also every other CA up to the root of the tree. After all, you may trust MyFavoriteInternetCA.com, but the CA certificate it has may have been issued by MI-31.mil.Andromeda, whom you don't trust at all. (They even have a non-existent domain name—the Andromedans are tricky....) Is it the real MyFavoriteInternetCA.com who certified the site you're talking to, or are you being tricked? The root of this tree is called the *trust anchor*, and though it may be turtles all the way down,[1] it has to be trust all the way up.

If there's only one CA in your universe, life is relatively simple. Unfortunately, that isn't the universe most of us live in. Most commercial operating systems, and especially web browsers, come equipped with a very large set of CAs built in. This implies that your vendor trusts them—but do you? Are they (your vendor *and* the CAs) honest? Competent? Most crucially, does their threat model match yours?

The existence of sub-CAs raises another thorny question: what is the permissible scope of activity of the sub-CA? If some company example.com is a sub-CA, it's perfectly reasonable for it to want to issue certificates to its own divisions (e.g., hr.example.com) or employees (e.g., Mary@hr.example.com). Can it legitimately issue a certificate for ARandomBrand.com? What if that corporation is a subsidiary of example.com? What if it was a subsidiary but has since been sold?

More subtly, sometimes an employee speaks for the corporation and sometimes he or she speaks personally. In a paper world, of course, you can't tell whether the person who signed a contract was authorized to do so by her employer. Should certificates embody that sort of authority? Can you tell? You might think that music.example.com was one division of some large media conglomerate, but it turns out that "Music" is the 6,304th most common surname in the United States;[2] perhaps the cert belongs to Mary Music's laptop. ("Lawyer" is #6,309. I think that that's a coincidence.)

---

1. "Turtles all the way down," https://en.wikipedia.org/wiki/Turtles_all_the_way_down.
2. "dist.all.last,"
   http://www.census.gov/topics/population/genealogy/data/1990_census/1990_census_namefiles.html.

There are special rules for special circumstances. In certificates representing owner-ship of IP addresses, for example, there are explicit rules for ensuring that certificates contain only address ranges that are subsets of those owned by the issuing CA or sub-CA [Lynn, S. T. Kent, and Seo 2004, Section 2.3]. Of course, the root CA has to have the right to those addresses before it can delegate them. That's a political issue; on the global Internet, those rights are held by the five *Regional Internet Registries (RIRs)*, those rights are assigned to them by the *Internet Assigned Numbers Authority (IANA)*.

Other special rules exist as well. There are standard ways to indicate that a certificate can be used for signing executables, or for email or web encryption. For CA certificates, there is a "Name Constraints" field; this means that a CA trusted to issue certificates for, say, *.example.com can't issue fake certificates for some other company. In general, though, the precise role of a certificate is not obvious, especially to a program.

Sometimes, the policies of a CA matter. CAs are supposed to document their policies in a *Certificate Practice Statement (CPS)*. In the real world, few people even know of the existence of CPSs, let alone try to read them, but since they're often very long and written in legalese it isn't clear that that matters much. More seriously, the party most likely to know about the CPS is the one to whom the certificate was issued, while the relying party—who is most affected by failures—is much less likely to even know of its existence. Let's put it like this: when you decide to do some shopping on the Internet, do you even look to see which CA issued the certificate to the site you're visiting? Do you examine the certificate thoroughly enough to find a pointer to the CPS? Do you then download and study it? Some CAs appear to claim that you're legally required to read their CPS before going to any site that uses it. Here's one from Symantec:[3]

> WHETHER YOU ARE AN INDIVIDUAL OR ORGANIZATION, YOU ("RELYING PARTY") MUST READ THIS RELYING PARTY AGREE-MENT FOR USER AUTHENTICATION CERTIFICATES ("AGREE-MENT") EACH TIME BEFORE VALIDATING A SYMANTEC-ISSUED USER AUTHENTICATION CERTIFICATE ("SYMANTEC CERTIFI-CATE") , USING SYMANTEC'S ONLINE CERTIFICATE STATUS PRO-TOCOL (OCSP) SERVICES, ACCESSING OR USING A SYMAN-TEC DATABASE OF CERTIFICATE REVOCATIONS OR RELYING ON ANY INFORMATION RELATED TO THE SYMANTEC CERTIFICATE (COLLECTIVELY, "SYMANTEC INFORMATION"). IF YOU DO NOT AGREE TO THE TERMS OF THIS AGREEMENT, DO NOT SUB-MIT A QUERY AND DO NOT DOWNLOAD, ACCESS, OR RELY ON

---

3. "Relying Party Agreement for User Authentication Certificates," https://www.symantec.com/content/en/us/about/media/repository/relying-party-agreement-user-authentication.pdf.

How Many CAs Does Your Browser Trust?

Still not convinced there's a problem? Let's look at the list of trusted CAs. As of October 2011, Microsoft listed 320 different root certificates.[a] It had been 321, but one was removed because the CA, DigiNotar, was hacked and its private signing key stolen, allegedly by parties linked to the government of Iran [Galperin, Schoen, and Eckersley 2011] (or maybe the NSA [Schneier 2013]). More than 100 different company names are represented (because of assorted mergers and acquisitions, it's difficult to tell just how many companies are actually involved) from 49 different countries. More than 30 of the certificates are explicitly listed as belonging to agencies of national governments. Does that give you a warm, fuzzy feeling?

Mozilla lists 150 different CAs, from about 60 different organizations. Their database does not have an explicit country indication, but 8 of the CAs are identified as belonging to government agencies.[b]

It's harder to assess Apple's list, since they don't appear to have a single web page; examination of the system certificate file on a computer running Mac OS X "Lion" (10.7.3) on April 12, 2012, shows about 180 different certificates, from at least 30 countries and more than 70 companies.

Note that any of these CAs can create unrestricted sub-CAs, which you can't even see listed in your browser. Any of these organizations can issue certificates for any site on the net.

Is that bad enough? It's worse: some vendors will "helpfully" update your trusted CA list automatically [Microsoft 2009]:

> Root certificates are updated on Windows Vista automatically. When a user visits a secure web site (by using HTTPS SSL), reads a secure email (S/MIME), or downloads an ActiveX control that is signed (code signing) and encounters a new root certificate, the Windows certificate chain verification software checks the appropriate Microsoft Update location for the root certificate. If it finds it, it downloads it to the system. To the user, the experience is seamless. The user does not see any security dialog boxes or warnings. The download happens automatically, behind the scenes.

What you're supposed to do instead is to add unwanted certificates to the "untrusted" list, through a fairly ghastly user interface.

---

a. "Windows Root Certificate Program — Members List (All CAs) — TechNet Articles — United States (English) — TechNet Wiki,"
   http://social.technet.microsoft.com/wiki/contents/articles/2592.aspx.
b. "Included Certificate List," http://www.mozilla.org/projects/security/certs/included/.

ANY SYMANTEC INFORMATION. IN CONSIDERATION OF YOUR
AGREEMENT TO THESE TERMS, YOU ARE ENTITLED TO USE
SYMANTEC INFORMATION AS SET FORTH HEREIN. AS USED IN
THIS AGREEMENT, "SYMANTEC" MEANS SYMANTEC CORPORA-
TION OR ANY OF ITS SUBSIDIARIES.

The shouting caps are all theirs. Note what it says: before "validating" or "relying" on
information in the certificates they issue, you "must read this" agreement. Your browser
did tell you that, right? No? I guess you're not allowed to buy things online.

All of this—the certificates, the trust anchors, the delegation rules, the revocation
mechanisms (see Section 8.4)—compose what we know as PKI. PKI is the subject of
a great deal of angst, fear, misinformation, disinformation, and downright mythology.
Unfortunately, the foci of all of this Sturm und Drang are generally the complexity and
security issues. While these are indeed of concern, we now see the crucial limitations of
certificates for most people:

- It is rarely clear to system administrators or developers which CAs are trusted for
  given applications. It is almost never clear to end users.

- It is rarely clear to anyone what a given certificate's intended use is.

- It is almost never clear how trustworthy or competent a CA is. Many years ago,
  Matt Blaze observed that a commercial CA would protect you from anyone from
  whom they wouldn't take money [2010]. This is a crucial point: if you trust a system's built-in CAs, you are in effect trusting some unknown set of third parties to
  vouch for someone else's identity (or attributes) and making access control decisions based on these third parties' opinions.

It helps here to reason by analogy. Suppose someone who claims to be an employee
wants to walk into your building. Rather than showing an employee ID card, they instead
pull out what appears to be a credit card in a real employee's name; this credit card
was issued by one of several hundred banks you've never heard of, possibly up to and
including the Bank of San Serriffe.[4,5] Do you think they should be admitted to your
building? Would you accept that as a login credential for your computer systems?

Any of these CAs can issue a certificate for any web site in the world—and your
browser will accept it.

---

4. "San Serriffe," http://www.museumofhoaxes.com/hoax/archive/permalink/san_serriffe.
5. "Knuth: The Bank of San Serriffe," http://www-cs-faculty.stanford.edu/~knuth/boss.html.

8.3   PKI versus PKI

Although, as I've shown, the standard Internet-wide PKI is unacceptably insecure, most of the tools and pieces can be used quite securely if we can reverse the three big problems listed above. That is, if we can construct a scenario in which everyone knows exactly who can issue a certificate and what the purpose of that certificate is, and if the issuer can be trusted to an extent commensurate with the resource being protected, we will have a secure (or secure enough) system, *while using the same software, syntax, and so on.* In particular, if we give up on the notion of the One True PKI and the One True List of CAs, and instead have a CA per access control point, we can reap most of the benefits of public key cryptography while avoiding the pitfalls. I call this concept PKI, to suggest small-scope CAs, rather than the large-scope CAs of a traditional PKI. To expand on the credit card analogy, enterprises generally issue their own employee credentials that are used to enter the building, rather than deferring to the bank. Furthermore—and I'll expand on this point—employee ID cards function as *authorization* tokens even more than they do as identification devices. It's your possession of the card (possibly as authenticated by your picture—a biometric—and perhaps knowledge of a PIN) that gets you in the door, rather than your name and address.

The key insight is that every function that requires (or would benefit from) use of certificates should have its own PKI. Thus, an IPsec gateway would issue its own certificates; these would be distinct from the certificates issued by, say, the corporate email service for use in encrypting and authenticating messages. Similarly, the outside company that handles procurement would issue a sub-CA certificate to the enterprise; this CA would in turn certify employees who are authorized to buy things.

Note how this solves the problems described in the previous section. The IPsec gateway CA is trusted for IPsec; your web browser won't believe certificates that it issues for, say, Amazon.com. The purchasing certificate from ReallyNiceCorporateToys.com comes from a CA that has the name ReallyNiceCorporateToys.com; no one will think it should let you use IPsec.

The trustworthiness issue is the most important distinguisher. By definition, PKI certificates are issued by the party that is entitled to grant access to some resource. It does not have to be—and is not—trusted to grant or withhold access to anything else. Furthermore, given that such parties are handing out access credentials, from a security perspective it does not matter whether these credentials are key pairs, passwords, or special thought symbols that are sensed by a magic crystal under the users' keyboards. The actual technologies used may have differing security properties, but the fact that public key technologies are used does not change the powers of the grantor. It is certainly possible to overload the meaning of a PKI certificate, just as (in the United States) drivers' licenses are used to gain access to airplanes and alcohol; the trick (and it's at least as much organizational as technical) is to resist the temptation and do things properly. Use these certificates only for the purpose for which they were issued.

A consequence of this is that running a PKI does not imply a need for excessive complexity or security. In describing a simplified approach to IPsec configuration [Srivatsan, M. Johnson, and Bellovin 2010], we wrote:

> Public key infrastructures (PKIs) are surrounded by a great mystique. Organizations are regularly told that they are complex, require ultra-high security, and perhaps are best outsourced to competent parties. Setting up a certificate authority (CA) requires a "ceremony", a term with a technical meaning [Ellison 2007] but nevertheless redolent of high priests in robes, acolytes with censers, and more. This may or may not be true in general; for most IPsec uses, however, little of this is accurate. (High priests and censers are definitely not needed; we are uncertain about the need for acolytes...)
>
> Much of the mystique is due to the general-purpose nature of PKIs and certificates. If a certificate is intended to attest to a person's identity, a lot of process may be necessary. The real danger from a compromised root key comes from the attacker's ability to create arbitrarily many fraudulent credentials.

This is crucially important: a PKI installation need not be surrounded by any more security than any other credential-issuing system. Some years ago, I heard a presentation from a PKI vendor; the speaker stressed how "court-certified videographers" recorded all root key ceremonies. Would you do the same when setting up your payroll system? Your ID card system? Of course not—but why is it needed for certificate issuance? In multi-organization situations, it could be defended as a mechanism to ensure trust; internally, that isn't needed.

A PKI avoids the central philosophical contradiction of general-purpose PKIs: the CA is not authoritative for the name space concerned. This means that there are two different entities that have to vouch for someone's identity, the actual name space owner—on the web, that's whoever controls the DNS name—and the CA. Much of the bureaucratic overhead of large-scale PKIs is dedicated to ensuring that their decisions match those of the name space owner.

Running a PKI instead of using a KDC or even, in some cases, a password file has another, more subtle advantage: successful attacks against your centralized infrastructure are less damaging. Secret keys and password files must be protected against disclosure. In other words, you have a confidentiality problem. By contrast, CAs need only authentication, a simpler problem. (Recall Table 7.1 and Figure 7.4: public key-based authentication is the most secure type available.)

Apart from hype and myth-making, there's another reason that many organizations refrain from issuing their own certificates: it seems like a very hard thing to do. There's some truth to that, albeit for a very bad reason. Let's face it: many of the readily available certificate-minting software packages are not only not user friendly, they're downright user hostile. Much of the complexity comes from asking for information that is generally irrelevant and often incomprehensible. Too many fields don't need to be user settable in 99.99% of cases. Do you really need to know (or want to know) what the difference is between the "keyUsage" and "extendedKeyUsage" fields? A vendor of cryptographic software is almost certainly more qualified than a typical organization to pick, say, appropriate algorithms, key lengths, expiration periods, and so on, but the poor soul who has to use the software has to read through (and understand) all of these options before concluding that the default values can be left alone. Other fields, such as Organizational Unit or City, might be necessary for identity certificates; they're generally irrelevant for the certificates I'm advocating, which are *authorization certificates*. That is, they give access to some resource, but by intent they give access to the holder of the corresponding private key. By contrast, identity certificates are used for authentication; after that, the user's name is matched against some form of access control list.

The ability to do something like this naturally suggests the idea of a company issuing certificates for its own internal web sites, rather than buying them from a commercial CA. It's not a bad idea, but alas it is probably not worth it. Yes, it's good that your own internal IT department is the one attesting to the identity of, say, the Payroll web site. Alas (and as described above), the risks arise because all of the other CAs your browsers trust can also issue such certificates; having your own CA doesn't change that. You could try deleting them, but then you're faced with the challenge of keeping up with the deletions, that is, knowing every machine in the company (including all of the mobile devices people are using), knowing what browsers are in use, knowing how to delete CAs from all of these, actually having the authority to do so, keeping up with "helpful" vendor functionality that restores CAs (see the box on page 153), and so on. An organization with a highly centralized, all-controlling IT group may be able to accomplish this (except, perhaps, working around that excessive helpfulness), but excessive rigidity has its own disadvantages [Perrow 1999].

Some companies do, in fact, do this, for a somewhat different reason: their firewalls want to inspect all traffic, even if it's HTTPS-protected. To do that, they use local CAs that issue fake certificates for any web site; this permits the firewall to decrypt and then reencrypt all traffic. There are interesting liability questions if this is done to, say, banking web sites, but of course many organizations bar all non-work usage. (On the other hand, I once worked for an organization that explicitly based its computer usage policies on

Deuteronomy 25:4: "You shall not muzzle an ox while it is threshing." A modest amount of personal usage was explicitly permitted.)

There's one more bad idea in this space that should be disposed of. Some people will get the notion that they should delete all CAs that have issued certificates for Facebook and other sites on which employees "waste" time. It won't work. People who want to get to such sites will just click through all of the bloodthirsty warnings their browsers will display; you'll only succeed in training people to ignore security pop-up messages.

If you don't want to rely on a PKI or a PKI, there's another way to get a great deal of safety: *key continuity* (also known as *certificate pinning* or *key pinning*). Key continuity relies on a simple concept: public keys rarely change. Accordingly, applications can record the key sent by a peer; if there's a difference on successive connections, it's quite possible that some evil party is trying to play nasty games. On the other hand (and as shown in the error message in Figure 8.1), key changes can also occur for perfectly benign reasons. In fact, this situation *will* occur. Knowing how to deal with it—and training users how to react *when* they see such errors—is crucial; you do *not* want your users to become acclimated to clicking through error messages. A variant checks whether the issuing CA has changed; while less likely to generate false alerts—organizations don't change their CA vendors that often—such changes are by no means impossible. Indeed,

```
@@@@@@@@@@@@@@@@@@@@@@@@@@@@@@@@@@@@@@@@@@@@@@@@@@@@@@@@@@@@@@@
@    WARNING: REMOTE HOST IDENTIFICATION HAS CHANGED!      @
@@@@@@@@@@@@@@@@@@@@@@@@@@@@@@@@@@@@@@@@@@@@@@@@@@@@@@@@@@@@@@@
IT IS POSSIBLE THAT SOMEONE IS DOING SOMETHING NASTY!
Someone could be eavesdropping on you right now
(man-in-the-middle attack)!
It is also possible that the RSA
host key has just been changed.
The fingerprint for the RSA key sent by the remote host is
c5:10:e6:70:18:65:22:6f:48:71:26:26:3f:6d:2b:07.
Please contact your system administrator.
Add correct host key in /Users/smb/.ssh/known_hosts to get
rid of this message.
Offending key in /Users/smb/.ssh/known_hosts:150
RSA host key for some.host has changed and you have requested
strict checking.
Host key verification failed.
```

Figure 8.1: A key continuity failure message.

making it hard to switch CAs would create a serious vendor lock-in problem. The key or CA change problem, and the question of protecting initial contacts, has limited the use of key continuity; to my knowledge, the only popular non-web application that uses it is ssh. Still, it is a powerful tool in the right hands.

The IETF has recently created an HTTP extension for key pinning [Evans, Palmer, and Sleevi 2015]. The new header fields defined can specify the length of time for which a pin should remain active. In addition to permitting pinning of the certificate itself, it permits pinning to a particular CA, thus allowing for easy issuance of new certificates for the site. In addition, there is provision for a reporting URL, so that the web site owner can be informed of spoofed certificates. This will work well for some sites; it remains to be seen how well it will work in general.

Another way to look at the PKI problem is that it has created a technical decoupling of trust from user-accessible concepts. That is, users try to connect to a service (e.g., the web) on some specific domain. They thus implicitly trust the DNS to give them the proper IP address. If we add DNSSEC [Arends et al. 2005a; Arends et al. 2005b; Arends et al. 2005c] to the mix, this is a reasonably secure process. With today's PKI, though, trust is coming from the collection of root CAs. If the sites' certificates (or the hashes thereof) were stored in the DNS and protected by DNSSEC, there would be no need to trust the CAs; each site could control its own cryptographic fate. This is the approach being taken by the IETF's *DNS-based Authentication of Named Entities (DANE)* working group [Barnes 2011; Hoffman and Schlyter 2012]; however, it is crucially dependent on DNSSEC, which has not yet seen widespread adoption. It is too soon to predict what will happen here.

Earlier, when I spoke of PKI CAs issuing certificates to users, I know that some of you were practically jumping out of your seats and raising your hands to ask about usability. It's a serious issue: in a world of multiple devices per person, how can normal users securely store and manage a large collection of private keys? Fortunately, with a bit of software assistance, it's not a show-stopper.

Recall that in Section 7.3, I discussed password managers. The same concept (and much of the same code) can be used to handle private keys, while encrypting them for storage in some convenient place, for example, a cloud provider. Again, if a private key is simply an access token for a single service, it does not need to be protected more strongly than a password would be for the same service. It would be nice if there were secure, convenient, portable key storage devices that worked well with our laptops, phones, tablets, smart light switches, and the like, especially for high-value keys, but such tokens have been just around the corner for well over a decade.

DANE versus Certificate Transparency

Some people have practical or philosophical objections to DANE. DNSSEC responses are large, there are complex technical issues hindering its deployment, and there is serious reason to wonder whether DNS registrars understand the security challenges involved in running a CA-like service. One alternative proposal is a Google proposal, *Certificate Transparency (CT)* [Laurie, Langley, and Kasper 2013]: every CA would log all of the certificates it issue, thus permitting browsers to notice if two different CAs had issued a certificate for some site. For that matter, any company that wishes could monitor the various CT logs to see whether certificates appear in inappropriate places.

The trouble with CT is that it requires universal compliance; otherwise, there's no way to protect against a non-CT CA issuing the bogus certs. To date, most CAs have indicated that they are not enamored of CT, quite notably including Symantec, one of the major CAs.[a] It is unclear whether there will be sufficient participation for it to fly, though it has already detected one incident [Goodin 2015d].

The security concerns about registrars are quite plausible. With today's CA structure, as problematic as it is, someone attacking a secure web site has to subvert two independent mechanisms: the routing or DNS entry that controls where the traffic goes, and the CA. With DANE, anyone who can seize control of a company's DNS entry—and that has happened, even to security-savvy firms [Edwards 2000]—can replace the certificate. Is this better or worse than CT? A lot depends on your threat model, but there isn't room in the Internet for two solutions to the PKI conundrum.

---

a. "Upcoming changes to Google Chrome's certificate handling,"
   https://cabforum.org/pipermail/public/2013-November/002336.html.

8.4   Certificate Expiration and Revocation

Regardless of whether we use a PKI or a PKI, certificates do not last forever. After some time interval specified in the certificate (i.e., set by the CA), certificates expire. Alternatively, they can be revoked for any number of reasons, including if the private key is believed to have been compromised. Expiration and revocation seem straightforward. They're not, but before diving into the complexity, let's look at how certificates die.

Certificates can become invalid ("die") in one of two ways. First, they can expire; all certificates include an expiration date, after which they may not be used. Second, they can be revoked, that is to say, explicitly declared to be invalid. The latter may be done because of private key compromise, suspected or actual misbehavior by the holder of the private key, or fears for the strength of the cryptographic algorithms used.

There are three reasons for expiration. First, there is the sense (often a vague sense) that after a certain period of time, the likelihood of an undetected compromise of the private key has become unacceptably high. The mathematics of this policy are impeccable. Suppose that the probability of a compromise during a given time interval is p; further suppose that the intervals are independent. Obviously, then, the probability of security— that is, of no compromise—after n intervals is $(1 - p)^n$. Pick your trustworthiness probability threshold t and solve, getting $n = \frac{\log t}{\log 1-p}$; it's nice, simple, and mathematical. It's also a useless exercise, since no one has any good idea what p might be. A few years is a common choice, but the mathematical basis for that is nil.

The second reason for certificate expiration is that algorithms age. Back in the dawn of time when the web was young, CAs commonly issued certificates with 1,024-bit keys and MD5 as the hash algorithm. Both are now believed to be insecure; suitable choice of an expiration date protects against that. This, too, seems like an impossible decision—how can you know when an algorithm will be cracked?—but in reality, modern algorithms do not fail all at once. Generally speaking, cracks will show up years in advance. To give just one example, signs of weakness in MD5 were noted as early as 1996 [Dobbertin 1996], well before the 2004 crack [X. Wang et al. 2004]. People realized this, even without hindsight; to give just one example, Bill Cheswick, Avi Rubin, and I warned about it in *Firewalls* [2003, p. 347]. A certificate lifetime of a few years should allow enough time to change; your credentials based on insecure algorithms will probably expire and be replaced before the problem becomes critical.

Finally, certificates expire to ease bookkeeping with respect to revocations: there's no apparent need to keep track of the revocation status of an expired certificate because it is a priori invalid. As we shall see, though, that benefit is more illusory than real.

A party accepting a certificate can check for revocation in two different ways. The older mechanism uses a *Certificate Revocation List (CRL)* [Cooper et al. 2008], a file of revoked certificates signed by the issuing CA; the URL of this list is included in certificates. Those of a certain age may recall store clerks looking up credit cards in a book-format blacklist; conceptually, this is the same thing, save that CRLs include the time of the next update to provide warning of stale revocation lists. (Just what a relying party should do if a new CRL doesn't arrive on time is a difficult question. Clearly, something is wrong; quite possibly, a denial of service attack has been launched to prevent folks from learning of newly revoked certificates. Equally clearly, rejecting all presented certificates just because you can't retrieve a new CRL is very unlikely to be correct.)

The other way to check the validity of a certificate is via a network connection using *Online Certificate Status Protocol (OCSP)* [Myers et al. 1999]. The obvious analogy,

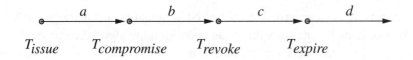

Figure 8.2: Timeline of certificate compromise, revocation, and expiration.

of course, is a modern credit card terminal. Don't stretch that analogy too far; credit card numbers are not self-checking the way certificates are. OCSP is used to verify the continuing validity of a certificate, rather than whether it was ever valid. OCSP can return Valid, Invalid, or Unknown status codes; again, the question of what to do if the OCSP server is unavailable or returns Unknown is a difficult one.

Intuitively, OCSP seems "more secure," in that it reduces the time between key compromise and effective revocation. The actual benefit, though, is much less. Consider the timeline in Figure 8.2. The effect of OCSP is to shrink interval b, the time between compromise and a "don't trust this" signal. Almost always, though, the time between $T_{compromise}$ and *discovery* of the problem is much longer than the time between discovery and effective revocation. Yes, OCSP reduces the effort needed for effective revocation, but realistically that's almost always a small percentage of the interval b.

Furthermore, the very concept of certificate death isn't as simple as it appears. Let's look at expiration first. It seems obvious—after a certain date D, the certificate may not be used—but "used" for what? Suppose that someone encrypts and signs a file at date $D-1$, when the certificate is still good. Are you allowed to verify the signature at $D+1$? Obviously, you should be; anything else would be absurd. What should happen, though, if the sender created the file at $D+1$? That shouldn't happen—but what should you, the recipient, do if it does, and how can you tell if you don't have access to the sender's clock? (The problem of clock synchronization between the sender and the recipient is an entirely separate can of worms.)

Digital signatures present an even more complex challenge. The point of a digital signature is to provide proof that some individual (more accurately, some private key) created a particular file or message. However, one reason why certificates expire is to deal with unsuspected compromise of its private key. How should a recipient handle a message that was signed with a now-expired key? The timestamp in the message itself may indicate that it was signed before the expiration date—but can you trust the signer's timestamp? After all, that value might have been set by the enemy. Equally problematic, how do you prove to a third party, such as a judge, just when the message was signed? There are schemes for timestamping documents—see, for example, [Haber and Stornetta 1991a; Haber and Stornetta 1991b]—but they're rarely used, at least in the United States.

Ultimately, the issue becomes a very deep question: when does your *reliance* on a signature expire? That is, when should you no longer take actions based on a message that was signed with some particular key? A case in point is a software package, such as a device driver, that was signed by the vendor. Depending on the package, a considerable amount of time may elapse between signature time and the time the signature is checked. A lot can happen between those two events.

Let's first consider an easier situation: receiving a digitally signed email message, perhaps containing an assent to a contract. There are four parties to consider: the CA, the signer, the relying party, and a judge who may be asked to rule on disputes. Look again at the timeline in Figure 8.2; the certificate was created at T_{issue}. If the message is received during interval a, clearly all is well; no compromise has yet happened. Interval b is the danger period: the private key has been compromised, but the certificate has not yet been revoked. The size of the interval depends on two different factors: how much time has elapsed between the actual compromise and its detection, and how long the various processes take to actually revoke the certificate.

Interval c is safe *if* the relying party actually checks for revocation. As we have seen, different revocation schemes have different properties here. Depending on the scheme and various environmental considerations, T_{revoke} can move to the right, effectively lengthening interval b. (Revocations do carry an explicit timestamp, but the meaning will vary; it may be the time of compromise as determined by the certificate holder, or it may be when the revocation was requested. You have to check the CPS for details.)

Interval d is unambiguous (everyone checks for expiration) in the sense that you won't trust a compromised certificate, though the exact value of T_{expire} depends on the clock skew between the CA and the relying party.

All this seems simple, but it's not. $T_{compromise}$ is uncertain and often unknowable; was the message signed during interval a or interval b? For that matter, suppose the signer regrets agreeing to the contract and deliberately leaks the key, but claims that it was available earlier? Is the signature genuine or not? What then? This matters if there's a dispute: who actually signed the message, the nominal signer or an attacker who has the compromised private key? Ultimately, a judge may have to decide.

The problem intended to be solved by digital signatures was described this way by Diffie and Hellman in their original paper [1976]:

> In current business, the validity of contracts is guaranteed by signatures. A signed contract serves as legal evidence of an agreement which the holder can present in court if necessary.

and

> That is, a message may be sent but later repudiated by either the transmitter or the receiver. Or, it may be alleged by either party that a message was sent when in fact none was. Unforgeable digital signatures and receipts are

needed. For example, a dishonest stockbroker might try to cover up unauthorized buying and selling for personal gain by forging orders from clients, or a client might disclaim an order actually authorized by him but which he later sees will cause a loss. We will introduce concepts which allow the receiver to verify the authenticity of a message, but prevent him from generating apparently authentic messages, thereby protecting against both the threat of compromise of the receiver's authentication data and the threat of dispute.

Unfortunately, the issue of key compromise has dimmed the luster of Diffie and Hellman's solution. The crucial advantage provided by digital signatures, non-repudiation, vanishes in the face of a deliberate key leak by the signer. This means that ultimately, the authenticity of a signature is a factual question, of the sort commonly handled by courts. Unfortunately, in this situation the crucial evidence—log files, forensic examination of the purported signing computers, and so on—is of a sort rarely handled well by courts and juries; the material is too technical. Your best defense is logging (Section 16.3) and insistence on logging by the other party; ideally, such logs are kept by an independent party. Think notary publics, moved to the digital world.

Life is even more complicated in other digital signature scenarios, where the actual dependency is considerably later than receipt of the signed message, or where "receipt" is not obvious. Consider, for example, a digitally signed device driver, written onto a CD and packaged with the hardware. The real dependency of the signature is not when you buy the device, but when the CD was burned (though of course you don't know whether the signature was checked at that point). A compromise later is quite irrelevant; no hacker, no matter how good, can affect an already created CD. (On the other hand, the Andromedans can launch a *supply chain attack* and tamper with nominally sealed boxes of hardware, substituting their own CD for the genuine one. They've done it in the past.) Sure, you can check whether the certificate has been revoked before you install the device driver, but that isn't a meaningful operation unless you're somehow informed that $T_{compromise}$ was before the CD was created—and of course you can't know that. Note carefully that none of this analysis applies to downloaded device drivers; for those, the situation is similar to the email situation. After all, a clever attacker can easily replace a signed device driver on a vendor's web site.

Generally, attackers aren't trying to tamper with software you know you're installing. Rather, they're trying to take advantage of the implicit *authorization* that some operating systems attach to the *authentication* of files signed by certain CAs. That is, they'll silently install code if the file is signed by a certificate issued by any of a vast number of parties. Stuxnet took advantage of this [Falliere, Murchu, and Chien 2011; Zetter 2014]; there have been other reports of signed malware using the same technique [Bijl 2011; Goodin 2012b; Hypponen 2011; IIJ 2012] as well as at least one accidental key compromise

---

Are Digital Signatures Legally Binding?

The formal status of a digital signature—that is, of the output of a series of calculations that can only be performed or verified by a computer—is of course a legal matter, not a technological one. In the United States, such signatures are binding, both as a matter of common law and as explicitly codified in the *Electronic Signatures in Global and National Commerce Act* of 2000.[a]

A signature "whether electronic or on paper, is first and foremost a symbol that signifies intent" [Smedinghoff and Bro 1999]. Identifying the signer and ensuring the authenticity of the signed document are described as "secondary purposes." A legal opinion from the Comptroller-General [1991] notes that "Because of its uniqueness, the handwritten signature is probably the most universally accepted evidence of an agreement to be bound by the terms of a contract... Courts, however, have demonstrated a willingness to accept other notations, not necessarily written by hand." In general, then, there is no reason that a digital signature cannot be used.

However—this is, as noted, a legal matter, and there are often exceptions, caveats, and different rules in different jurisdictions. Before assuming that a digital signature is legally binding, consult your own attorney or logomancer.

---

a. "Public Law 106-229," http://www.gpo.gov/fdsys/pkg/PLAW-106publ229/content-detail.html.

[Goodin 2015c]. As noted in the box on page 82, there is speculation that 512-bit RSA keys were factored in at least one case; with Flame, a new cryptanalytic technique—applied to certificates using MD5, which the CA should not have accepted—was used. In the other cases, it seems more likely that the private key was stolen.

Looking at things more formally, what we really need to consider is the relationship between T_{revoke} and T_{rely}, the time when you *use* the certificate. Ideally, of course, $T_{rely} < T_{revoke}$. The complexities discussed above occur when $T_{revoke} < T_{rely}$; problematic uses include file installation, showing the signature to a judge, and more. Absent more information, dilemmas are inescapable. That, however, points to a solution: more information.

If the digital signature includes a trustworthy timestamp (this will generally be the case for signed software; if you don't trust your vendors to tell the truth about the time, why are you installing their code?), this value can be compared with $T_{compromise}$ when it is learned. (Of course, if it's a fraudulent software package, it *isn't* from the vendor you trust.) If vendors would do things like publish a time-stamped list of signatures they've created, you could compare your signed files with that list, and with $T_{compromise}$ if and when you learn of it. (Some companies prefer not to reveal that they've been hacked [Yadron 2014].) I know of no vendors who create such lists, and few who publish the results of forensic examinations, but perhaps that will change. Better yet, the vendors could let an outside party maintain the list; that's better for things that someone may want to show to a judge. (If done properly, publishing a signature list doesn't reveal any sensitive information. The list doesn't have to have the signature itself, let alone the file being signed; rather, it can be the cryptographic hash of the actual signature.)

Now consider what happens if $T_{expire} < T_{rely}$. Is using the certificate at that time safe? As before, there isn't enough information to decide; what we really need to know is the relationship of $T_{compromise}$ to $T_{signature}$. Conceptually, this means that one might want to revoke an expired certificate, if the compromise isn't detected until much later. This can happen; see [Naraine 2012] for one example. The existence of a revocation message is an explicit statement of danger, rather than the more generalized feeling of concern that expiration times are intended to handle. Think of it this way: certain diseases are more likely to occur as we age, even though they can occur earlier. However, this general warning—when you reach age X, get tested for such-and-such—is very different than a doctor looking at some test results and delivering the bad news. When there's bad news—when a certificate is known to have been compromised—that fact has to be communicated explicitly, so that you can take appropriate action.

What it comes to is that revocation is rarely used or usable on the Internet. The semantics are unclear, and the very different models for what it means to "use" a certificate means that the effects of such an action are often unpredictable.

One more point bears mentioning: none of the conceptual problems with revocation are related to the difference between PKI and PKI. Those have to do with trust patterns; revocation suffers from complex semantics. Moreover, the complexity is inherent in the problem statement; they are not an artifact of current designs. A PKI limits the damage from a compromised key; it doesn't change the very difficult reasoning about what to trust and when.

8.5 Analysis

What possible changes might affect the recommendations of this section?

The heart of the web PKI problem is the "let a hundred CAs bloom" approach of browser and OS vendors. It seems unlikely that they will change their policies; unless and until either certificate transparency or DANE are deployed, there are no secure alternatives for initial contact. Besides, this is The Way Things Are Done; we are dealing with the Deity of Inertia. Finally, the political implications of having only one root CA—one all-powerful entity that decides who can and who cannot do secure web interactions—make it an extremely unacceptable alternative.

Key continuity as an add-on is relatively simple to add; however, the key change or CA change scenarios must be dealt with. This is a challenging problem in user experience design. A good solution would present users with comprehensible information about the old and new CAs. I suspect that a perfect solution is an intractable problem; even understanding the question "do you want to trust this change in certificate authorities?" requires a far deeper understanding of PKI than most users have, want to have, or should have. There are browser add-ons (e.g., Certificate Patrol for Firefox) that provide such functionality for sophisticated users; indeed, key continuity checking is how the DigiNotar hack was detected. On the other hand, the number of (apparent?) false alarms is so great that I've disabled it on my computers.

Google has implemented key continuity in Chromium, its open-source operating system and browser. However, the feature announcement came with a warning [Evans 2011]:

> You can now force HTTPS for any domain you want, and even "pin" that domain so that only a more trusted subset of CAs are permitted to identify that domain.
>
> *It's an exciting feature but we'd like to warn that it's easy to break things! We recommend that only experts experiment with net internals settings.* [emphasis in the original.]

Their own sites are protected by default, and we can assume that they would push out an update in advance of any change in their own certificates or CAs. That isn't a solution that is generally applicable.

It would be nice if users could easily download a different collection of CAs from some source that they themselves trust. Enterprises would like this; it would permit easy tailoring of the list to include corporate CAs. There is a downside, though; repressive governments could use it to insert their own CA in the list, at least for browsers distributed within their countries. It also poses a new problem: how is that download to be authenticated? Most likely, every browser vendor would use its own, hard-wired CA to protect such downloads; they would then issue certificates to anyone who wanted to supply a CA list, being careful only to verify the identity of the supplier. There is no strong need to verify their trustworthiness, at least if you assume that people who download the MI-31 CA list are only doing so voluntarily.

There are two other models of certificates that bear mentioning, the *web of trust* and *simple public key infrastructure (SPKI)*. Both are significant steps away from the hierarchical, name-based approach of traditional certificate authorities.

The web of trust, used by the *Pretty Good Privacy (PGP)* mail encryptor [S. L. Garfinkel 1995; Lucas 2006; Zimmermann 1995], certifies name/key bindings via an arbitrary directed graph rather than a tree. There are no keys specifically designated for use by CAs; rather, every key is simultaneously usable for certificate signing and for actual data encryption or signing.

The advantage of the web of trust is that no infrastructure is necessary to start using it; you and your friends can generate keys and sign each others', and you're off and running. You don't have to worry about Andromedan-run CAs; you're trusting your friends. On a small scale, it works well; you can even view it as a form of PKI. Problems appear when you need to make more than one hop. You probably trust your friend to vouch for her friends' identities, but do you trust them as much? Their friends, whom you don't know even at one remove? Have you ever met a friend of a friend who seemed rather sketchy to you, enough so that you wondered why your friend associated with such a person? Scale that up a little and it becomes obvious that trust drops off very rapidly with distance.

Revocation is even more problematic in web-of-trust systems than in hierarchical CAs, since there is no single CRL to consult. There are some well-known PGP key servers, but these are generally used to obtain keys, not to revalidate currently stored keys.

SPKI [Ellison 1999; Ellison et al. 1999] takes a different, even less conventional approach to certificates: it's based solely on authorization, rather than identity. The certificate may contain the name of the putative holder, but that's more a convenience; presentation of the certificate gives the authorization information for the holder, and the private key is (of course) used for authentication. The name is never looked up in any sort of access control list. This decision was made for a number of reasons, most notably because of the difficulty of constructing a single global, unique name space. SPKI also includes the notion of delegation, and a number of set-theoretic operations on collections of certificates to decide whether a particular one provides authorization for a given service; see [Ellison et al. 1999] for details. It's an interesting model, and it has been used in a few situations; it's unclear, though, how well it would function at Internet scale.

It is important to realize that the thorny problems in this chapter—the need to trust many CAs, and the meaning of revocation—are conceptual problems that are inherent in the overall solution space. Simple changes in technology, such as a different hash function or switching to elliptic curve signatures, don't affect them at all; these problems are not susceptible to easy technical fixes. It will take major breakthroughs to find fundamentally different solutions, and a multi-year effort to deploy them.

Chapter 9

Wireless Access

"They do not use lasers, they do not use radio, they do not use hyperwave. What are they using for communication? Telepathy? Written messages? Big mirrors?"

"Parrots," Louis suggested. He got up to join them at the door to the control room. "Huge parrots, specially bred for their oversized lungs. They're too big to fly. They just sit on hilltops and scream at each other."

Ringworld
—LARRY NIVEN

9.1 Wireless Insecurity Myths

Among the stories that one hears is that wireless, and in particular 802.11 (AKA *Wi-Fi*), is inherently and horribly insecure. Is it? As is often the case, the answer is "it depends."

The way to understand the Wi-Fi problem is to realize that there are really four different issues: ability to talk to wireless hosts (which, in this chapter, I'll refer to as "host access"), ability of the attacker to get on the wireless network ("network access"), ability to eavesdrop on the packets being carried on the net ("content access"), and ability to do traffic analysis ("metadata access"). The first affects whether you let traveling employees use Wi-Fi; the other three are about whether your enterprise should use it. The four problems are quite different; different solutions are needed for each. Furthermore, there are two different classes of popular wireless technology, Wi-Fi and mobile phones; Wi-Fi can be internal or external, and tech toys (i.e., smart phones and tablets) tend to live in multiple worlds. Because of their dual nature, I'll defer discussion of toys to Section 9.4. (There are, of course, many other wireless technologies in use; however, with the possible exception of Bluetooth, few are serious computer security issues.)

Let's look at content access first. There is no doubt that eavesdropping on unencrypted Wi-Fi traffic is trivial. Wi-Fi's advertised operational range is 100 meters; however, with a suitable external antenna, considerably longer ranges than that are quite easily achievable. The canonical do-it-yourself Wi-Fi antenna is based on an empty Pringles can; plans are widely available on the Internet.

If the Andromedans are after you, though, a conventional, wired network may not be any better. Someone I once knew put it like this: "All those Ethernet cables you've run? You call them wires; I call them antennas."

If you're dealing with a lesser enemy, there is little doubt that an unencrypted Wi-Fi network is easier to eavesdrop on than a wired one. Wired networks are switched; for the most part, machines receive only packets intended for them. Although this can't be seen as a security measure, let alone a strong one—there are well-known attacks, and even without them some packets are flooded to all ports as part of normal operations—it certainly is a help. With a wireless net, there may be many hosts connected to each access point, which is the only device whose location you really know and to which traffic is filtered by the switch.

Perhaps more seriously, wireless extends the perimeter of your network for active users, letting someone outside your building appear as if they are actually on your LAN. In other words, content access and network access are far easier with wireless nets than wired. Although this would seem to be a significant defect, it is fairly easily countered with proper cryptography.

What applies to access to content applies to access to the network: if your network isn't properly protected, the lack of a physical perimeter is a serious issue. However, the differential advantage is a lot less than one might suspect when dealing with skilled enemies; an enemy who has compromised any single machine on your LAN has amazing powers.

By playing games with ARP, MAC spoofing, and the like, it's relatively easy for a rogue machine to divert traffic to itself. In one incident I saw (the boxed story on page 172), the attacker was able to spoof any machine on the LAN, as well as intercept any traffic. An open access point might be useful in achieving initial penetration (indeed, Gonzalez [Chapter 3] and company did use such techniques), but in many situations, there are many other ways, such as spear-phishing, to achieve the same goal.

In other words, wireless networks are indeed somewhat less secure than wired nets. However, the odds of a single-machine penetration of your LAN, especially by a targetier, are sufficiently high that one should not skimp on internal protection. "The machine is on my LAN" is good enough access control only for low-value resources.

Proper use of cryptography—WPA2 Personal and especially WPA2 Enterprise—is a very effective defense. Put simply, the cryptography here works; it does the job it's intended to do. In fact, in one way it is arguably better than an unencrypted wired net: outsiders with fancy antennas can't read the data. The details, though, do matter.

To associate with a WPA2-protected network, a node needs a cryptographic key. With WPA2 Enterprise, a login and authenticator (often, though not always, a password) are needed as well. Using these and some randomly generated values, a separate session key is generated for each user. This means that other nodes on the same net can't read the data. There are two important caveats here, though. First, with simple WPA2 Personal, an attacker who is on-net before a target node joins can overhear the key exchange dialog and can calculate the session key just as well as the target can; eavesdropping is thus possible. This sounds like it takes a sophisticated adversary; in fact, there are popular open-source tools that do just that. WPA2 Enterprise prevents the attack, since the user's secret authentication data is also part of the session key calculation. Second, WPA2 encryption is *link* encryption, that is, between the wireless access point and the nodes. Traffic deliberately sent to an attacker's node (perhaps in the wake of an ARP-spoofing attack) will be encrypted to it, not to the proper recipient, so it will be readable by the attacker. To protect against this sort of diversion attack, you need to encrypt at Layer 3 or above. That, however, is identical to what can happen on a wired net.

The conclusion is that WPA2 Enterprise is somewhat *better* than wired LANs against content access and network access attacks. This applies even to the Andromedans with their souped-up Pringles cantennas. Plain WPA2 is slightly weaker than wired LANs, since many more nodes are associated with a typical access point than with a port on a wired switch, so machines using the same access point can eavesdrop on each other.

On the other hand, wireless networks are significantly more vulnerable to metadata access attacks. Even with encryption, the source and destination MAC addresses of packets are sent in the clear; anyone within range can pick them up. Yes, the Andromedans can do the same to a wired net, but it takes rather more unusual equipment. This is probably not an issue, though, for most enterprises; metadata access is rarely of interest to any threat level short of an APT (though even the lower grades of APTs will do it), and even though the bad guys gain some advantage from tackling a wireless net, doing so still requires reasonable proximity. Most attackers would probably find it easier to hack into a router or network management station and capture the NetFlow data.

The situation is rather different for external, public Wi-Fi nets. Here, use of encryption is extremely rare; the nets are, after all, *public*, and expecting Joe Sixclick, the proverbial mouse potato, to turn on encryption when visiting a local hotspot is simply not realistic.

An Active Attacker

Some years ago, my department's system administration group was notified by the campus network security people that one of our machines was infected: it was doing an address space scan across campus, trying to find vulnerable machines. Things like that happen; it's unfortunate, but it's hardly a surprise if a random desktop machine has been taken over. This one, though, was a shocker: it was the departmental FTP server, a tightly administered machine. Naturally, it was immediately shut down. Some hours later, the campus folks inquired why nothing had been done...

The sysadmins checked: it was powered off. To be sure, they physically pulled the plug and the network cable. "Still scanning?" "Yes..."

At this point, it seemed like a case of IP address spoofing, which is pretty easy for an on-net attacker. They checked the ARP tables, only to discover that the proper MAC address was being used. MAC address spoofing, though also easy, is much rarer, because MAC addresses aren't normally logged by hosts, and hence are of much less utility in network forensics. Fortunately, the campus networking people keep very detailed histories of the Ethernet switch management data. With the help of those histories, we were able to determine that the actual attacking machine was in another building entirely. Furthermore, it had been spoofing many different department hosts, at the MAC and IP layers, for at least six months. The final irony: the compromised machine was a small firewall... (When we cleaned up that firewall and some desktop boxes that were also compromised, the attacker retaliated by launching a denial of service attack against the department. How *dare* we take away his (her) toys!)

(I've seen published suggestions that hotspot login pages tell users to reconfigure to an alternate network name with a public WPA2 key. I strongly suspect that the people making such suggestions have never run any network larger than their own houses'. How much free customer care can you afford when your real business is selling coffee?) Network access is not a concern, of course, but access to content is much greater than on a typical switched network; as discussed below, use of a VPN or application-level encryption is absolutely mandatory. There is one area of concern to some network operators: the ease of sniffing MAC addresses complicates access control at paid hotspots; unscrupulous users can pick up addresses of people who have paid for the service and piggyback on them. (That's a bit more complicated than it sounds; see [Clayton 2005] for some details.)

What about danger to the hosts themselves? Are they at more risk on wireless nets than wired? The answer is a qualified "no."

For encrypted internal Wi-Fi networks, there is strong access control; thus, there should be no new attackers present. There is one more moving part—the key negotiation component—and it's quite conceivable that some implementations have exploitable security holes. I haven't seen any reported, but given how many other network entities have proved vulnerable it would be foolish to assume that it can't happen. Still, at this point at least the incremental risk seems to be low.

External networks are another matter. Attackers who set up fake access points or who play ARP games can capture content. If you're cautious, it should all be encrypted, so you shouldn't have any problems. Alas, there are complications.

The ideal form of encryption on a public network is a VPN, with all traffic going back to somewhere safe. In fact, what we really want to do is to lock down our hosts sufficiently well that they won't emit anything unencrypted. That turns out to be hard; most hotspots want your browser to talk to a login session first; often, you have to pay, and they want to show you more ads [Seltzer 2015]. (Most also want you to agree to a long laundry list of terms and conditions that their lawyers drew up, though even some prominent judges don't bother reading that kind of verbiage [Weiss 2010].) Perhaps more seriously, using encryption in such scenarios requires proper bilateral authentication; all too many software packages and users get this wrong. Besides, as discussed in Chapter 8, getting it right can be quite hard. The risk, then, is low under good conditions—proper software and well-trained users—but noticeable under other conditions.

Because outsiders—your potential enemies—have access to the same wireless net as you do, mobile hosts may also be at risk in two different ways. First, access to some of your traffic may enable an attack. It shouldn't—you should be using a VPN—but as noted, there is generally a brief period when that just isn't feasible, even if everything else is set up properly. Can a sophisticated attacker who fakes a login page send your browser nasty stuff via a drive-by download? It's almost certainly possible, though it's hard to assess the odds. The second risk is network scanning attacks: attacks intended to learn what hosts are present and what services these hosts are listening for. These are, of course, possible against wired nets, assuming that your attacker knows your IP address. Proper IPsec software should reject non-VPN packets; it isn't clear that all implementations do so properly, and some other types of VPN don't even try.

The real danger from use of external networks, wired or wireless, may be indirect. Suppose that a machine does become infected. The real risk is when that machine comes home and connects to your organizational network: will they bring the infection home? For that matter, if they only use their VPNs part of the time, will the infection traverse the tunnel when they do set it up? The incremental risks seem somewhat less today than a few years ago (possibly because machines are as likely to be infected from inside-your-walls web browsing and email as they are when traveling), but if you're worried about APTs and your employees are visiting Andromeda, special precautions may be indicated. Indeed, there are people who bring "burner laptops" with them when traveling to some countries, and they leave their smart phones home [Perlroth 2012]. The inconvenience is considerable, but so, apparently, is the threat.

Another way to look at the issue is to consider the Wi-Fi threats posed by our different classes of attackers. We will assume WPA2 for internal nets and no encryption for external ones.

Joy hackers If they're geographically very close (i.e., within 100 meters), they can use a wireless net more easily. Joy hackers are the group most easily defeated by Wi-Fi encryption.

Opportunistic attackers Random attackers, by definition, aren't likely to be particularly close in the physical world, so there is little difference in risk. You might stumble on one at a public hotspot; again, you want to use VPNs there in any event.

Targetiers Targetiers are the most interesting case. Many will have ways to penetrate at least one machine on your LAN. Some, in fact, will be disgruntled insiders and hence already have access. While they may also seek to gain initial entry via poorly protected wireless nets, they can do so much damage once they're on the inside that simple external access control will do little. In other words, there is little differential security for a Wi-Fi net.

On the other hand, poorly secured Wi-Fi nets have been entry points in the past. Again, though, WPA2 is a strong defense against network access attacks on internal nets; the more interesting question is host access attacks against roaming devices.

MI-31 There is little that can be done to prevent eavesdropping by the Andromedans; ubiquitous cryptography, at all layers, is the best answer. Although the use of Wi-Fi encryption will help deflect one entry point to your net, they have many other ways in. Wi-Fi does make metadata access easier, which they may find to be a significant advantage.

In other words, the usual recommendation for wireless security (using Wi-Fi encryption) is quite effective against most threats. If the Andromedans are not in your threat model, there is no reason to eschew wireless connectivity; the precautions you have to take on any network are more than sufficient to deflect common wireless threats.

There is one more aspect of wireless security that is rarely mentioned, but is familiar to many system administrators: finding the offending host when there's a problem. If you use managed switches (and except possibly for in-room use, an enterprise should use nothing else), and if you have good records about which switch ports are connected to which jacks, localization is easy: map the offending IP address to a MAC address, map it to a switch port, and look up the offender's location. (That's what was done in the story on page 172.) Except under unusual circumstances, that's much harder in a wireless world. Even without snack food container antennas, the range of an access point can be up to 100 meters; that's a lot of area to search for a malefactor, especially if the malefactor is actually a piece of malware living unsuspected on someone's machine.

What can you do? Sometimes, there are special circumstances. I recall one conference where nasty stuff was coming from someone's laptop. We knew from the switch logs which access point was involved; given the layout of the network, we were fairly certain what room the offending machine was in. Someone ping-flooded the machine, while someone else wandered around looking for the combination of a brightly lit indicator LED and the bewildered face of someone wondering why he suddenly couldn't get out to the net. . .

There are more general techniques, of course. Tao et al. describe using RF signal strength to localize machines within a few meters [2003], though it seems likely that directional antennas would defeat their scheme [Wallach 2011]. Generally speaking, the easiest thing to do is to blacklist the offender's MAC address; if it's an innocent party's infected machine, they'll complain soon enough. Better yet, put it on a separate VLAN, where any web page they try to visit tells them what's going on and how to get help. Some universities do that, especially for student machines in dorm rooms.[1] That won't block a skilled attacker who can change the machine's MAC address, but even pros can forget to do that [Williams 2010].

9.2 Living Connected

As we've seen, Wi-Fi is acceptably secure for internal use if proper cryptography is used. Let's take a deeper look at Wi-Fi link encryption. All Wi-Fi devices come with the ability to encrypt traffic. It costs little and should generally be turned on. However, there are different flavors of crypto available; which one you select matters a great deal.

The oldest form of Wi-Fi encryption, *Wired Equivalent Privacy (WEP)* is all but useless and should be avoided [Borisov, Goldberg, and Wagner 2001; Stubblefield, J. Ioannidis, and Rubin 2002; Stubblefield, J. Ioannidis, and Rubin 2004]. It has no redeeming virtues save for backwards compatibility with ancient hardware; any device manufac-

---

1. "PaIRS: Point of contact and Incident Response System," http://goo.gl/xhroc.

tured since, I suspect, the late Cretaceous period should support something better. WEP is a poor implementation of a weak cipher (RC4); in addition, it has the key distribution weakness discussed below.

There are two newer encryption standards, WPA and WPA2. WPA will run on older hardware; however, it generally uses RC4, which means that it can be cracked in about an hour [Vanhoef and Piessens 2015]. When available, WPA2 should be used. (If it's not available on some of your gear, upgrade the hardware and/or the OS; something that old probably has other security weaknesses as well.)

Any time you use cryptography, key management is a crucial question. Even apart from the cryptanalytic weaknesses of RC4, which were not known at the time WEP was designed, the architects made a very serious blunder: every authorized device has to have the same key. This in turn has two important consequences: first, departure of an employee or loss of any single device (a phone, a laptop, etc.) compromises the key for everyone, necessitating an immediate key change; second, *when* this happens it's extremely difficult to change the key in an organization of any size, since every device and access point have to be rekeyed more or less simultaneously, including the keys in gadgets belonging to telecommuters and road warriors, as well as the 12,345.67 nodes of yours that are currently out for repair. In a practical sense, this is impossible for organizations much larger than a family.

The right answer is enterprise mode. With it (and, to be sure, a RADIUS server), every user has a separate login. Individual keys can be revoked without interrupting connectivity for everyone else. You may think that setting up a RADIUS server is unnecessary work— but the first time you have to change a widely shared key, you'll wish you had done it. Besides, you probably need RADIUS anyway, for other access control decisions.

WEP: A Case Study in Bad Crypto

From a security perspective, WEP is all but useless and shouldn't be used. This advice is widely accepted, though not necessarily widely followed. (Sitting here in my house, I see 12 of my neighbors' networks. Nine use WEP, two use WPA2—and one is wide open. . . .) But how did WEP get that bad? It turns out that the flaw that finally impelled vendors to act was the only one that wasn't avoidable.

What were the problems with WEP?

- As noted, there's no key management. There was supposed to be, but according to rumor the standards group felt that that was a problem for another layer and hence another group—but it never happened.

- WEP uses RC4, a stream cipher. Stream ciphers, though, are a very bad match for an unreliable datagram network like Wi-Fi; they assume a reliable byte stream. To partially compensate for this, a so-called *initialization vector (IV)*—actually, a packet counter used as part of the key—is employed. But it's too small (only 24 bits), which causes collisions, which in turn lead to the very well-known problem of a stream cipher used to encrypt two different plaintexts with the same key. Decryption by the attacker becomes trivial. (More details on this issue can be found in [Borisov, Goldberg, and Wagner 2001].)

- Stream ciphers, when employed without authentication, permit predictable changes to received plaintext. This, too, can be employed to read the plaintext and to do all sorts of other nasty things. (Again, see [Borisov, Goldberg, and Wagner 2001].)

- RC4, despite its use on the web for many years, turned out to have a serious cryptanalytic weakness: it's vulnerable to *related-key attacks* [Stubblefield, J. Ioannidis, and Rubin 2002]. That is, if the attacker can intercept two or more packets whose keys differ in only a few bits, it's possible to cryptanalyze the cipher. While susceptibility to related-key attacks is considered a serious theoretical weakness in a cipher design, it rarely matters in practice; the key management layer normally prevents that. But not only does WEP not have a key management layer, the IV design *guarantees* the existence of many related keys. No one could have predicted the flaw in RC4; however, it could be turned into an attack on WEP [Stubblefield, J. Ioannidis, and Rubin 2002] only because of the other, avoidable design errors.

Why did these mistakes occur? The fundamental issue was cost, especially when Wi-Fi was first introduced: RC4 is very cheap, so it could run fast enough on low-end hardware. That, coupled with insufficient attention to the operational model and the threat model, led to the design decision. We are still paying for that mistake today, long after cheap, fast encryption hardware became readily available.

For external use, there is, of course, no access control. What then? As noted, the most important defense is a VPN. Always enable triangle mode (and disregard complaints about performance—but if you're a large, multinational corporation, give your employees access to all of your VPN nodes around the globe, unless some quirk of local laws makes that undesirable). Pay a lot of attention to bilateral authentication, in software you buy, in software you develop, and in user education and training.

It pays, of course, to ask who the threats are in this environment. With very few exceptions—some hypothetical Big Ear Bar outside a SIGINT agency, where off-duty spooks go to drink after work, or perhaps a conference or trade show at which some company will always have a significant presence—targetiers are rarely causes for concern here; there are just too many places for such an enemy to cover to have any real chance of success. MI-31 is of course a threat; knowing where employees of their targets tend to be is part of their stock in trade. Still, this is an expensive attack, even for them, since it requires people to be physically present for just the right amount of time—too little time and they'll miss their targets; too much and they'll stand out and be suspicious, especially to the counterintelligence folks who also hang out at the Big Ear Bar.

The biggest risk, then, is the opportunistic attacker, someone sophisticated enough to create fake access points complete with nastyware. While they're good, they don't come one per hotspot; the odds on encountering one are reasonably low. In other words—and if you're not being targeted by Andromedan agents—ordinary care (fully patched systems, VPNs, antivirus protection if indicated) and no more than the usual allotment of luck will keep you safe enough that excess paranoia isn't necessary.

9.3   Living Disconnected

> Now, there are few existential crises as unnerving for a geek like me (the original feral kind...) as being off the net.
>
> *The Apocalypse Codex*
> —Charles Stross

Suppose you think random Wi-Fi is too risky. What then? Are there risks you incur by eschewing it?

It's trite but true to observe that availability is generally considered a security property; thus, not being online for fear of Wi-Fi is by definition a problem. That may very well be; however, engineering is the art of picking the right trade-off in an overconstrained environment, and it's perfectly reasonable to decide that some (presumably small) sacrifice of availability is a better, if imperfect, choice. Are there more threats?

One issue is access to security updates. Sometimes, problems are urgent; indeed, as I was writing this section a news blog ran a story headlined, "Attention all Windows users: patch your systems now: A critical IE vulnerability Microsoft patched Tuesday is under active exploit" [Goodin 2012a]. A delay in installing a patch can be serious, especially for folks who are willing to insert others' USB drives.

If, as an organization, you still prefer to avoid Wi-Fi, keep it turned off on all laptops. Better yet, have the hardware surgically removed. Do NOT use Wi-Fi internally while barring it externally; it's just too easy for an attacker to set up a fake hotspot bearing your own organization's network identifier [Legnitto 2012], at which point employee laptops will automatically associate.

It is important to consider the organizational culture, personnel training, and actual usage demands before making such decisions. If the job demands some way to exchange files or deal with web sites or email when out of the office, most people *will* find some way to do that, be it flash drives, personal devices (with *your* data loaded onto them), and more. You may find that in reality, you're taking a greater risk by barring Wi-Fi than if you figured out how to lock down machines against all network threats.

There's one more point to consider, and it goes to the heart of this book's theme: is living disconnected worth it? Employees have laptops and network connections because there's a *business* need for such things, and not just to provide them with recreation in lonely hotel rooms or a cheap way to make a video call home. As always, the proper question is not "is Wi-Fi access safe?"; rather, it's "is the benefit to the business from having connectivity greater than or less than the incremental risk?"

9.4   Smart Phones, Tablets, Toys, and Mobile Phone Access

More and more people are carrying smart phones, tablets, iToys, and other forms of very portable connectivity. These devices can typically talk over both mobile phone and Wi-Fi networks. Are they safe?

The whole *Bring Your Own Device (BYOD)* issue is quite complex; I'll address other aspects of it in later chapters. For now, though, let's focus on connectivity.

When in Wi-Fi mode, the connectivity issues are, of course, the same as for any other device. When outside, though, toys will fall back to mobile phone networking. Indeed, depending on the vagaries of your access points and the Wi-Fi geography of your building, this can even happen when inside the office. As a consequence, toys, more than most devices, live in both worlds, and have to be able to function that way. In particular, access to essential resources, especially email, need to be readily and transparently available no matter where the toy is or which network it is using. The most secure way to accomplish this is via a VPN.

For phones in particular, it is often reasonable to bar outside Wi-Fi use; most emails that people will actually deal with on a phone are short enough that downloading over a phone network only is not a hardship. Folks will gripe (and often with good reason), but it's a trade-off worth considering. The big exception, of course, is for people who travel internationally; international data roaming prices are generally extremely high.

Of course, we haven't yet answered the question of whether mobile phone data networks are safe (or safe enough, or safer than Wi-Fi). Are they? Let's look at the same four categories.

For most people, including most attackers, it's a lot harder to intercept or modify phone traffic than Wi-Fi. Governments, though, including that of Andromeda, have already solved that problem; they have fake base stations that can trick phones and mobile hotspots into associating with them instead of with the real network [Department of Justice 2005; B. Heath 2015; Strobel 2007; Valentino-DeVries 2011]. In other words, the defensive technique fails against precisely the same class of enemy who can generally defeat Wi-Fi security. (If you still prefer this technology to Wi-Fi and want to connect from your laptop, make sure you use a dedicated USB modem instead of a portable Bluetooth- or Wi-Fi-connected hotspot. Why expand your attack surface?)

Traffic on mobile phone networks is generally encrypted these days. While the encryption isn't that strong [Biryukov, Shamir, and Wagner 2001]—indeed, the claim has been made that it was deliberately weakened by governments—it is strong enough that it's not the weak point in your defenses. Sure, MI-31 can cryptanalyze it, but they're the same folk who have the fake base stations or who can gain access to the wired part of the cellular network. In addition, the encryption is probably a good enough defense against metadata access to data packets.

We don't have to worry about the security of access to mobile phone networks. That's generally the concern of the carriers; very few organizations run their own such nets. All that said, it's pretty good; there are few technical attacks on phone authentication these days.

To sum up: mobile phone networks are reasonably safe against attackers short of APT status. The toys themselves carry some risks, but as noted I'll discuss those in Chapter 15 and Chapter 16.

9.5 Analysis

To provide coverage of 95 percent of the UK population we require a total of 8 million digitally networked CCTV cameras (terminals). Terminals in built-up areas may be connected via the public switched telephone network using SDSL/VHDSL, but outlying systems may use mesh network routing over 802.11a to ensure that rural areas do not provide a pool of infectious carriers for demonic possession.

The Atrocity Archives
—CHARLES STROSS

As can be seen from Table 9.1, the incremental risks from Wi-Fi are not great. There is some extra danger to mobile nodes, but this is often manageable, especially if you use VPNs and don't have to deal with annoying web login pages. (Those of you who realized that there should really be a 3-dimensional table, to match our threat categories, get an extra gold star on your copy of the book. I covered that in the text; besides, I don't think that having four different, near-identical tables would help comprehensibility.)

Inside an organization, WPA2 and especially WPA2 Enterprise are very effective forms of network control, if access to the network key is properly controlled. There is some risk if a device is stolen, but only until the affected login is disabled or its password changed. Of course, you can only do that with WPA2 Enterprise, but that's one reason you want to run it. Another risk is a rogue employee deliberately sharing her or his credentials, but the danger of folks setting up external tunnels is almost as great.

Looking at the table, the two areas of most concern are access to content and risks to the host when on external Wi-Fi nets. Both seem amenable to fixes. For the former, a well-implemented VPN should solve the problem. Most of the risks to the host come from the lack of such protection, especially when dealing with login screens. Those login screens won't go away; the reasons for their existence are not primarily technical. (There's already an IEEE standard for network authentication and access, 802.1x. I've encountered it exactly once, at an IETF meeting, and of course the IETF prefers to do things in a nice, standardized way. Most sites prefer to hijack an HTTP session.) A sandboxed browser, though, would help, especially if that browser were crippled in such a way as to prevent typing in a URL; that way, it could only talk to a fixed URL, and thus elicit the login screen. In the future, then, we should be able to switch those two entries to ✓. (Exercise for the reader: why do I say that this browser should be crippled?) This question is discussed in more detail in Chapter 10.

✦   ✦   ✦

Let's take a deeper look at the suggestion from Chapter 5 that mobile devices should live outside the firewall because of their risk of infection. If they're to be useful at all, the devices have to have access to some enterprise resources. That has security implications. What are they, and what can we do to minimize adverse consequences? Email is a good case study, since it's more or less a minimal requirement for device users. We need to consider both the high-level requirements and implementation-level attacks.

First, it's obvious that email connections need to be encrypted. It would be good to use a special VPN for this, but few devices support VPNs for some protocols but not others. As noted above, it's difficult to live in a pure VPN environment.

The other way to do it is to encrypt just the email protocols: SMTP for sending; IMAP and POP3 for reading. Fortunately, all of them support *Transport Layer Security (TLS)* (Chapter 6). TLS is quite secure, but it uses *public key infrastructure (PKI)* technology (Chapter 8), which carries certain risks unless handled and implemented very carefully. Certificate pinning would work well here, but few, if any, email clients support that. Unfortunately, some TLS implementations, notably OpenSSL, have quite a mixed security reputation; see, for example, [Baxter-Reynolds 2014; Bellovin 2014c; Ducklin 2014] on the goto fail bug or [Andrade 2014; Bellovin 2014b; Schneier 2014] on Heartbleed. It is worth considering moving your mail servers to be outside the firewall. More precisely, they may be better off in a DMZ where they can be reached from both the inside and the outside; this will limit the consequences to the rest of the organization if one is compromised.

Authentication is a second problem: attackers could launch online password-guessing attacks against the mail server. There are several obvious counters here: rate-limiting of guesses, strong email passwords, and so on. A better solution is cryptographic authentication, either as the sole form of authentication or as an adjunct to conventional password authentication. Client-side certificates—issued by the email service PKI, not a PKI—work well here; they provide strong authentication at the TLS level. If the client does not have

Table 9.1: The wireless security problems matrix. The symbol ✓ indicates "secure" (or rather, "about as secure as a wired LAN"), ✗ indicates "insecure," and ? means "it's complicated." A wired LAN is the standard for comparison. For internal Wi-Fi nets, assume WPA2 or WPA2 Enterprise.

	Access Type			
	Hosts	*Network*	*Content*	*Traf. Anal.*
Internal Wi-Fi	✓	✓	✓	✗
External (public) Wi-Fi	?	N/A	✗	✗
Mobile phone	✓	N/A	✓	✓

the proper certificate, it can't get to the SMTP or IMAP level, and hence can't launch password-guessing attacks or attacks against the implementations. It sounds great; unfortunately, support for client-side certificates is also lacking today.

I've carefully omitted one class of scenarios: a compromised or captured mobile device being used to attack the mail server, or even simply to retrieve email improperly. While those are certainly risks with mobile devices, they are not unique to external mail servers. If we insisted that mobile devices create a VPN to get inside the firewall before retrieving email, the risks would be greater, not less; not only would the email be at risk, but so would everything else inside the firewall. Indeed, it is precisely this situation that leads me to suggest moving email outside the firewall.

The same sort of analysis can be applied to other protocols. The requirements are straightforward: ubiquitous encryption, bilateral authentication, and cryptographic authentication. Web servers are the other class where this can be done fairly easily, if only there were a good solution to the PKI problem.

Chapter 10

Clouds and Virtualization

She had never driven through the clouds. It was an adventure that always she had longed to experience. The wind was strong and it was with difficulty that she maneuvered the craft from the hangar without accident, but once away it raced swiftly out above the twin cities. The buffeting winds caught and tossed it, and the girl laughed aloud in sheer joy of the resultant thrills. She handled the little ship like a veteran, though few veterans would have faced the menace of such a storm in so light a craft. Swiftly she rose toward the clouds, racing with the scudding streamers of the storm-swept fragments, and a moment later she was swallowed by the dense masses billowing above.

The Chessmen of Mars
—EDGAR RICE BURROUGHS

10.1 Distribution and Isolation

Two seemingly disparate technologies have gained increasing attention in recent years, cloud computing and *virtual machines (VMs)*. The only way to improve the buzzword level of a virtualized, cloud-enabled system is to add that other au courant word, "ecosystem," to it. Though the mechanisms are not precisely new—VM technology dates back to the 1960s [Meyer and Seawright 1970], and those of us of a certain technical age have to squint to differentiate "the cloud" from the time-sharing service bureaus of the same era—their importance has increased dramatically in recent years. Most of the attention has been on the economic and functionality impact of cloud services, albeit with much handwringing about its supposed insecurity.

Virtualization, on the other hand, has been hailed as the solution to security problems, ranging from sandboxing desktop apps to protection in the cloud. Even virus scanning, it is said, can be improved by VM architectures.

From a broader perspective, the two can be seen as complementary. The cloud seemingly creates new security problems, while virtualization solves them. Is this an accurate summary? Not quite. Each has a sphere of action that the other doesn't impinge on; in those places, the two are completely independent. Furthermore, even where they do interact the risks and benefits are not one-sided; cloud services have security advantages even without virtualization, and VMs can have their own set of risks.

In most situations, cloud computing is based on VM technology; I'll therefore discuss virtualization first.

10.2 Virtual Machines

The basic concept of virtualization is simple: Take an ordinary, off-the-shelf operating system, and, instead of running it in privileged mode on real hardware, run it as a user program in virtual address space provided by the *hypervisor*. When the *guest OS* attempts to execute a privileged instruction, it instead traps to the hypervisor, which examines the intended instruction and emulates it. Thus, if the virtualized OS is trying to write a block of memory to a disk drive, the hypervisor will take that block and schedule it to be written somewhere appropriate: a physical drive dedicated to that guest, a file taking the place of a disk drive, or even a network connection to a storage server. When the operation is complete, the hypervisor simulates an interrupt to the guest machine. Modern machines have special architectures and instructions to make this more efficient, but the basic concept is still the same.

As well as emulating privileged instructions, the hypervisor creates and destroys VMs, allocates and manages resources of the underlying hardware (e.g., disk, RAM, CPU time), separates different VMs from each other, and so on. It has an interface (sometimes command line, sometimes graphical) to let users control such actions, and to do things like press the virtual reset button. There are also *hypervisor calls* (*hypercalls*) that allow VMs to make explicit requests; these might be for things like copy and paste between the guest OS and the underlying system.

Consider this in light of the virtual instruction set and effective target environment concepts introduced in Chapter 4. The virtual instruction set presented to the guest OS includes all of the real hardware instructions, emulated if necessary, as well as the facilities made available by hypercalls. The effective target environment is the set of physical or virtual resources allocated to it by the hypervisor. If this sounds familiar, it should; it is quite clear that a hypervisor *is* an operating system, and can even have its own privilege escalation vulnerabilities (see, for example, [CERT 2012]). (Although today's VMs generally consist of a few extra kernel and user-level modules on a familiar OS such as Windows or Linux, it doesn't have to be done that way. In fact, the very first VM hypervisor, CP-67 [Meyer and Seawright 1970], was extremely specialized and provided none of the facilities commonly associated with an OS. It didn't even have a file system; through at least the early 1980s, system administrators creating user VMs had to manually specify absolute ranges of disk cylinders to be assigned to each virtual disk.)

In most typical configurations, individual VMs are strongly separated from each other; this is the property that has led some people to propose that VM technology is the solution to our security woes. This is at best partly true, and even the part that is true will hold only under certain circumstances.

A guest OS is, of course, an OS; guest Windows is Windows, guest Linux is Linux, and so on. These do not magically become less vulnerable because of the existence of a hypervisor between them and the silicon; an SQL injection attack against a virtualized web server will succeed or fail in the same way as it would on the same configuration and server without a hypervisor. The same care is necessary, the same feeding is necessary, and the same patches are necessary. In fact, if nothing else in the environment changes, VMs can be *less* secure because the sudden increase in the number of operating systems can create a very large bump in the system administration load.

On the other hand, the isolation between guest VMs on a single box is much stronger than the isolation between two different users on a conventional OS; as such, the effective target environment for any malware is less. A VM can thus help contain an intrusion. This breaks down, however, when VM technology is used as a *sandbox* technology (see Section 10.3) for user applications. The trouble is that there needs to be too many interactions and connections. A virtualized web browser still needs to be able to save downloaded files and pass mailto: URLs to the mailer; a virtualized mailer needs to talk to the web browser to handle embedded URLs, etc. The degree of protection provided by virtualization in that kind of environment can be quite limited [Bellovin 2006b].

At best, a VM is about the equivalent of letting your enemy have a machine in a rack in your data center. Even without the added risks of cache timing attacks and bugs allowing escape from the virtualized environment, this is probably not the sort of thing you'd be enthusiastic about. On the other hand, if the network connectivity from that machine were limited, say by VLANs and/or internal firewalls, the incremental risk is low.

If a hypervisor is just an OS, why should it be more secure than a conventional OS? After all, an ordinary operating system is supposed to separate different users' programs from each other; why, if these fail, should one think that a VM architecture will succeed?

The answer is the nature of the virtual instruction set. From the perspective of the hypervisor, there are very, very few (and perhaps no) privileged operations, which in turn means there are very, very few (and perhaps no) opportunities for mistakes. Yes, there are resource access requests, for example, attaching a virtual disk drive, but these are generally done by the VM's operator using its command interface; the VM itself may not have the ability to make such requests, valid or not.

A related reason is the absence of privileged VMs. Historically, very few security holes have been in the kernel (though this is changing); rather, they've been due to buggy applications that are either tricked into abusing their privileges or are themselves exploited. Exploitation of a VM, though, is a guest OS issue and with no VMs having any special abilities there is no way to trick one into misusing its powers.

The strong separation provides for another advantage: the hypervisor can do intrusion detection and virus scanning of the guest OSs without fear of interference from a successful attack. Such interference is quite common, ranging from simple measures—adding entries to /etc/hosts to direct virus signature update requests to the wrong place to sophisticated rootkits, collections of programs and tools that hide intrusions. My favorite example involved a sabotaged version of /sbin/init, traditionally process 1 on Unix-like systems. This program is invoked from the kernel at boot time; all other processes on the system are direct or indirect descendants of it. Naturally, a simple scan for changed files (e.g., by Tripwire [G. Kim and Spafford 1994a; G. Kim and Spafford 1994b; G. Kim and Spafford 1994c]) would detect the modified version of /sbin/init, so it took precautions: it modified the kernel's file system code to include a module that looked for requests to open /sbin/init. If the processID was 1—that is, if it was the OS itself trying to boot and hence invoke init—the hacked version was loaded. All other requests, including Tripwire's, would get the original, unmodified version.

Putting the scanner in the host OS solves this problem if we assume that the infection cannot spread. If the IDS knows a lot about the setup of the VM and knows something about the guest OS, it can do the scans. There are difficulties, but they can be surmounted; see, for one example, [T. Garfinkel and Rosenblum 2003].

10.3 Sandboxes

Sandboxing, sometimes known as *jailing*, is a class of techniques designed to limit the access rights—the effective target environment—of a program. The intent, of course, is to limit the damage that that program can do if it is evil, infected, or subverted. The concept has been around for many years. Bill Cheswick used a jail (and apparently coined the usage) when we were monitoring the attacker he dubbed "Berferd" [Cheswick 1992; Cheswick 2010; Cheswick and Bellovin 1994]. Cheswick's fundamental isolation primitive was chroot(), a system call that has been in Unix since the late 1970s. Sandboxing has become of much more interest in the last few years, since both Microsoft and Apple have made it a central part of their desktop architectures, most notably for browsers but also for other high-risk applications.

Quite a variety of mechanisms have been used to implement sandboxes. For our purposes here, though, those details aren't important. From an architectural perspective, there are three interesting questions:

1. What restrictions are imposed on the sandboxed program? Alternatively, what sensitive resources are still accessible?

2. What is the granularity of exceptions to the general restrictions?

3. How easy is it to use correctly, that is, how hard is it to configure and maintain?

Naturally, the questions interact. VMs, for example, restrict more or less every form of access, but they're hard to maintain (you have an entire extra OS to patch). Similarly, fine-grained security policies require a lot of detailed work to understand exactly what resources are needed; this provides a lot of flexibility, but it's easy to get it wrong. If you restrict too much, you may find that under unusual circumstances the application doesn't run; restrict too little and you create security holes. Leaving some of the decisions to system administrators or (worse yet) end users is generally an invitation to trouble.

In practice, strong isolation is relatively easy: put the suspect code on a VM. Apart from the maintenance issues, the isolation is often too strong; it's too hard to share information, even aside from the problem of creating the policy specification. This strong isolation alone is why VMs are not good general-purpose sandboxes.

There are two issues with sharing items across the boundary of the sandbox. The first, as noted, is the policy specification issue. The second is more subtle: there is now a communications channel between the untrusted application and the outside world. You have to be extremely suspicious of anything coming out of the sandbox; conceptually, that program is under the control of your enemy (and of course, the more skillful your enemy is the more you have to worry). Consider just a simple bidirectional stream. This is *exactly* equivalent to a network connection, but we already know that nasty things can happen via Internet connections; streams from the sandbox are no better. The situation almost feels like the Schrödinger's cat experiment [Trimmer 1980]: until you look at the sandboxed process, in some sense nothing has happened—but here, it's the observer who may end up dead instead of the cat.

For a case study, let's look back at my suggestion at the end of Chapter 9, that the signon to a public wireless network be done via a sandboxed browser. Why would a sandbox help? More importantly, what sort of sandbox is appropriate? What sort of communication to and from the sandbox is necessary?

The risk we were worried about was unpleasant things happening to a roaming laptop on a public wireless network. A strict VPN, where all outbound traffic was encrypted and no inbound traffic was accepted if it were not cryptographically protected, was the solution I suggested. However, that left no way to sign on to the public network, so I suggested a sandboxed browser.

Assuming that the VPN does its job, the specific issue is what can happen to the sandboxed browser. That suggests one characteristic of the sandbox: it should permit no other network I/O than by the browser and its utterly necessary adjuncts, such as DNS queries. It would be nice if the browser itself were minimally configured, with no Java, no JavaScript, no Flash, and so on, but that's not realistic; too many login screens need one or both of the latter two. Still, the network capabilities of the sandbox should be strictly limited.

Another characteristic is that to a first approximation, we don't need any output from the sandbox; that tremendously improves security. Unfortunately, that is just a first approximation; there are many strange and wondrous varieties of login systems. As Ted Lemon has noted, "The ingenuity that is applied to breaking the Internet by hotel Internet providers is genuinely inspiring. If only they would use their powers for good...."[1] I've seen screens where the first login attempt gives you a password you need for subsequent uses. I've seen pop-up windows that give live countdown timers for your session; if you close that window, you're assumed to have logged off. I've seen screens that show your credit card receipt, which you really need to save to be reimbursed for the expenditure. The details vary, but it seems clear that some way to save the output from such a session, if only as an image file, is necessary. Though not ideal, it is still reasonably safe.

The third characteristic, though, is more problematic: the browser may need access to your password manager (Chapter 7). Often, you're logging on to a network run by a service provider for which you have an account; that account needs a password, and of course you want your password manager to keep track of it for you. How should you implement this?

The wrong answer is to run your regular password manager in the sandbox. Doing so would imply that an untrusted environment—the browser that's running in the sandbox precisely because it's doing dangerous things—should have access to all of your credentials. It may be acceptable to have a separate instance of the password manager there, one that only knows about network access credentials, but that implies the need for persistent storage across instantiations of the sandbox. That's undesirable, because it means that

---

1. "Ted Lemon—Google+—The network at World IPv6 forum has a captive portal which intercepts port 80," https://plus.google.com/108428495411541457022/posts/2782SLV9Fe2.

infections can persist, too; you want to be able to discard the sandbox when you're done logging in. Still, this is an option that may be useful for some people.

The other extreme is to do it manually: run the password manager in your regular environment, look up the password you need, and type it into the sandbox. Alternately, you can probably use copy and paste; that's possible with most hypervisors. You lose something, though: automatic selection of the proper password based on the URL you've visited, which is a useful guard against phishing attacks.

It's tempting at this point to try to devise a custom solution, a specialized channel that would allow for precisely the proper queries. Is there some way to export the actual URL from the sandbox and import the proper login details? It can be done, but it's probably not a good idea.

Assume some sort of channel back from the browser—the compromised browser, running in a thoroughly p0wned sandbox—to the password manager. The first risk is the obvious one, as discussed above: is the code that is listening to this channel trustworthy? Let's assume that it is. It's still a dangerous situation. For obvious reasons, the browser can't be allowed to make direct queries—"here's a URL, give me the login credentials"— as opposed to popping up some sort of dialog box asking the user to permit the action. Visualize that request, in the context of this somewhat tongue-in-cheek definition of a dialog box: "A window in which resides a button labeled 'OK' and a variety of text and other content that users ignore."[2] In other words, too often (and probably far too often) users will ignore the URL in the dialog box and just give their assent to their password being collected. This sort of habituation to security warnings is very well known (see, e.g., [Egelman, Cranor, and Hong 2008]). If a user is expecting a password dialog box and is not expecting an attack, all too frequently the user will simply assent to the request and not bother reading it.

We are faced with an unpleasant dilemma here: do we trust the user to notice which URL is being requested, and copy and paste the proper password, or do we trust the user to notice a bogus hostname in a dialog box? We can resolve it by looking at the comparative harm from the two failure modes. In the first case, the malware will get the password to the network the user is trying to access; in the second, it will receive some arbitrary password of the user's. The former is of comparatively low value; the latter could be high value, but the success of the attack depends in part on the attacker's ability to guess for which sites the user has passwords. There are some obvious guesses that will often be successful—a Google or Facebook login, or something like American Express in an airport, to name just a few—but a targetier or MI-31 is likely to *know* what sites you connect to. Looked at this way, the choice is quite clear: a custom interface to the password manager from the sandbox is far riskier, especially against sophisticated adversaries.

---

2. "Glossary—W3C Web Security Context Wiki," http://www.w3.org/2006/WSC/wiki/Glossary.

It's also worth realizing the limitations of sandboxing. In this scenario, it does nothing to prevent you from connecting to a phony access point or being asked to enter your credit card details to a bogus access server. A sandbox is designed to protect your host against software you wish to run; these threats represent evil on external boxes.

10.4   The Cloud

Is the cloud "secure"?

The question as I have just phrased it is unanswerable because neither "secure" nor (especially) "cloud" have rigorous definitions. We also have to ask the first question in any security dialog: "what are you trying to protect, and against whom?" And there's one more question that is asked all too infrequently: secure compared with which alternatives? This last question is often the most interesting.

Intuitively, the cloud can provide computing cycles (e.g., Amazon's EC2) and/or re-mote storage (see Section 10.7); this latter can be just for the owner, or it can permit sharing. For "security," we can use the usual trio of confidentiality, integrity, and avail-ability. Our questions, then, are these: for remote storage and computing, does the cloud provide more or less confidentiality, integrity, and availability, across a wide spectrum of attackers, compared with providing the same functionality yourself?

Availability is probably the easiest to answer. I assert that despite occasional well-publicized failures, a professionally run cloud service is *more* available than a typical in-house solution. There are more redundant resources that can be used to resolve outages, whether malicious or accidental in origin. A good cloud service will use RAID disks and back them up. (How recent are your backups? When did you last test your ability to recover from a disk crash?) Put it this way: do you have more servers than Amazon? Do you have more bandwidth than Google? Yes, a failure at a large provider will affect more users [Brodkin 2012]; conversely, we hear about such failures more than we hear about the routine (and frequent) outages at typical corporations. The difficult issue is whether your enterprise can function if all of its computer capability is cloud resident; diversity is always a good thing. But should you seek diversity in your own environment or via different cloud providers? If you need very high availability, you can't just accept a cloud provider's word that all will be well.

Integrity and confidentiality are somewhat harder to assess. Most (though of course not all) penetrations result from exploitation of holes for which patches are already avail-able. Is your own in-house staff conscientious about installing all available fixes? Are your systems properly configured, especially for sharing data? Would a service provider do better? The questions aren't easy to answer. If the reason for a delay in patching is lack of resources, the cloud provider is likely to be better. On the other hand, many enterprises delay until they can assess the compatibility of their own in-house applications with the new system—and cloud providers have very many applications to worry about. Sharing resources with outsiders is almost certainly better done via the cloud; their access control mechanisms are tuned for that sort of scenario, and they've dealt with the complexity of the underlying platforms.

In-house computing probably has the edge when considering possible attackers. Apart from a provider's own employees turning to the dark side, you run the risk of being collateral damage when some other customer is being targeted. There are also legal issues to consider: under the laws of many different countries, you arguably have less protection against "subpoena attacks" when your data isn't stored in house [Maxwell and Wolf 2012].

I do not claim that the answer to cloud computing is simple. I do assert that running your own systems is not inherently better, even from a security perspective. You need to think about the problem without preconceptions and do a detailed assessment for your own particular situation.

10.5   Security Architecture of Cloud Providers

Although there are many different ways to build a cloud provider, from a security perspective there are three interlinked pieces: the service platform, the administration and provisioning system, and the corporation. A failure in any of these pieces or in the people associated with them can lead to trouble for customers.

The service platform is what gets all of the security attention, but there are questions that have to be answered. Is it Windows or Linux? How is virtualization done? Where are files stored? How are network segments partitioned? What security mechanisms are used for the switches and routers? How much bandwidth is available? What flavor of hypervisor is used? What auxiliary services, such as credit card services, are provided? Who has physical access to the data centers? How are they screened? All of these are important; the answers should be addressed in reasonable detail in provider documentation, for example, [Amazon 2011].

The service platform isn't the only risk, though. The administration and provisioning system—the mechanisms, both web-based and programmatic, by which customers request and configure services—are quite important, too. The issue is not so much abuse of the direct mechanisms (can Customer A request access to B's files? What if C's password is stolen?) as what can happen if the provisioning system is penetrated. This is a very plausible threat. If nothing else, a provisioning system obviously requires databases, and many, many web sites have fallen to SQL injection attacks. Beyond that, of course, there's the human element: are the people who program, maintain, administer, and operate these systems screened to the same extent as those who deal with the service platform?

The third piece of the security puzzle is the corporation itself. Cloud providers are like any other corporation, complete with marketing departments, human resources departments, clerks, lawyers, system administrators, and vice presidents in charge of dispensing administratium [DeBuvitz 1989]. The risk here is indirect but nevertheless very real: the people who run the service and provisioning platforms are employees and thus have to deal with internal web servers and computers run by the IT group (as well, of course, as shoveling the administratium out of their offices). If an attacker can penetrate an internal system, it can be used to infect a system administrator's computer. If the same computer is used to talk to the service platform, *vae victis*!

The obvious defense against this scenario is an airgap: give such employees two computers, one for general corporate computing and one for work that gets near the service platform, with no connection between them. This is obviously not foolproof—again, remember Stuxnet [Falliere, Murchu, and Chien 2011; Zetter 2014]—but from a customer's perspective, the questions are whether it's even attempted, and how well employees actually follow good practices.

We've seen similar penetrations in the real world. Consider how Twitter was hacked a few years ago [FTC 2010]. In one incident, the bad guys launched a password-guessing attack against an administrative login. In another case, an attacker penetrated the personal email account of an employee. Two similar passwords were stored in plaintext in this account. With this data, the hacker was able to guess the employee's Twitter administrative password and used it to commit mischief.

10.6   Cloud Computing

Computation, especially on small amounts of data, is one of the simpler and more straightforward uses for the cloud. You lease a machine (typically a VM) with a particular operating system, upload the input data, run your programs, and download the results. Depending on the cloud provider, you may find it easy to lease many VMs. Typically, you only pay for the CPU time and data transfers you actually use. What are the security risks?

The first thing to realize is that a VM is, as noted, a computer with an operating system, with all of the risks appertaining thereto. If a given OS is insecure if run on bare silicon, sprinkling it with cloud dust does not magically secure it. The surrounding environment may provide some protection (see below), but an OS is an OS.

There has yet to be a perfect, bug-free, secure operating system; given that, it is obvious that it will be necessary to apply patches on occasion. Who will maintain the OS for your VMs? There are different models possible. Sometimes, you, the user will be responsible; in others, the cloud provider will do it. Neither is intrinsically better; while it's nice to be rid of the responsibility, OS patches can break your applications (Chapter 13).

Beyond the simple OS, some cloud providers supply interfaces to common applications and services: databases, credit card billing systems, content management systems, even shopping carts for small online stores. These programs can also have security bugs, which will also require patches. The provider will generally handle that, though of course with some risk of breaking code of yours that talks to these services.

Suppose, though, that you're on your own, and the cloud provider does not patch your OS and applications for you. What then? The cloud provides three things: a large amount of computing capacity, surge capacity for peak loads, and (in theory) higher availability than most stand-alone data centers. Against that, you take the risk of a penetration from another customer, from the provider's staff, or from some hacker who has penetrated the cloud provider, and in particular their support systems. It is difficult to measure any of these risks, especially that of insider attacks; such crimes are rarely detected, let alone reported. There may also be some extra advantages if you don't provide enough physical security for your own data centers; there may also be better tools for managing large numbers of VMs.

Cloud computing is an especially good place to treat security as an economic issue. There is certainly some incremental risk; on the other hand, running a data center sized for peak loads can be quite expensive, particularly when you include the costs of electricity and cooling. Furthermore, you have your own insiders to worry about; do you vet your personnel as well as a cloud provider does for its people?

10.7   Cloud Storage

Storage is a particularly important special case of cloud computing. Computation is generally private; users want as much isolation from other customers as is feasible. VMs are thus a good approach, since the strong isolation they provide is all to the good.

Storage is another matter. Cloud storage is desirable precisely because it makes data sharing easy. Services like Dropbox, Box.net, Google Drive, and more make it easy to share files, either broadly or selectively. Is this a safe thing to do?

One question is why organizations might prefer to use these external services for external file sharing, rather than doing it in house. After all, all major operating systems (and most minor ones) have some form of file-sharing ability. There seem to be at least three reasons, apart from the lovely automagic synchronization some of these services provide. First, someone has to manage the authorization name space: if you want to let some external parties view your files, you have to have a way to name them; this in turn means that they have to have some sort of login and credentials on some part of your system. Cloud providers handle that for you; all you have to know is the login name your partners use. Second, file sharing is obviously quite delicate from a security perspective, and several of the popular networked file systems have had a long, sad history of security problems. It's better not to rely on such systems in a high-threat environment. Finally, and partly for this reason, corporate file servers tend to live behind the firewall, where they're unavailable to legitimate outside users. Indeed, many corporate firewalls will even block outbound requests for such protocols; by contrast, most cloud storage services use HTTP or HTTPS, which are allowed through.

The first reason is valid. Managing such logins is a difficult matter, and more so procedurally than technically; it's not at all unreasonable to want to let someone else have the headaches. The other two, though, are troubling. Why should cloud storage vendors be able to produce more secure storage access code than Microsoft, Apple, Oracle, et al.? Perhaps more to the point, can they? Do we have any strong evidence that they've actually succeeded? There is some reason for optimism; the cloud protocols were specifically built for one purpose, secure Internet-wide sharing; at least two of the local solutions, Oracle's NFS and Microsoft's CIFS, were built on top of very general and problematic *Remote Procedure Call (RPC)* protocols and had authorization mechanisms aimed at local users, making them harder to secure.

On the other hand, at least one cloud storage vendor, Dropbox, has experienced a serious security failure [Singel 2011]. Somehow, a bug in a program change let it accept any password and gain access to any file at all. The flaw was in the authentication mechanisms, not the file access protocol itself, but as I've noted over and over again, security is a systems property; you cannot restrict your attention to just one component.

The third reason for the popularity of cloud storage is the most worrisome. When our security mechanisms exclude valid uses and force use of external solutions that evade— there is no milder word—the firewall, there is something seriously wrong with our protocols, our firewalls, our policies, or (most likely) all of the above. It is possible to bring such services in house—see the discussion in Section 11.3—but it takes a fair amount of effort and care.

Flaws in the design or implementation of the authentication and file access protocols are the two obvious failure modes. There are several other possibilities as well, the most serious of which are the cloud provider being hacked or suffering an insider attack. They're tempting targets for skilled attackers because a single penetration exposes the resources of many other organizations. (Per the threat classification matrix, the provider would be the victim of a targeted or APT attack; its customers would probably be opportunistic victims.) The usual approach to the latter has been via process: the provider uses stringent procedures to limit the number of employees who can get at user files. A better solution to both, from a technical perspective, is to encrypt and decrypt files on the client machines. This, however, makes sharing much more difficult. It takes a moderately complex cryptographic protocol, especially if you want to be able to revoke access—and you almost certainly do.

Another theoretical issue is transport security. Most providers have used the obvious solution, HTTPS rather than HTTP, but it's something to watch for. Note, though, that unless the developers were quite cautious, cloud storage over HTTPS is susceptible to the same PKI flaws as a web browser. A cloud client could easily do certificate pinning, but it's unclear which, if any, products actually implement that. Many mobile apps have trouble doing even basic TLS [Fahl et al. 2012; Georgiev et al. 2012].

The biggest risk, though, has nothing to do with clouds, cumulo-silicon or otherwise. Rather, it is intrinsic to the sharing process: getting the *access control list (ACL)* correct. I'm not even talking about the risks of client-side insider misbehavior. Every shared object is potentially accessible by anyone with a valid login on the server, in that they can construct requests to read or write the file. This is limited by ACLs, but there is a large body of research showing that ACLs are extremely hard to manage, especially in complex situations [Madejski, M. Johnson, and Bellovin 2012; Reeder, Kelley, et al. 2008; Reeder and Maxion 2005; Smetters and Good 2009]. In a cloud scenario, where many different people may set controls on many shared resources, this is a recipe for disaster. Let me give just one scenario. Suppose your company shares many files with an outside vendor; you then switch vendors. The initial set of ACLs were created and maintained by someone who has since left your company, and because of changes in your system design in the years since the original contract was signed there was a lot of churn in exactly what files needed to be shared. How will you revoke all of the access rights held by the first company?

It is worth repeating that this last issue would arise even if you used your own, internal file servers. The only saving grace, were you to do it in house, is the increased ability to write custom scripts to search your file system—more likely, *file systems*—for all such files; you may not have that ability with a cloud provider. Their ability to help you solve problems like this may be the biggest single security difference between otherwise similar offerings.

10.8 Analysis

By now, it is clear that there is not and cannot be any simple answer to the question of cloud!security. There are too many types of cloud services and usage patterns; each has its own risks and benefits. Do not believe any blanket assertions about the security or insecurity of "the" cloud; there is simply no such thing. The same is true of sandboxing and virtualization; not only are there different uses (and hence different security properties), there are different implementations.

The risk/benefit trade-offs for cloud storage seem to favor using it, especially for sharing data with external parties. Even if there were similar protocols for in-house cloud storage, the problem of managing the external username space is daunting. The gain from outsourcing that responsibility, though, comes with a potentially serious cost: you have little control over the authentication mechanisms used for your own employees, let alone for your partners'. As noted in Chapter 7, there are many ways to do it poorly. The issue, though, is not the cloud per se, but how a particular service is provided; the risk would be the same if you made the same poor choices yourself.

A very serious concern is unmanaged use of cloud storage by your own employees. If people want to take work home—and many people do—cloud storage can be much more convenient than flash drives. Either may be against corporate policy; both are hard to stop. Fundamentally, though, this is a people problem and a cultural problem more than a technical one. Yes, you can get add-on products that limit use of USB drives, at which point you've made life difficult internally. (Have you ever handed a memory stick with a presentation to a colleague? I sure have, and before that CDs and floppies; slide shows to go are de rigeur in large organizations [Bumiller 2010].) Similarly, you can try to add firewall rules that block unauthorized connections to popular cloud services, but it's easy to set up relays on external private servers and work around the blockages. The real issue is the mismatch between employee work habits or desires (and, perhaps, how people are evaluated) and corporate security policies. Unless you're being targeted by the Andromedans, you're probably better off finding a secure way to let people use cloud storage than trying to ban it.

There's an interesting trade-off here. Which is better, a private file server available internally and externally, or a commercial cloud storage provider? As noted, common network file system protocols do not have a great reputation for security; however, commercial providers have a relatively large attack surface, per Section 10.5. You would have the same attack surface but you may be less tempting to targetiers; besides, you *know* what precautions you've taken.

A possible solution to some of the security issues posed by a private store is to put it on an external network, but make it accessible only via a VPN, even from inside your organization. The trick will be finding VPN software flexible enough (and comprehensible enough) to allow for two or more secure networks—one for general "phone home" access and one for the file store—and automatic enough that users don't have to think about how to use it. (That's why you want encrypted access even from the inside: you want the user's behavior to be as similar as possible, inside or outside.) The fundamental precept here is to make it easy for people to do the right thing; forcing them to fight menus of soul-wrenching complexity will not endear your system to your colleagues.

If your security policies do permit some sharing of material, you're probably better off trusting your users [M. Johnson et al. 2009]. When official mechanisms are too complicated, people will ignore them and resort to the aforementioned work-arounds.

If one looks only at security, cloud computation is a tougher problem than cloud storage because there's no issue of external logins that need to be maintained. Cloud storage can give you new functionality—shared access—while cloud computation merely saves you money. That, then, is how the question should be answered: is the expected difference in loss from relying on a cloud computation provider more or less than what you save by employing such facilities? Unfortunately, as posed that question is unanswerable, since measuring security isn't possible even without trying to measure the probability of an attack in different situations [Bellovin 2006a]. A different approach is needed.

Start by comparing, as best you can, the security of each of the provider's three components (Section 10.5) with your own equivalents. Pay no attention to mechanisms designed to separate different customers from each other; you don't have the equivalent. You'll probably find that your provisioning component is minimal; if you can't find your own instance, consider the provider's as part of their service platform.

Most of the time, a cloud provider will win on availability and physical security. In many cases, they'll also do better on personnel security, especially for the delivery platform; that is, after all, what they're selling, and many businesses do not do much in the way of background checking. For technical security issues, while you can't measure your security proactively, you can get a good handle by looking retrospectively. Select some pieces of software you run, including the operating system, and do a deep dive into its vulnerability list over the last year. Don't restrict yourself to the vendors' bug lists; much of the time, vendors don't post security holes until patches are available. Check official compendia like the *Common Vulnerabilities and Exposures (CVE)* list (http:// cve.mitre.org/cve/index.html) and especially the *National Vulnerability Database (NVD)* (http://nvd.nist.gov/), as well as sites like bugtraq and Full Disclosure. When were the vulnerabilities known? When were patches available? When did you install them? For how long were you vulnerable? You won't find it easy to get similar data from providers, but now you know what questions to ask. Try this one: what do they do when a bug report shows up on one of those lists? If they don't monitor them—well, that's an answer, too. (On the other hand, do your security people monitor those lists?) Don't forget to ask about auxiliary services offered by the provider; you may not use them, but if they're hacked do they provide an entrée into your systems?

Life gets more interesting when you factor in threat models. Ordinary care should shield both you and cloud providers against joy hackers. Against targetiers, there are advantages in both directions. On the one hand, you may prefer an external service, precisely because it is external and hence less known to insiders; on the other hand, a popular cloud provider may attract outsiders who think there are fruitful pickings once they break in. The really interesting questions, though, are posed by the more skilled attackers, the opportunistic hackers and the Andromedans.

A cloud provider is a *very* tempting target because if someone penetrates it they gain a lot. They have not only the immense power of the provider's platforms, they have access to the systems of many different customers. This can turn some opportunistic hackers into targetiers—and a skilled targetier is, of course, an APT. Perhaps they're at the lower left of that quadrant (given the nomenclature in this book, shall I say that they're from the Lesser Magellanic Cloud?), but they are in the quadrant, with all that implies. Your systems may be collateral damage to such an incident, but that's small comfort. The conclusion is that a cloud provider has to be held to higher security standards than most companies.

Finally, what if your own threat model includes attacks from Andromeda? Does reliance on a cloud provider make things worse? If the cloud provider is good, they're already trying to build defenses at that level. Your problem is that your attack surface has increased, and from a direction against which you have few defenses. MI-31 is the sort of organization that can find hypervisor bugs, bribe or extort employees, and so on. They're also quite capable of setting up a fake company that purchases services from your provider, giving them closer connections to you. This is a serious threat model, which means that you need a really good cloud provider. The best rule of thumb here is to select one whose security—technical, people, and process—is better than your own.

✷   ✷   ✷

It is harder to do a blanket analysis on sandboxing per se because there are many kinds of sandboxes and many applications that can benefit from it. The trick is to match the scenario to the available protective technology. The other big issue is the system administration overhead necessary to set up the sandbox; VMs, in general, need as much care and feeding as do regular ones, so the expense will depend on how efficient your organization is at system administration.

Some characteristics that are a good fit for a VM sandbox include few channels to the outside world, simple policies controlling those channels, and infrequent creation and destruction of the sandbox. A standing service—say, an inbound mail handler—is a good example. By contrast, it does not make sense to spin up a VM for each message; the rate is far too high.

A departmental file server passes the creation rate test, if it instantiates a sandbox per client, but it fails the policy test: complex access control rules that govern which users can perform which operations on given files. Web browsers fail both tests, if you want a separate sandbox for each site visited.

Another issue is what resources are available within the sandbox. VMs provide many; they're great at keeping misbehaving code away from other machines' files, but they don't restrict network access, they have plenty of privileged code lying around, etc. If you need fine-grained restrictions, some sort of jail technology may be better. On the other hand, if all you need is a restriction on its network reach, you could use an inward-facing firewall to block that and get the other advantages of virtualization.

Note the implication here: often, the right choice is to use more than one sandbox mechanism. Thus, a browser may run with reduced privileges overall, but still use separate userids for different sites [S. Ioannidis and Bellovin 2001; H. J. Wang et al. 2009]. That provides intrabrowser protection.

All of the major operating systems have their own sandbox scheme, though the design principles vary tremendously. In general, the choice is between simplicity—of design and implementation, and hence of the implementation and configuration of sandboxed applications—and flexibility. This means that it's relatively hard to port a sandboxed application between OSs unless it assumes minimum granularity and is coded accordingly. (That's one reason that Firefox is sometimes called the least secure browser [Anthony 2014]: it doesn't use a sandbox, because its many different platforms have very different sandboxing paradigms.) A consequence of that is that the same program may be less safe on one OS than on another, which in turn means that flexibility in choice of OS might be appropriate in some deployments.

I sometimes ask my students which operating system is the most secure. It's the wrong question; the proper one is "which OS makes it easiest to write secure applications?" Sandboxing is part of the answer.

Part III
Secure Operations

Chapter 11

Building Secure Systems

"All through that century, the human race was drawing slowly nearer to the abyss—never even suspecting its existence. Across that abyss, there is only one bridge. Few races, unaided, have ever found it. Some have turned back while there was still time, avoiding both the danger and the achievement. Their worlds have become Elysian islands of effortless content, playing no further part in the story of the universe. That would never have been your fate—or your fortune. Your race was too vital for that. It would have plunged into ruin and taken others with it, for you would never have found the bridge."

Karellen in *Childhood's End*
—Arthur C. Clarke

Basic technologies are all well and good, but what we really want are systems—and, if you're reading this book, *secure* systems. Systems security comprises four very different aspects: good basic technologies (the subject of Part II), correct coding, proper design, and secure operation. All of these are necessary; a weakness in any can spell disaster. I've already covered the most important basic technologies. Entire books can be and have been written about correct coding; accordingly, I'll just touch on it. I'll spend more time on system building and its close cousin evaluation—how do you put the various pieces together?—though that's really a topic big enough to merit its own book. Finally, I'll discuss secure operation, a vital topic usually lumped under the headings of "simple system administration" or those "!@#$%^& [l]users." There's more to both of those topics; I'll cover those, too, in subsequent chapters. As always, the stress is on how to think about the problem; other than the fundamental limitations of human beings, the specifics will vary over time but the basic problems remain.

It is important to remember, of course, that there are no foolproof recipes for security. No matter how good you are nor how carefully you follow my advice, you can still experience a failure. In other words, a good design includes consideration of how to limit the damage from any single breach.

11.1 Correct Coding

There are many books and papers on how to write correct, secure code; I don't propose to recap them or replace them here. Let it suffice to say that the usual advice—avoid buffer overflows, sanitize your inputs, watch out for cross-site scripting errors, the usual seemingly endless list—is sound. A few points are worth stressing, however.

The first is that the threat model—the kinds of bugs that can be exploited, or defenses bypassed—is not static. Once upon a time, if you'd offered defenders "canaries" to protect against stack-based buffer overflows [Cowan et al. 2003] and made data space non-executable, everyone would have exclaimed, "Problem solved!" Of course, it wasn't. Heap overflows are exploitable, too, and things like *return-oriented programming (ROP)* [Pappas 2014; Shacham 2007] showed that there are other attack techniques possible. No one in the security field is betting that there aren't more that no one has bothered to discover yet.

The "solution" sounds simple: write correct code. Of course, it's neither simple nor even feasible, which is why I put the word in quotes. Nevertheless, it's a goal to aim for, which in turn means that anything that improves correctness improves security. This includes the whole panoply of software engineering processes, with all that implies: design documents, design and code reviews, unit and system tests, regression tests, and so on.

Those techniques alone won't solve the problem, though, because many security requirements are quite different than the usual. Take "tainting": the concept that input from an untrusted source must not be used to do certain things without certain context-specific checks. It certainly makes sense, but how this should be done is heavily context-dependent. Let's consider the differences between web servers and mailers.

Both have to watch out for problems, but the problems can differ, even when they're addressing the same underlying issue. One favorite example—favorite because programmers *still* get it wrong, even though it's been recognized as a problem for decades, is the ".." problem: filenames that contain enough '/../' strings to move up the tree beyond the nominal base for that activity. How you achieve this, though, is very different; accordingly, the specific rules programmers must follow (and hence the specifications for the application) will vary.

For web servers, all files must be under a directory known as the *document root*. Avoiding too many instances of /../ sounds simple, but it isn't. For one thing, some instances are correct practice in setting up web sites, which means that they must be accepted and processed correctly; something like html/../art/pic.jpg should be rewritten as art/pic.jpg; however, html/../../docroot/art/pic.jpg is invalid, even if it would ultimately point to the same file. There are also the myriad ways to represent /, such as %25 and &#0025;—to say nothing of all of the Unicode characters that look like a /, such as ߼, which is technically the "fraction slash" rather than the more usual "solidus." (If that's not bad enough, imagine a Unicode-encoded URL that includes something like iana.org<fractionslash>othernastystuff.com, which can easily be mistaken for something really on the iana.org web site rather than on othernastystuff.com.)

The problem with mail is more subtle. It's not so much people sending email directly to files, since that's easy to handle simply by checking inbound messages against the list of legal recipients (few computers will accept messages for /etc/passwd@example.com or even smb/../../etc/passwd@example.com) as it is the ability on some systems for users to specify a filename to receive their own email. That is, I can (sometimes) say that mail for me should be written to /home/smb/funky-mail. That sounds simple, too; the mailer should simply permit writing to files that I have write permission for. It isn't; I'll skip the details (again, this isn't a book on secure coding), but in a very similar situation the Apache web server does about 20 different checks.[1] A useful simplification, then, might be to allow delivery to any files below /home/smb, but that in turn brings in the .. problem. (Bonus points to all readers who spotted the other very serious security problem inherent in that very bad idea. Don't do this without a lot more care; it doesn't do what you want.) There's a lot of security complexity here no matter how you slice it, but given that /../ adds to the conceptual workload and that there aren't strong reasons to permit it, it's not at all unreasonable to bar it in this situation.

There's one more variant worth mentioning: an FTP server. Those typically log users in, and then rely solely on the access controls of the underlying OS. Because of the way in which the login takes place, it's more similar to an ordinary user login than a mailer is, which simplifies things; accordingly, FTP servers don't even have to consider the issue— unless the server supports pattern-based access control (some do), in which case the situation is similar to but simpler than for web servers.

We can see, then, that the proper handling of this string is very much context and specification dependent. A simple set of rules is in fact simplistic.

What programming language you use probably matters, too. C is notorious for its susceptibility to buffer overflows, uncontrolled pointers, and more; using a more modern language would eliminate whole classes of problems. Clearly, this is the right thing to do.

---

1. "suEXEC Support," http://httpd.apache.org/docs/2.4/suexec.html.

Or is it? It turns out that scientific evidence for this proposition is remarkably hard to come by. A 1999 National Academies study noted [Schneider 1999]:

> There is much anecdotal and little hard, experimental evidence concerning whether the choice of programming language can enhance trustworthiness. One report [Computer Science and Telecommunications Board 1997] looked for hard evidence but found essentially none. Further study is needed and, if undertaken, could be used to inform research directions in the programming language community.

The cited report discussed many studies, but there were always confounding factors that called the results into question.

There's another factor to consider: are these modern languages too complex? Remember Hoare's warning about Ada, which was being adopted as the standard programming language for US Department of Defense projects [1981]:

> The next rocket to go astray as a result of a programming language error may not be an exploratory space rocket on a harmless trip to Venus: It may be a nuclear warhead exploding over one of our own cities. An unreliable programming language generating unreliable programs constitutes a far greater risk to our environment and to our society than unsafe cars, toxic pesticides, or accidents at nuclear power stations. Be vigilant to reduce that risk, not to increase it.

On balance, most security people feel that moving away from C and C++ is probably the right answer, but the answer is less clear-cut than I'd like.

Ultimately, perhaps Brooks' analysis was the most accurate [1987]:

> I predict that a decade from now, when the effectiveness of Ada is assessed, it will be seen to have made a substantial difference, but not because of any particular language feature, nor indeed of all of them combined. Neither will the new Ada environments prove to be the cause of the improvements. Ada's greatest contribution will be that switching to it occasioned training programmers in modern software design techniques.

Training, though, is an important part of process as well: programmers do need to be taught how to write correct, secure code.

✳   ✳   ✳

Virtually everything I've just described, with the exception of some of the requirements, applies to all large-scale software development projects. Security, though, is different;

there are malicious adversaries. In ordinary code, one can say "no records are longer than 1,024 bytes" and not worry. In security-sensitive code, though, that's a recipe for disaster; attackers will happily construct longer records for the precise purpose of overflowing your buffers if you're not careful. How do you know if you've been careful enough?

C, of course, is part of the problem. Since strings do not have explicit length fields, many string functions—copying, comparison, and more—come in two forms, such as `strcpy()` and `strncpy()`; one uses the conventional zero byte delimiter and one takes an explicit length as well. Passing lengths around everywhere isn't always convenient, especially in old code that's been updated over the years; is it ever safe to use functions like `strcpy()`?

It is perhaps unfortunate that the answer is "yes": sometimes, they are safe as well as convenient. If the answer were "no," they could be deleted or flagged with bloodthirsty warnings by the compiler, much as `gets()` is. If the program has already verified that the string lengths are safe, or if the input comes only from trustworthy sources like a sysadmin-specified file, there's no strong reason not to use these functions. The problem is how to tell the difference, and in particular how to audit your code.

I took a very quick look at the source to a recent version of the Firefox web browser. By actual count of the lines emitted by `fgrep -wR` I found 303 instances of `strncpy()` and 735 instances of `strcpy()`. Does that imply that Firefox is terminally insecure? Probably not; most of those instances will be false positives—but that's an awful lot of code to review by hand.

Beyond that, there are many common errors that cannot be detected that way. The simplest example is a type mismatch between modules, which is especially easy to do in C. Another example is the difficulty of *taint analysis*: given how a variable can be referred to directly or via a pointer, determining where something came from is very difficult.

The answer is to use a specialized *static analyzer*, a program that looks at programs and finds certain classes of mistakes. Static analyzers are old—lint dates back to the 1970s [S. C. Johnson 1978]—but newer ones are much more comprehensive. If nothing else, they've been tuned to detect security-sensitive misbehavior.

This book is not the place for a comprehensive discussion of such programs. (If you're interested, I recommend [Chess and West 2007; McGraw 2006]. Microsoft has developed many tools that can cope with systems as large as Windows or Office [Ball et al. 2004; Larus et al. 2004].) I will note three caveats about using them:

- Static analyzers aren't panaceas. Bad code is bad code, and creatively bad programmers can outwit the best tools. (Chess and West's book also gives a lot of very sage advice on mistakes to avoid.)

- Vulnerabilities—in this context, that means programming errors—increase all the time. Newly discovered attacks, new operating environments, and new languages will all have their quirks; code that was once effectively safe can become unsafe. Consider format string attacks, which were completely unknown before around 1999. Old code has to be revisited with newly updated tools.

- Static analysis is just one more part of the development process, along with code reviews, testing, and so on. Simply having a tool, or using it casually, will not suffice. Again, process matters.

✷   ✷   ✷

There's a reason, then, that this section is named "Correct Coding" rather than "Correct Programming": the problem is far deeper than just writing the programs.

11.2   Design Issues

Let's start our discussion of security design principles by considering a typical—but simplified—example: a modern web server. Major sites' web servers today don't serve static files; rather, they're controlled by *content management systems*, which in turn are database driven. That is, a reference to a page will generally invoke a script that processes a template for the page; the template, in turn, will contain database references and/or invocations of other scripts. The database will contain structured files for all of the content: the title and actual text of the requested page, information about other links to show on that page ("most e-mailed," "trending," video or audio adjuncts, and so on), related content, and more. For that matter, the database will likely contain information about users, the kinds of ads they should receive, and more.

Figure 11.1 shows the layout of a typical high-end web server. There are several points about it worth noting. First and foremost, all of the major components are replicated; this is done for reliability and load sharing. There are two border routers, each perhaps homed to a different ISP. There are multiple web servers, each fed by load balancers. There are multiple databases; here, some of the separation is likely because of different roles and access characteristics. Even the networks are replicated; no single failure should be able to take this site off the air.

The second point worth noting is the inherent security in the design. The load balancers, which are also inverse proxies, feed only ports 80 and 443 through to the web servers. They're not intended as firewalls per se; nevertheless, they function as such. Similarly, an attacker who has somehow compromised the load balancers or the routers on ei-

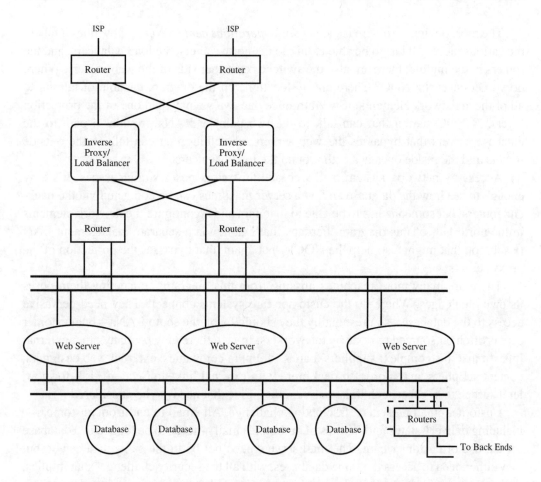

Figure 11.1: The layout of a typical web server and its associated databases.

ther side of them still can't get to the databases; the web servers are just that, web servers, and they don't route IP packets between their "north" and their "south" Ethernets.

The third thing we notice is that "minor" link in the southeast to "back ends." That's probably the most dangerous part of the system as shown, unless there are strong security protections between the web servers and databases and these undescribed back-end systems.

The fourth item is that the diagram is seriously flawed; there are many more vital functions that can't be integrated into this scheme without breaking the nice security properties I just outlined. Note carefully what I'm saying: it's not that I've omitted details (that's inevitable in such a high-level view); rather, it's that when you add in some of these details, a lot of their security properties are *inherently* compromised.

The most obvious problem is the *network operations center (NOC)*: how does it talk to the various pieces? It has to be able to talk to the north routers, the load balancers, and the routers in the middle; there are also the switches on either side of the web servers. Where do you connect the NOC? There are *no* locations on the diagram capable of talking to all of those network elements; if we introduce one, we've bypassed one of the protection layers. A NOC station that can talk to the two pairs of LANs provides a path to the database servers that bypasses the web servers; something that can talk to the outside routers and the inside ones is a path around the load balancers.

Access by network, system, and web administrators poses similar issues. It's easy enough to see how the database and web server machines can be contacted via the back-end routers, but someone has to be able to maintain and reconfigure the network elements in the north half of this diagram. Perhaps that's done via a separate management LAN (a solution that might also help the NOC)—but again, that bypasses the protection of the proxy servers.

There are many more machines missing from this diagram; connecting them poses its own challenges. Where do the customer care systems connect? They need pervasive access to the databases, so presumably they should be on the south LANs—but customer care is often outsourced or done by teleworkers. In fact, there may be many other external links to just this complex: suppliers, banks, shipping companies, external web designers, content suppliers, and more. I'll deal more with external links in Section 11.3; for now, let it suffice to say that such links raise another issue that needs to be considered.

Customer email presents a fascinating challenge. All email to and from customers—including delivery status and failures of outbound email—needs to be logged in a database for the use of customer care. The mail servers need not be in the same data center, but they either need to access the same databases, with all the security challenges that implies, or the separate databases they do use must be accessible to customer care and somehow linked to what is done via the web servers.

There are many more types of access needed: (tape?) backup machines, along with the interfaces needed to restore files; the backup data center, which may be on the other side of the planet but needs up-to-the-minute databases; the console servers; the environmental sensing and control networks (if your machine room gets too hot, you really want to shut things down); your authentication server, which in turn should probably be linked to your personnel machines so that they know whether an employee has left the company—the list goes ever on. A few years ago, I looked at the high-level schematic for a large company's billing system. It had four different databases and 18 other processing elements. One of those databases held the sales tax rates for every relevant jurisdiction; that, of course, implies a real-time link to some vendor who is responsible for tracking changes in rates and rules, and updating the database as needed. Real-world systems are infinitely complex—and if someone shows you a diagram without such complexity, the proper response is "what aren't you showing me?"

Security people don't get to pick what functions exist, nor do they decide which are handled in house and which are outsourced. We do, however, have the responsibility of securing it all, even when the rest of the organization decides to change things around.

11.3 External Links

Out of all design issues, the most difficult is external connectivity: the many, many links to other companies. Make no mistake about it: there are *very* many links. I once asked a top network security person at a major American corporation how many authorized links there were to other companies: "at least a thousand." And how many unauthorized links did he think existed? "At least that many more." These links exist not because of carelessness or lack of security awareness; rather, they're there because they're necessary for the business. As such, the security question is not whether they should exist, but how to secure them. You'll occasionally win a fight on that issue; more often, you'll not just lose, you'll be shunted aside as someone who doesn't understand the business.

How should external links be secured? Many people's immediate reaction is to say, "Set up an encrypted VPN from the outside company to our network." It's not a bad suggestion, and I'd likely include it among my own recommendations, but let's take a deeper look at it: why should you encrypt this link, and what does it cost? For that matter, we should look more closely at just how the encryption should be deployed.

Encryption protects against eavesdropping; it also provides authentication of received packets. Who, though, is going to engage in such activities? In a business-to-business connection, both ends have dedicated connections to their ISPs. Eavesdropping on either the access links or ISP backbones isn't easy. The Andromedans can do it; few others are capable of it. Put another way, if your threat model includes surveillance by intelligence agencies, encrypting such links is vital. That's by no means a preposterous concept, but it's also not a universal threat model. VPNs are cheap and easy—but if they're problematic in your environment for some reason, it's worth thinking hard about who your enemies are. Hold on a moment, though, before you rip out your crypto: there are two more things to consider.

I'll defer discussing one until the end of the section, but I've already alluded to the other: cryptography can authenticate packets without relying on the source IP address. Again, this goes back to threat models: who is capable of forging addresses? Although it's still a sophisticated attack, it's much easier than eavesdropping. One mechanism is a *routing attack*: someone announcing someone else's IP addresses via BGP. It's rare but feasible; there have been reports of spammers doing it [Ramachandran and Feamster

How to Say "No"

Despite what I said on page 213, sometimes it's necessary to fight against a thoroughly bad idea. Under certain circumstances, you're not just acting in the interests of your own integrity, you're acting in your employer's interests as well. The trick is conveying the message in the right way. There are two things to remember. First, since the idea you're opposing was propounded for business reasons, you have to show business reasons why it's a bad idea. Don't say, "Oh, no; we'll be hacked!" Instead, show how much money a security breach in that spot can cause. If the scheme in question is likely to earn €100,000,000, saying, "There's a 3% chance we'll be hacked and it will cost €100,000 to clean it up," is not going to get any traction; the expected value of a successful hack is far lower than the profits, and the hack is only modestly likely. On the other hand, if you can point to a situation like Target's—40 million credit card numbers were stolen; some analysts estimate that the total cost to the company may run into the *billions* [Abrams 2014; Riley et al. 2014]—you'll be taken rather more seriously.

Second, although the argument is nominally about money, discussions like this are always political. That means that you have to approach it politically, with all that implies: finding allies, speaking their language, and so on. I know that that doesn't come naturally to many technical people, but we live in a wetware world. . .

Come prepared to discuss the technical risks in a comprehensible fashion. Don't speak of cross-site scripting attacks; instead, speak of the effects: "The attacker can steal our users' login credentials, and we'd be liable." Demonstrate *exactly* how the security failure could occur: "We're relying on the same software package that was apparently responsible when the Bank of San Serriffe was hacked last year, so we know that the capability is out there."

Your message will be heard more sympathetically if you can show an alternative that is more secure while still satisfying the business need. Adding components may increase costs only slightly, while significantly improving security and still preserving the original business advantage. Compromise might be in order, too. I participated in one security review where the result was very, very clear to everyone: the risk was obvious, the consequences severe, and there was no feasible recovery strategy after the inevitable breach. The outcome, though, was not to cancel the project; rather, it was to do a very limited scale beta deployment while the flaw was repaired. The scale was limited enough that the risks were acceptable, the product group would learn how well things functioned otherwise, and there would be enough time for a proper fix before large-scale use.

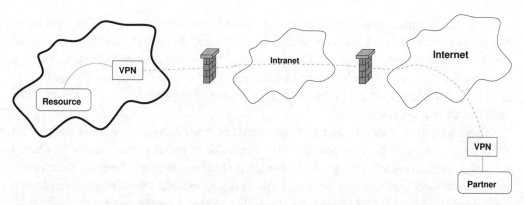

Figure 11.2: A shared enclave: an internal firewall protecting the rest of the organization from externally accessible partners that may have been penetrated.

2006; Vervier, Thonnard, and Dacier 2015] and an apparent Bitcoin thief [Greenberg 2014; Litke and Stewart 2014], and I've heard of other incidents from Reliable Sources. Another way to do it is by attacking the DNS, either directly via a *cache contamination attack* [Bellovin 1995; Kaminsky 2008] or by hijacking a site's DNS records via their registrar [Edwards 2000]. Note that these would be targeted, reasonably sophisticated attacks; we're into the upper right quadrant of our threat matrix, though not all the way to Andromeda.

The more mundane threats demand more of our attention. The real risk is that you're letting others inside your network: what can they do, and what can you do to protect yourself? The answer is very much context dependent, but there are some standard approaches.

The most obvious, if you can do it, is to apply firewall rules to the interconnection. That is, restrict what hosts and services of yours the external machines can reach. Note that there may be a conflict between your cryptography and the need for firewalling: you can't filter IPsec-protected traffic based on actual destination addresses and port numbers, so that has to be done after decryption or integrated with it.

A problem, though, is that the resource of yours being accessed is still vulnerable; if it is penetrated, the rest of your network is at risk. Thus, and if the threat model so indicates, a more interesting way to approach the solution is what I call the *shared enclave* model: walling off the resource behind a firewall, a firewall that protects the rest of the company from the enclave. This is shown in Figure 11.2. The main corporate firewall permits the external traffic into the corporate network, but only to the internal VPN gateway. The traffic then passes through the second firewall to the decryption gateway; from there, the actual resource can be reached.

Note the problem: how does the rest of your organization reach it? The answer, of course, is to have special rules on that internal firewall permitting such access. What are the necessary types of access? Obviously, that's somewhat situation dependent, but it's clear that essentially, we've more or less replicated the configuration shown in Figure 11.1, and hence all of the problems that go with it. That's not to say that this is a bad idea; however, it comes at a cost.

There's another reason to adopt shared enclaves: your partner may insist on it. After all, if you set up a VPN, your partners are vulnerable to attacks from your side. (Yes, I know that your firewall's strength is as the strength of ten firewalls because your hearts are pure, but your partners may not realize this.) Enclaves limit which of your employees have access to the VPN and hence have the ability to endanger your partner.

Taking this one more step, you may need to insist on an enclave architecture at their end, for the same reason. Even if you trust their honesty, do you trust their competence at network security? After all, it is highly unlikely that your site is the only external connection they have. Unless there are further protections, you're exposed not just to your partners but to all of the other companies to whom they talk, ad infinitum. There's a word for this sort of transitive closure of connected networks: the Internet.

Note how we derived the shared enclave architecture. It came from a combination of three factors: the resource to be protected, a threat model that assumed that the computer hosting this resource might be penetrated, and (to some extent) a need to protect the partner organization from other failures within your site. The second factor is the most crucial here: if your shared resource, perhaps a special-purpose web or database server, is strongly enough protected, you don't need the extra layers of protection. If it may be weak, or if it is very exposed to the outside (perhaps you're a big wholesaler and it's handling orders from a very large number of retail outlets), a stronger security posture is indicated.

✴   ✴   ✴

Sometimes, partners need to access far more than a single cluster of easily segregated servers. I know of one situation where a company was legally compelled to engage an outside auditing firm to check on certain classes of transactions. This firm therefore required access to a fair number of internal databases: the data architecture had of course not been designed without outside auditing in mind, so information was scattered hither and yon. How should this be handled?

Again, we go back to our threat model: how much do you trust the outside firm? If they're honest and competent, a simple set of firewall rules will suffice. That is, create an access control list that allows this outside company to reach some set of database servers within your network. (See the box on page 218.) Use standard database facilities, such as GRANT and VIEW, to limit what parts of the database they can see. If they're honest but perhaps not competent enough, the right solution might be an enclave on their side, not yours. How do you enforce that? You enforce it the same way you enforce many other things in the real world: by a contract with suitable penalty clauses, rather than just by technology.

If that isn't sufficient protection, the best approach is often an application gateway. The obvious starting point is an SQL proxy that filters out dangerous things, per Figure 2.1. It then implements a *federated database* [Josifovski et al. 2002], which treats multiple independent databases as a single one. Again, the standard SQL restriction mechanisms can and should be used. More specifically, use them to restrict what this *proxy* can reach; this provides some protection against database access control implementation flaws since the outside party can't even reach the actual databases.

Again, note that the proper design is driven by resource and threat models. If the resource is extremely valuable or the threat is great, stronger protections are indicated. Often, though, ordinary commercial practices will suffice.

11.4 Trust Patterns

As noted, the criteria used to select different protection schemes are resource value and threat model. What, though, makes the different schemes more or less secure? Why does a shared enclave give more protection than a set of firewall rules? Why do all of the necessary but missing connectivity requirements in our model web server complex hurt security? The answer to these questions—*trust patterns*—is at the heart of how one designs secure *systems*.

What do I mean by *trust patterns*? Who talks to whom? Who can talk to whom? What might they do? What do you trust them to do and to which other machines, all modulated by the strength of any security controls that are applied?

Let's consider a simple case and a variant: two hosts, A and B, on a network, and the same two hosts separated by a firewall that permits only port 80 to pass from A to B. What is the difference? If B trusts that A will only try to connect to port 80 on B—and not to any other port, nor to any port on host C—there is no difference, and the firewall is irrelevant. If B does not have that much trust in A, whether because A has nasty tendencies or because B thinks that A might be penetrated by nasty outsiders, the firewall enforces B's trust assumption: that the only connections that A will make will be to B:80.

We see here two essential design and analysis principles: that a system design can make certain assumptions about what will happen, and that external components can be used to enforce those assumptions. We can see this in some of the design alternatives dis-

Managing Firewall Rules

Circa 2000, I was asked to audit a firewall configuration. It was pretty straightforward, save for one thing: there were about 500 different rules. I told the organization that their design was terminally insecure; there was no way that anyone could understand the ruleset, so it was bound to have holes. I was right—but in fact I was wrong; I ignored the very strong business need for the connectivity. The correct answer would have been a design for how to do it safely.

Fundamentally, a firewall ruleset is a program that decides which connections should be permitted. If we approach the problem from this perspective, the shape of a solution starts to emerge: we employ all our tools for correct programming. Those include modularization, version control, "compilers," code review, testing, and more.

Modularization is one of the most crucial. In a situation like this, most sets of rules come from different internal groups. Perhaps the billing department has one set of exceptions, Personnel has another, and so on. If they're non-interfering, they can be analyzed independently, and even stored in different files; one job of the compiler is to combine the different files into a single ruleset.

The crucial word in the previous sentence is "non-interfering": how can the compiler tell? The answer is fairly straightforward: if the IP address ranges don't overlap, the rules don't interfere. If you have two different rule modules that do interfere, the compiler should flag that as an error. (One more caveat: multiple IP addresses for the same machine can also be problematic under certain circumstances. Analyzing that is left as an exercise for the reader.)

Ideally, a site would have good firewall rule analysis tools. These have been built [Bartal et al. 2004; Mayer, Wool, and Ziskind 2000], but they don't seem to be in common use. Too many products consider a really great GUI to be a better idea. Therein lies danger.

All rule modules should be tracked back to a particular request by a particular organization. This is easily done with a standard ticket-tracking system. Rules should have an expiration date; they should be reviewed periodically and removed when no longer needed.

There's one more trick you can use to keep rulesets manageable: have every outside partner talk over a different router interface, and have their rulesets tied to that interface. This need not (and probably is not) a separate physical interface, but a virtual one—an MPLS channel, a GRE tunnel, or an IPsec VPN—works just as well. In many cases, in fact, that will be the real benefit of using IPsec for external connectivity: it provides a convenient hook on which to hang the proper firewall rules.

cussed earlier. Let's revisit Figure 11.1 from this perspective; in particular, let's consider the effects of the existence of a NOC that has to be able to speak directly to each network. There are two essential security assumptions here: that the web servers will only be contacted on ports 80 and 443, and that there's no way to reach the database servers without going through the web servers. The former property is enforced by the reverse proxies, and the latter by the topology of the configuration.

The existence of the NOC invalidates both assumptions: there is now a path to the web servers that does not pass through the proxy servers, and there is a path to the database servers that does not go through the web servers. These violations do not inherently render the configuration insecure; however, they force us to take a deeper look. The original design required that the web servers trust the proxy servers and did not require any trust assumptions by the database servers. Now, we require an additional two assumptions: that the NOC itself will not attempt improper connections (and "improper" may have a more complex meaning), and that the NOC is itself sufficiently secure that it does not create a bypass path for attackers.

The former assumption is probably safe. If your NOC engineers can't be trusted, you probably have bigger security problems. (Can they be trusted? See Section 16.3, on logging, for precautions you can take.) The more interesting questions are whether the NOC machines are secure enough, and what to do if they're not.

Roughly speaking, a computer can be penetrated in one of two ways: either there's a flaw in something that's listening to (i.e., reachable via) a network port, or the user of the computer has inadvertently downloaded something dubious. Standard Windows and Mac OS X boxes tend to be listening to too many ports out of the box to be high assurance. They may very well be secure, but you don't *know* that; some form of remediation is indicated. (How to prevent external connections to those ports can be a bit tricky, since the operational needs of a NOC tend to conflict with standard firewalls, but the details of what to do are out of scope for this book. For now, let it suffice to say that it can be done.) Inadvertent downloads can be dealt with both by policy—"Thou shalt not browse the web from thy NOC console"—or by technology: delete all browsers from those boxes. If you can't delete the browsers because they're needed to configure or monitor certain things, force all browsing to go through a proxy that enforces your rules and logs exceptions.

To sum up: analysis of the more realistic server complex configuration shows that there are additional nodes and paths that have to be trusted. These may not be not fully trustable; however, with a bit of extra work we can achieve high-enough levels of security.

What did we do here? The essence of the analysis was looking at who could talk to whom, and deciding whether a simple connection was secure enough. Depending on the situation—the resources being protected, the threats, the topology, and the inherent properties of the systems and configurations—we may need to take actions and/or add components to ensure security.

Let's make another change to the topology and to the threat model and see what happens. Suppose that one of the databases is at a remote location. That is, instead of the database server being connected to the two south LANs, we instead have a router with a direct link to another router at some other site; at that site, we have another LAN with our database server. (For simplicity, I'll omit the reliability aspects of this variant, but of course there would be lots of replication.) How does this change our security analysis?

To a first approximation, it doesn't; we only have to assume that the new routers and links are secure. However, there are two potential issues. First, we need high assurance that the other site is indeed secure and that there is no way for other machines at this site to gain access to the distant database. Second, I noted the need to assume that the links are secure—but if your enemy is a major government, that may not be a valid assumption [Timberg 2013].

Encryption is the solution to both issues, but how we deploy it may differ. If the only risk is from the Andromedans, a link encryptor will suffice. On the other hand, if you're worried about what's going on at your remote site (and you probably should be, since it's distant and you have to rely on the sysadmins there), you probably want something like the enclave strategy discussed above, with a VPN link to it. (Fairly obviously, if you're not worried about governments but are worried about remote configurations, an unencrypted tunnel to the enclave will suffice—but using encryption won't hurt, and it will protect you if you've gotten the threat model wrong.)

When analyzing trust patterns, what is a node? There is no simple answer; it can be a process, a computer, or some combination of the two. Ideally, it is just a process; however, the analysis has to include the risks of privilege escalation attacks by that process should it be subverted, other active processes on the machine that may be penetrated via network activity, and so on. Similarly, defenses include file access permissions, sandboxes, virtual machines, and other host-centric concepts. Security and especially insecurity are systems properties; looking too narrowly is a classic mistake.

11.5 Legacy Systems

For all my fine words about design, I've been quite silent about one very ugly subject: legacy systems. There are very few greenfield designs in this business, ones where you get to build everything from scratch. We rarely have that luxury. There's often some Paleolithic mainframe off in a corner somewhere, one that contains a database vital to the project, but you can't talk to it securely because there are no COBOL implementations of TLS. What then? As it turns out, our analytic tools still work, but there will generally be more need for additional components.

Again, we start by assessing trust patterns. Do we trust the legacy systems or the path to them? Not infrequently, the answer to both questions is "no"; however, you will have neither the budget nor the time nor the authority to touch the systems. (Even if you had unlimited budget and authority, "do not touch" is probably the right answer. If you tried to rewrite every legacy system your project relied upon, the resulting disaster would make a lovely case study for a software engineering class. The system would end up far too large and far too complex to even work.) The best you can do is treat the legacy systems the way you would other unpleasant but necessary components (such as the NOC): they exist, you have to talk to them, and they have certain immutable properties. Your job is to engineer around the potential insecurity.

The best answer, in general, is a front end or proxy that you control. This box, which has known and acceptable properties, is the only one allowed to talk or listen to the legacy system. In essence, it's a proxy firewall that provides protection in both directions. It's not unreasonable to add some extra functionality, such as syntactic transformations like converting from XML to a punch card-oriented format, but that should be done with care: adding too much extra complexity to a security box always weakens it. Bear in mind, though, that this sort of conversion still has to be done somewhere. This is a difficult architectural decision: is this a legacy system interface box, a security gateway, or both? There are sound reasons for saying "both," but that in turn implies a need for care in just how this box is implemented. Should technologies like sandboxing be used?

There is one important disadvantage to this proxy strategy: information is lost. Specifically, the legacy system no longer has authoritative information on who initiated particular transactions; this affects both access control and logging. It is tempting, in some instances, to let the proxy impersonate individual users, but that may be infeasible or have other bad side effects. For one thing, how does the proxy server get the credentials to impersonate users? For another, the legacy system may not be designed for that many logins; $O(n^2)$ algorithms are perfectly acceptable when n is small but not when it's far larger than anyone had ever anticipated. Consider, say, a payroll system. Back when the world was young and punch cards walked the earth, employees probably filled out paper time sheets; these were sent to the keypunch pool and the resulting card decks were fed into the system. No logins were necessary. A tech generation later, departmental administrative folk would have something like an IBM 3270 terminal for interactive entry; at this point, logins and passwords would have been added, but only one per department. In today's world, of course, every employee would do it, via a web browser or a special smart phone app. That's at least an order of magnitude more users; can the system handle it?

From an access control perspective, the answer is to give the proxy full permissions on the mainframe's database. This, though, hurts logging (Section 16.3): the mainframe no longer knows and hence can no longer record the actual userid that initiated a particular transaction. This isn't good, but it is an inevitable consequence of what is often an unavoidable course of action. The only solution is to do copious logging at the proxy, with—if possible—enough information to permit automated correlation of the proxy's log file entries with the legacy system's.

11.6 Structural Defenses

There is a remarkable but subtle theme running through the last three sections: the designs we encounter are driven much more by application logic than by threat model. That is, the interconnection of web servers, database machines, service hosts, and so on is largely independent of what enemies might try to do. A high-end web site has a database because that's the best way to build the web site; it has nothing to do with the desire to separate a more critical resource from the highly exposed web server. The threat model comes into play when we decide what defenses to put in different spots: encryption, packet filters, hardened hosts, and more. Can we do better? We can, if we divide the logic differently and build the databases in a fashion that reflects the threats.

Let's consider an e-commerce site where the primary threat is high-end, targeted criminal activity. That is, the design is not intended to counter the Andromedans; rather, it's dealing with folks who just want money. There are three primary threats: theft of credit card numbers, fake orders to be delivered to a hacker-controlled address, and the financial and PR loss to the company if customer personal data is stolen. A common response to a data breach is for the affected company to pay for credit monitoring for the affected people. It's hard to say how much that costs per person, but it seems to be about $5 [Burke 2015]. That is not a trivial amount of money for most companies. Let's take the threats one at a time.

From this analysis, it is clear that the biggest threat is to the databases and in particular to their contents. That is, our protections should focus on certain fields; other components, such as the web server itself, are of much lower importance.

Credit card number theft is probably the biggest threat. If we can believe the estimates for Target's loss [Abrams 2014; Riley et al. 2014], it cost them about $50 per card number compromised. In other words, it's worth a considerable amount of effort to ensure that this failure *never* happens, no matter what else is compromised.

The first approach is to use database access controls, as outlined above, to make sure that the web server can never read the credit card number. The web server is the likely point of entry for a direct attack. If the database server itself is compromised, though, its access control mechanisms may not stand up—and the data on it is so central to business operations that it's likely very exposed to someone who has already gained access to the corporate network. Only one computer really needs to read the credit card number, though, and that's the one that actually sends the billing information to the bank. Accordingly, let's use public key cryptography to encrypt the credit card numbers; only the billing computer will have the decryption key. This computer is extremely specialized, and hence can be locked down a lot more than most other machines. If it's still too vulnerable, or if you can't afford the public key decryptions, have a specialized encrypt/decrypt computer: the web server or the database machine can ask it to encrypt credit card numbers using, say, AES; only the billing computer can request decryptions.

There is an alternative design that merits analysis: store credit card numbers in a separate databases, one that could perhaps be locked down more tightly. While better than storing card numbers in the primary database, it's not as good as this design. First, if the billing computer does the decryption itself, the card numbers are never exposed except at the single point where they are actually needed. Regardless of anything else, there must be exposure at this point; more or less by definition, any other scheme must be strictly weaker. Second, database servers are inherently more complex than the encryption/decryption server in the alternate scheme; probabilistically, this makes them considerably less secure. (There's another wrinkle I won't analyze in detail: many merchants use credit card numbers as customer identifiers; this lets them link online and offline purchases by the same person. There are a number of ways to deal with this, including using salted hashes as the identifier.)

We can use a similar strategy against the second threat: delivery to false addresses because of a database penetration. (Takeover of a user account is a separate issue.) Shipping addresses are not particularly sensitive, so they don't necessarily need to be encrypted (but see below); however, they do need to be authenticated. The crucial point here is the encryption the key that should be used: one derived from the user's password. More specifically, the user's password is used as a private key for the *Digital Signature Algorithm (DSA)* or its elliptic curve equivalent. From it, a public key is derived and is sent to a certificate authority (CA) server. The private key is used to sign all shipping addresses; the certificate, which is stored in the user profile database, authenticates them.

Note how this works. An attacker with control of the web server or even the database server cannot create a valid shipping address. Doing that can only be done for an account that is actively shopping on the site at that time. In fact, a user would be prompted for a password any time a new shipping address is entered; this is already routinely done by some sites for high-value purchases. The crucial machine is the CA server; as with the card number decryption server in the first scenario, it is a specialized machine that can be locked down far more tightly than a database server can be.

We deal with the third problem, theft of other personal information, by encryption: we encrypt all such information with the user's password. It is thus fully exposed to the web server when the user is logged in, but is protected otherwise. Certainly, information can be captured while a web server is compromised, but most accounts are not active most of the time.

This scheme poses a few interesting trade-offs; in particular, password reset and "big data" analysis become tricky. Let's take these one at a time.

If user profile data is encrypted with the user's password and that password is lost, the data is lost. There are at least two approaches to dealing with this. The first is to treat it as an advantage: one common cause of password reset is a compromise of the customer's email account, in which case the attacker can use that account to reset passwords on other interesting accounts and thus gain access to them. Forcing the user to reenter important data, such as credit card numbers, can actually be an advantage. A second approach is to keep a backup copy of the data, encrypted with a different key. This works if the password reset server—which cannot be the web server—is the only one that can decrypt this copy. It's a riskier approach, in that this is not nearly as simple a process as, say, the credit card number decryption server postulated earlier; still, it's at least somewhat stronger than keeping the data in the clear all along. Is this worth it? That's a business decision; this scheme is more costly (and not super-strong); is it worth it to avoid the customer annoyance of reentering profile data? How costly would the loss of the data *you* store be? (Not storing too much data can be a cost-saving measure as well as privacy-preserving.) If you don't use separate protection for credit numbers, as outlined earlier, it would seem prudent to use this variant for them at least.

There are other business costs as well. Another sensitive item is the user's email address; if a list of email addresses is stolen, it's valuable to the spammers. (Email addresses were the goal of some people allegedly linked to a penetration of JPMorgan Chase [Goldstein 2015].) That suggests that it should be encrypted. On the other hand, many companies like to send email to their customers, especially those who haven't been active lately. This may or may not be spam from the perspective of the recipient; nevertheless, very many companies perceive this as a useful (i.e., profitable) thing to do. This is a classic trade-off of security costs versus business opportunities and has to be evaluated as such, for each company's needs.

Big data analysis is easier to deal with. The analyses of interest generally deal with a set of categories, rather than raw personal data; user data can be categorized appropriately before encryption. Consider, for example, a company that wants to match its customers against the vast stores of information accumulated by data brokers [FTC 2014]. The desired information can be extracted (and perhaps hashed) when the user is logged in; later analyses can be done against this secondary information, without reference to the cleartext identity. The problem, of course, arises when you conceive of new analyses to do, ones for which you have not previously extracted the necessary data from the plaintext record.

⁂   ⁂   ⁂

I call these defenses "structural" because they're a reflection of the inherent structure of what needs to be protected. *If* your assets can be made to fit such a model, and *if* you can find ways to isolate the sensitive information while still fulfilling the primary organizational purposes, you can achieve very strong security against certain threats. However, these two "ifs" are very big ones indeed; except for passwords (which, as discussed in Chapter 7, are generally salted and hashed), this is not a common defensive approach. Often, though, that's because it hasn't been thought about. It should be.

11.7   Security Evaluations

> For now I'm a judge
> *And a good judge, too*
> Yes, now I'm a judge
> *And a good judge, too*
> Though all my law be fudge
> Yet I'll never, never budge
> And I'll live and die a judge
> *And a good Judge too*

> *Trial by Jury*
> —W. S. GILBERT AND ARTHUR SULLIVAN

The converse of design is analysis: given a system, is it secure? If it isn't, where are the problems and how can they be fixed or at least remediated?

Organizations can conduct security reviews at many different points. They may be done at various points during implementation, shortly before initial customer release, during periodic audits of the IT infrastructure, or even after a breach in some other system has awakened management.

Reviews have a lot in common with initial design. There's a business need; there are also likely some very necessary security risks. As before, while you must be honest, it's still sometimes necessary and always difficult to say "no." The advice on page 214 applies here, too: instead of saying, "I have a bad feeling about this," show precisely what the problem is and how to fix things.

There is one very important difference between design and review, though. A designer has a free hand to choose different components, including for reasons as mundane as "we'll get a better discount from vendor K if we buy more of their gear this year," or for important but non-security reasons such as the ability to run on the −48V DC that the backup battery plant provides. (Why −48V DC? That's an old telephone company central office standard; even today, gear intended to run in telco central offices will support that voltage. This is especially true for generic hardware such as routers and network switches.) The analyst has to work with the design as it exists, and not as he or she thinks it should have been built. The best analogy here is an architect versus the controlled demolition experts who bring us those really cool building implosion videos. Both need to understand the strength of materials, how many columns must fail to bring down a wall, and so on. The architect, though, will worry about aesthetics, the client's budget, how the space will be used, and more; the demolition expert takes all that as a given and figures out how many explosive charges detonated in what sequence will cause the proper collapse. The exterior wall cladding, carefully selected for its color, reflectivity, and thermal efficiency, is utterly irrelevant unless its strength or other physical properties affect the amount of plastique to use.

When doing the analysis itself, the most important thing to remember is that attackers don't follow the rules (Chapter 2). More specifically, they don't follow your notion of what can happen; they'll attack where they can. *Always* look more broadly. Consider, for example, a single node that the diagram labels "web server." The naive approach is to look at the HTTP server itself: Apache or IIS, which version, what configuration options are supported, and so on. Those questions are necessary but are by no means sufficient. The attacker would be just as happy to use an ssh port that was left unprotected, or to penetrate the firm to which you've outsourced your web site design; they'll then upload backdoored scripts *using the authorized connection*, which may involve FTP or something else unusual. You have to consider the computer as a whole—and if it's a virtual machine, you have to consider the hypervisor as well.

For that reason, I'm not fond of using attack trees or other top-down methodologies for security analysis. Those start by saying "to attack X, one must first penetrate Y or Z." Certainly, penetrating Y or Z will suffice, but that approach tends to favor known paths. Instead, go bottom-up: look at each computer, assume that it's been compromised, and see what can happen.

I approach system security analysis by *boxes and arrows*—a directed graph (not a tree!)—that shows input dependencies. (This approach is similar, though not identical, to Rescorla's "protocol models" [Rescorla and IAB 2005]. Also, see the "data flow diagrams" in [Shostack 2014].) A module with many arrows pointing to it is harder to secure because there are many avenues from which an attack can be launched; by extension, input from such modules should be treated with suspicion because it's much more likely to have been corrupted.

The process is iterative; neither boxes nor arrows are indivisible. If, notionally, an arrow represents a TCP connection, you need to ask how that TCP connection is protected and what other TCP connections can be created. Similarly, a box labeled "web server" on a high-level diagram may in fact run a content management system based on several SQL databases.

Resist the temptation to reify such a diagram by attaching weights and penetration probabilities. There are no reliable numbers on just how trustworthy a given component is; indeed, given how heavily dependent vulnerability is to the type of attacker and the assets being protected, it's far from clear that reliable numbers would be useful if used in a different context.

Here is where defenses come into play. First, we look at what nasty things are being prevented. Let's go back to Figure 11.1 and assume that the web server has somehow fallen. In that diagram, the database servers are now very much at risk. What mechanisms are in place to protect them? Are there access control lists or other firewall-like mechanisms on the LANs to keep the web servers from any ports other than SQL itself? Is the database configured to restrict access appropriately? To give one trivial example, there is no reason whatsoever that a web server should be able to read a customer's stored credit card numbers; it should only be able to write them. (If your user interface design includes the display of the last four digits of a card number, that should be a separate column, written by the web server at the same time as it writes the actual card number. How to ensure that the two fields are always consistent requires annoying but not overly hairy programming.)

It is, of course, fair to ask the chances of a particular computer being compromised. An analysis that simply says, "Very bad things will happen if Q is compromised," but does not explain how that could happen is fatally flawed. A statement like that is at most a caution—Q must be strongly protected—but says nothing about the actual risk. This part of the analysis, assessing the strength or weakness of any given computer, is the one most dependent on the experience and judgment of the analyst; it is also the one most dependent on the abilities of the adversary. Is Linux more secure than Windows? Is Debian Linux 5.0 more secure than Windows 8.1? Does the answer change depending on the patch installation strategy, or on external protections such as packet filters? What is the reputation of installed third-party software, such as Apache or MySQL? What can a realistic attacker do with physical access to some component? There are no easy or obvious answers to even simple questions like these, let alone more difficult ones about MI-31's stash of 0-day exploits or about attacks involving combinations of software weaknesses.

One approach to subsystem security analysis is the *Relative Attack Surface Quotient (RASQ)* [Howard, Pincus, and Wing 2005]. RASQ does not try to assign an absolute security value to a component; rather, it compares different designs for a subsystem to evaluate which is more secure. The evaluation is done by looking for attack opportunities along a set of different dimensions, such as open communications channels or access rights. RASQ is not a perfect solution, and it does require two or more versions of a subsystem to evaluate; still, it is useful when assessing design alternatives or changes to an existing system architecture.

Operational considerations matter, too. Recall the story from Chapter 2 about the guest login on a gateway. One can't anticipate a chain of failures quite like that, but it's entirely fair to ask what provisions are present for emergency access. Are they secure? I once reviewed a design that stated, "No console access except from the computer room." That's a lovely thought, and in the 1980s it might have been a sensible precaution. Today, though, servers live in lights-out data centers, often with no one on-site. Indeed, the actual code may run on some cloud provider's infrastructure. What, then, is "the" computer room? And if there really is no other access, what will happen in an emergency? The system I was reviewing would have been more secure in real life if they planned ahead for secure, available console access.

You may find, if you push, that there are actually more components than are shown on the diagram you've been given, just as we saw when analyzing Figure 11.1. Drill down! Ask questions about such things! (But do it tactfully: don't say, "What else are you hiding from me?" after some extra component is disclosed. . . .) It's quite normal for system architects to show a design with only their components; the boring operational pieces are left to the data center folk who are accustomed to dealing with console servers, NOCs, and so on. Attackers, of course, don't care about this organizational boundary.

Understanding and evaluating a system is not a simple task. Indeed, just understanding the threats is difficult; whole books (like the excellent [Shostack 2014]) have been written on the subject. The essence is to approach the questions systematically. A very high percentage of failures occur because designers or evaluators completely overlooked some aspect of the architecture, or because they underestimated the skills and resources of potential enemies. If you look at every component and every link, asking yourself who could compromise it and what the effects would be, you're much more likely to get the right answer.

Chapter 12

Selecting Software

Most demons are as dumb as a sackful of hammers. This does not mean they're safe to mess with, any more than a C++ compiler is "safe" in the hands of an enthusiastic computer science undergrad. Some people can mess up anything, and computational demonology adds a new and unwelcome meaning to terms like "memory leak" and "debugger."

The Jennifer Morgue
—CHARLES STROSS

12.1 The Quality Problem

When it comes to software, the choice is buy or build. Given the complexity of most products, the large majority of software today is purchased, not locally built; this includes almost all operating systems, word processors, web servers, web browsers, compilers, databases, and a vast assortment of other applications. That means that our security is critically dependent on the vagaries of vendors—and too much of their software is insecure.

Broadly speaking, product quality (not just software quality) improvement is driven by three different factors: market pressures, liability, and regulation. All three have failed here. Let's take them one by one.

In at least the short term and probably the medium term, most software products have a pretty constant market share. Some products are effectively monopolies. Microsoft has *no* competitors for enterprise desktop computing; even Apple (let alone Linux) has a minuscule market share. Nor is this necessarily wrong; it's not clear that competing alternatives are really ready. Enterprise desktop computers are not managed one at a time the way that home computers are; rather, a vast array of tools are used by system administrators. The tools for Windows are simply far better developed.

Even if the tools existed, switching would still be very hard. Software is "sticky"; replacement products are rarely 100% compatible, either technically or in terms of user experience. Changing mail servers, for example, sounds simple: everything speaks IMAP, right? Well, no. Apart from the fact that many organizations use Microsoft Exchange's own protocols (thus necessitating client configuration changes at the very least), different implementations of IMAP support different optional features, have different mail-filtering languages, require very different configurations, and—most seriously—have their own mail-storage formats. It's certainly possible to switch, but doing so is neither simple nor cheap.

The net effect, then, is that there are considerable technical barriers to switching software products. Some of this is inherent in the concept, but it's also true that incumbent vendors like it that way and often take conscious actions to lock in their customers even more. The net effect is that the market can't fix security nearly as much as we'd like, even apart from the market externalities of many breaches.

Liability (and its usual adjunct, liability insurance), the second common driver, has also failed, for two very different reasons. One is pervasive: virtually all software comes with an *end-user license agreement (EULA)* that disclaims all liability for more or less anything, up to and including possession of your computers by demons from beyond the abyss. Here is some sample text from Apple's EULA for Mac OS X (shouting caps as in the original):

> B. YOU EXPRESSLY ACKNOWLEDGE AND AGREE THAT, TO THE EXTENT PERMITTED BY APPLICABLE LAW, USE OF THE APPLE SOFTWARE AND ANY SERVICES PERFORMED BY OR ACCESSED THROUGH THE APPLE SOFTWARE IS AT YOUR SOLE RISK AND THAT THE ENTIRE RISK AS TO SATISFACTORY QUALITY, PERFORMANCE, ACCURACY AND EFFORT IS WITH YOU. C. TO THE MAXIMUM EXTENT PERMITTED BY APPLICABLE LAW, THE APPLE SOFTWARE AND SERVICES ARE PROVIDED AS IS AND AS AVAILABLE, WITH ALL FAULTS AND WITHOUT WARRANTY OF ANY KIND, AND APPLE AND APPLE'S LICENSORS (COLLECTIVELY REFERRED TO AS APPLE FOR THE PURPOSES OF SECTIONS 7 AND 8) HEREBY DISCLAIM ALL WARRANTIES AND CONDITIONS WITH RESPECT TO THE APPLE SOFTWARE AND SERVICES, EITHER EXPRESS, IMPLIED OR STATUTORY, INCLUDING, BUT NOT LIMITED

TO, THE IMPLIED WARRANTIES AND/OR CONDITIONS OF MER-
CHANTABILITY, SATISFACTORY QUALITY, FITNESS FOR A PAR-
TICULAR PURPOSE, ACCURACY, QUIET ENJOYMENT, AND NON-
INFRINGEMENT OF THIRD PARTY RIGHTS. D. APPLE DOES NOT
WARRANT AGAINST INTERFERENCE WITH YOUR ENJOYMENT OF
THE APPLE SOFTWARE AND SERVICES, THAT THE FUNCTIONS
CONTAINED IN, OR SERVICES PERFORMED OR PROVIDED BY, THE
APPLE SOFTWARE WILL MEET YOUR REQUIREMENTS, THAT THE
OPERATION OF THE APPLE SOFTWARE OR SERVICES WILL BE UN-
INTERRUPTED OR ERROR-FREE...
8. Limitation of Liability. TO THE EXTENT NOT PROHIBITED BY AP-
PLICABLE LAW, IN NO EVENT SHALL APPLE BE LIABLE FOR PER-
SONAL INJURY, OR ANY INCIDENTAL, SPECIAL, INDIRECT OR
CONSEQUENTIAL DAMAGES WHATSOEVER, INCLUDING, WITH-
OUT LIMITATION, DAMAGES FOR LOSS OF PROFITS, CORRUP-
TION OR LOSS OF DATA, FAILURE TO TRANSMIT OR RECEIVE
ANY DATA OR INFORMATION, BUSINESS INTERRUPTION OR ANY
OTHER COMMERCIAL DAMAGES OR LOSSES, ARISING OUT OF
OR RELATED TO YOUR USE OR INABILITY TO USE THE APPLE
SOFTWARE OR SERVICES OR ANY THIRD PARTY SOFTWARE OR
APPLICATIONS IN CONJUNCTION WITH THE APPLE SOFTWARE
OR SERVICES, HOWEVER CAUSED, REGARDLESS OF THE THEORY
OF LIABILITY (CONTRACT, TORT OR OTHERWISE) AND EVEN IF
APPLE HAS BEEN ADVISED OF THE POSSIBILITY OF SUCH DAM-
AGES... In no event shall Apple's total liability to you for all damages (other
than as may be required by applicable law in cases involving personal injury)
exceed the amount of fifty dollars ($50.00). The foregoing limitations will
apply even if the above stated remedy fails of its essential purpose.

Microsoft's disclaimers are similar in spirit (boldface as in the original):

**The manufacturer or installer, and Microsoft exclude all implied war-
ranties, including those of merchantability, fitness for a particular purpose, and non-infringement...**
**Except for any refund the manufacturer or installer, or Microsoft, may
provide, you may not recover any other damages, including direct, consequential, lost profits, special, indirect, or incidental damages.** If you
have any basis for recovering damages from Microsoft, you can recover only
direct damages up to the amount that you paid for the software (or up to

$50 USD if you acquired the software for no charge). The damage exclusions and limitations in this agreement apply even if repair, replacement or a refund for the software does not fully compensate you for any losses or if the manufacturer or installer, or Microsoft, knew or should have known about the possibility of the damages. Some states and countries do not allow the exclusion or limitation of incidental, consequential, or other damages, so those limitations or exclusions may not apply to you.

Even the *GNU Public License (GPL)* acts this way (LaTeX formatting from the original!):

15. Disclaimer of Warranty.

THERE IS NO WARRANTY FOR THE PROGRAM, TO THE EXTENT PERMITTED BY APPLICABLE LAW. EXCEPT WHEN OTHERWISE STATED IN WRITING THE COPYRIGHT HOLDERS AND/OR OTHER PARTIES PROVIDE THE PROGRAM "AS IS" WITHOUT WARRANTY OF ANY KIND, EITHER EXPRESSED OR IMPLIED, INCLUDING, BUT NOT LIMITED TO, THE IMPLIED WARRANTIES OF MERCHANTABILITY AND FITNESS FOR A PARTICULAR PURPOSE. THE ENTIRE RISK AS TO THE QUALITY AND PERFORMANCE OF THE PROGRAM IS WITH YOU. SHOULD THE PROGRAM PROVE DEFECTIVE, YOU ASSUME THE COST OF ALL NECESSARY SERVICING, REPAIR OR CORRECTION.

16. Limitation of Liability.

IN NO EVENT UNLESS REQUIRED BY APPLICABLE LAW OR AGREED TO IN WRITING WILL ANY COPYRIGHT HOLDER, OR ANY OTHER PARTY WHO MODIFIES AND/OR CONVEYS THE PROGRAM AS PERMITTED ABOVE, BE LIABLE TO YOU FOR DAMAGES, INCLUDING ANY GENERAL, SPECIAL, INCIDENTAL OR CONSEQUENTIAL DAMAGES ARISING OUT OF THE USE OR INABILITY TO USE THE PROGRAM (INCLUDING BUT NOT LIMITED TO LOSS OF DATA OR DATA BEING RENDERED INACCURATE OR LOSSES SUSTAINED BY YOU OR THIRD PARTIES OR A FAILURE OF THE PROGRAM TO OPERATE WITH ANY OTHER PROGRAMS), EVEN IF SUCH HOLDER OR OTHER PARTY HAS BEEN ADVISED OF THE POSSIBILITY OF SUCH DAMAGES.

No one reads these license agreements (even US Chief Justice Roberts doesn't [Weiss 2010]), but you're bound by them nevertheless. They all say the same thing: vendors aren't liable, no matter if their software leads to demonic possession of your computer.

Suppose, though, that there was some liability. That would almost certainly lead to cyberliability insurance, but the insurance industry would have problems, too. For one thing, there's not enough actuarial data to use in setting rates; most intrusions are never detected, and many that are detected aren't reported. For another, this sort of insurance works best if it leads to improvement in the underlying artifact—electrical codes, for example, were originally a creation of the fire insurance industry—but we as a profession don't know enough about the actual, detailed causes of failures [Bellovin 2012]; this is itself a problem.

The third force for improving quality is regulation, but regulation is quite problematic when it comes to software. Apart from the reluctance of many governments to impose regulations on a very dynamic industry, it's quite unclear what regulations should say. "Don't commit buffer overflows"? "Don't be insecure"? "Don't use C or C++"? "Here is the One True Model for software development"? The possible rules are either too trite or venture into areas where there isn't any agreement at all on how to do it.

To be fair, software has improved. When I started in this business, it was normal for a mainframe to crash one or more times per day. Here's how long one of my computers has been up:

```
$ uptime
 1:28PM up 1124 days, 9:35, ...
```

The improvement is visible for security, too. As I've noted, both in this book and elsewhere, Microsoft has expended a tremendous amount of effort on software security, and the effects have been quite noticeable. Apple's efforts, though less specifically publicized, have resulted in improvements to its codebase as well. However, software stickiness, the need for backwards compatibility with previous (sometimes bad) designs, and general difficulties in upgrading enterprise software means that problematic code persists for a very long time.

12.2   Selecting Software Wisely

Given all that, how should one select software wisely (or should I write s€£ect $oftware wisel¥)? As I imply, it's a question of money. More precisely, it's a question of how you minimize your total outlay over time.

The first question to ask, though, is this: does the software do what you need it to do? Perfectly secure software that doesn't meet your requirements is rather useless. Sure, you won't get hacked via it—but you also won't get its benefits. In fact, maybe you will get hacked *because* of it: if you have to write your own code to make up for the

Security Rap Sheets

Periodically, some piece of code will seem to be the focus of a disproportionate number of security incidents. In 2001, for example, the Gartner Group released an advisory that said, in part:[a]

> Enterprises using Microsoft's IIS web server software have to update every IIS server with every Microsoft security patch that comes out—almost weekly. However, Nimda (and to a lesser degree Code Blue) has again shown the high risk of using IIS and the effort involved in keeping up with Microsoft's frequent security patches.

The code was seriously buggy; Gartner recommended that its clients stop using it.

Was it really worse? Why were so many bugs found? Very often, this is not just random chance; it reflects the fundamentally low quality of some piece of code, and the concomitant focus on it by the hacker community. If a program is poorly written, it will probably have many bugs, and not just one or two; ordinary efforts by the bad guys will tend to expose them. By contrast, fixing a large, buggy program while maintaining backwards compatibility is a major undertaking; often, the best thing to do is to scrap the old code and write it afresh, though that will almost certainly cause transition woes.

It is perfectly reasonable to take such history into account when evaluating a system. Why not? After all, the hackers do that when deciding where next to chip away. It is, however, important to stay current; my list of risky software is not the same as it was ten years ago, or even five. New pieces of crudware take the place of old ones; old ones can be repaired if the vendor puts in enough effort. Take IIS, for example. That Gartner Group warning was one of the catalysts that made Microsoft get religion and launch a massive code and system quality effort. They've done an admirable job, a cleanup job worse than what Heracles did on the Augean stables, but it's paid off; their code is now among the best in the business. The IIS warning was retracted in 2004.[b]

---

a. "Nimda Worm Shows You Can't Always Patch Fast Enough,"
   https://www.gartner.com/id=340962.
b. "Management Update: IIS Is No Longer the Problem in Web Server Security,"
   https://www.gartner.com/id=464817.

missing functionality, will it be written securely? If you don't have experience with secure development, this is a serious risk indeed.

Let's assume, then, that the product has the right functionality. Can you trust it? Alternately, if there are several competitive products, all of which can do more or less what you need and all of which are comparable in total cost of ownership, which will be the most secure? Unfortunately, it's very, very hard to tell.

One starting point is the product's reputation (see page 234). If used judiciously, it's a reasonable starting point; a series of security flaws tends to indicate fundamental lack of care during development, and there's no reason to think that the last flaw found is the last one present. On the other hand, flaws found are often a reflection of attention paid rather than underlying code quality. For example, more holes are reported in Windows than in Apple's OS X—but is that a reflection of code quality or of Windows' vastly greater market share? Attackers aren't stupid; if they're going to go to the effort of finding an exploit, they're likely to prefer one that's useful against many more victims.

Some people tout the virtues of open-source software. After all, "given enough eyeballs, all bugs are shallow" [Raymond 2000]. Unfortunately, the adage is at best an oversimplification and at worse dangerously misleading. First, the eyeballs actually have to *look* at the code and not simply download it. Second, they have to be capable, motivated eyeballs—do they belong to a person who actually knows how to evaluate code? Third, simply looking at code is far from enough. Secure code is the output of a sophisticated development process; lots of tools, testing, and far more go into it than just reading the code. As I've argued elsewhere [Bellovin 2009b], many open-source projects do not have the resources or the discipline for secure software development. This is arguably the primary cause of the very public failures in OpenSSL.

All that said, open-source packages do have a crucial advantage: you can look at the source code, not so much to find specific holes as to get an overall feeling for the quality of the code.

There's one important caveat that you should factor into your own analysis: who is your enemy? If you're being targeted, it may very well be worth an attacker's while to develop an exploit aimed at you, no matter what OS you run. Similarly, a high-end attacker is likely to have existing frameworks and toolkits into which a new vulnerability can be plugged. In other words, the further your adversaries are from the origin of our threat model graph, the less you're protected by running an unusual operating system or suite of applications. It is worth remembering that Stuxnet and the remote bugging exploit in the "Athens Affair" [Prevelakis and Spinellis 2007]—two incidents generally attributed to intelligence agencies—involved malware running on very unusual platforms indeed. (The Athens Affair has also been blamed on the United States [Bamford 2015].)

There are other factors that you can look at beyond reputation. One is how well the product handles its own security-relevant components. Does it use encryption where it should or could? If so, is the selection of algorithms reasonable? Does it need root or Administrator privileges to run? If so, why? If you can examine a trial installation, look at file permissions—is everything locked down properly? Or are there world-writable files and directories? Sometimes, there's a good reason for such things; more often, they're a sign of lazy or security-clueless programmers. Does the product use multiple security contexts when appropriate? Apache, for example, though it runs as user www, is installed with its files owned by some other userid.

Can you talk to the company's security group about specific concerns? Do they seem knowledgeable? Even if the design isn't perfect from your perspective, do they have good reasons for it? I had a long email interchange with the top security person at the company that developed the password manager I use—I'd noted an oddity, and had a few concerns. He was very responsive—the oddity was my error, and he was already aware of my concerns. It turned out that there were trade-offs that they had to consider, in terms of market (it's a multi-platform product), usability, supportability, and legacy code. I don't know that I'd have made all of the same decisions, but their choices were not unreasonable, and they did not compromise the essential security of the product.

Try applying the evaluation methodology described in Section 11.7. How many different components comprise the product? How do they talk to each other? Can an attacker send or intercept messages on those channels? How does one component of the product authenticate the source of messages? Consider, for example, a Unix-based system that uses multiple processes. If they communicate via pipes, the channel is quite safe. If they use Unix domain sockets, the risk is at most from on-machine attackers, and perhaps not even them. On the other hand, if Internet-domain sockets are used, there may be a considerable risk—and in one case, that decision led to regulatory action against a company.[1]

Perhaps most important, what do you know of the company's development and security practices? How do they themselves assess security? What sort of security analysis and testing do they do? Remember that security has to be built in, not bolted on. Do they do this?

There are some security certifications; however, their relevance to most organizations is questionable. First and foremost, certifications apply to a given security model. If it does not match your needs, you will reap few, if any, benefits from software designed to meet that model, with or without a certification. Years ago, when I was fairly new to the security business, I tried applying the Department of Defense's Orange Book's principles [DoD 1985a] to a standard commercial setup: multiple users, (non-web) server, database,

---

1. "In the Matter of HTC AMERICA, Inc., a Corporation,"
   http://www.ftc.gov/sites/default/files/documents/cases/2013/07/130702htccmpt.pdf.

and so on. It didn't work. It didn't come close to providing any useful protection because the Orange Book was designed for the military's setup for classified information (Top Secret, Secret, and Confidential, plus compartments), and that wasn't at all what I was trying to do. Furthermore, certification takes time (which means you'll be well behind the cutting edge—not always a disadvantage!) and often applies only to very particular hardware configurations.

All that said, and especially if you're working in a classified environment, you may need such things. Note that those environments correlate well with serious threat models, which in turn should affect your choice of software.

Ultimately, you cannot predict what's going to happen with any given program or program product. If there is a security problem, there are three questions to ask. How responsive is the vendor when problems are found? Does your overall system architecture protect most of your assets, even if this component fails? Finally, how easily and quickly can you replace it with something else, while not creating more problems for yourself in the process?

Chapter 13

Keeping Software Up to Date

A wandering minstrel I—
   A thing of shreds and patches,
   Of ballads, songs and snatches,
And dreamy lullaby!

Nanki-Poo in *The Mikado*
—W. S. GILBERT AND ARTHUR SULLIVAN

13.1   Holes and Patches

Of all of the tools in the technical workshop, few are as loathed as the security patch. On one hand, they're a nuisance that tends to introduce entropy into the original code base. On the other hand, patches are utterly necessary. Software is always imperfect; when imperfections manifest themselves as holes, there are few choices but to spackle them, sand them, and paint them. The alternative—the sysadmin equivalent of moving some furniture in front of the hole, if I may continue my metaphor—is not just unattractive, it reduces architectural flexibility and leaves you vulnerable to attackers who are closer to the wall than you are.

Let's skip the flowery imagery. Any time you have a security bug—and if your system is at all complex, you do—you can either repair it or mitigate it. Mitigations can include putting another access mechanism—a firewall or equivalent—between the hole and would-be attackers; alternately, you can assume that a penetration will occur and prepare for detection and recovery in the usual way, by taking extra backups, creating specialized

239

intrusion detection scripts, and so on. Finally, under extreme circumstances, you can shut down the vulnerable systems until one of the other alternatives become feasible.

Some would opt for a final alternative: ignore the problem and hope that you're not hit. This isn't a strategy, it's wishful thinking. Maybe you won't be hit, but if you're not watching carefully you'll never know if you were right or not.

Deciding between these choices requires complex analyses and calculations, calculations that are always imperfect because the necessary data is unobtainable. Though there have been tries at general quantitative solutions—see [Beattie et al. 2002] for an excellent attempt—the answers are at best probabilistic and at worse meaningless because of inadequate data. Furthermore, the existence of targeted attacks skews the results; you're no longer dealing with a random function.

There are a number of factors to consider. Some are generic security questions; other are specific to the particular hole.

Attacker motivation Are you being targeted? If so, by whom? Answers of "no" are rarely definitive; answers of "yes" should be taken seriously.

Attacker capability For this specific hole, how much sophistication is needed to launch an attack? If, say, it reduces the complexity of finding a cryptographic key from 2^{256} operations to 2^{70}, you're probably safe from all but the Andromedans. On the other hand, if there's a kit out there that merely requires a script kiddie to click "P0wn!", the risks are considerably higher.

Exploit availability How widespread is exploit code? If the hole was originally reported on public mailing lists like bugtraq and Full Disclosure, it's a pretty good bet that anyone who wants it, has it. Holes that were closely held by the vendor until patch release are less likely to be exploited initially, but the likelihood goes up with time: attackers study the patches to learn what new things they can do to unpatched systems. Indeed, some people use the phrase "Exploit Wednesday" for the day after Microsoft's regular monthly "Patch Tuesday" security update [Leffall 2007].

On the other hand, if there's a report that a 0-day is in active use, that's a strong indication that you should move very quickly to install the patch when it becomes available and to mitigate its impact until then.

Patch quality How good is the patch? Does it really solve the problem? Does it create new problems? Patches are software; therefore, they can be buggy. Furthermore, since there is often pressure to ship patches quickly, they may undergo less testing than base code.

Security and functionality problems with patches are far from unknown. Sometimes, they don't fix the problem [Greenberg 2012]; other times, they can introduce new ones [Gueury and Veditz 2009]. Speed of response to a newly announced hole is good, but not if it comes at the expense of quality and hence security [Bellovin 2009b].

Patch timing When has the patch become available? At the start of (your) workday early in the week? 3:00 AM on a holiday weekend? It's tempting to try to compare that to the attackers' work schedule, but that's probably fruitless. If nothing else, the Andromedans' ritual calendar is derived from the rotation of a distant pulsar, the product of two random twin primes, and the current state of health of Schrödinger's cat [Trimmer 1980]. More seriously, attackers can be anywhere in the world; if they're serious attackers (and in particular if they're targeting you), they'll strike when they can, and not take the weekend off.

Damage potential What is the potential for damage if a system is hacked? Will sensitive data be compromised? Does the data on system fall within the ambit of mandatory breach notification laws?

Importance of availability How vital is it that the system be available? To whom, under what conditions? Is it mission critical—for an online store, the web site *is* the business—or is the system just running a background task that is looking for "a message in eleven dimensions hidden deep inside the number pi" [Sagan 1985]? Can you do without it for a while? Which is worse, having it unavailable now or during cleanup and recovery if it's hacked?

Suppose you can't patch immediately, either because no patch is available or for any of the other reasons listed above. Now what? How to proceed next is very situation dependent. Apart from the questions above, how you proceed depends on just how much you know about the exploit and how it is used.

Under certain circumstances, the right response might be procedural. For example, if there's a 0-day PDF exploit in the wild, you might be able to protect yourself by telling members of the organization not to open suspicious PDFs. It might work, but absent further instructions or controls it's a very risky approach. A lot, though, depends on the precise nature of the attack.

Few people ever knowingly open something that's boobytrapped. The trick, though, is telling people how to recognize fraudulent messages. Perhaps most people will recognize phony airline ticket receipts, package tracking notices, and the like. Skillfully crafted spear-phishing attachments are much harder to detect, unless all of your employees are the type to peruse Received: lines on inbound email.

Another approach might be purely technical: drop or reject all messages with attached PDF files, or strip such attachments from any inbound messages. This is, of course, a self-inflicted denial of service; to work around it, employees may try to evade the ban by shipping around URLs to cloud-based storage services, having PDF-containing email sent instead to personal accounts and importing the attachments via flash drives, etc. Curiously enough, under these circumstances and threat model—spear-phishing attacks exploiting a 0-day hole in PDF viewers—this behavior may not create a security hole. Consider: if the files in question are from known correspondents, it would take two-way communications to set up the alternate channel. This, though, means that the sender is verified, at least by email address. The spear-phishing incidents we've seen thus far involve passive impersonation, not account hijacking or the like. While one can certainly imagine that MI-31 is reading such emails and can adapt accordingly, that would represent a considerable escalation in the typical attack effort.

These, as noted, are work-arounds. Really, though, you want to patch holes as soon as you can. The trick is being able to do so effectively.

13.2   The Problem with Patches

Apart from the issue of whether the patch actually fixes the security problems to which it is addressed, there are two aspects of patches that merit caution. First, of course, patches are software and are thus subject to the "thousand unnatural shocks that [code] is heir to" [Shakespeare 1603]. That is, they themselves can be buggy, insecure, and so on, just as the base code can be. In fact, patches can be worse. When you're writing new code, you have a relatively clean slate and can design appropriate interfaces to do what (you think) you need to do. By contrast, a patch is a change to a flawed but extant code base; the structure of that code may not let you easily do what you want. Consider a simple example: you realize that a procedure needs to check its inputs more carefully and pass back an error indication if there's a problem. It sounds simple enough—unless that procedure had no provision for returning any status indication; worse yet, it's invoked from many places, some of which are not well-suited to error handling. Now what? Any experienced programmer can think of several solutions in less time than it took me to type this; the fact remains, though, that the code won't be as clean as it could have been had the need been recognized initially. Furthermore, one of the obvious methods—passing back an "impossible" value as its normal output—could cause problems for some of those other pieces of code, especially if "impossible" turns out to be an overstatement.

A second problem, especially serious in large enterprises, is that often, specialized (and perhaps locally written) applications are incompatible with the patch: they relied, implicitly or explicitly, on old, buggy behavior. Your CEO will not be happy if you explain that the corporation can't function because you pushed out a security patch. For that matter, you won't be happy, either, if one of the affected applications is the payroll system that writes your paycheck.

The solution, of course, is testing, by the software vendor and by you in your own test lab. Historically, the first round of testing has not always been high quality; more than one patch has caused serious problems [Goodin 2013] or failed to fix the security hole it was intended to close [Greenberg 2012]. Beyond that, vendor testing is more or less by definition inadequate for your environment: the vendor doesn't know your precise configuration or applications. You have to test things yourself, and make sure that the applications you care about continue to work; that in turn means that you have to have a good-enough test lab and the resources to use it. Even that's not a guarantee, of course; "Program testing can be used to show the presence of bugs, but never to show their absence" [Dijkstra 1970].

So: patches can be incomplete or buggy, the vendor may not have tested them well enough, it's a nuisance for you to test them, even that won't show all problems—and you absolutely have to install them. The bad guys often reverse-engineer patches [Leffall 2007; Naraine 2007] (and the Andromedans certainly do), which means that once the patch is out you're at increased risk, though from whom and by how much depends on the threat model.

There are related issues surrounding new versions of a product: when should you install them? Any experienced sysadmin has heard and uttered the mantra "never install .0 of anything;" the advice is quite sound for production systems. In the long run, though, you don't have a choice; vendors don't want to support old codebases forever and will *end of lifetime (EOL)* them at some point. Once a product has been EOLed, there will be no more security patches for it, and the one thing worse than installing security patches is not having any patches to be installed. If that's not enough to force your hand, what will you do when some other upgrade—a new version of your OS, or newer hardware that isn't supported by your old OS—forces your hand? You can often get away with skipping a version, but at some point you *will* have to upgrade. The proper response is to plan how to do it (and lobby upper management for the necessary budget and staff), not to deny the necessity.

13.3 How to Patch

Assuming that a decision to install a security patch has been made, there are three important procedural steps:

- Deciding on a per-machine schedule for installation

- Actually installing the patch

- Tracking which machines have or have not had the patch installed

This applies to all patches. The situation for security patches is different, though, since there's a cost to not installing them other than a noticeable loss of functionality from running on a buggy platform.

Deciding when to install a patch depends on four different factors. The first, of course, is how much confidence you have that it won't be harmful. If you're highly confident that it won't break anything (perhaps because of your testing, or perhaps because the affected modules are not ones that you use), there's no reason to hold off. Conversely, if the patch affects mission-critical code and you haven't tested it, you should hold off.

A second critical factor is whether the security hole is actively being exploited. Often, this will be in the technical press, for example, [Goodin 2012a] or on social media or security mailing lists. At other times, you might hear this from colleagues or from some government agency, as happened with a recent Internet Explorer (IE) bug [Rosenblatt 2014]. Obviously, you have to take remedial action very quickly in a case like this.

You have to be very careful about your threat model, though. A report by Microsoft gives some figures on when various new holes are exploited and by whom. They looked at 16 new vulnerabilities found over a two-year period. Only two ever made it into exploit kits used by ordinary criminals, and that was a rather late development—but nine of them were used very early in targeted attacks [Batchelder et al. 2013, p. 9]. In other words, ordinary care in patching, rather than crash programs, will generally suffice, except in rare cases *or* if you're being attacked by MI-31.

Sometimes, you may have other defenses that you can rely on until you're ready to patch your system. In the case of that IE exploit, you may be able to configure your web proxy (which your firewall forces all employees to use) to block external web browsing by IE users. Microsoft's *Enhanced Mitigation Experience Toolkit (EMET)*[1] is reputed to be highly effective at blocking exploits even after they're downloaded. Relying on this is a delicate dance, though; you have to be sure that all exploit paths are blocked. You may know, for example, that your mail gateway will detect and delete some particular nasty file, but do you know it won't be downloaded via the web or carried in on a USB drive?

Finally, you may know that your organization isn't at risk. Perhaps there's a bug in the encryption module used by web browsers and an instant messaging program, but it's only exploitable in the latter. Your organization doesn't use instant messaging, so you're not at risk; you do rely on encrypted web browsing, though, so you don't want to risk breaking it.

Suppose you've decided that a given patch should be installed. In an ideal world, you just tell that to your database-driven sysadmin platform (Section 15.3), good magic happens, and all is well. (If you don't have such tools and you're a large organization—well, you should. Go read Chapter 15 and then come back here. I'll wait.) Decentralized

---

1. "The Enhanced Mitigation Experience Toolkit," https://support.microsoft.com/kb/2458544.

or open organizations have a harder time; they're more reliant on users doing the right thing, to wit, installing the patches when they're told to.

The more different platforms in use, the harder job the sysadmin group has. They need the time, test machines, and expertise to evaluate patches from multiple vendors and make the right decisions. The usual (and generally correct) response is segmentation: a small list of fully supported platforms, with others permissible on an at-the-users'-own-risk basis. Consider the following statement by my own university's IT group:

> Currently, Administrative Applications are not certified to run on Windows 8. Additionally, Windows 8 is only an install supported product; CUIT does not support Windows 8 functionality at this time.

They don't say don't run Windows 8; they simply say it's not certified or supported. It may work (and in fact probably does work very well)—but if there is a problem, it's *your* problem, not theirs. This is a university, about as open an environment as one can imagine. There's at least one of every imaginable system here (and some unimaginable ones as well); there's an obvious limit to what the IT group can do.

In corporations, there is rarely that much flexibility about what computers are used. However, there's one growing exception: the Bring Your Own Device (BYOD) movement, where employees are allowed to use their own equipment, especially smart phones. The organization is very limited in what it can do about patch installation: the gear is, after all, employee owned. Often, the best that can be done is to insist that people run a company-supplied audit tool, one that ensures that the system is fully up to date on patches and antivirus software before it is allowed to connect to the corporate network. Such software exists, especially for Windows machines.

The final important aspect of patch installation is tracking which machines have or have not been patched. Always-on, in-building desktops and servers are the easy case; they'll almost always be up to date. Mobile devices, home equipment, and systems that are out for repair are more challenging. Automated sysadmin tools generally handle this without undue trouble, but if you're not using one you need some other recording and audit mechanism. An unpatched machine, especially a mobile machine that can wander outside the firewall, is a risk to the entire organization. (The August 2001 IETF meeting was in the middle of the Code Red worm outbreak. I looked for attacks originating from the meeting LAN. There were at least a dozen infected laptops there, laptops that were tunneling back to their home networks and/or would be physically connected to it the following week. Code Red should not have penetrated any properly designed and administered firewall, but virtually every corporation had it on the inside of their networks. This is likely one reason why.) If you can't track installation automatically, the use of auditing tools is probably your best option.

Chapter 14

People

"Uh, yes, well, it turns out that if you face a secured console to an outgoing console, you can read off Security files from anywhere in the vid net. Of course, you have to have somebody inside HQ who can and will aim the consoles and call up the files for you. And you can't flash-download. But I, uh, thought you should know, sir."

"Perfect security," said Count Vorkosigan in a choked voice. Chortling, Miles realized in startlement.

Illyan looked like a man sucking on a lemon. "How did you," Illyan began, stopped to glare at the Count, started again, "how did you figure this out?"

"It was obvious."

"Airtight security, you said," murmured Count Vorkosigan, unsuccessfully suppressing a wheezing laugh. "The most expensive yet devised. Proof against the cleverest viruses, the most sophisticated eavesdropping equipment. And two ensigns waft right through it?"

Goaded, Illyan snapped, "I didn't promise it was idiot-proof!"

Count Vorkosigan wiped his eyes and sighed. "Ah, the human factor. We will correct the defect, Miles. Thank you."

The Vor Game
—Lois McMaster Bujold

14.1   Employees, Training, and Education

Some years ago, I gave a talk at a Three-Letter Agency. At lunch, I commented to my hosts that at least they worked at an organization where people took computer security seriously. They gave me these pained looks; finally, someone said, "Well, parts of the organization do."

A couple of years later, I ran into someone who also worked at TLA.gov and told her that story. She replied, "Damned straight—I have my job to do." The security rules were getting in her way, and she was evaluated on (and took pride in) her actual job, which had nothing to do with whether or not she followed security rules. She and her colleagues were right, in that the rules were intrusive and interfered with the important work they were doing. But this was the TLA, and the Andromedans really were out to get them. Those rules, for all of their intrusiveness, (probably) helped with security.

In a second corner, we have willful disobedience of security policies. John Deutch, the former Director of Central Intelligence, was found to have used unclassified Agency-issued computers to prepare classified materials [Snider and Seikaly 2000]. In addition, some other family members used the machine; investigators found that "high risk Internet sites" were visited by someone other than Deutch himself [Snider and Seikaly 2000, p. 31]. News reports suggest that the computer was used to dial up AOL to contact adult web sites [Powers 2000]. This incident represents a people problem, not a technology problem; still, a security policy has to account for such behavior.

In the last corner of our triangular room we have employee mistakes, people clicking on things that they should have left alone. That's how RSA was penetrated [Richmond 2011], via a well-crafted email message that contained a boobytrapped spreadsheet [Rivner 2011]:

> The attacker in this case sent two different phishing emails over a two-day period. The two emails were sent to two small groups of employees; you wouldn't consider these users particularly high profile or high value targets. The email subject line read "2011 Recruitment Plan."
>
> The email was crafted well enough to trick one of the employees to retrieve it from their Junk mail folder, and open the attached excel [*sic*] file. It was a spreadsheet titled "2011 Recruitment plan.xls. [*sic*]

That attack was probably from an APT—among other things, the attached file really was a spreadsheet that contained a 0-day exploit—but more mundane examples show up constantly, ranging from purported nude celebrity pictures to package tracking notices to vague threats about pictures allegedly posted to social networking sites.

What these incidents all have in common is that there is a human, not technical, link in the chain of weaknesses that can lead to trouble. It is tempting to try to fix such problems via technical means. For better or worse, that's not always possible. The answer is three-fold: training, education, and incentives. Sadly, most companies stop after the first.

Let's look at the OED. Both "train" and "educate" have many definitions; these are the ones I'm using:

train To cultivate or develop (the mind, the spirit, a faculty, etc.), esp. for a specified purpose; to accustom to performing a specified function.

educate To help or cause (a person, the mind, etc.) to develop the intellectual and moral faculties in general; to impart wisdom to; to enlighten.

Training focuses on a "specified purpose"; education is broader. Training says "pick strong passwords" and tells you how to; education shows you what the attacks are and how password guessing works, and may teach you to write your own such program.

Education is more time consuming and expensive than is training; perhaps more seriously, people who aren't security geeks are probably uninterested in attack minutiae. Both are valid objections; there's a fine line between imparting enough information to be useful and wasting the time of (and boring) people who have better things to do for a company than listening to people like me. There's a third reason, though, one that is not valid: when it comes to security matters, there seems to be a reflexive urge for secrecy. After all, if you talk about weaknesses you'll teach the bad guys how to attack, right? As was noted long ago [Hobbs 1857], "Rogues are very keen in their profession, and already know much more than we can teach them respecting their several kinds of roguery." It's counterproductive to hide attacks from your own employees, because doing so prevents them from distinguishing between rules that are desirable and rules that are really important. There is, of course, a difference; witness the efficacy of rule-book slowdowns.

There's a well-known historical incident where the lack of appreciation of the importance of security procedures had important consequences: one attack the British used against the German Enigma machine took advantage of cipher clerks' ignorance and laziness [Kahn 1991]:

> The cryptanalysts of the Luftwaffe Enigma coined the term "cillies"—either the name of the girlfriend of an Enigma cipher clerk used as a key or just a burlesque of "sillies"—for some of the foolish things that Enigma operators persisted in doing, despite regulations to the contrary. One was to use as message keys a sequence from their keyboard, such as QWE or NBV, or the first three letters of a girlfriend's name, or an obscene word. Another form of cilly occurred when a lazy encipherer chose as his message key the position that the rotors were in at the end of the encipherment of the previous message.

Note carefully that cillies occurred "despite regulations to the contrary." The clerks (and more or less everyone else) were kept ignorant of cryptanalytic techniques; consequently, they didn't know how serious their errors were.

How could this last problem have been fixed? Today, it's done technically: the crypto box picks its own session ("message") keys, and users have no opportunity to make such mistakes. Given that the Enigma operated mechanically, that probably wasn't an option without a radically different design. They had a people problem; the British were able to exploit it. The Germans were not sanguine about the risk. Their solution was to have traffic monitors who looked for procedural violations. It wasn't a bad approach, but it couldn't scale to deal with wartime traffic volumes—and the German traffic was read.

Sometimes, the answer lies in the incentive structure. You can try negative incentives —punishing people who break the rules—but positive incentives not only work, they improve morale and productivity. Consider the first story in this chapter, about TLA.gov. You could say, "Let me make it impossible for her to violate security," or you could impose penalties for noncompliance with the rules. A better approach, though, is to say, "What technology would improve her productivity without hurting security?" or even "Can we ease the rules somewhat and concentrate on what's really important?" The usual rationale for eschewing the last of these approaches is cost. Often, though, that's a hangover from when computers were expensive. Today, they're not; people are.

Intentional disregard of rules can be another matter. In the Deutch case, the Inspector-General found that [Snider and Seikaly 2000, p. 3] "Deutch was aware of prohibitions relating to the use of unclassified computers for processing classified information. He was further aware of specific vulnerabilities related to the use of unclassified computers that were connected to the Internet. Despite this knowledge, Deutch processed a large volume of highly classified information on these unclassified computers, taking no steps to restrict unauthorized access to the information and thereby placing national security information at risk." This wasn't just a desire to be more productive, or a case of overly strict rules [Powers 2000]: "But Deutch's character also includes impatience, dismissing the concerns of others, roughness in argument, refusing to listen as soon as he disagrees— all of those attributes summed up as arrogance by the people who worked with him at the Pentagon and the C.I.A. Every last one of them said it was arrogance that got him into trouble: he knew the rules, but he didn't think they applied to him." To quote Marcus Ranum [Cheswick, Bellovin, and Rubin 2003, p. 202], "You can't solve people problems with software."

The hardest problem to deal with is when a user has been tricked. You can say that more education or training would have helped, or perhaps better adherence to rules. It's not that simple. Security is an adversarial process, which means that you're pitting experts in deception—the attackers—against people who may be very competent at their own jobs but who aren't security experts. Furthermore, the advantage is with the attacker, who only has to win once. You can try for improved technical measures—could that infected spreadsheet have been caught by a better antivirus scanner?—but sometimes (as in the RSA case) you can get hit by a 0-day. Maybe more training would help—recall that the employee had to retrieve the email from the Junk folder; was that proper procedure?—but again, there's a limit to how far that can take you.

The proper answer here, as in so many other situations, is maintain a sense of balance: how often will you be penetrated by such schemes, what will those incidents cost you, and how does that figure compare to what you would spend on more training and gadgetry (and lost productivity)? If you think that you're being targeted by the Andromedans and that the potential losses are high, you need to escalate your defense, including airgaps and very strict procedures surrounding your crucial assets. In the RSA incident, it seems likely that keying material for their tokens was taken; this was later used to attack Lockheed [Drew 2011]. If you assume the inevitability of a failure involving human behavior, the avoidable flaw was in the protection of this keying material.

14.2 Users

In Section 14.1, I focused on the security aspects of employees. If, however, you have any customer-facing resources that are security sensitive—and that category includes both web sites with logins and environments (e.g., ISPs) where your business is providing a security-sensitive service—you have a very different class of problem to deal with. Make no mistake—users are people, too—but your relationship to them is very different. In a nutshell, you need them, and you can't tell them what to do.

You can send employees to classes. You can insist that they complete (endure?) web-based training sessions, complete with online quizzes. You can create and often enforce policies on web sites that they may or may not visit. You can even discipline them for egregious security violations.

None of that is true for users. You can enforce some minor things, like password strength. You can make educational material available. However, businesses that persistently annoy their customers are not going to flourish. (Strictly speaking, that's not completely true; businesses with an effective monopoly, e.g., broadband ISPs in much of the United States, can get away with such misbehavior for a while. However, they end up disliked and as the target of jokes—and very vulnerable to a technological or economic change that destroys their monopoly. Until that happens, they may also find themselves in hot water with regulators.)

To see how to handle this, it's necessary to divide security issues into three categories: those that affect the company directly, those that cause indirect economic harm, and those for which the company is more or less caught in the middle.

One obvious case of direct harm is abuse of user accounts that have stored credit card numbers. Visa, for example, warns [Visa 2008] that "Many merchant agreements now include provisions that hold businesses liable for losses resulting from compromised card data if a business (or its service provider) lacks adequate data security." In other words, if your security isn't strong enough and a customer account is compromised, you may be responsible for any credit card charges to accounts belonging to your customers. The onus is on you to provide strong enough security in the face of lack of cooperation or outright misbehavior from users.

There's an interesting business decision here. Companies want (need) customers, but a customer who costs you money is not very attractive. This suggests deploying strong security up front, especially security mechanisms whose cost is independent of the number of users. There are two caveats. First, some mechanisms can drive away users, either because they're too hard to use or because they're too intrusive or otherwise unpleasant. Ask your favorite search engine for articles on shopping cart abandonment—most surveys indicate that one significant cause is requests for too much information, information you may need to reduce fraud. Second, some mechanisms do have a significant cost, especially if human intervention is needed to resolve the issue.

Indirect expense comes from things like users with virus infections. You didn't do anything wrong, but you're being hurt: someone is pounding on your web site (and hence overloading it), or too much of your bandwidth is being consumed. (Aside: on this last point, your mileage may vary. Some ISPs see excess bandwidth usage as a benefit: they get to sell fatter pipes to their customers. That's up to them, though of course it's improper to infect your customers deliberately as a sales tactic.) Again, the biggest expense will come if humans have to intervene; people are much more expensive than pipes.

The name of the game here is cost avoidance: what can you deploy that will ameliorate your problem? Some universities do this very well; they detect infected machines and relegate them to a recovery VLAN, where all they can do is download instructions, patches, and antivirus software.[1] The economic trade-off is primarily the cost of these mechanisms versus the expenses they prevent.

The third category is the most annoying: you didn't do anything to cause the problem, and you're not being hurt yourself, but others are asking you to solve it, or at least to be part of the solution. Consumer ISPs see this constantly: when one of their users misbehaves or is experiencing security problems, they get to help their customers solve the problem. If there's a virus infection that's causing a user's machine to attack other sites, the ISP will get the complaint. What do you do?

---

1. "PaIRS: Point of contact and Incident Response System," http://goo.gl/xhroc.

One approach, of course, is cost avoidance: do enough filtering to avoid bringing down the wrath of others. A very important special case of that is port 25-blocking: as an anti-spam measure, most residential ISPs prevent their customers from talking directly to other sites' SMTP servers. Too much of that is a bad idea, though, especially on inbound traffic; it interferes with the evolution of the Internet [Hagino 2003].

In a competitive market, it's often possible to use security as a marketing advantage. Supplying antivirus packages at a discount is one popular strategy; indeed, that can be cost-effective even without competition, simply to decrease the number of help desk calls and emails. You can't always use that option—even if your acceptable use policies prohibit, say, file sharing, users who want to do it won't perceive filtering or blocking software as an advantage.

One thing you need to keep an eye on is the legal environment. This will differ in different countries, of course. The United States imposes very few security requirements on ISPs, but there is some chance that that will change. [Lichtman and Posner 2006], for example, say:

> Internet service providers control the gateway through which Internet pests enter and reenter the public computer system. They should therefore bear some responsibility for stopping these pests before they spread and for helping to identify individuals who originate malicious code in the first place.

They then give legal reasoning showing that "rules that hold one party liable for the wrongs committed by another are the standard legal response in situations where, as here, liability will be predictably ineffective if directly applied to a class of bad actors, and yet there exists a class of related parties capable of either controlling those bad actors or mitigating the damage they cause." This is not currently the law in the United States—but that might change.

Ultimately, the security problem posed by users is much less tractable than the employee problem. They have no duty to you, nor do you have much influence over them save for pulling the plug. Annoying your customers is very rarely good business strategy.

14.3 Social Engineering

There's a particularly nasty variant of attacks called *social engineering* that is aimed at humans rather than computers. The attackers may try to tempt you or may try to scare you; fundamentally, they're trying to con you.

There are as many variants of social engineering attacks as there are situations where people can be tricked into doing something that they shouldn't. Rather, there are more attacks; for any situation, there are many possible ways to con someone.

One of the classic examples involves use of an attractive woman. This can range from a purely fake online presence all the way to all the way. Kahn relates the story of a spy code-named CYNTHIA [1967], who worked "not for money but for thrills." She seduced assorted diplomats, and persuaded them to betray their countries' naval codes. The practice isn't dead; the Soviets loved doing such things. In East Germany, the Stasi turned it around. Reasoning that many men had been killed during World War II, and thus leaving many women without prospective partners, they employed attractive male agents to seduce vulnerable targets [Knightley 2010]. Nor are such shenanigans limited to heterosexual temptations; in many cultures, a homosexual affair is an even better lever to use [Milmo 2006].

There are obvious online equivalents. Imagine an online porn site—better yet, a kinky porn site—set up by would-be blackmailers. Best of all, imagine a legitimate web site that uses ads and the full panoply of modern web-tracking technologies to identify the habitués of porn sites. I haven't heard of this being done for blackmail, but given the incidence of malware on such sites [Wondracek et al. 2010] it's hardly a stretch.

Many spam emails employ much more mundane forms of social engineering. Whether the emails appeal to cupidity, with a promise of the unclaimed riches of a deposed dictator, fear ("Click here to see your overdue bill before it's referred to a collection agency"), or lust ("Nude pictures!"), the concept is the same: the spammer is trying to trick someone into doing something they shouldn't, such as clicking on an attachment (Figure 14.1). Most of these emails seem too blatant to be plausible, but even very intelligent people have fallen for them [Ellement 2004].

Spear-phishing is even more dangerous. These emails are carefully crafted to appeal to specific people; they'll often include very specific details such as knowledge of internal projects and the recipients' associates. The attack on RSA, described earlier in this chapter, was one such case. Many experts fear that the penetration of the US *Office of Personnel Management (OPM)* computer systems [Zetter 2015] will lead to more spear-phishing attacks; the OPM databases included detailed personal information about people with security clearances. In terms of our threat matrix, ordinary phishing attacks are opportunistic, while spear-phishing messages are targeted attacks.

Social engineering still happens offline or by phone, even in the high-tech world. Mitnick [2002] relates many such scams that he pulled, back when he was on the wrong side of the law. Clever con artists can talk people out of amazing amounts of information. In one recent corporate scandal, private investigators impersonated HP's board members—a technique known as *pretexting*—in order to obtain their phone records [Darlin 2008].

There are no—repeat, *no*—strong technical defenses against social engineering, especially when it happens offline. The essence of the problem is an authorized person being tricked or coerced into doing something permissible but for improper reasons. Some-

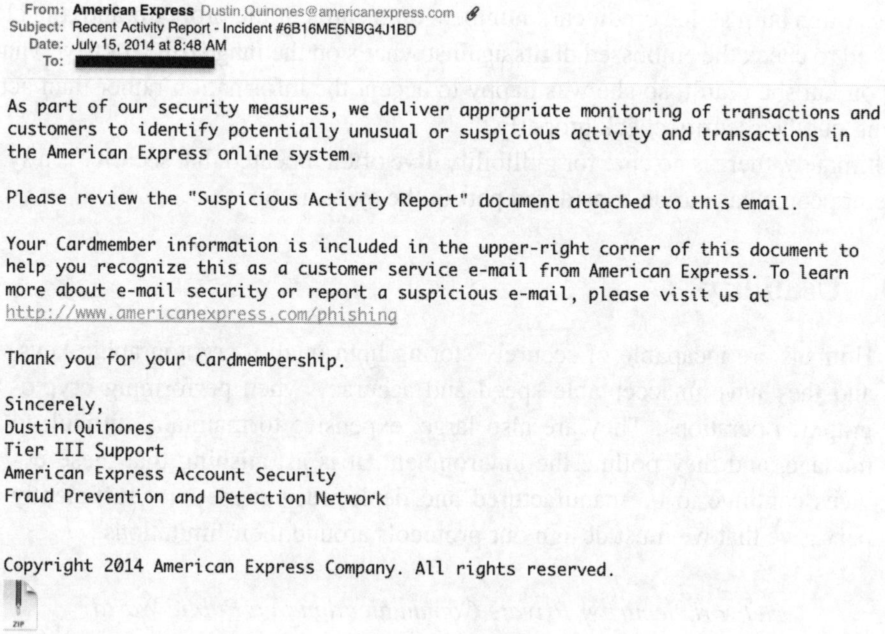

From: **American Express** Dustin.Quinones@americanexpress.com 📎
Subject: Recent Activity Report - Incident #6B16ME5NBG4J1BD
Date: July 15, 2014 at 8:48 AM
To: ███████████████

As part of our security measures, we deliver appropriate monitoring of transactions and customers to identify potentially unusual or suspicious activity and transactions in the American Express online system.

Please review the "Suspicious Activity Report" document attached to this email.

Your Cardmember information is included in the upper-right corner of this document to help you recognize this as a customer service e-mail from American Express. To learn more about e-mail security or report a suspicious e-mail, please visit us at http://www.americanexpress.com/phishing

Thank you for your Cardmembership.

Sincerely,
Dustin.Quinones
Tier III Support
American Express Account Security
Fraud Prevention and Detection Network

Copyright 2014 American Express Company. All rights reserved.

Figure 14.1: An amusing phishing email I recently saw. The link to the American Express phishing web is actually accurate, though that URL actually redirects to one that uses HTTPS. The zip file, not surprisingly, contains a .exe file rather than the purported malicious activity report.

times, process will help, but if and only if people follow it religiously. I once heard a story about a general who walked up to an entrance to a sensitive facility. The private on guard saw his stars, came to attention, and saluted. The general returned the salute, walked past, then turned around and reamed out the private. "Why didn't you shoot me?" he demanded. "Sir?" the private quaked. "I walked past you; you didn't ask for an ID. How do you know where I got this uniform?" The general understood the problem; the private was too afraid of offending a high-ranking officer to do what he knew he should have done.

Sometimes, logging will help. If someone is accessing resources they shouldn't, or accessing many more resources they're authorized for, that should show up in the log files. Of course, log files don't help if you don't look at them.

Education can help. Once, when I was buying something at a local big box store, I swiped my credit card in the terminal and put it away. The clerk asked for it; she told me she needed to see the last four digits. I recited the digits; she compared that to what was on her screen and was happy. She was happy—but I could have been scamming her.

Thieves often burn stolen credit card numbers onto cards of the proper brand; the clerk is supposed to check the embossed digits against what's on the mag stripe. I knew what was going on but she didn't, so she was happy to accept the information rather than actually carrying out the security check properly.

Ultimately, there is no cure for gullibility. I've often repeated that security is a systems problem; people have to be considered part of the system, too.

14.4   Usability

> Humans are incapable of securely storing high-quality cryptographic keys, and they have unacceptable speed and accuracy when performing crypto-graphic operations. They are also large, expensive to maintain, difficult to manage, and they pollute the environment. It is astonishing that these de-vices continue to be manufactured and deployed, but they are sufficiently pervasive that we must design our protocols around their limitations.
>
> *Network Security: Private Communication in a Public World*
> —CHARLIE KAUFMAN, RADIA PERLMAN, AND MIKE SPECINER

It's a fact—perhaps dismaying to some of us computer types, but a fact nevertheless—that the users of our computer systems are, almost without exception, people. This in turn implies that our systems (and that includes security systems) should be designed for use by people. To ignore that is to invite trouble.

Don Norman expressed this very well some years ago in an essay—he called it a "lecture," though "rant" might be more accurate—in *RISKS Digest* [Norman 2003]:

> If we assume that the people who use technology are stupid ("Bubbas") then we will continue to design poorly conceived equipment, procedures, and software, thus leading to more and more accidents, all of which can be blamed upon the hapless users rather than the root cause—ill-conceived software, ill-conceived procedural requirements, ill-conceived business prac-tices, and ill-conceived design in general. This appears to be a lesson that must be repeated frequently, even to the supposedly sophisticated reader/ contributor to *RISKS*.
>
> It is far too easy to blame people when systems fail. The result is that over 75% of all accidents are blamed on human error. Wake up people! When the percentage is that high, it is a signal that something else is at fault—namely, the systems are poorly designed from a human point of view. As I have said

> many times before (even within these *RISKS* mailings), if a valve failed 75%
> of the time, would you get angry with the valve and simply continual [*sic*] to
> replace it? No, you might reconsider the design specs. You would try to figure
> out why the valve failed and solve the root cause of the problem. Maybe it is
> underspecified, maybe there shouldn't be a valve there, maybe some change
> needs to be made in the systems that feed into the valve. Whatever the cause,
> you would find it and fix it. The same philosophy must apply to people.

Precisely. Security systems have the same sorts of failure modes; when they're not designed for *people,* failures are inevitable.

We see this most clearly when people, be they customers or employees, are asked to perform security-sensitive tasks. Will they perform these tasks correctly? Will they realize they don't know how to? Or will they, with all of the best intentions in the world, do the wrong thing?

The classic example, of course, is the entire panoply of rules, customs, and beliefs surrounding passwords. The specific details are discussed in Chapter 7; what is important to note here is that the underlying issue is a mismatch between the system design—reliance on a set of strings that are either guessable or impossible to remember—and ordinary human abilities. From this perspective, it is clear that the correct solution is to do away with passwords; as outlined earlier, that notion often runs afoul of economic constraints.

Interfaces aimed at sophisticated users are no better. Figure 14.2 shows the dialog box for setting file permissions on Windows 7. The number of errors is staggering. What happens if neither "Allow" nor "Deny" is checked? What is the difference between "Write" and "Modify"? Is "Full Control" all of the other permissions shown (including "Special Permissions," whatever they are), or is it something different? How do user permissions interact with group permissions if there's a conflict? All of these questions have answers, but I suspect that even most programmers don't know what they are. An experiment by Reeder and Maxion [2005] on Windows XP, which had a very similar interface, has shown just how hard it is to use this interface correctly: a majority of users couldn't carry out some relatively simple tasks. By contrast, their redesigned interface, with no changes to the underlying security mechanisms, achieved a fourfold improvement in the error rate.

This is a relatively simple case, in that the underlying mechanisms are not in question. That is, Reeder and Maxion showed that a certain task can be accomplished better in one way than in another, but did not ask, let alone answer, the question of whether the actual security model can accomplish what is actually necessary. Other situations present that question more squarely: given human behavioral characteristics, how should information be presented when the right answer isn't completely clear?

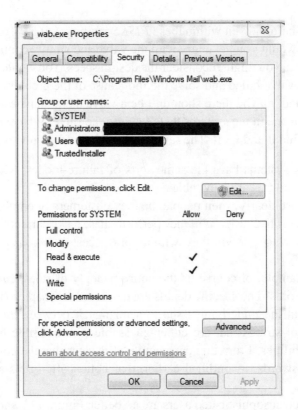

Figure 14.2: The dialog box to set file permissions on Windows 7.

To look at that question, it is instructive to compare certificate warning messages from several popular web browsers: Safari, Firefox, Google Chrome, and Internet Explorer (IE) 10 on Windows 7; all are shown in Figure 14.3. (To be precise, this is Safari 6.1 and Firefox 25.0 on Mac OS 10.8.5, and Chrome 31.0 on a Chromebook.) The particular situation is an attempt to visit a site with a self-signed certificate, that is, one signed by some certificate authority not known to the browser. Comparing them from a usability perspective seems straightforward.

The Safari message (Figure 14.3(a)) speaks of "certificates," a concept foreign to normal people. There is no default action choice, but if you think that certificate-spoofing is a serious risk (and it sometimes is), "Cancel" should be the default. The only other choice, other than continuing, is to display the certificate, but the results of that activity are, shall we say, likely to prove mystifying to most ordinary users.

Firefox's message box (Figure 14.3(b)) is much better. It speaks of "trusted identification," which is comprehensible to non-cryptographers. It gives you some guidance on

(a) Safari

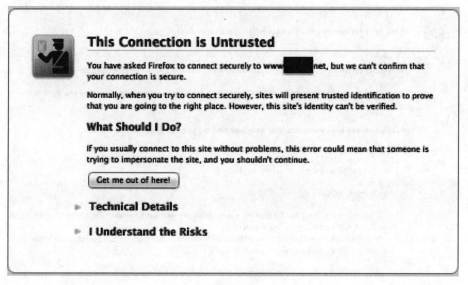

(b) Firefox

Figure 14.3: Warning messages for self-signed certificates from some browsers.

The site's security certificate is not trusted!

You attempted to reach **www.net**, but the server presented a certificate issued by an entity that is not trusted by your computer's operating system. This may mean that the server has generated its own security credentials, which Chrome cannot rely on for identity information, or an attacker may be trying to intercept your communications.

You should not proceed, **especially** if you have never seen this warning before for this site.

Proceed anyway | Back to safety

▸Help me understand

(c) Chrome

There is a problem with this website's security certificate.

The security certificate presented by this website was not issued by a trusted certificate authority.

Security certificate problems may indicate an attempt to fool you or intercept any data you send to the server.

We recommend that you close this webpage and do not continue to this website.

🛡 Click here to close this webpage.

🛡 Continue to this website (not recommended).

🔺 More information

  • If you arrived at this page by clicking a link, check the website address in the address bar to be sure that it is the address you were expecting.
  • When going to a website with an address such as https://example.com, try adding the 'www' to the address, https://www.example.com.

For more information, see "Certificate Errors" in Internet Explorer Help.

(d) Internet Explorer

Figure 14.3: Warning messages for self-signed certificates from some browsers (*continued*).

understanding the error message: that if this is abnormal for you for this site, it could be a sign of trouble. Finally, it presents the three choices—to abort, to look more deeply, or to continue—in a comprehensible form. "Get me out of here!" is clearly the preferred choice, "I Understand the Risks" acknowledges the situation, and "Technical Details" is for those who understand what's going on. (To be fair, I suspect that most people would understand "Show Certificate" to mean that something incomprehensible was about to happen.)

Chrome and IE 10 (and every other version of IE I tried) are about as bad as Safari; they, too, speak of certificates issued by some entity. They are better in one respect: they make a clear recommendation about what the user should do. On the other hand, their text is pure geek-speak, especially in IE. Safari, at least, makes it clear that the issue is identity verification. Chrome offers a bit of guidance on how to assess the situation.

Chrome will also give a comprehensible explanation of what " is actually going on if you click "Help me understand." The IE "More information" text advises you to check the URL or to consult the help subsystem for information on "certificate errors"; if you do, you can read the marvelously illuminating statement that "Certificate errors occur when there's a problem with a certificate or a web server's use of the certificate."

So far, so good. Firefox wins points for an initial comprehensible message; Chrome, though more obscure to start, does a better job at presenting the full picture. Safari and IE trail, the former for giving no explanation and making no recommendation, and the latter for giving redundant, repetitive, and redundant technobabble and a generally negative attitude. The "More information" button is even worse, since its suggestions imply that the issue is a minor configuration or user error. That may very well be, but it's inconsistent with the strong warnings against proceeding.

Remember, though, that security is a systems property. The initial warning, though important, is not the end of the story. What happens if you click through the warnings, not just once but twice or more? Chrome and Safari let you through on subsequent visits; IE goes through the same warning dialog. Firefox gives you a choice to make the exception permanent or not, but the default—which most people will accept—is to accept the site and its certificate in the future. Which is the right choice? To accept the choice as permanent, to persist with the "You cannot pass" attitude [Tolkien 1954, Book II, Chapter 5], or to ask the user?

Punting to the user has its issues, but per Chapter 8 against a serious adversary the web's PKI isn't even much of a speed bump. How should a browser behave, either on initial contact or on subsequent attempts?

An initial warning seems correct. The semantic definition of the web's PKI demands that *something* be said, though of course one can argue that the PKI is so weak that it doesn't matter much.

How a browser should behave on subsequent connections is a harder call. One approach is to go back to our threat matrix: what classes of attackers would be most likely to engage in behavior that could result in self-signed certificates showing up? The answer, oddly enough, is those of middling competence. A joy hacker might not know what a certificate was, let alone how to create a bogus one and lure someone to the web site presenting it; the Andromedans could hack into a trusted root CA and obtain a certificate that would be accepted without a warning [Galperin, Schoen, and Eckersley 2011]. Our other axis, targeting, adds little. A web server is out there for all to connect to. A targetier might know what sites someone would be likely to visit, or be more able to lure someone there, but this is the usual advantage of a targetier.

Note that there are a significant number of self-signed certificates on the net. One survey found that more than a quarter of all web sites had technically invalid certificates [Ristic 2010, p. 23]; 16% of all sites used certificates from "untrusted" CAs. Almost certainly, the overwhelming majority of these are non-malicious. A change in a site's presentation is a stronger indication of malicious behavior than a first occurrence. The warnings from Firefox and Chrome both get this right. This also justifies their practice (and Safari's) of making this override "sticky," though how to change that status later is often obscure and of course varies from browser to browser.

Internet Explorer, though, does not offer an option to continue to accept such certificates except during the current browser session. Microsoft has made a determination that visiting such sites is inherently unsafe, and while you can do so it won't make the process easy. Users (or their system administrators) can add new root certificates, if desired; alternately, they can continue to click through the warnings. Doing that, however, has a human factors cost: it habituates users to clicking through security warnings.

I've already mentioned the W3C Wiki defining "Dialog box." Users *will* click through warnings they don't understand if doing so is necessary to accomplish what they're trying to do. The question is not whether Microsoft is right about the dangers of such certificates, but whether the danger from them is greater than the danger of reinforcing the click-through habit. This is a very different question, and one that is much harder to answer. It is especially hard to answer because browsers have to operate in very different environments, ranging from wide-open hotspots to homes to tightly run organizational networks. The risks from either course vary accordingly.

The rise of mobile devices has made matters worse; the small screen size has resulted in warnings that are even less informative or less readable. Figure 14.4 shows the initial and "Details" pop-ups on an iPhone or iPad. Contrast how little information there is compared with Apple's own desktop browser (Figure 14.3(a)), itself not a model of clarity. The magic word "certificate" isn't used, which is good, but users get no sense of just what the problem is or what the risks may be. (For all of the flaws in Chrome's and IE's warnings, the dialog boxes they display on phones is the same as on full-size computers.)

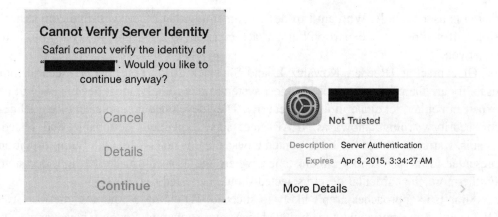

Figure 14.4: The initial and "Details" warning from iOS for an untrusted certificate.

14.5 The Human Element

To paraphrase assorted religious texts, computers are made for people and not people for computers. Our systems—our total systems, including the training and other processes involved—cannot succeed if we forget this point.

A shift in viewpoint explains this well: people-related security problems represent bugs in system operation, rather than in architecture or code. Such problems should no more be ignored than the more traditional bugs that security architects worry about. The fact that they are probabilistic in nature—not every user will make the same mistake—does not matter; race condition attacks are probabilistic, too, and have a much lower success rate than do social engineering scams. It is no more reasonable to ignore the human element in security designs than it is to ignore buffer overflows. The only real question is how to find a suitable solution.

The first aspect, of course, is the obvious one: match your system designs to human capabilities. Unlike technology, these are relatively static; as noted earlier, *homo sapiens 2.0* will not be released any time soon. There can be some changes—in some environments, education, training, or procedures (Chapter 16) can compensate—but by and large, people's reactions and perceptual limits will remain the same.

The second aspect of a solution is not quite as obvious: although there are usability design principles (and they're useful and important), blindly following them is not a substitute for expertise. Face it: most computer types are not experts on what normal people find usable. (Me? I think that regular expressions are extremely clear and obvious, and that *vi* is user friendly. Who am I to design something that others will find comprehensible?) If you're not as expert on human factors as on security, find someone who is to assist you.

Of course, as [Reeder, Kowalczyk, and Shostack 2011] note, neither security nor usability are the primary purpose of most systems; accordingly, most developers will be expert in neither, let alone in usable security. They developed a simple set of guidelines for security warnings known as NEAT: Necessary, Explained, Actionable, and Tested. That is, warnings should not be presented unless there is no choice, with full information presented to the user under circumstances where the user can make the right decision. Furthermore, the particular design selected should be tested rigorously.

Simplistic approaches aren't likely to succeed. Wrapping a complex interface in a GUI may (or may not) make the myriad choices more apparent; it won't, however, necessarily make them comprehensible. The only way to really know is by user studies—and those take expertise as well.

Finally, remember that usability, like most of the rest of security, is a systems problem. That is, all parts of it interact, even from a usability perspective. The difference between employees and users is fairly clear; other aspects are less so. Consider the timing of password change requests (and ignore for now the follies of password aging discussed in Section 7.2). On some systems, this happens at login time. The problem with this was noted long ago by Grampp and Morris [Grampp and Morris 1984]: "Picking good passwords, while not very difficult, does require a little thought, and the surprise that comes just at login time is likely to preclude this. There is no hard evidence to support this conjecture, but it is a fact that the most incredibly silly passwords tend to be found on systems equipped with password aging." That is, the timing itself was problematic.

People-centered risks depend to some extent on the threat model. Offline attacks tend to be more targeted, if only because of their expense. They're even more serious than usual if the Andromedans are involved; intelligence agencies have far more skill at manipulating humans than is generally realized. (Most spies are in fact professionally trained con artists. They don't actually break into secure buildings and steal secrets; rather, they manipulate people who already have the proper access [Bellovin 2014a].) Worse yet, few sites outside the defense and intelligence communities have anywhere near the expertise required to detect and counter such attacks.

Often, remote changes can cause usability troubles. More precisely, they can result in unusable interfaces suddenly becoming visible and important. Mechanisms intended to cope with spam and unsafe attachments are irrelevant, until the recipients' email addresses become "popular." Desktop firewall and filtering rules matter little at home if Internet access is solely through a NAT, but when the local ISP turns on IPv6 there will be direct access. Direct access to home machines is often a good thing, but only if appropriate access control mechanisms can be turned on by the users.

All of this needs to be taken into account when assessing the role of humans in a security setting. It is the people and their background, the technology and when it is used, and it all *changes*.

Chapter 15

System Administration

"He kept asking me stupid questions, was too dumb to learn from his own mistakes, made work for other people to mop up after him, and held a number of opinions too tiresome to list. He shouldn't have been in the course and I told him to tell Dr. Vohlman, but he didn't listen. Fred was a waste of airspace and one of the most powerful bogon emitters in the Laundry."

"Bogon?"

"Hypothetical particles of cluelessness. Idiots emit bogons, causing machinery to malfunction in their presence. System administrators absorb bogons, letting the machinery work again. Hacker folklore—"

The Atrocity Archives
—CHARLES STROSS

15.1 Sysadmins: Your Most Important Security Resource

<RANT>
A good system administrator's value, to misquote a line from Proverbs 31, "is far beyond that of rubies." Proper system administration can avert far more security problems than any other single measure. Your sysadmins apply patches, configure firewalls, investigate incidents, and more. Being a system administrator is a high-stress but often low-status position. The job is interrupt-driven; there are generally far too many alligators for them to even think of draining the swamp, even when they know exactly how to do it. Sysadmins

typically have too few resources to do the job properly, but are blamed when the inevitable failures occur. They're often on call 24×7, but frequently report to someone who equates running Windows Update on a single computer with keeping a modern data center on the air. Of course, all of these issues are magnified when it comes to security, since it's often very hard to tell whether a given preventive measure actually accomplished anything. But management wants things to work perfectly, even though the people responsible for that aren't given the resources—or respect—necessary.
</RANT>

Rants aside, I'm 100% serious about the importance of system administration. If nothing else, most security problems are due not just to buggy code, but to buggy code for which patches already exist. Sysadmins are, of course, the people who install such patches; per Chapter 13, it's not a simple process in a mission-critical environment. To people who have had hands-on involvement in operations, whether of data centers, networks, or services—and I've done all of these—the importance of doing this well is self-evident. How to accomplish it is a trickier question.

I do not claim to be a management expert. That said, the single biggest complaint I've heard from sysadmins is lack of respect from their user community and by extension from upper management. Some of this is inevitable. When something almost always works, it's natural to ignore it most of the time, and only pay attention when there's a failure—and at that point, people are generally looking for someone to blame. In the same vein, many users perceive that a similar-seeming service at another location or company works better; again, the sysadmins play the role of goats, even if the difference is either not present or is due to factors beyond their control. Strong leadership, including managers who can act as buffers and shields, is vital, as (of course) are more tangible tokens of recognition such as good salaries.

Why is this relevant to this book? It's quite simple: system administrators are the front-line soldiers in the fight for security. They implement many of the security mechanisms selected by system architects, and of course take care of patch installation and system upgrades. They're also the people most likely to notice security problems, whether from looking at logs, noticing performance anomalies, or fielding user complaints. Furthermore (and of necessity), a good system administrator has to know a fair amount about real-world security issues and threats. (A remarkable number of really good security people drifted into the field from the sysadmin world.) The question this chapter is tackling is how to apply this book's principles to system administration, and vice versa.

15.2 Steering the Right Path

Aside from setting security policies—the subject of most of the rest of this book—one of the most crucial decisions a system administrator has to make is how much control to exercise. Both extremes, the Scylla of complete anarchy and the Charybdis of totalitarianism, have disadvantages, including security weaknesses.

The security risks of anarchy—of not setting policies, of too easily acceding to requests for variances, of not enforcing policies—are fairly obvious. In a world where something as simple as a flash drive can wreak havoc [Falliere, Murchu, and Chien 2011; Kenyon 2011; Mills 2010], it is clear that first, there must be policies, and sometimes stringent ones, and second, that these really need to be enforced.

On the other hand, too much stridency about minor matters also has to be avoided. Sysadmins are (generally speaking) human, too; Lord Acton's dictum about the corrupting influence of power is applicable. Far too often, the real need for security is instantiated as inflexibility, pointless rules, and deafness to legitimate needs. This stereotypical administrator, depicted by Scott Adams in his *Dilbert* cartoon strips as "Mordac, the Preventer of Information Services," has its roots in the real world, too.

The problem with rules that are too strict is, as I've noted before, that people will evade them. The story on page xiii about the modems is true (yes, I know at which company it happened, and I know people who were there at the time); it's an example of what happens when a security policy is too strict for the culture. A security policy has to represent a balance between four different interests: the security folk, who understand the threat models; the system administrators, who know what's feasible to implement (and what it will cost); the business managers, who understand what the organization is supposed to be doing; and the line managers, who understand what employees will and won't put up with. (It would be better to ask the employees themselves, but that's often infeasible.)

Deciding on the policy is an iterative process, where several people play more than one role. A sysadmin might say, "Yes, I can enable that function, but only if we upgrade the desktops to a newer release of the OS, because that version implements it securely." Both sets of managers will object to the budget hit for the upgrade (though the line managers may, on behalf of the employees they manage, endorse bright, shiny new hardware as long as they don't have to pay for it), but everyone is in trouble if there's a major penetration. Too often, the argument will come down to a culture war—the geeks against the bean counters, the technical folk against the suits—which helps no one, especially since it's the sysadmins who take the opprobrium for "needless" restrictions on what people can do.

There's no deterministic algorithm for settling this, of course. The best approach is for all sides to come equipped with numbers and alternatives. What are the benefits—in dollars, euros, zorkmids, what have you—to the company's business of the managers' preferred strategy? What are the costs and risks of the (nominally more secure) alternatives? What assets are at risk if there is a penetration? Who are the possible enemies, and which of those assets would each group be interested in? What are the odds on one of those groups attacking, and via which paths? How strong are the defenses? How bad will the morale hit be if certain measures are implemented? Will this manifest itself in lowered productivity and/or higher turnover?

As I'm sure you realize, few of these questions can be answered with any degree of accuracy or confidence. The business folk—yes, the much-reviled suits and bean counters—are likely to have the best numbers, where "best" includes "most accurate." (There's a certain irony in them, and not the geeks, being the most quantitative.) I'm not saying that their market or development cost projections are always correct—I'm talking about profits, not prophets—but on balance, they do far, far better than security people can on their projections. Besides, they're much less likely to view a failure as a sin, rather than as a simple economic misjudgment. The essence of what they do is taking calculated risks; security folk, on the other hand, generally live for risk avoidance.

Implicit in the previous paragraphs is that the system administrators are more or less neutral parties. It's not their product that will be affected by security-imposed delays, nor are they responsible for the overall security architecture of the product. Of course, they'll get the blame if the upgrade goes badly wrong or if there is a penetration.

✦   ✦   ✦

A recent issue that illustrates this nicely is the so-called Bring Your Own Device (BYOD) movement: employees purchase and use their own equipment rather than using company-issued phones, laptops, etc. There may be financial advantages to the company—employees will often foot much of the bill—and perhaps morale benefits (Mac aficionados tend to be unhappy when forced to use Windows machines and vice versa) and functionality challenges (Does vital corporate software work on random computers running random releases of random operating systems? How is it to be maintained?), but in this book let's restrict our attention to a much simpler question: is BYOD secure? Let's look at it.

The first big issue is system administration: who is ensuring that user-owned devices are administered properly? Penetration by 0-days is rare; the overwhelming majority of attacks use vulnerabilities for which patches exist. As we've seen, patching isn't easy, but with company-administered machines there is someone responsible for dealing with the trade-off. Does the corporate sysadmin group have the right to install patches on employee machines? Does it even have the ability to do so, especially if they have no competence in or infrastructure for some kinds of devices? What about antivirus software? Is it installed? Is it up to date? Is it even necessary or possible? (At the moment, at least, it isn't possible for third parties to write functional antivirus software for Apple's iOS—there are no kernel or application hooks for it, and the same mechanisms that are intended to prevent installation of unapproved applications also block AV software. That may or may not play well with corporate policies that *demand* the installation of such packages.)

Naturally, threat models have to be considered. If you're dealing with the Andromedans, the precise device may not matter as much. A government-controlled mobile phone company in the United Arab Emirates pushed an update containing spyware out to its BlackBerry customers; presumably, this was intended to work around the strong encryption used by *Research In Motion's (RIM)* devices [Zetter 2009b]. Travelers to China often eschew laptops and smart phones [Perlroth 2012]. It is hard to see how corporate system administration would be an adequate counter to this class of attack. It isn't even clear that other countries' equivalents of MI-31 can mount a credible defense, as the Iranians have learned.

Against lesser threats, though, good administration does make a difference. Most users do not upgrade their software [Skype 2012]. More subtly, users are not prepared to assess the comparative risks and benefits of different software packages. Which browser is most secure, Internet Explorer, Firefox, Safari, Chrome, or Opera? Suppose the comparison was between Internet Explorer 6 and Firefox 14? Internet Explorer 9 and Firefox 3? With what patches or service packs installed? On what releases of what operating systems?

Even assuming that all of the administration is done as well by the user as a pro would manage, there's another issue: what else is installed, and what web sites does the user visit? It's one thing for corporate policy to say "thou shalt not" for company-owned machines; it's quite another to insist on it for employee-owned devices that may be shared by other family members. Don't get me wrong; there are legitimate concerns here. It is not an exaggeration to say that "adult" web sites often host the computer equivalent of sexually transmitted diseases [Wondracek et al. 2010]; religious and ideological sites are even worse [P. Wood 2012].

From the above analysis, it would seem clear that BYOD is a bad idea. It's not so simple. Again, recall the distinction between insecurity as a sin and insecurity as a financial risk. There are monetary and morale benefits to BYOD; this benefit must be weighed against the potential costs. How to choose?

As always, we cannot do a strict quantitative analysis; the risks are too uncertain. Still, there are guidelines that are helpful. Start by making two assessments: how strict is your security policy, and how much knowledge, overall, does your sysadmin group have? Sites with loose policies, for example, many universities, take relatively little additional risk by permitting BYOD; by contrast, defense contractors probably should not. Most sites, though, are somewhere in the middle. That's where the sysadmin group comes in. Can you buy or build a tool to do a minimal evaluation of a user's system, for all variants of major interest? (This seems daunting, but in reality there are only a handful of choices for which there will be very much employee demand.) Insist that this tool be installed as a minimum precondition for connecting to the network, and use it to assess the essential security state of these devices. (I should note that it is vitally important to be honest about what such a tool does and to be scrupulously careful to limit its abilities; betraying employee trust is a surefire route to all sorts of bad outcomes.)

Developing and using such a tool properly isn't easy. In general, large organizations will have large-enough sysadmin groups to manage it. Small organizations, unless they're supported by honest and reasonably priced consultants, probably cannot. If you can't, consider treating employee-owned devices as semitrusted, per the analysis in Section 9.4. The same suggestion applies to devices where an assessment tool is difficult, such as many smart phones.

Again, though, remember the threat model. The more serious the threat, the less safe BYOD is. This should be used as a discount factor to the sysadmin clue quotient. In particular, an evaluation tool is precisely the sort of atom blaster that can point both ways [Asimov 1951]; by definition, it detects certain security problems on a computer. This is wonderfully useful information to an attacker.

15.3 System Administration Tools and Infrastructure

There's a diagram floating around the net (Figure 15.1) that shows a lot of the trouble with system administration. Much of it is routine but interrupt-driven: a disk has crashed, or the print spooler isn't working right, or some vendor has released an urgent security patch. At the same time, the background work of upgrading the LAN switch to gigabit Ethernet, moving Legal to its own VLAN, and installing the new 32-terapixel display in the CEO's conference room has to continue.

Geeks and repetitive tasks

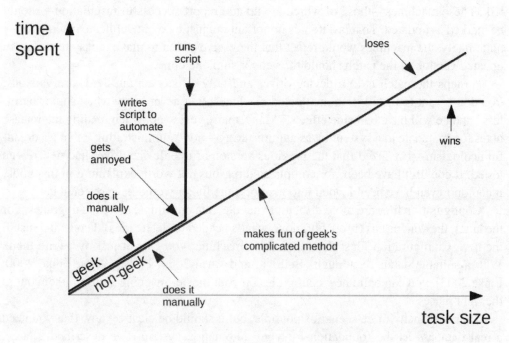

Figure 15.1: The advantage of automation.

While there are many facets of system administration that can benefit from automation, this is a security book, so I'll restrict my focus to security issues. The importance of all of these is proportional to the size of the organization; spending the time to write scripts and build infrastructure is less cost-effective for smaller sites. There are, broadly speaking, three relevant activities: shipping out patches and software upgrades; routine log collection and analysis; and sending specific queries to many machines while investigating or analyzing a (suspected) incident. (More generally, there are a number of good books on system administration, such as [Limoncelli, Hogan, and Chalup 2007].)

The starting point for all of these efforts is a good database of computers, not just the ordinary one of machines and IP addresses, but also hardware information and which versions of which software packages are installed on each. Furthermore, you want each machine marked by role; you want to be able to differentiate, say, mission-critical machines from less vital ones. Suppose some vendor releases a critical patch to some package. On which machines do you install it? You don't necessarily want to install it everywhere immediately; as noted earlier, patches carry their own risks (Chapter 13). Instead, your patch distribution system should do a database dip and select the machines that are at serious risk. These machines—those of which are up and report successful installation—should be marked as updated. That last item is important not just to avoid duplicate installation— quite likely, the machines would reject that themselves—but to make it easy to install an updated version of the patch should the vendor ship one out.

Perhaps the patch is to a device driver and only affects certain hardware versions. You don't want to install it on unaffected machines; you never know when some "harmless" update will have bad side effects. (Many, many years ago, when reading the release notes for an update to a system I was administering—*not* "administrating"; that's a dreadful neologism—I realized that the previous version of one device driver had never been tested. It couldn't have been; for complicated reasons not worth explaining in this book, it couldn't even have been loaded into memory; the linker would have rejected it.)

Configuration files are more difficult to handle than are simple software upgrades. For the latter, the vendor has (probably) done what's needed to delete the old code and install the new. Configuration files, though, are per-machine; you cannot just overwrite them. With a suitable database, though [Bellovin and Bush 2009; Finke 1997a; Finke 2000; Finke 2003], you can build new config files on your master machine and ship them out to the right places.

There are many more scenarios possible, but it should be clear by now that you need a real database as the foundation for your automation system. I've described a large, complex system, but even a much simpler version will go a long way towards simplifying the task. However, do *not* confuse a simple GUI form with a database; they're not the same. (More generally, there is a persistent but erroneous notion that anything with a full-screen interface instead of a nasty command line is a priori and ipso facto user friendly. Good sysadmins are pickier about their friends; they'll gladly trade a bit more time up front learning things and in exchange get a lot more power to do what they really want to do.) When you use a GUI, your options are limited to those anticipated by the forms' designer. Your configurations and needs may not match.

Building and maintaining the proper database is neither easy nor cheap. Operations that were once simple, such as installing a single package on a single machine, are now more complicated and more expensive. You can't just double-click on the distribution file; instead, you have to copy the file to your master sysadmin box, update the database to say where you want it, create templates for the configuration files, and then click the "Make it so" button. This is clearly not worthwhile if you're running just a few computers, but if you've got a few hundred to deal with it's another story.

There are, of course, plenty of large installations where this kind of setup makes sense. It's done all too rarely, though, because of the aforementioned interrupts and alligators. Put another way, the sysadmin group rarely has the resources—people, money, and time—to build the infrastructure necessary to operate efficiently. Given that "efficiently" often translates to "securely," this is a crucial deficiency. Foresighted management realizes this.

Alas, even if you get to build the necessary pieces, short-sightedness in the executive suite can doom the effort. I know of one group that did such a good job on their database-driven administration that the sysadmins appeared to be underemployed. The group was pared back sharply, the database moldered into uselessness—and suddenly, the sysadmins were overloaded and they had to ramp up again. By this time, though, the really competent people with vision were long gone. (The company itself? It's now out of business, though not because of system administration woes.)

There's a more subtle advantage to database-driven sysadmin tools: ultimately, you'll need less code. Code is bad: it's buggy, needs maintenance, etc. The more things you do via special-purpose tools, the more programs you'll need to maintain. A new kind of device, or even a new version of an existing device, can require an entirely new program. By contrast, a database-driven design may require only new templates. If new code is needed, it's likely to be small snippets in well-defined places; much of the complex, controlling logic is in the driver program that can remain unchanged.

As discussed in Section 16.3, automated log file analysis tools are necessary, too. I won't belabor the point here, save to note that sysadmins are, as always, on the front lines when it comes to using these tools and analyzing their output.

15.4 Outsourcing System Administration

Given how vital system administration is to security, and given how difficult it can be to do it well, the question naturally arises of outsourcing the function. Is it a good idea? Often, the answer is "yes," but there are some caveats.

As noted, system administration isn't easy. If, however, you have the resources to build the necessary tools and databases, it can be done effectively and efficiently. Note, though, the conditional: *if* you have the resources, you can do it well. Note also what I said at the start of this chapter about the status of system administration in typical organizations: do you have the resources?

It would seem, then, that for most organizations it would make sense to outsource system administration. The issue, though, is not so simple, for one reason: policy. What are the policies of the providing organization? This includes not just security policies, though those are obviously crucial. The other (and often more important) issue is which versions of which operating systems and applications are supported, and with which configurations.

Consider an absurd generalization: a Linux-oriented site will almost certainly be unhappy with a provider that specializes in Windows. More plausible cases are both more likely and more problematic. Suppose, for example, that you have a crucial application that only runs on a particular release of a particular OS. Will the providing company support that version for long enough to permit you to migrate safely? This is the canonical example, but it's almost too easy; you can always repatriate a single machine and run it yourself. Too much of that, though, and you have the worst of both worlds: expensively outsourced administration of desktop machines—the ones that are easy to handle with vendor tools or simple scripts—and homegrown (and probably manual) handling of the more complex servers. Alternately, consider conundrums like BYOD or telecommuting, where part of the trade-off is employee productivity or morale versus (perhaps notional) security: is your evaluation the same as some provider's?

The trade-offs here are inherent in the problem. System administration at scale requires automated tools; automation, in turn, thrives on uniformity. This is, of course, as true for home-built automation as for a provider's. The provider, operating at larger scale, may even support more flexibility than you can—but is it the *right* flexibility? Can they support the trade-offs and compromises that are right for your organization and your goals?

The decision is even more complex when one looks ahead. For the foreseeable future, there will be more heterogeneity, not less, in both device choice and configuration options. Which solution will be better able to adapt? Will you want to move ahead more slowly or more quickly than the provider?

There cannot be a single answer to any of these questions. What is essential is to understand the choices. Almost certainly, a good provider of system administration services can operate more efficiently than all but the largest, most sophisticated organizations can on their own. On the other hand, that efficiency can come at a serious price in *your* necessary functionality.

15.5   The Dark Side Is Powerful

No discussion of system administration is complete without a mention of the potential dangers posed by rogue system administrators. Sysadmins are generally all-powerful; that means that they're all-powerful for evil as well as for good. On systems with all-powerful administrative logins, such as root on Unix-like machines, a sysadmin can access every single file, no matter the file permissions. Nor will encryption help if the rogue sysadmin also controls the machine on which decryption will take place; installing a keystroke logger or other form of key-stealing software is child's play for any decent superuser. The threat is exactly the same as described in Section 6.4, only here the enemy is a highly privileged insider.

In the absence of other controls, then, one must assume that a system administrator has access to every file and resource accessible (or potentially accessible) to any member of the organization. The usual organization solution to protecting high-value resources is some form of two-person control: make sure that another system administrator approves any changes. There have been research approaches to this problem [Potter, Bellovin, and Nieh 2009], though commercial solutions are few and far between. However, even if they do exist they may be only a theoretical fix; the realities of human behavior may vitiate the protection, especially in a small organization. Consider: one administrator—a person who, per the above, is probably overworked and underappreciated—is being asked to assume that a close colleague (who is suffering from the same slings and arrows of outrageous management) isn't trustworthy. Will the (potential) rogue's changes be checked carefully, with all the insult that that implies, or will the checker simply click "OK" without reading it? Nor is handing off just the double-checking to another organization's administrators likely to work; too many routine changes require too much context for easy evaluation by an outsider.

The NSA realized the danger posed by rogue or subverted system administrators long ago [[Redacted] 1996]:

> In their quest to benefit from the great advantages of networked computer systems, the U.S. military and intelligence communities have put almost all of their classified information "eggs" into one very precarious basket: computer system administrators. A relatively small number of system administrators are able to read, copy, move, alter, and destroy almost every piece of classified information handled by a given agency or organization. An insider-gone-bad with enough hacking skills to gain root privileges might acquire similar capabilities. It seems amazing that so few are allowed to control so much—apparently with little or no supervision or security audits. The system administrators might audit users, but who audits *them*?

> This is not meant as an attack on the integrity of system administrators as a whole, nor is it an attempt to blame anyone for this gaping vulnerability. It is, rather, a warning that system administrators are likely to be targeted—increasingly targeted—by foreign intelligence services because of their special access to information...

> ...if the next Aldrich Ames turns out to be a system administrator who steals and sells classified reports stored on-line by analysts or other users, will the users be liable in any way? Clearly, steps must be taken to counter the threat to system administrators and to ensure individual accountability for classified information that is created, processed, or stored electronically.

Note carefully the part about targeting, and consider which class of enemies might do this. The NSA, of course, has always worried about APTs.

If you can't check the work, can you check the people? That is, will employee background checks weed out the bad apples? While they may identify the obvious misfits, they're by no means a guarantee; even the NSA has had its failures [Drew and Sengupta 2013]. Heath offers an interesting analysis [2005, p. 76], by comparing the societal rate of disqualifying factors with the rate found by investigators. In the 1960s, the NSA felt that it had to extirpate homosexuality from its ranks, since such "deviance" was an "obvious" security weakness. Despite an intensive effort, they found about 1% of the people they should have found. Some of that could, perhaps, be explained by self-selection bias, but probably not all of it. Furthermore, she notes that there is no good data showing the predictive value of any of the standard issues of concern such as heavy alcohol use.

The best answer is a combination of remedies. Certainly, for high-security enterprises some level of background checking is a good idea; banks, for example, are generally well advised to avoid hiring people with a lengthy criminal record for embezzlement. Similarly, some amount of two-person control can help, even if only done randomly. Finally, and perhaps most important, there should be some amount of auditing: what changes were made, and why? This in turn requires that *all* privileged operations be done in response to trouble tickets. These may be self-created—a good sysadmin will frequently detect problems that have not (or not yet) been noticed (or at least identified) by ordinary users; it's preposterous to insist that such problems not be fixed—but the entry must exist nevertheless. (Should you insist that another sysadmin fix such problems? Perhaps, but the learning curve to understand the details of the issue may be steep.) Finally, *all* privileged operations must be carried out via an interface that logs precisely what was done. If a script is run, a copy of the script should be filed away. If new files are used to replace old ones, save both copies. This sort of structure will permit later analysis by an auditor.

No discussion of rogue system administrators would be complete without mentioning the most infamous one of all, Edward Snowden. The story isn't complete; a good summary up to a certain point can be found in [Landau 2013; Landau 2014]. Without going into the larger issues raised by Snowden's activities, there are some purely technical ones: how did he accomplish what he did, what safeguards should have been in place, and what could or should have been done by the NSA to prevent or detect such behavior, or at least figure out after the fact what was taken? None of these are easy. Here, though, it was a perfect storm of threat models: very sensitive data, a system administrator who turned to the Dark Side and impersonated other users [Esposito, Cole, and Windrem 2013], and more.

Chapter 16

Security Process

In the Laundry we pride ourselves on our procedures. We've got procedures for breaking and entering offices, procedures for reporting a shortage of paper clips, procedures for summoning demons from the vasty deeps, and procedures for writing procedures. We may actually be on track to be the world's first ISO-9000 total-quality-certified intelligence agency.

The Atrocity Archives
—CHARLES STROSS

16.1 Planning

Security doesn't just happen. It takes organized effort, planning ahead, and *process*. If you're a geek like me—and you probably are one (or at least a geek at heart) if you've made it to page 279 of a rather technical book—those words probably strike horror into your heart. Nevertheless, and very reluctantly, I've concluded that process is a very necessary component of secure operation. Sigh...

The first issue is very simple: who makes which decisions about security? Even in a tiny organization, it requires some thought: the sole sysadmin may be the one to implement a policy, but it's management that has to set the shape of the policy. Larger organizations, of course, have more complex management structures, and hence more complex arrangements for creating policies. Actually setting policy is, as outlined in Chapter 15, an interactive process. There are at least four different players: the manager who sets the overall flavor, the manager whose bailiwick will be affected by a policy or policy change,

the security person who knows the threats, and the sysadmin who handles the actual technical aspects.

In some situations, such as the aftermath of a penetration, many more people have to get dragged in, up to and including the Legal and Personnel departments. In smaller organizations, these distinct jobs may not exist; that said, the roles are always there.

A second important issue is the resources—money—to be devoted to security. Security is always an expense; it is never a profit center. Worse yet, and unlike expenditures on, say, machinery, security doesn't help productivity. In fact, the necessary mechanisms often hurt. You need to spend money on security, just as you need to spend money on other parasitic expenses such as insurance, audits, employee background checks, and more. The problem with security, though, is twofold: as noted, it can hinder and annoy employees, and you never really know whether the money you've spent on it has done you any good. This is a crucial negotiation: as a security person, you're the one who best understands the threat model, but again, security is a parasitic expense.

There are many other aspects of security where advance planning and process can help. One is the role of employee training—it's often boring and frequently ignored, but you can't do without it. If nothing else, it can be a legal necessity: part of the US Federal Trade Commission's settlement with Twitter included several requirements for employee training.[1] Procurement strategy can matter: is it worth paying more for hardware and software that you think is more secure, or that your sysadmin staff can handle better? And of course, creating an ongoing mechanism for tracking changes in the threat model will clearly help, even if the intelligence group does end up annoying the sysadmins by insisting on constant reevaluation of security mechanisms.

Finally, there's bookkeeping—keeping track of all the little things that can make or break security in the real world: what systems have or haven't been updated, when certificates are due to expire, where all the external links go, and more. None but the smallest of sites can do without that, even if it does require more pixelwork by everyone else.

16.2   Security Policies

Where do security policies come from? More precisely, what factors should go into creating them? I'll start by showing how to create firewall rules, but the concepts generalize.

It's an empty truism to say, "Derive them from overall corporate policy" or "Negotiate with all stakeholders." Apart from the fact that the overall mechanism should have been established earlier, per Section 16.1, it begs the questions: how are those policies established, or how are the stakeholders identified? Ultimately, it boils down to balancing

---

1. "Twitter Settles Charges . . . ," http://www.ftc.gov/opa/2010/06/twitter.shtm.

opportunities, risks, and the threat model—but that's almost as empty a truism. A more structured process is needed.

Most organizations will have a "deny by default" basic policy. Thus, we start by identifying the desired functionality. Note carefully: "allow inbound connections to TCP port X" is not "functionality"; rather, it's a way to achieve it. We're not up to that decision yet. Per Section 11.3, there are often several possible mechanisms to achieve the desired results; at this point, all of them should be on the table.

The next step is to evaluate the different options for both cost and security risks (Section 11.7). For large-enough projects, it may pay to bring in Legal: can some of the risks be ameliorated by a contract with some external party? Should you impose some security requirements on that party? Remember that the goal is not security at any cost, it's security commensurate with the cost/benefit trade-off. If you never lose your bet—that is, if you never suffer a breach—perhaps you're being too conservative.

On the other hand, don't neglect worst-case analyses. Estimates of penetration probability have a very high degree of uncertainty, and systems are often far more porous than anyone would like [Perlroth 2014]. Ask yourself this: what if there is a serious penetration because of this new hole? Can you contain the resultant damage?

Your threat model comes in here, in a non-obvious way. A sophisticated adversary (and we're well into the upper-right quadrant now, though not quite to the level of the Andromedans) will seek out and exploit indirect paths in. Your security may be top-notch, but what of your partners? Target was reportedly hacked via a link to the contractor that ran its HVAC systems [Krebs 2014].

At this point, you can select and start to deploy a solution, but we're not done with process yet. You need a process for logging the original request, including requester, justification, alternatives considered, relevant threat model aspects, and what exceptions to your normal rules you made to fulfill the request. Why should all this be written down? At some point, things will change and you'll need to revisit the exception. Maybe the project is over and you can remove it all. Alternately, perhaps the threat model or your own internal topology (and hence defenses) have changed; this may dictate a change in which solution you should prefer. Yes, changing a deployed system isn't easy, but that's the sort of thing software people do all the time. If there's a security case for changing it, compatible with the business case, it can be done.

If your policy is "default accept"—many, though not all, universities are that way—you need a somewhat different process. Start with the assets to be protected and the threats to them, then lay out the defensive options. "Install a firewall" isn't an answer; a firewall is a way to enforce a certain policy, not a policy in and of itself.

Organizations with a mostly open net generally have a culture to match. That in turn means that there's an organizational cost to tightening security: people will resent it, and in particular will resent the loss of ability to do things they had been accustomed to doing. This suggests looking for options that cause minimal disruption: protecting only a few servers, blocking the most-abused TCP ports, and so on. Unfortunately, one critical asset isn't easily isolated: staff time to clean up intrusions. There are no simple answers, but the basic question and the basic trade-offs are the same as always: is the increase in security worth the cost? Here, some of the cost is in morale, which is harder to quantify; it is a cost nevertheless.

The morale issue can easily arise when considering non-firewall security policies, too, such as software installation and BYOD. The analysis probably starts with the benefits of the technology. We proceed more or less as above: what does the technology do for the organization, which can include both increasing productivity and improving morale? Against that, there are the risks and costs, especially whether this will hurt security. Manageability and staff time are crucial cost factors, too. Suppose someone wants some non-standard software installed. The benefits to that staffer may be obvious, but is it secure enough to use? That evaluation, which may be time-consuming, has to be done by the sysadmins and/or the security group. Is it worth their while to even start the process?

The security issues and cost trade-offs surrounding BYOD are somewhat different. Apart from the security question, an employee-owned device is just that: employee owned. This raises difficult questions about manageability: not just who has what rights on the device (though that's a difficult question), but also on the ability of the sysadmin group to carry out its usual management processes. The classic case, of course, is Blackberries versus iPhones and later Android phones. Blackberries were designed from the start for centralized administration: the corporate IT group configures them, decides what apps users can or cannot use, and so on. (Blackberries have other features intended for corporate use and centralized management, such as integration with calendar, address book, and voice mail systems. These are not security issues [though they profoundly affect the sysadmins], so I won't discuss them further, save to note that their lack may affect the benefit side of the cost/benefit equation.) By contrast, iPhones and Android phones were designed for personal use; the central management features, especially initially, simply weren't as good. Does this lack affect security? Assuredly. Is this a fatal flaw? That's a harder question; there are advantages that have to be considered as well. Morale is one factor, of course, but many people feel that they are more productive with the newer devices. And of course, if employees are using their own toys the company does not have to spend the money buying the devices—though prices have dropped so far that the expense is not a particularly significant increase to the fully loaded cost of a professional-grade employee.

The most difficult issue, though, is the fact that the organization cannot set or enforce its normal policies. Some insist on company-supplied software that verifies that patches and antivirus software is up to date; this is largely unobjectionable. Other corporate policies might be seen as more intrusive, such as a ban on visiting adult web sites. As noted [Wondracek et al. 2010], even from a purely security perspective this isn't unreasonable—but it's also a fact that lots of people visit such sites despite that. There are more problematic issues with personally owned machines. Some games include anti-cheating modules that appear to spy on other activities on the user's computer [Ward 2005]:

> But Mr Hoglund found that The Warden also scans the text in the title bars of any Window for any other program.
>
> Writing in his blog about what he found Mr Hoglund said: "I watched The Warden sniff down the e-mail addresses of people I was communicating with on MSN, the URL of several websites that I had open at the time, and the names of all my running programs."

It's easy to see why corporations might find that troubling, but it's also easy to see why some employees might want to own computer games.

There are other difficult policy questions that can arise even today, and more will certainly show up in the future. What's important is to have a structured methodology for dealing with them. A reflexive "no" answer can be just as bad as a reflexive "yes," and business pressures will make the latter strategy far more plausible than would have seemed likely even a few years ago.

16.3 Logging and Reporting

Few automated systems work well without feedback, and computer security systems are no exception. You need to know what's going on on your systems; the way to learn is your log files. There are three fundamental questions: what do you log, how do you log it, and what do you do with your logs?

The two obvious answers to the first question are "security-sensitive events" and "everything." Neither is quite correct, though the latter is closer to the mark. The problem with trying to restrict what you log to security-sensitive information is that you don't always know in advance what will be relevant. The limits, then, on collection are primarily load based, though care should be taken to avoid logging or retaining privacy-sensitive information without strong operational reasons.

Once upon a time, disk space was the primary bottleneck; obviously, that's a lot less true today. CPU time is more of an issue, at least when it comes to fine-grained logging (e.g., every "open file" operation) on busy hosts. The biggest issue, though, is how much data you can actually make sense of: do you have enough CPU power, RAM, and so on, to do the necessary correlations?

Given all that, the proper strategy is twofold. First, set logging to "high" on all of your boxes; back off if and as necessary. Second, and equally important, set up your system administration databases (Section 15.3) to be able to turn things back to "high" in an emergency. This sort of prepositioning (which I'll return to in the next section) is essential for rapid response.

How to log is conceptually more straightforward, though the engineering issues may require a fair amount of attention. There are two primary requirements: that an attacker who has penetrated a system be unable to wipe its logs, and that the logs be available in one place for analysis. Both of these point in the same direction: a centralized logging machine. Of course, for a large site you can't do that all in one place; the link and disk bandwidths are probably inadequate. The trick—that is, the engineering effort—goes into figuring out the right way to divide things up.

As explained below, log information is best stored in a database, not a flat file. This suggests that at a minimum, a federated database [Josifovski et al. 2002] be used to permit access to all records if necessary. More often, you'll want to limit your queries to single databases if possible; this in turn means grouping together related records, ones that might be needed in a single query. An obvious starting point is your service replicas: logs from all web servers, or all VPN servers, or all authentication servers should go to the same log database, especially if the replicas are providing identical services.

A diagram is shown in Figure 16.1. Various system elements create log file entries; these are sent to a parser/demultiplexer. The parser is, I fear, an ugly piece of code: it has to take text strings—all the myriad types of messages produced by every version of every box you have—and convert them into useful database entries. Once that's done, a configuration file specifies which databases should receive which entries—and it's perfectly reasonable to replicate some entries to help performance during queries.

Both the parser and the databases need to be replicated. One reason, of course, is reliability; a second, as we shall see, is to aid in forensic analysis.

How you implement log file queries and polling is very OS dependent. On Unix-like systems—Linux, Solaris, Mac OS X—the built-in utilities make it easy to do data reduction on each end system; on Windows, you may find it easier to pull the files back to your monitoring server and crunch them there. Alternately, you could install a script language (e.g., Python or Perl) on each machine. The existence of portable application packages such as Apache makes that an attractive idea.

It's time for an example. Here's a (lightly edited) log file entry from a colleague's small hosting center:

```
Jul 23 19:45:17 r0/r0 32773: Jul 23 19:45:16.206:
    %SEC-6-IPACCESSLOGP: list serial-out4 denied
    tcp 10.13.0.22(65276) -> 69.16.175.10(80)
```

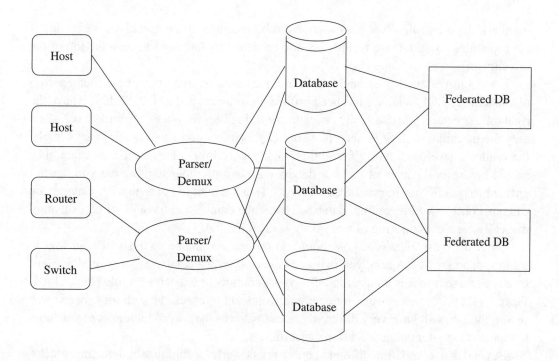

Figure 16.1: Putting log file entries into a database.

His routers are configured to block all packets to or from network 10/8, since that address block is reserved for intrasite use [Rekhter et al. 1996]; this message was produced by a Cisco router. Suppose we wanted to investigate the real origin of that packet. What database queries might we want to issue?

One path would be to try to figure out on which computer the offending packet originated. To do that, we'd want a query asking all switches if they saw 10.13.0.22 as the source IP address on any ports. (Some Ethernet switches log that information; others do not.) If there are other routers in the data center, check their traffic matrices to see whether they saw any such traffic. Note that these queries presume that other, non-logging information has been added to the databases: a network management server should periodically use SNMP to dump the traffic data from assorted network elements.

We could also check which users were logged in at the time. This is a straightforward query—whose login times span the period of interest?—but it requires login data from every machine. Another way the packets could have entered the network is via a VPN: which VPN sessions were active at that time? It's generally not reasonable to do full-packet logging (and a privacy risk besides) and few sites do full process accounting these days, but those are good options to be able to turn on quickly if weird things are happening. Again, these records need to be added to databases to ease the job of the investigator.

Let's consider another example. Suppose, for example, that you believe that a particular machine's SQL database has been probed by someone at 192.0.2.42. If you have the right infrastructure, you can easily check the SQL log files for queries from 192.0.2.42 on only the machines with SQL servers. (Your SQL servers don't have such logs? Clearly, the vendor's developers haven't read this book yet. Tell them they need to. In fact, they should buy several copies of it. Your database system provides logging but you haven't enabled it yet on your internal SQL servers? That's a simple configuration change you can push out via your sysadmin database; the same database entry will, of course, automatically enable monitoring of that newly created log file.)

Other than investigations, you should do routine automated analysis of your logs to try to spot anomalies. Again, you're much better off with a database, for several reasons. One is because it makes it easier to tailor your monitors to a machine's role [Finke 1994; Finke 1997b]. On web servers, for example, you want to check the web logs. A test web server, though, will have very different contact patterns than a production one; you want to tune and tag your collection efforts accordingly.

Beyond that, correlating different entries is a powerful technique for detecting attacks; see, for example, [Abad, J. Taylor, et al. 2003; Abad, Y. Li, et al. 2004; Kruegel and Vigna 2003]. While the math behind sophisticated intrusion detection systems can be complicated (Section 5.3), the basic concept is straightforward: combinations of various activities can be revealing. Proper log file analysis may be the only way that Manning or Snowden could have been caught. They were authorized to access many and possibly all of the files they downloaded, but the volume of their activities was certainly suspicious [Toxen 2014]:

> The NSA should monitor how many documents one accesses and at what rate, and then detect and limit this. It is astonishing, both with the NSA's breach and similar huge thefts of data such as Target's late-2013 loss of data for 40 million credit cards (including mine), that nobody noticed and did anything. Decent real-time monitoring and automated response to events would have detected both events early on and could have prevented most of each breach.
>
> The open source Logcheck and Log-watch programs will generate alerts of abnormal events in near real time, and the Fail2Ban program will lock out the attacker. All are free and easily can be customized to detect excessive quantities of downloads of documents. There are many comparable commercial applications, and the NSA certainly has the budget to create its own.

The notion of automated examination of log file entries for security monitoring is not new [S. E. Hansen and Atkins 1992; S. E. Hansen and Atkins 1993]. Too few sites do it, even today; they treat their log files as something to examine after a breach. Of course, if they don't monitor their logs they probably won't notice that they've been hacked.

16.4   Incident Response

What will you do when your site is hacked? Not "if," "when." If you run a decent-sized site, you'll almost certainly have to face the issue at some point. Planning and preparation can make a huge difference in how things turn out and in how quickly you're back on the air.

Some of the issues are non-technical. When an attack is detected, who should be notified and when? Note that sometimes, you're uncertain about whether you're dealing with an attack—when do you pass the possibly bad news up the ladder?

Obviously, the details will vary depending on the size of the organization. In large companies, the *Chief Information Security Officer (CISO)* will make the hard calls, but that means looping in the CISO fairly early in the game. In smaller organizations, it will probably be the head of the IT group (or maybe the one and only sysadmin) who handles things. However, penetrations are *not* just a technical issue; a lot of different people (or roles) have to get involved:

CEO Penetrations can be serious; companies have gone out of business because of them [Butler 2014]. There can also be major impact on your company's reputation [Ziobro and Yadron 2014] and even on the Board of Directors [Ziobro and Lublin 2014].

Legal Depending on your industry and what happened, breaches may have legal consequences. In most US states, for example, companies are required to notify people if their personal information has been stolen [Stevens 2012]. If the hack is serious enough to affect the share price, the public has to be notified [Michaels 2014].

Some companies prefer to delay any public mention of the breach [Yadron 2014]; in at least one, Urban Outfitters, the legal department calls the shots [Yadron 2014]:

> After a hack involving consumer data, her first call isn't to her boss, who is Urban's technology chief. Instead, it's the company's general counsel, a shift the company made post-Target to cloak the conversations under attorney-client privilege. Then, according to the plan, an outside investigator, whom she declined to name, is due at Urban headquarters within 24 hours, Ms. Hutchinson said.

I'm on record as opposing too much silence [Bellovin 2012], but I'm neither a CEO nor a general counsel.

Public Relations Expect press inquiries once the story gets out. In fact, if you're unlucky, that's how you'll find out: an enterprising journalist has turned up evidence of the hack and will contact your company. (What should you say about the incident? My advice is honesty; as Shakespeare noted, "truth will out" [1596].) That said, initial impressions of the problem will almost certainly be wrong; bear that in mind when crafting your strategy.

Personnel If an all-employee advisory is needed, it's probably up to the Personnel folks to handle it. If it's an inside job, they'll certainly need to be involved.

Physical Security I've seen hacks where *every* employee's password had to be reset and patches installed on their computers. The security guards at the doors were the ones who handled the logistics of this.

Production Department Heads It may become necessary to shut down certain production systems, even ones that are customer facing. That's probably a joint decision, but even if it's strictly up to the CISO, the production folks need to know.

It is instructive to read how complicated the logistics were even in the 1980s [Eichin and Rochlis 1989; Stoll 1988]. They're more complicated now.

Both of those papers make another point: it's important to be able to communicate when you can't use email. It may be unavailable (Is your mail server still up? Still reachable?), or you may need to refrain from using email to avoid alerting the attackers. Translation: everyone relevant needs to have a list of phone numbers—printed on paper. The list should include home and mobile phone numbers, especially if your office phones use VoIP. Naturally, there needs to be a known, well-defined policy on when this list should be used—but when it's needed, it's *really* needed.

The larger the company, the more need there is for a notification and reaction flowchart, and perhaps even rehearsals. Even small organizations need to think about the problem in advance; at a minimum, anyone who might be called should be aware of the possibility.

There are purely technical precautions to take, too. Specifically, you need to know what to do to monitor an ongoing problem, assess the damage, and restore full, uninfected functionality. The latter is largely up to your own group; the former two items may be outsourced, in which case you need to know whom to call. To do it yourself, you'll likely need special software and perhaps hardware. Monitoring a network? What computer will you hook up to the monitoring ports on the relevant switches or routers? How will you reconfigure that node to start feeding the right stuff to the monitoring port? How will you distribute that data or its analyses to all of the right people, when you don't want to email it? How will you preserve the data in a form that may be useful in a prosecution?

Find out in advance who the proper legal authorities are for your industry and jurisdiction. Talk to them; find out what they'd want you to do in case of an incident. Your lawyers should talk to prosecutors about what logging should be like to best preserve useful evidence. Your local police department may be the wrong choice; many don't have the expertise to handle computer intrusions originating from a foreign country. Similarly, there are often industry-specific information-sharing organizations; these can keep you apprised of ongoing threats and probably know who the proper law enforcement agencies are.

Even if you have no interest in prosecution, a full forensic analysis is mandatory: you need to know what the damage was, how the attackers got in, and whether you've cleaned them out. The canonical advice on disinfecting a system—reformat the disk and reinstall—is inadequate; if you don't change something, you'll end up reinstalling the vulnerability. To quote the old folk definition, insanity is doing the same thing over and over again and hoping for a different result. You probably do need to reinstall, but that's not sufficient. Reinstallation, though, means that you need access to installation media and your backups, and you need some way of knowing which backups are clean and which contain attacker-installed back doors.

This is where your logs will earn their keep: they're your only way of knowing when and how the initial penetration took place. A dose of humility is need, as well as confirmation by inspecting the systems suggested by the log. Don't act too hastily, though; take time to think it through. Recovery is never a fast process. At a minimum, you're installing a lot of systems and applications (and possibly using this as an opportunity to upgrade to new versions), and testing your new setup. If you don't move to new versions, you'll certainly want to install pending patches. You won't have the usual luxury of time in a test lab, but you're also not doing yourself any favors if you don't take some time to test. You'll need spare machines and disks, so you can continue operations while the rebuilds take place; that, too, requires advance procurement. Recovery is an all-hands-on-deck event, with plenty of overtime for everyone. (Maybe the CFO should also be on the notification list?)

Dealing with an intrusion is never easy and is rarely fun. (Bill Cheswick, Avi Rubin, and I described our experiences in Chapter 17 of [Cheswick, Bellovin, and Rubin 2003]. We were lucky; it was a largely unused experimental machine.) Knowing what to do and having the necessary hardware and software on hand makes life a lot easier.

Part IV

The Future

Chapter 17

Case Studies

> "You understand these are all hypothetical scenarios," T.J. had said. "In all these cases, the net refused to open."
>
> *To Say Nothing of the Dog*
> —CONNIE WILLIS

Let's put this all together now and examine a few scenarios. More precisely, let's look closely at some quasi-realistic case studies: the high-level paper designs of various systems and the effects that some equally hypothetical changes in technology, needs, or operating environment can have on the system architecture and in particular on its security.

Don't take the designs too literally. I'm presenting realistic scenarios, but I've often omitted important details that aren't relevant to the exact points I'm trying to illustrate. What is most important is the thought process: How did we arrive at our answer?

17.1 A Small Medical Practice

More than almost any other small businesses, medical practices have critical needs for secure and rapid access to information, at more or less any time of day; at the same time, few outside of major hospitals have any dedicated IT staff, let alone security specialists. In other words, such practices pose a major challenge for today, let alone in the future.

While there are many variations, especially for larger practices, one common setup is a small, network of computers, usually (but not always) running Windows. Backup is to a local file server. There is probably Internet connectivity; this is used for email, electronic prescriptions (via special web sites), and the like. Someday, this link will be used to transfer electronic health records; right now, though, the various brands of systems don't talk to each other very well, so that's still a ways off [Pear 2015].

There are many ways that a system like this could evolve. Given the increasing complexity of the information environment in medicine, it's far from clear that such small networks will remain economically viable. Still, let's look at one near-term change: the need for doctors to access patient records remotely, perhaps to deal with aelectronic health records!remote access patient request or emergency at times when they're not in the office.

There are two main constraints here. First, security is crucially important. Even in the United States, which has comparatively weak privacy laws, the *Health Insurance Portability and Accountability Act (HIPAA)* requires doctor's offices to exercise great care when handling patient information.[1] The technical requirements include access control, auditing, integrity mechanisms, and transmission security. The rules are so strict that some companies explicitly prohibit their customers from using their facilities for HIPAA-covered information. To give just one example, the terms of service for Pair.com's cloud offering explicitly states that their clientele may not "[p]ost, store, publish, transmit, reproduce, or distribute individually identifiable health information or otherwise violate the USA Health Insurance Portability and Accountability Act (HIPAA) and The Patient Safety and Quality Improvement Act of 2005 (PSQIA) or the privacy protection equivalent of these USA laws adopted in any other relevant jurisdiction."[2] There's a reason for this restriction: regardless of their technical abilities, they almost certainly do not have the procedures and processes in place to comply with the legal requirements set by HIPAA.

The second major constraint is the technical capability of the practice: they have very little. Undoubtedly, they rely on contract IT support; this in turn means that sophisticated solutions are inadvisable. Even if they worked initially, they're likely to break in short order. In other words, we need a solution that will be robust without constant care and attention.

There are two classes of solution that are worth considering: bring the outside machine to the office network, or store the data in a secure cloud environment. Each has its advantages and disadvantages.

The first has a conceptually easy solution: set up a VPN gateway on the office network, and set up VPN software on each external client. Setting up the VPN in the first place can be contracted out; if the client software works well, there shouldn't be many problems.

1. "Summary of the HIPAA Security Rule,"
   http://www.hhs.gov/ocr/privacy/hipaa/understanding/srsummary.html.
2. "- pair Networks," https://www.pair.com/company/hosting-policies/paircloud_contract.html.

Alas, life is not that simple. Often, VPN software does not play nicely with the NAT boxes installed in hotels, hotspots, and the like. I personally have—and need—several different VPN setups, just to cope with the many different failure modes I've encountered. To give just one example, I sometimes connect to a VPN server running on TCP port 443, to work around networks that only want to permit web browsing. This isn't ideal—running a TCP application on top of a TCP-based VPN can lead to very weird performance problems—but it's (often) better than nothing. If the doctors will only be connecting from a few places that have known characteristics, for example, their homes, a VPN can work well; otherwise, they're dicey. We thus have a solution that is secure but often not usable.

Using a secure cloud storage service can solve this problem. By "secure" I mean one where the client machines encrypt the data before uploading it and decrypt it after downloading it. The service itself does not have the decryption keys; thus, data stored there is protected even if the service itself is hacked. The only issue is configuring the various medical applications to look for their data in the directories that are shared via the cloud; generally, this is not a difficult matter.

Cloud storage services are generally simple to use. The hard part is the server, but that's managed by the provider, not the end users. Furthermore, the client programs generally use HTTP or HTTPS to communicate; as noted earlier, those are the universal solvents that can get through most NATs.

There are two flies in the ointment for either of these solutions; both concern the client computers that doctors will use. First, are they adequately secured? A computer used for general-purpose Internet work is probably not safe; there are too many nasties floating around the Internet. There is guidance on the subject from one US government agency [Scholl et al. 2008, Appendix I], but it basically boils down to "run your computer securely." It's safer to use a records-only computer—and laptops are cheap enough today that it's not an unreasonable burden. (Conversely, of course, the computers in the doctors' offices should not be used for general work, either.)

The second issue is more problematic: are the doctors using phone apps to access patient records? In general, phones and phone apps are less configurable than desktop and laptop equivalents; it may not be possible to play cloud storage games. In that case, the VPN solution might be the only choice.

17.2 An E-Commerce Site

Let's consider an e-commerce site of the type discussed in Chapter 11. There is a web server that is a front end for several databases; one of these databases contains user profile information, including addresses and credit card numbers. There are other important databases, including ones for billing, order tracking, and inventory.

The site now wishes to expand dramatically and act as a sales hub for other sites, much as Amazon and several other companies do. This implies links from this site, which I'll dub VeryBigCo.com, to, say, VerySmallCo.com, a representative of its ilk. What changes should we make to VeryBigCo's site architecture to do this safely? (Naturally, the discussion here is only about the security changes and not about things like a mismatch in database semantics.)

This isn't the place for a complete design; there are far too many elements and messages in a real system. Still, by looking at the kinds of events that take place, we can understand the broad shape of the security issues we must address. In other words, we look at the boxes and arrows (Chapter 11) of the functional design.

The first question to ask is the usual first question one should ask when doing security: "What are you trying to protect, and against whom?" E-commerce sites live and die by the confidentiality and integrity of their databases; therefore, that's what we need to defend most strongly. Furthermore, this is an ordinary e-commerce site, rather than one selling defense gear; we thus don't have to worry about MI-31. Our enemies are primarily opportunistic hackers, though there may be some element of targeting.

Protecting the databases is a matter of application security, not network security. (That said, per the discussion in Section 11.3 encryption is probably a good idea but not necessarily vital.) The enclave strategy suggested in Chapter 11 is a good start, but here it is not sufficient; what's really important here is making sure that the database operations *on the intentionally shared systems* are correct. In other words, protecting the database *computer* is not enough; we must ensure that only legitimate changes are made to the database.

Another question is which site's security should have priority. Suppose we can't come up with a single design that protects VeryBigCo.com and VerySmallCo.com equally. Which is more important? There are several possible ways to address this question. One is to note that that customers are dealing with VeryBigCo.com; therefore, it will be held responsible for any errors. A second approach is to assume that the larger company is more technically capable, and hence should make the decisions. That assumption, of course, is dubious; besides, a big site is more likely to be targeted. We could, of course, use the pragmatic, power-politics approach: VeryBigCo.com is bigger than VerySmallCo.com and hence can get its way.

This, however, is a technical book, so we can look at a technical security metric: which solution is *simplest* and hence most likely to be secure? Even with that approach, business considerations do enter into our analysis. As it turns out, the solution we'll devise is symmetric. The larger company has more reason to deploy it, and is probably more capable of doing so, but this design is symmetric.

We start by assuming that the standard precautions—enclaves, encryption, care in parsing input messages, and so on—are already in place. What more do we need to do to protect VeryBigCo.com's databases, and in particular to protect their *contents*? Phrased this way, the goal becomes clear: How do we ensure that only *legitimate* changes are made? This translates very directly to a design requirement: some component must assure the semantic consistency of requests from VerySmallCo.com with VeryBigCo.com's understanding of the state of transactions. For example, there cannot be a message saying, "We have just shipped 17 widgets; please pay us €437.983¼" unless someone has actually placed such a order. How is this to be enforced?

The wrong way to do this is to add logic to VeryBigCo.com's database systems. Those are already complicated enough; adding more complexity will hurt security. Furthermore, the last thing you want to do is to allow an untrusted party (VerySmallCo.com) that close to the crown jewels of the company. Instead, there should be a small proxy gateway that validates all transactions. This is an application firewall; it is the actual border between the two companies.

It is tempting to combine this proxy box with whatever code is necessary to translate between the different parties' databases. Don't do it. First, the translation is a difficult but unprivileged function. If it's done by the firewall, there is more risk of the firewall being penetrated. Second, the translation is partner-specific, so it should be closer to the partner. (If you work for the large company you may even be able to tell your smaller partners, "Here's what we're sending and receiving; if your databases don't work this way, you can do the translation, not us.") Third, the validation logic is not partner-dependent; you want to be able to use the same module (more precisely, another instance of that module) to do the proxying for all of your partners. This is much harder to do if the validation logic is inextricably entwined with the translation logic. A corollary is that you want to do your validation on concepts that your system understands; these, of course, are actions against your type of database.

Doing the validations requires that the proxy firewall check the transactions against your side's notion of the current state. There is an interesting tradeoff here. If the proxy queries the master database, it will learn the definitive status of all transactions; on the other hand, it means that this exposed box has to have very broad access. The alternative, having a separate transaction status database, eliminates that risk but it means that you will have the same information in two different places. This is always a dubious practice. On balance, the first alternative is likely better, since the proxy by intent has to have fairly broad access if it's going to pass through validated commands. If, on the other hand, your database has sensitive fields that will never be used by the proxy, you may feel that the other approach is better.

There's one more thing to consider: logging. Per Section 16.3, your proxy should log all inputs and outputs. Furthermore, its log files should be on a machine outside of the enclave; this way, they're protected in case the proxy is penetrated.

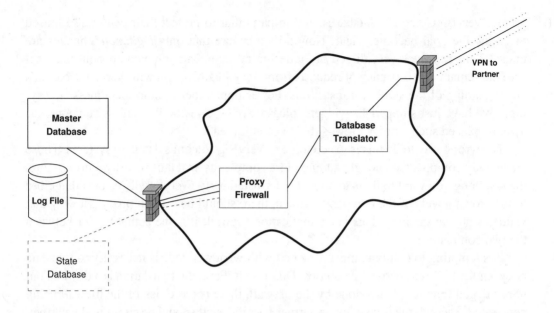

Figure 17.1: The enclave design for linked e-commerce sites.

The final architecture is shown in Figure 17.1. There is an enclave with a VPN to your partner. Inside the enclave, you have two computers: your database translation computer and your proxy. Exactly two types of outbound connections are allowed from the enclave: to the logging server and to your database. If you opt for two databases, you have to permit access to both or put the state database inside the enclave. That's a bad idea, for reasons that should be obvious by now. (Hint: ask yourself two questions: "Who has to write to this database? What are the consequences if it's hacked?")

The important thing about this design is how we arrived at it. Per Section 11.7, we drew our boxes: initially, these were just your database and the other side's query module. We then asked, "What can happen if the other side is evil?" The answer, that your database could be corrupted, led to the need for a proxy. The protection against its failure is the log file; the need to protect it leads us to put it outside of the enclave.

17.3 A Cryptographic Weakness

It's going to happen: no matter how sound your design, no matter how careful your users, some day you'll read of a new security hole (e.g., Heartbleed [Bellovin 2014b; Schneier

2014]) or cryptographic weakness (e.g., the serious attack on RC4 [Vanhoef and Piessens 2015]). What do you do? What should you have done earlier?

The first step is simple: don't panic [Adams 1980]. Many problems are not nearly as easily exploitable as the trade press would have you believe; there is no need for an emergency response. The second step, then, is to get sound technical information on the problem. Exactly what is wrong, and under exactly what conditions can an attacker use it against you? Third, consult your sysadmin database (Section 15.3) to learn which of your computers might be susceptible.

The analysis that follows should not be taken as a recommendation of what you should do right after reading this section. I'm describing how to respond to a particular attack; by the time you read this, there may be a more powerful one. Rather, take this as an example of how to do the necessary analysis when the next break comes along.

Let's start with a cryptanalytic attack on RC4. RC4 is commonly used in two contexts, TLS and WPA-TKIP. (The *Temporal Key Integrity Protocol [TKIP]* is the RC4-based encryption protocol used with WPA. *Wireless Protected Access [WPA]* is a now-obsolete standard that replaced WEP, but could run on hardware that is too slow for the newer, AES-based WPA2 standard.) Where do you use these? Your mail and web servers probably use TLS; you may also have other software that uses it. WPA-TKIP, of course, was employed to protect Wi-Fi networks. Your system administration databases should point you to all of these; for WPA, though, you may find that your employees are using it at home.

The next part of the analysis is to consider your threat model. Wi-Fi signals have a normal range of 100 meters; even with a good antenna, it's still likely that an attacker would have to be within a couple of kilometers. In other words, a remote attacker, no matter how skilled, can't exploit WPA's use of RC4. The Andromedans could probably get someone close enough to your building, and a targetier might try, but many targetiers are insiders anyway, with legitimate access to the wireless LAN. Suppose, though, that you are being targeted by MI-31. Are they likely to send someone that close, thus risking physical exposure? It can certainly happen, but one of the big advantages of Internet espionage is that you don't have to risk sending people into dangerous environments.

Of course, there's another place that WPA-TKIP might be used, one that probably won't be in your databases: your employees' home networks. For the most part, the same logic applies; there is still no remote threat. An employee's network is somewhat more likely to be hit by an ambitious joy hacker, one who has found a clever new cryptanalytic tool. Direct traffic to your company should still be safe—you are using a VPN, right?— but there may be some risk. Per the analysis in Chapter 9, your employee's computer is now sharing a LAN with an attacker. This might expose the machine to on-network attacks, just as in a public hotspot. Worse yet, the attacker might go after *other* devices on the LAN and use them to attack the employee's machine indirectly. Imagine, for example, putting an infected executable file on a home file server. This poses more of a risk than the same technique used against an organization's LAN, since the organization's file server is probably run much more securely.

We see, then, that the direct risks to a company from the RC4 crack are relatively low. By all means move away from it (and yes, that may require hardware upgrades), but for most organizations it isn't a crisis. Your database will point you at exactly which boxes need to be replaced. Home networks probably pose more of a risk, though likely only from attackers in the upper right quadrant of our chart. It is worth considering whether the company should purchase new gear for employees with insecure home networks.

Our analysis of the risk to TLS proceeds along similar lines. First, though, remember two things: in general, eavesdropping on communications links isn't easy (Section 11.3), and very few attackers other than the Andromedans attack the crypto (page 82). To have a problem, we need a combination of two circumstances: an attacker good enough to do cryptanalysis and use of RC4 on a link that this attacker can tap.

There is little doubt that that MI-31 can tap more or less any link, even underwater cables [Sontag and Drew 1998]. Even lesser attackers can listen to the Wi-Fi traffic in a public hotspot, though, and that poses a real threat: hotspots are popular places for people to check their email. An externally available mail server, then, is at risk.

Here's where a thorough understanding of the attack comes in. As of when I'm writing this, the best public attack on TLS with RC4 is designed for recovering web cookies, not for spying on IMAP [Vanhoef and Piessens 2015]. Furthermore, it requires injected JavaScript and 52 hours of monitored traffic. Even the most hypercaffienated employee won't run up that much coffeeshop time overnight. In other words, although the problem is real, it's not a critical emergency; you don't need to turn off your webmail servers instantly. And that brings up the last point to consider: what is the cost of reacting?

If you turn off a service, people can't use it. What is the cost to your business if employees can't read their email? How much money will you lose if customers can't place web orders? How many customers will you lose permanently if you disable RC4, because their browsers are ancient and don't support anything better? Will users fall back to plaintext, thereby making monitoring trivial? Even bad crypto can be better than none; again, most attackers are stymied by any encryption.

These is the sort of analysis you need to go through when you learn of a new flaw. Ask what is at risk, from whom, under what conditions, and what the cost of responding is. Sometimes, there are emergencies, such as when new flaws are found in popular applications and exploits are loose in the wild [Goodin 2015a; Krebs 2013; Krebs 2015]. More often, though, you do have a bit of time to *think*.

17.4 The Internet of Things

"Things flow about so here!" she said at last in a plaintive tone, after she had spent a minute or so in vainly pursuing a large bright thing, that looked sometimes like a doll and sometimes like a work-box, and was always in the shelf next above the one she was looking at. "And this one is the most provoking of all—but I'll tell you what—" she added, as a sudden thought struck her, "I'll follow it up to the very top shelf of all. It'll puzzle it to go through the ceiling, I expect!"

But even this plan failed: the "thing" went through the ceiling as quietly as possible, as if it were quite used to it.

Through the Looking-Glass, and What Alice Found There
—LEWIS CARROLL

Let's now try to apply our methodology to something that doesn't really exist yet in any final form, the so-called *Internet of Things (IoT)*. The Internet of Things is the name given to a future where many objects (which I'll just call "Things") contain not just microprocessors but networked processors, thus allowing remote monitoring and control. We're already seeing its start, what with Internet-enabled thermostats, fitness-tracking devices, and the like; we're almost certainly going to see more of it. What should a security architecture look like for the IoT?

We have to start by understanding the different components. While there are many possible design choices, in the near term the design space is constrained by current technologies and current business models. All of that can and will change, of course, but for my purposes here it suffices to set out a plausible model rather than a prediction.

- Things will have very poor user interfaces, which will complicate their security setup. Many will speak via a private protocol to a home-resident hub/charger; it will speak IP for its Things.

- Because of the shortage of globally routable IP addresses, very few, if any, Things will have their own unique address. Rather, they'll have local addresses [Rekhter et al. 1996] and live behind some NAT box such as a home router. The advent of IPv6 will eliminate this need for it but probably will not eliminate the home NAT; per the box on page 67, to some extent NATs serve as firewalls. This need will not go away in the near term. They are thus unable to be contacted directly from outside the house LAN.

- Given this, most Things will report up to and be controlled by some vendor's (cloud) server complex. Yes, it's possible to punch holes in NATs. Few people do it because every home router is different and most people don't have the skill or the time. If you're a vendor, it's far easier to have your Things phone home frequently.

- Since these vendor-supplied servers will exist and will capture a lot of data, the temptation to monetize the data will be overwhelming for many such companies. Ignoring the privacy aspects (at least in this book), this means that a large database of personally sensitive information will exist, and hence will need to be protected.

- There will be multiple vendors, and hence multiple server complexes. They'll need to talk to each other, at least partially as a proxy for the Things talking to each other. Some static Things in the home may try to communicate directly with each other, but other Things will be mobile and will have to go via the cloud. ("Hey, Hot Water Heater—this is Robin's Phone. Based on her heart rate, speed, and route, she's probably out jogging. She'll be home and ready for a shower in 20 minutes; better heat up some water." "Thank you, Phone, but based on the current temperature and the timing of hot water demand earlier this morning, I think I'm ok.")

- The consequences of a Thing being hacked may or may not be very serious; it depends on the Thing. A "smart TV" generally has a microphone and camera; it can be abused to spy on people in their homes (and we know that some bad guys like to do things like that [N. Anderson 2013]). A coffee pot is much less dangerous— unless its protection against overheating is controlled by software. A hacked toy might be annoying, but if it contains a microphone that talks to cloud servers, like some dolls do [Halzack 2015], it's also dangerous. And then there are hacked cars [Greenberg 2015b] and rifles [Greenberg 2015a]...

Our architecture, then, has several levels: Things, hubs, and servers. Things should speak only to the proper hub. Hubs can speak locally to other hubs or to hubless Things. All hubs communicate over the Internet with their assigned servers; these servers talk to each other. What are the security properties we need to worry about?

Let's start by looking at a hub. A hub has to register with a server; this registration somehow has to be tied to ownership. I should be allowed to control my thermostat, but not my neighbor's. The details of how this is done will vary, but the need to do this securely will always exist. For that matter, hubs have to be on the home's (probably Wi-Fi) network; this means provisioning an SSID and a WPA2 password. There are some interesting usability challenges here. A compromised hub can attack other local hubs, its own Things, and the server complex to which it connects. For that matter, since it has Internet connectivity, it could be turned into a bot and even send spam.

All connections from the hub should be encrypted, with the possible exception of very short range wireless connections to its associated Things. Although the link over the Internet is hard to tap (and Andromeda is probably not interested in monitoring your laundry cycles), there will be authentication data sent over the home Wi-Fi network; any compromised computer in the home (including another hub) could grab it.

Server-to-server links should also be encrypted. Per the discussion earlier in this chapter, that's more for authentication than confidentiality. That said, in the large mass of data from many people, there might be information of interest to MI-31, such as the location of a person of interest.

A corrupted server could attack hubs and Things. The most devastating thing it could do would be to replace the firmware on them, though just what this evil firmware could do would obviously be Thing-dependent. There are all of the other usual issues involving servers, such as compromise of its authentication database, its other personal data, and so on.

There is a delicate architectural question involving server-mediated Thing-to-Thing communication: who trusts whom? Consider the phone-to-water heater conversation presented above: how should this message be authenticated? The obvious solution—giving the phone a login on each Thing to which it may talk—doesn't work; the administrative hassles for consumers are appalling. If the phone and the water heater both talk to the same server, perhaps there's a trust relationship that can be assumed: the server knows that both belong to Robin. If, though, they're homed to different companies' cloud-resident servers, we have a problem. Communication should be allowed to take place if both Things belong to the same person, but how is that to be established? Should the servers trust each other? That might be the simplest answer, assuming suitable contracts (and suitable liability and indemnification clauses) between the IoT companies. If that doesn't work, we need complex cryptographic protocols for hubs to use to authenticate requests, or share key pairs, or what have you. This issue—how to establish and manage trust, across the acquisition and disposal of hubs, Things, homes, and servers companies—has many possible solutions. Most of these will be quite delicate; evaluating the security of any such architecture will be a considerable challenge.

Managing access control is another issue. Permissions on Things can be complex. Parents may not want their teenagers to be able to adjust the thermostat; they may want to permit house guests to do so. They may also want the thermostat to change itself automatically when a selected set of phones come within a certain radius of the house—this ability is on the market today. As I've discussed, managing access control lists is hard, but it's an essential part of the IoT, and vendors can't ignore usability.

We may find that part of the solution is another box: a household Thing manager. The manager needs LAN access to all Things, including phones (which will have to have

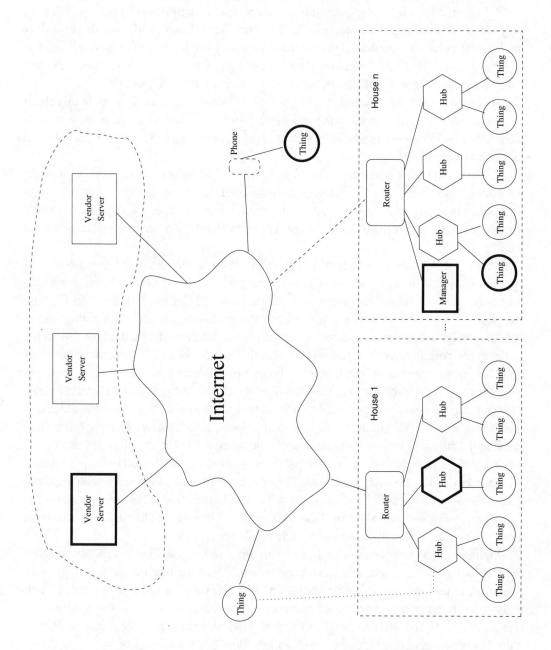

Figure 17.2: A possible IoT configuration. Objects drawn in bold may be compromised.

the proper apps). Maybe the manager is built into some hubs, and contacted by a web browser; this, of course, means that more passwords need to be set and managed.

Hubs and Things run software; this software will sometimes be buggy and will need to be updated. This means that there needs to be a bidirectional trust path; servers will have to authenticate themselves to the devices. This may conflict with some people's desire to reprogram their own gadgetry, much like they jailbreak iPhones. How shall this be handled?

The early returns are distressing. Many current devices don't do even rudimentary encryption [Barcena, Wueest, and Lau 2014]; my own analysis of some thermostats show similar weaknesses. The analytic methods I've described here seem adequate, though; they let us see the sensitivity of different elements and links, and understand where we need to put defenses.

A topology that fits these constraints is shown in Figure 17.2. Every house has a set of hubs; houses may or may not have Thing managers. Mobile Things are presumed to be associated with some hub; alternately, some may be managed directly by an associated phone, which in turn would likely maintain a quasi-permanent connection to a vendor's server. Let's see what happens if different components are compromised. I've drawn a few in "bold" to reduce ambiguity.

We will assume that all links are cryptographically protected. This prevents both eavesdropping and impersonation via the net. If the links are not encrypted, the effect is more or less the same as a compromise of one of its endpoints.

Let's look first at defending the servers. It turns out that that's a hard thing to do. By design, they're talking to many customer-controlled Things; they're also talking to other servers. They're dealing with a very heterogeneous (and constantly growing) set of Things; this in turn implies the need for frequent updates, probably by many parties. Servers are thus quite vulnerable, much more so than, say, manufacturer development machines.

Suppose that a vendor server has been taken over. What are the implications? Per the discussion, it has several abilities: it can send malicious commands to its associated Things, it can send bad firmware to Things, and it can steal authentication data. We need defenses against each of these threats and against the server itself being compromised.

There is not much that can be done directly about bad commands; by design, Things will listen unconditionally to their servers. However, it is possible to incorporate hard-wired limits that prevent dangerous behavior. The Nest thermostat, for example, has "safety temperatures": if these values are exceeded, either because it's too cold or too warm, the thermostat will activate the appropriate device, even if the thermostat has been turned off. At least some versions of the device will also ignore requests that seem inappropriate:

Note that your Nest Thermostat [*sic*] will never cool when the temperature
is below 45°F/7°C or heat when the temperature is above 95°F/35°C. These
limits cannot be changed.

That text appeared in an earlier version of their web site; it is unclear why the current web
site does not say the same thing.[3]

IoT Design Property 1 *Things should reject dangerous requests. To the extent feasible,
these limits should be enforced by hardware, not software.*

We can do a better job of defending against nasty firmware. As noted, servers are
vulnerable machines. We're therefore better off if firmware files are digitally signed by
the manufacturer. This isn't a perfect defense: Attackers could replay older, and perhaps
buggier firmware versions but they would find it very hard to make arbitrary malicious
changes to the firmware if the server were the only machine compromised. Note that this
is not the same as an "app store only" model. That all firmware be signed is a security
requirement; which signatures should be accepted is a policy decision that is separable
from this requirement.

IoT Design Property 2 *All firmware must be digitally signed by the manufacturer; the
signing key must not be accessible to the servers.*

Finally, authentication data is at risk. This completely rules out the use of passwords
for Thing-to-server authentication, if for no other reason than that we know that people
will use the same, easy-to-remember passwords for all of their Things (and lots of other
stuff besides). Things, however, are computers, not people; they can remember large numbers and do complex calculations. Accordingly, some form of cryptographic authentication seems best. Users will need to talk to the servers' web interface, though; there's not
much that can be done save to follow the advice in Chapter 7. Finally, since Thing-to-
Thing communication will go via the servers, authentication between them should be end
to end; that way, a compromised server can't interfere with such messages. This in turn
suggests the need for a "house PKI": issue each customer a certificate; this certificate will
in turn be used to issue certificates to all of her hubs and Things.

IoT Design Property 3 *Use cryptographic authentication, and in particular public key-
based cryptographic authentication, to authenticate Thing-to-server and Thing-to-Thing
messages.*

---

3. "How Safety Temperatures Work," https://web.archive.org/web/20140205203310/http:
//support.nest.com/article/How-do-Safety-Temperatures-work.

If servers are compromised, many clients could be at risk. By putting authorization in the house—that is, at Things and hubs, rather than on vendor servers—this risk is minimized.

IoT Design Property 4 *Authorization is done by Things and hubs, not by the servers.*

There is one last line of defense: server complexes are professionally run; as such, they can be equipped with sophisticated intrusion-detection systems, separate authentication servers, competent sysadmins, and more. In other words, with a bit of luck and ordinary competence many breaches will be avoided, and others will be detected and remedied quickly.

Home devices, such as hubs and Things, do not have those advantages. What if a hub is compromised? It turns out that there is not much new danger here. A hub is largely a message relay; if the messages are protected end to end, a compromised hub can't tamper with them. Hubs do have another role, though: they act as the agent for newly acquired Things and perhaps even issue them their certificates. They may also handle authorization on behalf of their Things—it makes much more sense to have a lighting controller regulate who can turn on a given lamp than to have to reconfigure access rules every time someone replaces a burned-out light bulb. For very low-powered Things, the hubs may even be the endpoint for all encryption. In other words, the Things trust them completely and don't even have an alternate communications path over which they can yell for help.

Hubs are on the local LAN and can generally be attacked from within the house or by a compromised server. They're generally not reachable directly from the outside, nor do they engage in risky activities such as browsing the web. The best defense, then, is intrusion detection: hubs should look for probes or nasty stuff coming at them from their servers, and alert the device owners if something appears wrong. It is possible that compromised hubs will need to be replaced; at the least, they'll need to be reset to the factory-shipped configuration.

IoT Design Property 5 *All hubs should incorporate intrusion detection. They should be able to upload and download configuration files, even across software versions.*

Things themselves may be compromised. A compromised Thing could attack its hub or associated phone; it could also send attack messages through the hub to its server or to other Things. Servers, being professionally run, have to protect themselves. The hubs, though, could perform an intrusion detection function on relayed messages if they're not encrypted end to end. However, messages must still be authenticated end to end. This demands complex key management scenarios, a possible danger point.

IoT Design Property 6 *Thing-to-Thing messages should be authenticated end to end. However, they are encrypted Thing-to-hub, hub-to-hub, and hub-to-Thing, to permit intrusion detection by the Hubs. Messages to servers may or may not be encrypted end to end.*

The last component of interest is the Thing manager, whether it's a stand-alone box or a component built into a hub. Managers are controlled by users via web browsers; user computers are, of course, at great risk of compromise, which in turn puts the manager (or at least the configurations it manages) at risk. Note that the manager will have to have a way to authenticate users; this is almost certainly going to be password based and without the opportunity for external authentication servers. There is also the very thorny issue of password reset: what should be done with the configurations (including private keys; the manager is probably the house CA) and authorizations stored in the manager? It seems likely that they should be retained, since someone who sets a new password could reset all access permissions anyway, but there may be privacy issues to consider.

IoT Design Property 7 *Managers are at great risk of attack from compromised user machines. The best they can do is strongly protect passwords and keys, and perhaps look for anomalous change requests—but it is hard to see whom to notify if the apparently authorized user is doing strange things.*

Needless to say, a full Internet of Things design would be far more complex than this sketch. Even at this level, though, looking at each type of box lets us analyze the risks to each component and some necessary defensive measures.

Chapter 18

Doing Security Properly

"You are ready, children, for everything that will have to be done. You have not come to your full maturity and power, of course; that stage will come only with time. It is best for you, however, that we leave you now. Your race is potentially vastly stronger and abler than ours. We reached some time ago the highest point attainable to us: we could no longer adapt ourselves to the ever-increasing complexity of life. You, a young new race amply equipped for any emergency within reckonable time, will be able to do so. In capability and in equipment you begin where we leave off."

Mentor of Arisia in *Children of the Lens*
—E. E. "DOC" SMITH

18.1 Obsolescence

If you've read this far, some of the preceding sections may already be obsolete, and the book as a whole may be moving towards obsolescence. There's no choice. Not only is high-tech a very dynamic field; the threat model also changes. Part of that latter is due to technical changes—new devices, new services, and so on will continue to appear for the foreseeable future—but it's also due to changes in who the attackers are and what they want. It's hard to imagine a more serious threat than a major government, but what these governments are interested in can and will vary. Nevertheless, the primary purpose of this book is to teach how to think about change; in that sense, its merits should, I hope, outlast the specific facts cited.

All that said, some changes are more likely than others and deserve specific mention. That's not to say that specific ideas will pan out—if I knew for sure what would be hot in the future, I could make a lot more money consulting for venture capitalists than I can as a professor—but rather that certain broad technical trends seem all but inevitable. Hardware, for example, will almost certainly continue to get smaller and cheaper; even if there are no amazing new gadgets, we almost certainly have a fair number of years before Moore's Law is repealed. Similarly, it seems all but certain that five or ten years from now we will all be using services that haven't been invented yet. I'm writing this in 2015, when the iPhone was only eight years old, and Twitter and Facebook were nine and ten, respectively. It is hard to remember when they didn't exist, but they're that young. Nevertheless, they've changed the face of computing and with that the threat model. If you doubt the effect of the latter two, consider how much easier Facebook makes it for an attacker to answer "security" questions. Twitter, of course has brought down a Congressman [Barrett 2011] and arguably entire regimes [Saletan 2011]. Anything that powerful *will* attract the interests of governments and their militaries.

Threats change, too, though that evolution is driven as much by economics and politics as by technology. Stuxnet was developed not just because it was possible, but rather because some highly skilled, motivated adversaries wanted to damage an Iranian nuclear centrifuge plant. Similarly, Shamoon, which attacked Saudi oil company computers [Goodin 2012c; Leyden 2012], was quite likely a response to cyberattacks on Iran, rather than the outcome of a new technological development. Commercially motivated attacks are by definition motivated by money—but where the money is is changing. There are already reports of sophisticated hacks to steal Bitcoins [Greenberg 2014; Litke and Stewart 2014].

Prophecy is difficult; we cannot say with any confidence what will happen next. What we can talk about are possible new characteristics that will cause trouble in the future.

18.2 New Devices

Fewer bets are more certain than that hardware will continue to improve for the next several years. While there may be unpleasant surprises, similar to the heat death of the megahertz race, it seems clear that substantial progress will continue. Perhaps significantly, disk capacity has improved even more than CPU price/performance. There are several conclusions we can draw from this.

First, cheaper and smaller computers are deployable in more places. Furthermore, these CPUs will almost certainly be networked, which poses some obvious security issues. Although some of the risks are low—illicit access to the chip in a toothbrush or bathroom scale raises at most minor privacy concerns—anything that is tied directly or indirectly to an actuator is more worrisome.

Small, specialized computers are also harder to manage directly. They won't have traditional input or output devices; indeed, even learning the MAC address will often be challenging. Sometimes, of course, these devices are easily firewalled. Digital toothbrushes, for example, will almost certainly have to be placed into a docking station, if only to recharge their batteries; this docking station can manage access control policies. Other devices, though, will need broader connectivity, without an obvious chokepoint, per the discussion of the Internet of Things (Section 17.4).

It would be nice, of course, if the programmers of such devices took proper care for security. This means not just basic access control—the need for that is generally understood by now—but also proper care in programming and some way to tie the widget into a larger policy framework. We can't even count on encryption being used, let alone used properly [Barcena, Wueest, and Lau 2014]. Experience suggests that this will rarely be the case, which in turn means that security people are not likely to be out of a job any time soon.

There is an important corollary here: we don't get to design the network protocols used by these new computers. This in turn means that when trying to devise security mechanisms for them, we have to take them as is, warts and all. This can't be viewed just as a bug; rather, it's likely to be reality.

The future, then, will be even more challenging for security. We can expect orders of magnitude more computers to protect; many of these will be more difficult to handle than today's. The primary challenge will be understanding who is supposed to talk to whom, and how.

18.3 New Threats

Predicting new threats is hard. It's not so much the concept that's difficult to imagine as the context. Cyberespionage isn't new; arguably, it existed more than 25 years ago [Stoll 1988; Stoll 1989]. The modern incarnation, though, became possible because the desired information moved online: you can't hack into a typewritten page. It was economics that changed the situation: the productivity advantages of creating and storing industrial and defense information on networked computers were overwhelming; to refrain would have made no sense. Nevertheless, the move has had consequences.

It is important to remember that conceptually, most "new" threats aren't new; rather, they become real or they become real at scale. Software tinkering with bank accounts, for example, was described almost 50 years ago in a science fiction book, albeit via a sentient computer [Heinlein 1966]. Cybersabotage was described by Reed [2004]. Deliberately destructive viruses were imagined by Gerrold [1972] and as a weapon of war in the myth of the so-called "Iraqi printer virus" [G. Smith 2003]. None of these are quite how it's done today, but the basic concepts are old.

It is clear that we can think of all sorts of futuristic threats, ones that may never come to pass. Consider, for example, self-driving cars [R. Wood 2012]. It's easy to imagine nightmare scenarios from hacked automobiles, especially when you realize how insecure today's car networks are [Koscher et al. 2010]. However, attacks (and especially serious attacks) don't happen simply because they're possible; rather, they happen because someone somehow gains something from the attack. Recall the definition of a threat cited in Chapter 3: "an adversary that is motivated and capable of exploiting a vulnerability." You need all three to have a problem: the vulnerability, the capability, and the motivation. Looking at this through a purely technological lens makes you focus on the first two, but the third is equally critical.

Predicting new threats, then, requires three steps. First, be aware of new services and gadgets. (Yes, it is indeed a job requirement that you acquire and play with lots of new toys. You have my permission to tell that to your boss.) Second, follow the security literature (including, of course, blog posts and newsletters) to learn about the new attacks and holes, and how easy or difficult they are to exploit. (The press often overhypes new holes.) Finally, pay attention to the news to see who might benefit from some new attack. Remember to factor in both the skill level required as well as whether the attack makes sense in terms of the possible perpetrator's goals.

18.4   New Defenses

The ultimate goal of security research, of course, is to find some strong, new defenses, ones that resist attacks old and new. Most likely, some fundamentally new design principle will be needed. As noted many times in this book, most security problems are due to buggy code. It is hard to imagine what a defense against that might look like, given that every other panacea proposed over the last several decades has failed.

Wulf and Jones noted that the security field has not had any really new ideas in quite a long time [2009]. They're quite right. Most of our systems are based on what I call the "walls and doors" principle: a strong wall between security contexts, and a door, an opening in the wall for selected requests. We're pretty good (though not perfect) at building walls, that is, at separating contexts. Doors, though, are problematic. They're not supposed to pass just any request; rather, they should do so only in accordance with a policy. Unfortunately, both specifying and implementing suitable policies is difficult.

Consider a simple web-mediated database search for a person's name. It sounds like a simple security policy: accept a name, and nothing else. However (and as memorably explained by xkcd; see Figure 2.1), it seems to be very hard to get that right. Admittedly, handling names properly is hard [McKenzie 2010], but there is no excuse for SQL injection attacks today. Nevertheless, they happen and with distressing frequency.

It is likely, of course, that at some point technology will render SQL attacks a minor concern. Somewhat greater programmer awareness coupled with new APIs will make it easier to do the right thing than the wrong one. These attacks will thus decrease in importance, just as has happened with buffer overflows, what with the development of improved training and better tools (e.g., *Address Space Layout Randomization [ASLR]* [Shacham et al. 2004] and stack canaries [Cowan et al. 2003]). What's next? There have been many different kinds of attacks over the years. What is significant is how many of them are against door wardens, the programs charged with enforcing a safe policy. In the 1990s, mailers were a popular target, because they had to pass information from one security context to another. These days, attacks involving active content, notably JavaScript and Java, are legion. (Microsoft says that about 75% of exploit kits in 2013 targeted Java, and about another 10% went after Flash [Batchelder et al. 2013].)

To complicate things, there are generally no defenses within the walls. This could be considered a matter of definition; alternately, one could envision an architecture with interior walls, walls of perhaps lesser strength but still with well-guarded doors. This would help with the "brittleness" problem [Bellovin 2006a], that our defenses shatter under attack so that one security bug can result in the complete penetration of a system and the compromise of everything in it.

How could such a resilient system be built? I outlined one scheme for protecting e-commerce sites in Chapter 11, involving encrypted database records. This isn't a complete solution—e-commerce sites have many more databases than just those holding customer records, and there are many other types of vulnerable systems—but the approach is illustrative.

There are certainly other possibilities. One might use a cryptographic scheme—fully homomorphic encryption [Gentry 2010]? functional encryption [Boneh, Sahai, and Waters 2012]?—though care must be taken to avoid simply changing the policy question from "What may pass through the door?" to "Who can have access to the keys?" If the underlying logic is the same, the bugs are likely to be the same as well.

It seems clear, though, that relying on walls and doors will not succeed. More precisely, it has not succeeded despite decades of effort; we need a new paradigm. Naturally, I hope that the principles explained in this book will help us adapt to such a paradigm if and when it arises.

18.5 Thinking about Privacy

This book is about computer security, not privacy. Nevertheless, a few comments about privacy are in order.

First, privacy is increasingly important. Governments around the world are enforcing more and more stringent requirements. Companies that fail, even inadvertently, have been sanctioned.[1] Consumers care more and more.

As it turns out, and despite some important differences, many of the design principles are the same. If nothing else, a system that can't protect data confidentiality can't protect user privacy; anyone who hacks the system can get at all of the data.

More importantly, just as proper security behavior changes with technology and attackers, so, too, do threats to privacy. Once, fairly simple schemes sufficed to anonymize data; today, deanonymization techniques are sufficiently advanced (see, e.g., [Narayanan and Shmatikov 2008]) that they have drawn legal attention [Ohm 2010]. The advances in technology have been accompanied by changes in the threat model: more people, especially advertisers, are willing to go to great lengths to track consumers [Valentino-DeVries and Singer-Vine 2012].

This does not by itself call into question such principles as "privacy by design" [Cavoukian 2009]. It does, however, mean that particular design choices must either be based on firm mathematical foundations or explicitly evaluated against a given state of technology and threat. For example, Chapter 2 of [Cavoukian 2009] advocates "biometric encryption": converting a biometric to a key to protect personal data. This is fine in principle; however, as [Ballard, Kamara, and Reiter 2008] points out, it's hard to evaluate the security of proposed constructs; indeed, several proposed schemes have later fallen to attacks. This doesn't mean that a privacy design based on biometric encryption is a bad idea; it does mean that the privacy guarantees are not absolute and will undoubtedly grow weaker over time.

18.6   Putting It All Together

If there is one single principle underlying this book, it is that security designs can only be evaluated against a particular point in time. Given that, and given the rate of change of technology, it is vital that we learn to ask, "What next?"

This is a practice that has largely been ignored by the security community, with the notable exception of (good) cryptographers. I have yet to see a system analysis that makes explicit what the time- or threat-bound assumptions are. Nevertheless (and as should be very clear by now), these assumptions underlie the conclusions—and some day, the assumptions will be wrong and the security illusory.

One practice that is, fortunately, becoming more common is to do new security reviews for major revisions of a product. That's good, but all too often, these new reviews

---

1. See, for example, http://www.ftc.gov/opa/2010/06/twitter.shtm, which describes a settlement between the US Federal Trade Commission and Twitter.

don't go far enough. Quite naturally, they focus on the new features, the new components, and the new interfaces. This is good as far as it goes, since anything new might have a wide-open door with a sign saying, "Welcome, Hackers!"; however, it doesn't go far enough. These reviews only rarely go back and look at the previous review, and if they did they'd likely search in vain for explicit upper bounds on the assessed security. Reviews, like cartons of milk, should come with expiration dates.

Large projects carry their own challenges. A major, enterprise-wide software deployment can take man years to design, develop, and deploy; see, for example, [R. Stross 2012] and [Israel 2012] for discussions of two failed megaprojects. It is sobering to compare these timescales with how short a time smart phones have been around. Agility is crucial.

I've occasionally muttered about a magic wand that I could wave that would fix all of today's security problems. It would have to be a very big wand, of course, carrying a very potent spell. The image, though, is wrong. The spells would have to be strengthened and recast continuously, and the wand kept continually in motion. There are and can be no final answers to security because the problem keeps changing. All we can do is to keep studying, keep improving our systems—and keep waving that wand.

> The old man leaned forward again. "Go, Tony! I throw the torch to you. Your place is the place I occupied. Lead my people. Fight! Live! Become glorious!"
>
> *After Worlds Collide*
> —PHILIP WYLIE AND EDWIN BALMER

References

Abad, C., J. Taylor, C. Sengul, William Yurcik, Y. Zhou, and K. Rowe (Dec. 2003). "Log Correlation for Intrusion Detection: A Proof of Concept." In: *Proceedings of the 19th Annual Computer Security Applications Conference*, pp. 255–264. DOI: 10.1109/CSAC.2003.1254330. (Cit. on p. 286).

Abad, Cristina, Yifan Li, Kiran Lakkaraju, Xiaoxin Yin, and William Yurcik (2004). "Correlation between NetFlow System and Network Views for Intrusion Detection." In: *Workshop on Link Analysis, Counter-terrorism, and Privacy, Held in Conjunction with SDM*. (Cit. on p. 286).

Aboba, B. and W. Dixon (Mar. 2004). *IPsec-Network Address Translation (NAT) Compatibility Requirements*. RFC 3715. http://www.rfc-editor.org/rfc/rfc3715.txt (cit. on p. 95).

Abrams, Rachel (Aug. 6, 2014). "Target Puts Data Breach Costs at $148 Million, and Forecasts Profit Drop." In: *The New York Times*. http://www.nytimes.com/2014/08/06/business/target-puts-data-breach-costs-at-148-million.html (cit. on pp. 214, 222).

Adams, Douglas (1980). *The Hitchhiker's Guide to the Galaxy*. First American edition. New York: Harmony Books. (Cit. on p. 299).

Adrian, David, Karthikeyan Bhargavan, Zakir Durumeric, Pierrick Gaudry, Matthew Green, J. Alex Halderman, Nadia Heninger, Drew Springall, Emmanuel Thomé, Luke Valenta, Benjamin VanderSloot, Eric Wustrow, Santiago Zanella-Béguelin, and Paul Zimmermann (2015). "Imperfect Forward Secrecy: How Diffie-Hellman Fails in Practice." In: *Proceedings of the 22th ACM Conference on Computer and Communications Security (CCS)*. https://weakdh.org/imperfect-forward-secrecy.pdf (cit. on pp. 83, 100).

Allen, Peter (Feb. 22, 2012). "British Drone Secrets Stolen from Paris Train Station." In: *The Telegraph*. http://www.telegraph.co.uk/news/worldnews/9099410/British-drone-secrets-stolen-from-Paris-train-station.html (cit. on p. 136).

Amazon (May 2011). *Amazon Web Services Overview of Security Processes*. White paper. http://d36cz9buwru1tt.cloudfront.net/pdf/AWS_Security_Whitepaper.pdf (cit. on p. 193).

Anderson, Nate (July 26, 2007). "Deep Packet Inspection Meets 'Net Neutrality, CALEA." In: *Ars Technica*. http://arstechnica.com/gadgets/2007/07/deep-packet-inspection-meets-net-neutrality/ (cit. on pp. 66, 71).

—— (Mar. 11, 2013). "Meet the Men Who Spy on Women through Their Webcams." In: *Ars Technica*. http://arstechnica.com/tech-policy/2013/03/rat-breeders-meet-the-men-who-spy-on-women-through-their-webcams/ (cit. on p. 302).

Anderson, Poul (1966). *Ensign Flandry*. Philadelphia: Chilton Books. (Cit. on p. 107).

Anderson, Poul (1983). "A Tragedy of Errors." In: *The Long Night*. Story originally published in *Galaxy*, 1967. New York: TOR. (Cit. on p. 6).

Andrade, Jose (Apr. 12, 2014). "What is Heartbleed, Anyway?" In: *Engadget*. http://www.engadget.com/2014/04/12/heartbleed-explained/ (cit. on p. 182).

Anonymous (Dec. 2011). Private communication. (Cit. on p. 83).

Anthony, Sebastian (Mar. 17, 2014). "Firefox is Still the Least Secure Web Browser, Falls to Four Zero-Day Exploits at Pwn2Own." In: *ExtremeTech*. http://www.extremetech.com/computing/178587-firefox-is-still-the-least-secure-web-browser-falls-to-four-zero-day-exploits-at-pwn2own (cit. on p. 201).

Appel, Andrew W. (Sept. 2011). "Security Seals on Voting Machines: A Case Study." In: *ACM Trans. Inf. Syst. Secur.* 14.2, 18:1–18:29. ISSN: 1094-9224. DOI: 10.1145/2019599.2019603. http://doi.acm.org/10.1145/2019599.2019603 (cit. on p. 55).

Apple (June 2015). *iOS Security*. https://www.apple.com/business/docs/iOS_Security_Guide.pdf (cit. on p. 128).

Arends, R., R. Austein, M. Larson, D. Massey, and S. Rose (Mar. 2005a). *DNS Security Introduction and Requirements*. RFC 4033. http://www.rfc-editor.org/rfc/rfc4033.txt (cit. on pp. 91, 159).

——— (Mar. 2005b). *Protocol Modifications for the DNS Security Extensions*. RFC 4035. http://www.rfc-editor.org/rfc/rfc4035.txt (cit. on pp. 91, 159).

——— (Mar. 2005c). *Resource Records for the DNS Security Extensions*. RFC 4034. http://www.rfc-editor.org/rfc/rfc4034.txt (cit. on pp. 91, 159).

Arnold, Ken and James Gosling (1996). *The Java Programming Language*. Reading, MA: Addison-Wesley. (Cit. on p. 23).

Asimov, Isaac (1951). *Foundation*. New York: Doubleday & Company. (Cit. on p. 272).

Baez, John, William G. Unruh, and William G. Tifft (Oct. 21, 1999). "Ask the Experts: Is Time Quantized?" In: *Scientific American*. http://www.scientificamerican.com/article.cfm?id=is-time-quantized-in-othe (cit. on p. 98).

Ball, Thomas, Byron Cook, Vladimir Levin, and Sriram K. Rajamani (2004). "SLAM and Static Driver Verifier: Technology Transfer of Formal Methods inside Microsoft." English. In: *Integrated Formal Methods*. Ed. by EerkeA. Boiten, John Derrick, and Graeme Smith. Vol. 2999. Lecture Notes in Computer Science. Springer Berlin Heidelberg, pp. 1–20. ISBN: 978-3-540-21377-2. DOI: 10.1007/978-3-540-24756-2_1. http://dx.doi.org/10.1007/978-3-540-24756-2_1 (cit. on p. 209).

Ballard, Lucas, Seny Kamara, and Michael K. Reiter (Aug. 2008). "The Practical Subtleties of Biometric Key Generation." In: *Proceedings of the 17th Annual USENIX Security Symposium*. http://cs.unc.edu/~fabian/papers/bkgs.pdf (cit. on pp. 124, 314).

Bamford, James (Mar. 15, 2012). "The NSA Is Building the Country's Biggest Spy Center (Watch What You Say)." In: *Wired: Threat Level*. http://www.wired.com/threatlevel/2012/03/ff_nsadatacenter/all/1 (cit. on p. 99).

——— (Sept. 29, 2015). "A Death in Athens." In: *The Intercept*. https://theintercept.com/2015/09/28/death-athens-rogue-nsa-operation/ (cit. on p. 235).

Barcena, Mario Ballano, Candid Wueest, and Hon Lau (July 2014). *How Safe is Your Quantified Self?* Symantec Security Response. http://www.symantec.com/content/en/us/enterprise/

media/security_response/whitepapers/how-safe-is-your-quantified-self.pdf (cit. on pp. 305, 311).

Barker, Elaine, William Barker, William Burr, William Polk, and Miles Smid (July 2012). *Recommendation for Key Management—Part 1: General (Revision 3)*. Tech. rep. 800-57. NIST. http://csrc.nist.gov/publications/nistpubs/800-57/sp800-57_part1_rev3_general.pdf (cit. on p. 100).

Barnes, R. (Oct. 2011). *Use Cases and Requirements for DNS-Based Authentication of Named Entities (DANE)*. RFC 6394. http://www.rfc-editor.org/rfc/rfc6394.txt (cit. on p. 159).

Barnett, Emma (Mar. 18, 2009). "Top 10 Worst Computer Viruses." In: *The Telegraph*. http://www.telegraph.co.uk/technology/5012057/Top-10-worst-computer-viruses-of-all-time.html (cit. on pp. 53, 59).

Barrett, Devlin (June 2011). "Weiner Calling It Quits: Lawmaker's Resolve to Keep Seat Withered Under Pressure from Top Democrats." In: *The Wall Street Journal*. http://online.wsj.com/article/SB10001424052702304186404576389422646672178.html (cit. on p. 310).

——— (July 23, 2015). "U.S. Plans to Use Spy Law to Battle Corporate Espionage." In: *The Wall Street Journal*. http://www.wsj.com/articles/u-s-plans-to-use-spy-law-to-battle-corporate-espionage-1437688169 (cit. on p. xii).

Bartal, Yair, Alain Mayer, Kobbi Nissim, and Avishai Wool (2004). "Firmato: A Novel Firewall Management Toolkit." In: *ACM Transactions on Computer Systems (TOCS)* 22.4, pp. 381–420. https://www.eng.tau.ac.il/~yash/infosec-seminar/2005/tocs04.pdf (cit. on p. 218).

Barth, A. (Apr. 2011). *HTTP State Management Mechanism*. RFC 6265. http://www.rfc-editor.org/rfc/rfc6265.txt (cit. on p. 138).

Batchelder, Dennis, Joe Blackbird, David Felstead, Paul Henry, Jeff Jones, Aneesh Kulkami, John Lambert, Marc Lauricella, Ken Malcomson, Matt Miller, Nam Ng, Daryl Pecelj, Tim Rains, Vidya Sekhar, Holly Stewart, Todd Thompson, David Weston, and Terry Zink (July 2013). *Microsoft Security Intelligence Report*. SIR Volume16. http://www.microsoft.com/security/sir/default.aspx (cit. on pp. 37, 244, 313).

Baxter-Reynolds, Matt (Mar. 19, 2014). "Apple's 'goto fail' Tells Us Nothing Good About Cupertino's Software Delivery Process." In: *ZDnet*. http://www.zdnet.com/apples-goto-fail-tells-us-nothing-good-about-cupertinos-software-delivery-process-7000027449/ (cit. on p. 182).

BBC (Apr. 23, 2014). "Profile: Private First Class Manning." In: *BBC News*. http://www.bbc.com/news/world-us-canada-11874276 (cit. on p. 73).

Beattie, Steve, Seth Arnold, Crispin Cowan, Perry Wagle, Chris Wright, and Adam Shostack (2002). "Timing the Application of Security Patches for Optimal Uptime." In: *Proceedings of the USENIX 16th Systems Administration Conference*. http://www.usenix.org/publications/library/proceedings/lisa02/tech/beattie.html (cit. on p. 240).

Bellare, M., R. Canetti, and H. Krawczyk (1996). "Keying Hash Functions for Message Authentication." In: *Advances in Cryptology: Proceedings of CRYPTO '96*. Springer-Verlag, pp. 1–15. http://citeseerx.ist.psu.edu/viewdoc/summary?doi=10.1.1.44.9634 (cit. on p. 140).

Bellovin, Steven M. (Sept. 1992). "There Be Dragons." In: *Proceedings of the Third Usenix Unix Security Symposium*, pp. 1–16. https://www.cs.columbia.edu/~smb/papers/dragon.pdf (cit. on p. 71).

Bellovin, Steven M. (June 1995). "Using the Domain Name System for System Break-Ins." In: *Proceedings of the Fifth Usenix Unix Security Symposium*. Salt Lake City, UT, pp. 199–208. https://www.cs.columbia.edu/~smb/papers/dnshack.pdf (cit. on p. 215).

——— (July 1996). "Problem Areas for the IP Security Protocols." In: *Proceedings of the Sixth Usenix Unix Security Symposium*, pp. 205–214. https://www.cs.columbia.edu/~smb/papers/badesp.pdf (cit. on p. 86).

——— (1997). "Probable Plaintext Cryptanalysis of the IP Security Protocols." In: *Proc. of the Symposium on Network and Distributed System Security*, pp. 155–160. https://www.cs.columbia.edu/~smb/papers/probtxt.pdf (cit. on p. 97).

——— (Nov. 1999). "Distributed Firewalls." In: *;login:* pp. 39–47. https://www.cs.columbia.edu/~smb/papers/distfw.pdf (cit. on pp. 62, 64).

——— (Apr. 1, 2003). *The Security Flag in the IPv4 Header*. RFC 3514. http://www.rfc-editor.org/rfc/rfc3514.txt (cit. on pp. 49, 79, 106).

——— (July–Aug. 2006a). "On the Brittleness of Software and the Infeasibility of Security Metrics." In: *IEEE Security & Privacy* 4.4. https://www.cs.columbia.edu/~smb/papers/01668014.pdf (cit. on pp. 199, 313).

——— (Oct. 2006b). "Virtual Machines, Virtual Security." In: *Communications of the ACM* 49.10. "Inside RISKS" column. (Cit. on pp. 59, 187).

——— (Feb. 2009a). *Guidelines for Specifying the Use of IPsec Version 2*. RFC 5406. http://www.rfc-editor.org/rfc/rfc5406.txt (cit. on p. 94).

——— (Apr. 29, 2009b). "The Open Source Quality Challenge." In: *SMBlog (blog)*. https://www.cs.columbia.edu/~smb/blog/2009-04/2009-04-29.html (cit. on pp. 235, 241).

——— (Sept. 27, 2010). "Stuxnet: The First Weaponized Software?" In: *SMBlog (blog)*. https://www.cs.columbia.edu/~smb/blog/2010-09/2010-09-27.html (cit. on p. 38).

——— (May–June 2011a). "Clouds from Both Sides." In: *IEEE Security & Privacy* 9.3. ISSN: 1540-7993. http://dx.doi.org/10.1109/MSP.2011.48 (cit. on p. 380).

——— (July 2011b). "Frank Miller: Inventor of the One-Time Pad." In: *Cryptologia* 35.3. An earlier version is available as technical report CUCS-009-11, pp. 203–222. http://dx.doi.org/10.1080/01611194.2011.583711 (cit. on p. 122).

——— (Nov.–Dec. 2012). "The Major Cyberincident Investigations Board." In: *IEEE Security & Privacy* 10.6, p. 96. ISSN: 1540-7993. DOI: 10.1109/MSP.2012.158. (Cit. on pp. 233, 288).

——— (May–June 2013). "Military Cybersomethings." In: *IEEE Security & Privacy* 11.3, p. 88. https://ieeexplore.ieee.org/stamp/stamp.jsp?tp=&arnumber=6521321 (cit. on p. 29).

——— (July–Aug. 2014a). "By Any Means Possible: How Intelligence Agencies Have Gotten Their Data." In: *IEEE Security & Privacy* 12.4. https://www.cs.columbia.edu/~smb/papers/possible.pdf (cit. on p. 264).

——— (Apr. 11, 2014b). "Heartbleed: Don't Panic." In: *SMBlog (blog)*. https://www.cs.columbia.edu/~smb/blog/2014-04/2014-04-11.html (cit. on pp. 182, 298).

——— (Feb. 24, 2014c). "Speculation About Goto Fail." In: *SMBlog (blog)*. https://www.cs.columbia.edu/~smb/blog/2014-02/2014-02-24.html (cit. on p. 182).

Bellovin, Steven M. and Randy Bush (Apr. 2009). "Configuration Management and Security." In: *IEEE Journal on Selected Areas in Communications* 27.3, pp. 268–274. https://www.cs.columbia.edu/~smb/papers/config-jsac.pdf (cit. on p. 274).

Bellovin, Steven M. and Russ Housley (June 2005). *Guidelines for Cryptographic Key Management*. RFC 4107. http://www.rfc-editor.org/rfc/rfc4107.txt (cit. on p. 85).

Bellovin, Steven M. and Michael Merritt (May 1992). "Encrypted Key Exchange: Password-Based Protocols Secure against Dictionary Attacks." In: *Proc. IEEE Computer Society Symposium on Research in Security and Privacy*. Oakland, CA, pp. 72–84. https://www.cs.columbia.edu/~smb/papers/neke.pdf (cit. on p. 141).

——— (Nov. 1993). "Augmented Encrypted Key Exchange." In: *Proceedings of the First ACM Conference on Computer and Communications Security*. Fairfax, VA, pp. 244–250. https://www.cs.columbia.edu/~smb/papers/aeke.pdf (cit. on p. 140).

Bellovin, Steven M. and Eric K. Rescorla (2006). "Deploying a New Hash Algorithm." In: *Proceedings of NDSS '06*. https://www.cs.columbia.edu/~smb/papers/new-hash.pdf (cit. on p. 84).

Bellovin, Steven M., Jeffrey I. Schiller, and Charlie Kaufman, eds. (Dec. 2003). *Security Mechanisms for the Internet*. RFC 3631. http://www.rfc-editor.org/rfc/rfc3631.txt (cit. on p. 101).

Bernstein, Daniel J. (2006). "Curve25519: New Diffie-Hellman Speed Records." In: *Public Key Cryptography (PKC 2006)*. Springer, pp. 207–228. http://cr.yp.to/ecdh/curve25519-20060209.pdf (cit. on p. 101).

Bernstein, Daniel J., Tung Chou, Chitchanok Chuengsatiansup, Andreas Hülsing, Tanja Lange, Ruben Niederhagen, and Christine van Vredendaal (July 22, 2014). *How to Manipulate Curve Standards: A White Paper for the Black Hat*. http://safecurves.cr.yp.to/bada55/bada55-20140722.pdf (cit. on p. 101).

Best, D.M., R.P. Hafen, B.K. Olsen, and W.A. Pike (Oct. 2011). "Atypical Behavior Identification in Large-Scale Network Traffic." In: *IEEE Symposium on Large Data Analysis and Visualization (LDAV)*, pp. 15–22. DOI: 10.1109/LDAV.2011.6092312. (Cit. on p. 52).

Best, Martin (2011). *The CIA's Airlines: Logistic Air Support of the War in Laos 1954 to 1975*. http://www.vietnam.ttu.edu/airamerica/best/ (cit. on p. 58).

Bester, Alfred (1953). *The Demolished Man*. Chicago: Shasta Publishers. (Cit. on p. 81).

Biham, Eli, Alex Biryukov, and Adi Shamir (1999). "Cryptanalysis of Skipjack Reduced to 31 Rounds Using Impossible Differentials." In: *Proceedings of the 17th International Conference on Theory and Application of Cryptographic Techniques*. EUROCRYPT'99. Prague, Czech Republic: Springer-Verlag, pp. 12–23. ISBN: 3-540-65889-0. http://dl.acm.org/citation.cfm?id=1756123.1756126 (cit. on p. 104).

Bijl, Joost (Nov. 21, 2011). "RSA-512 Certificates Abused in the Wild." In: *Fox-IT International Blog*. http://blog.fox-it.com/2011/11/21/rsa-512-certificates-abused-in-the-wild/ (cit. on pp. 82, 164).

Biryukov, Alex, Orr Dunkelman, Nathan Keller, Dmitry Khovratovich, and Adi Shamir (2010). "Key Recovery Attacks of Practical Complexity on AES-256 Variants with up to 10 Rounds." In: *Advances in Cryptology–EUROCRYPT 2010*. Springer, pp. 299–319. (Cit. on p. 103).

Biryukov, Alex, Adi Shamir, and David Wagner (2001). "Real Time Cryptanalysis of A5/1 on a PC." In: *Fast Software Encryption*. Ed. by Gerhard Goos, Juris Hartmanis, Jan van Leeuwen, and Bruce Schneier. Vol. 1978. Lecture Notes in Computer Science. 10.1007/3-540-44706-7-1. Springer Berlin / Heidelberg, pp. 37–44. ISBN: 978-3-540-41728-6. http://dx.doi.org/10.1007/3-540-44706-7_1 (cit. on p. 180).

Bishop, Matt (2007). *Overview of Red Team Reports*. For full details, see http://votingsystems. cdn.sos.ca.gov/oversight/ttbr/red-overview.pdf. http://votingsystems.cdn.sos.ca.gov/ oversight/ttbr/red-overview.pdf (cit. on p. 55).

Bittau, Andrea, Michael Hamburg, Mark Handley, David Mazières, and Dan Boneh (2010). "The Case for Ubiquitous Transport-Level Encryption." In: *Proceedings of the Usenix Security Symposium*. http://www.usenix.org/events/sec10/tech/full_papers/Bittau.pdf (cit. on p. 88).

Blaze, Matt (Nov. 1993). "A Cryptographic File System for Unix." In: *Proceedings of the First ACM Conference on Computer and Communications Security*. Fairfax, VA, pp. 9–16. http: //www.crypto.com/papers/cfs.pdf (cit. on p. 90).

———— (Mar. 24, 2010). "The Spy in the Middle." In: *Exhaustive Search (blog)*. http://www. crypto.com/blog/spycerts/ (cit. on p. 154).

Boehret, Katherine (Nov. 23, 2011). "Galaxy Nexus: An In-Your-Face Android Phone." In: *The Wall Street Journal*. http://online.wsj.com/article/SB10001424052970204531404577054233 319145676.html (cit. on p. 125).

Bogdanov, Andrey, Dmitry Khovratovich, and Christian Rechberger (2011). "Biclique Cryptanalysis of the Full AES." In: *Proceedings of ASIACRYPT*. http://www.springerlink.com/content/ j5h1350162456m29/ (cit. on p. 103).

Boneh, Dan, Amit Sahai, and Brent Waters (Nov. 2012). "Functional Encryption: A New Vision for Public-Key Cryptography." In: *Commun. ACM* 55.11, pp. 56–64. ISSN: 0001-0782. DOI: 10.1145/2366316.2366333. http://doi.acm.org/10.1145/2366316.2366333 (cit. on p. 313).

Borisov, Nikita, Ian Goldberg, and David Wagner (2001). "Intercepting Mobile Communications: The Insecurity of 802.11." In: *Proceedings of MOBICOM 2001*. http://www.cs.berkeley.edu/ ~daw/papers/wep-mob01.ps (cit. on pp. 175, 177).

Bowen, Brian M. (2011). "Design and Analysis of Decoy Systems for Computer Security." PhD thesis. Columbia University. http://academiccommons.columbia.edu/download/fedora_ content/download/ac:132237/CONTENT/Bowen_columbia_0054D_10190.pdf (cit. on p. 74).

Bowen, Brian M., Shlomo Hershkop, Angelos D. Keromytis, and Salvatore J. Stolfo (2009). "Baiting Inside Attackers Using Decoy Documents." In: *Proceedings of the 5th International ICST Conference on Security and Privacy in Communication Networks (SecureComm)*. http: //www.cs.columbia.edu/~bmbowen/papers/DecoyDocumentsCameraReadySECCOM09.pdf (cit. on p. 74).

Brainard, John G., Ari Juels, Ronald L. Rivest, Michael Szydlo, and Moti Yung (2006). "Fourth-factor Authentication: Somebody You Know." In: *ACM Conference on Computer and Communications Security*, pp. 168–178. http://www.rsasecurity.ca/rsalabs/staff/bios/ajuels/ publications/fourth-factor/ccs084-juels.pdf (cit. on p. 123).

Broad, William J., John Markoff, and David E. Sanger (Jan. 15, 2011). "Israeli Test on Worm Called Crucial in Iran Nuclear Delay." In: *The New York Times*. http://www.nytimes.com/ 2011/01/16/world/middleeast/16stuxnet.html (cit. on p. 37).

Brodkin, Jon (June 18, 2012). "Annals of Bad Luck: When Primary, Backup, and Second Backup Power Fail." In: *Ars Technica*. http://arstechnica.com/information-technology/2012/06/ annals-of-bad-luck-when-primary-backup-and-second-backup-power-fail/ (cit. on p. 192).

Brooks Jr., Frederick P. (Apr. 1987). "No Silver Bullet: Essence and Accidents of Software Engineering." In: *Computer* 20.4, pp. 10–19. ISSN: 0018-9162. DOI: 10.1109/MC.1987.1663532. (Cit. on p. 208).

Bryant, B. (Feb. 8, 1988). *Designing an Authentication System: A Dialogue in Four Scenes*. Draft. http://web.mit.edu/kerberos/dialogue.html (cit. on pp. 81, 84).

Bujold, Lois McMaster (1990). *The Vor Game*. New York: Baen. (Cit. on p. 247).

Bumiller, Elisabeth (Apr. 27, 2010). "We Have Met the Enemy and He Is PowerPoint." In: *The New York Times*. http://www.nytimes.com/2010/04/27/world/27powerpoint.html (cit. on p. 198).

Burke, Kathleen (June 10, 2015). "'Free Credit Monitoring' After Data Breaches is More Sucker than Succor." In: *MarketWatch*. http://www.marketwatch.com/story/free-credit-monitoring-after-data-breaches-is-more-sucker-than-succor-2015-06-10 (cit. on p. 222).

Burroughs, Edgar Rice (1920). *Thuvia, Maid of Mars*. Chicago: A.C. McClurg & Co. http://www.gutenberg.org/ebooks/72 (cit. on p. 36).

———— (1922). *The Chessmen of Mars*. Chicago: A.C. McClurg & Co. http://www.gutenberg.org/ebooks/1153 (cit. on p. 185).

Butler, Brandon (June 24, 2014). "A Wakeup Call for the Cloud." In: *NetworkWorld*. http://www.networkworld.com/article/2366862/iaas/a-wakeup-call-for-the-cloud.html (cit. on p. 287).

Capehart, George (May 13, 2012a). "The Wikileaks Brouhaha: Shooting the Messengers and Ignoring the Elephants, Part 1." In: *Daily Kos*. http://www.dailykos.com/story/2012/05/14/1091460/-The-WikiLeaks-Brouhaha-Shooting-the-Messengers-and-Ignoring-the-Elephants-Part-1?detail=hide (cit. on p. 73).

———— (May 15, 2012b). "The Wikileaks Brouhaha: Shooting the Messengers and Ignoring the Elephants, Part 2." In: *Daily Kos*. http://www.dailykos.com/story/2012/05/15/1091858/-The-WikiLeaks-Brouhaha-Shooting-the-Messengers-and-Ignoring-the-Elephants-Part-2?detail=hide (cit. on p. 73).

———— (May 16, 2012c). "The Wikileaks Brouhaha: Shooting the Messengers and Ignoring the Elephants, Part 3." In: *Daily Kos*. http://www.dailykos.com/story/2012/05/17/1092355/-The-Wikileaks-Brouhaha-Shooting-the-Messengers-and-Ignoring-the-Elephants-Part-3?detail=hide (cit. on p. 73).

———— (May 19, 2012d). "The Wikileaks Brouhaha: Shooting the Messengers and Ignoring the Elephants, Part 4." In: *Daily Kos*. http://www.dailykos.com/story/2012/05/19/1093112/-The-WikiLeaks-Brouhaha-Shooting-the-Messengers-and-Ignoring-the-Elephants-Part-4?detail=hide (cit. on p. 73).

———— (June 11, 2012e). "The Wikileaks Brouhaha: Shooting the Messengers and Ignoring the Elephants, Part 5." In: *Daily Kos*. http://www.dailykos.com/story/2012/06/11/1096025/-The-Wikileaks-Brouhaha-Shooting-the-Messengers-and-Ignoring-the-Elephants-Part-5 (cit. on p. 73).

Carroll, Lewis (1872). *Through the Looking-Glass, and What Alice Found There*. London: Macmillan and Co. https://www.gutenberg.org/ebooks/12 (cit. on pp. 3, 301).

Cavoukian, Ann (2009). *Privacy by Design: Take the Challenge*. Ann Cavoukian. http://www.privacybydesign.ca/content/uploads/2010/03/PrivacybyDesignBook.pdf (cit. on p. 314).

CERT (June 12, 2012). *SYSRET 64-Bit Operating System Privilege Escalation Vulnerability on Intel CPU Hardware*. Tech. rep. VU#649219. US-CERT. http://www.kb.cert.org/vuls/id/649219 (cit. on p. 187).

Chan, Casey (Oct. 21, 2011). "Anyone with a Smart Cover Can Break into Your iPad 2." In: *Gizmodo*. http://gizmodo.com/5852036/how-to-break-into-any-ipad-2-with-just-a-smart-cover (cit. on p. 7).

Checkoway, Stephen, Ruben Niederhagen, Adam Everspaugh, Matthew Green, Tanja Lange, Thomas Ristenpart, Daniel J. Bernstein, Jake Maskiewicz, Hovav Shacham, and Matthew Fredrikson (Aug. 2014). "On the Practical Exploitability of Dual EC in TLS Implementations." In: *23rd USENIX Security Symposium (USENIX Security 14)*. San Diego, CA: USENIX Association, pp. 319–335. ISBN: 978-1-931971-15-7. https://www.usenix.org/conference/usenixsecurity14/technical-sessions/presentation/checkoway (cit. on p. 100).

Chen, Shuo, John Dunagan, Chad Verbowski, and Yi-Min Wang (2005). "A Black-Box Tracing Technique to Identify Causes of Least-Privilege Incompatibilities." In: *Proceedings of NDSS 2005*. http://research.microsoft.com/en-us/um/people/jdunagan/leastprivilegetracing-ndss-2005.pdf (cit. on p. 42).

Chess, Brian and Jacob West (2007). *Secure Programming with Static Analysis*. Upper Saddle River, NJ: Addison-Wesley. (Cit. on p. 209).

Cheswick, William R. (Jan. 1992). "An Evening with Berferd, in which a Cracker is Lured, Endured, and Studied." In: *Proc. Winter USENIX Conference*. San Francisco, CA. http://www.cheswick.com/ches/papers/berferd.ps (cit. on p. 188).

——— (2010). "Back to Berferd." In: *Proceedings of the 26th Annual Computer Security Applications Conference*. ACSAC '10. Austin, Texas: ACM, pp. 281–286. ISBN: 978-1-4503-0133-6. DOI: 10.1145/1920261.1920303. http://doi.acm.org/10.1145/1920261.1920303 (cit. on pp. 70, 188).

Cheswick, William R. and Steven M. Bellovin (1994). *Firewalls and Internet Security: Repelling the Wily Hacker*. 1st ed. Reading, MA: Addison-Wesley. http://www.wilyhacker.com/1e/ (cit. on pp. 11, 22, 61, 81, 188).

Cheswick, William R., Steven M. Bellovin, and Aviel D. Rubin (2003). *Firewalls and Internet Security; Repelling the Wily Hacker*. 2nd ed. Reading, MA: Addison-Wesley. http://www.wilyhacker.com/ (cit. on pp. 61, 62, 161, 250, 289).

Clark, Sandy, Travis Goodspeed, Perry Metzger, Zachary Wasserman, Kevin Xu, and Matt Blaze (2011). "Why (Special Agent) Johnny (Still) Can't Encrypt: A Security Analysis of the APCO Project 25 Two-Way Radio System." In: *Proceedings of the Usenix Security Symposium*. http://www.usenix.org/events/sec11/tech/full_papers/Clark.pdf (cit. on p. 105).

Clarke, Arthur C. (1953). *Childhood's End*. New York: Ballantine Books. (Cit. on pp. 205, 380).

Clarke, Richard A. and Robert K. Knake (2010). *Cyber War: The Next Threat to National Security and What to Do About It*. New York: Ecco. (Cit. on pp. 17, 18, 74).

Clayton, Richard (2005). "Anonymity and Traceability in Cyberspace." Also published as technical report UCAM-CL-TR-653. PhD thesis. University of Cambridge, Darwin College. http://www.cl.cam.ac.uk/techreports/UCAM-CL-TR-653.html (cit. on p. 172).

Cohen, Fred (1986). "Computer Viruses." PhD thesis. University of Southern California. https://all.net/books/Dissertation.pdf (cit. on p. 46).

———— (1987). "Computer Viruses: Theory and Experiments." In: *Computers & Security* 6.1, pp. 22–35. (Cit. on p. 49).

Comerford, Richard (Oct. 1998). "State of the Internet: Roundtable 4.0." In: *IEEE Spectrum* 35.10, pp. 69–79. ISSN: 0018-9235. DOI: 10.1109/MSPEC.1998.722325. (Cit. on p. 5).

Comptroller General (Dec. 13, 1991). *Public Law 106-229—Electronic Signatures in Global and National Commerce Act.* http://www.gpo.gov/fdsys/pkg/PLAW-106publ229/content-detail.html (cit. on p. 165).

Computer Science and Telecommunications Board (1997). *ADA and Beyond: Software Policies for the Department of Defense.* Washington, DC: National Academy Press. http://www.nap.edu/catalog.php?record_id=5463 (cit. on p. 208).

Conti, Gregory and James Caroland (July–Aug. 2011). "Embracing the Kobayashi Maru: Why You Should Teach Your Students to Cheat." In: *IEEE Security & Privacy* 9.4, pp. 48–51. http://ieeexplore.ieee.org/xpl/articleDetails.jsp?arnumber=5968086 (cit. on p. 26).

Cooper, D., S. Santesson, S. Farrell, S. Boeyen, Russ Housley, and William Polk (May 2008). *Internet X.509 Public Key Infrastructure Certificate and Certificate Revocation List (CRL) Profile.* RFC 5280. http://www.rfc-editor.org/rfc/rfc5280.txt (cit. on pp. 150, 161).

Cowan, Crispin, Steve Beattie, John Johansen, and Perry Wagle (2003). "Pointguard: Protecting Pointers from Buffer Overflow Vulnerabilities." In: *Proceedings of the 12th Conference on USENIX Security Symposium - Volume 12.* SSYM'03. Washington, DC: USENIX Association, pp. 7–7. http://dl.acm.org/citation.cfm?id=1251353.1251360 (cit. on pp. 206, 313).

Crossman, Penny (June 10, 2013). "New Breed of Banking Malware Hijacks Text Messages." In: *American Banker.* http://www.americanbanker.com/issues/178_111/new-breed-of-banking-malware-hijacks-text-messages-1059745-1.html (cit. on p. 123).

Cui, Ang and Salvatore J. Stolfo (2010). "A Quantitative Analysis of the Insecurity of Embedded Network Devices: Results of a Wide-Area Scan." In: *Proceedings of Annual Computer Security Applications Conference (ACSAC).* http://www.hacktory.cs.columbia.edu/sites/default/files/paper-acsac.pdf (cit. on p. 54).

———— (Dec. 27, 2011). "Print Me If You Dare: Firmware Modification Attacks and the Rise of Printer Malware." In: *The 28th Chaos Communication Congress.* http://ids.cs.columbia.edu/sites/default/files/CuiPrintMeIfYouDare.pdf (cit. on p. 64).

Darlin, Damon (Sept. 7, 2008). "Hewlett-Packard Spied on Writers in Leaks." In: *The New York Times.* http://www.nytimes.com/2006/09/08/technology/08hp.html (cit. on p. 254).

Daugman, John (2006). "Probing the Uniqueness and Randomness of IrisCodes: Results from 200 Billion Iris Pair Comparisons." In: *Proceedings of the IEEE* 94.11, pp. 1927–1935. http://www.cl.cam.ac.uk/users/jgd1000/ProcIEEEnov2006Daugman.pdf (cit. on p. 124).

Debar, Hervé and Andreas Wespi (2001). "Aggregation and Correlation of Intrusion-Detection Alerts." In: *Recent Advances in Intrusion Detection.* Ed. by Wenke Lee, Ludovic Mé, and Andreas Wespi. Vol. 2212. Lecture Notes in Computer Science. 10.1007/3-540-45474-8_6. Springer Berlin / Heidelberg, pp. 85–103. ISBN: 978-3-540-42702-5. http://dx.doi.org/10.1007/3-540-45474-8_6 (cit. on p. 50).

DeBuvitz, William (Jan. 1989). "New Chemical Element Discovered." In: *The Physics Teacher.* http://www.lhup.edu/~DSIMANEK/administ.htm (cit. on p. 194).

Denning, Dorothy E. and Giovanni M. Sacco (Aug. 1981). "Timestamps in Key Distribution Protocols." In: *Communications of the ACM* 24.8, pp. 533–536. (Cit. on p. 86).

Department of Justice (June 2005). *Electronic Surveillance Manual*. Original from http://www.justice.gov/criminal/foia/docs/elec-sur-manual.pdf. https://www.cs.columbia.edu/~smb/Thinking_Security/docs/elec-sur-manual.pdf (cit. on p. 180).

Dierks, T. and Eric K. Rescorla (Aug. 2008). *The Transport Layer Security (TLS) Protocol Version 1.2*. RFC 5246. http://www.rfc-editor.org/rfc/rfc5246.txt (cit. on pp. 82, 104).

Diffie, Whitfield and Martin E. Hellman (Nov. 1976). "New Directions in Cryptography." In: *IEEE Transactions on Information Theory* IT-22.6, pp. 644–654. (Cit. on pp. 104, 149, 163).

Dijkstra, E. W. (Apr. 1970). "Structured Programming." In: *Software Engineering Techniques*. Ed. by J. N. Buxton and B. Randell. http://homepages.cs.ncl.ac.uk/brian.randell/NATO/nato1969.PDF (cit. on p. 243).

Dobbertin, Hans (Summer 1996). "The Status of MD5 After a Recent Attack." In: *CryptoBytes* 2.2. (Cit. on p. 161).

DoD (1985a). *DoD Trusted Computer System Evaluation Criteria*. Tech. rep. 5200.28-STD. DoD Computer Security Center. http://csrc.nist.gov/publications/secpubs/rainbow/std001.txt (cit. on pp. 49, 236).

——— (1985b). *DoD Password Management Guideline*. Tech. rep. CSC-STD-002-85. DoD Computer Security Center. http://csrc.nist.gov/publications/secpubs//rainbow/std002.txt (cit. on p. 114).

Dodis, Yevgeniy, Leonid Reyzin, and Adam Smith (2007). "Fuzzy Extractors: A Brief Survey of Results from 2004 to 2006." In: *Security with Noisy Data*. Ed. by Pim Tuyls, Boris Skoric, and Tom Kevenaar. Berlin: Springer. http://www.cs.bu.edu/~reyzin/fuzzysurvey.html (cit. on p. 127).

Domin, Rusty (May 23, 2007). "2 Sentenced in Coke Trade Secret Case." In: *CNN Money*. http://money.cnn.com/2007/05/23/news/newsmakers/coke/ (cit. on p. 20).

Drew, Christopher (June 4, 2011). "Stolen Data Is Tracked to Hacking at Lockheed." In: *The New York Times*. http://www.nytimes.com/2011/06/04/technology/04security.html (cit. on pp. 132, 251).

Drew, Christopher and Somini Sengupta (June 23, 2013). "N.S.A. Leak Puts Focus on System Administrators." In: *The New York Times*. https://www.nytimes.com/2013/06/24/technology/nsa-leak-puts-focus-on-system-administrators.html (cit. on p. 278).

Ducklin, Paul (Feb. 24, 2014). "Anatomy of a 'goto fail'—Apple's SSL Bug Explained, Plus an Unofficial Patch for OS X!" In: *Naked Security*. http://nakedsecurity.sophos.com/2014/02/24/anatomy-of-a-goto-fail-apples-ssl-bug-explained-plus-an-unofficial-patch/ (cit. on p. 182).

——— (Sept. 28, 2015). "Why Word Malware is BASIC: SophosLabs Takes Apart a Booby-Trapped Document." In: *Sophos Blog*. https://blogs.sophos.com/2015/09/28/why-word-malware-is-basic/ (cit. on p. 56).

Duff, Tom (Spring 1989a). "Experiences with Viruses on UNIX Systems." In: *Computer Systems* 2.2, pp. 155–171. http://www.usenix.org/publications/compsystems/1989/spr_duff.pdf (cit. on p. 46).

——— (Winter 1989b). "Viral Attacks on UNIX System Security." In: *Proceedings of the Usenix Conference*. (Cit. on p. 46).

Eastlake 3rd, D. (Mar. 1999). *Domain Name System Security Extensions*. RFC 2535. http://www.rfc-editor.org/rfc/rfc2535.txt (cit. on p. 91).

Eastlake 3rd, D. and T. Hansen (May 2011). *US Secure Hash Algorithms (SHA and SHA-based HMAC and HKDF)*. RFC 6234. http://www.rfc-editor.org/rfc/rfc6234.txt (cit. on p. 101).

Eastlake 3rd, D., J. Reagle, and D. Solo (Mar. 2002). *(Extensible Markup Language) XML-Signature Syntax and Processing*. RFC 3275. http://www.rfc-editor.org/rfc/rfc3275.txt (cit. on p. 104).

Eastlake 3rd, D., Jeffrey I. Schiller, and S. Crocker (June 2005). *Randomness Requirements for Security*. RFC 4086. http://www.rfc-editor.org/rfc/rfc4086.txt (cit. on p. 122).

Editorial Board, New York Times (July 19, 2015). "Defining 'Employee' in the Gig Economy." In: *The New York Times*. http://www.nytimes.com/2015/07/19/opinion/sunday/defining-employee-in-the-gig-economy.html (cit. on p. 77).

Edwards, M. (Feb. 15, 2000). "Something Old, Something New: DNS Hijacking." In: *Windows IT Pro*. http://windowsitpro.com/networking/something-old-something-new-dns-hijacking (cit. on pp. 160, 215).

Egelman, Serge, Lorrie Faith Cranor, and Jason Hong (2008). "You've Been Warned: An Empirical Study of the Effectiveness of Web Browser Phishing Warnings." In: *Proceedings of the Twenty-Sixth Annual SIGCHI Conference on Human Factors in Computing Systems*. CHI '08. Florence, Italy: ACM, pp. 1065–1074. ISBN: 978-1-60558-011-1. DOI: 10.1145/1357054.1357219. http://doi.acm.org/10.1145/1357054.1357219 (cit. on p. 191).

Eichin, M. W. and J. A. Rochlis (May 1989). "With Microscope and Tweezers: An Analysis of the Internet Virus of November 1988." In: *Proc. IEEE Symposium on Research in Security and Privacy*. Oakland, CA, pp. 326–345. http://dl.acm.org/citation.cfm?id=63528 (cit. on pp. 46, 288).

Electronic Frontier Foundation (July 1998). *Cracking DES: Secrets of Encryption Research, Wiretap Politics & Chip Design*. O'Reilly & Associates. ISBN: 1-565-92520-3. (Cit. on p. 102).

Ellement, John (Apr. 1, 2004). "Bail Set a [*sic*] $600,000 for Former Researcher." In: *The Boston Globe*. http://www.boston.com/news/education/higher/articles/2004/04/01/bail_set_a_600000_for_former_researcher/ (cit. on p. 254).

Ellison, Carl (Sept. 1999). *SPKI Requirements*. RFC 2692. http://www.rfc-editor.org/rfc/rfc2692.txt (cit. on p. 168).

——— (2007). *Ceremony Design and Analysis*. IACR eprint archive 2007/399. http://eprint.iacr.org/2007/399.pdf (cit. on p. 156).

Ellison, Carl, B. Frantz, B. Lampson, Ronald L. Rivest, B. Thomas, and Tatu Ylönen (Sept. 1999). *SPKI Certificate Theory*. RFC 2693. http://www.rfc-editor.org/rfc/rfc2693.txt (cit. on p. 168).

Esposito, Richard, Matthew Cole, and Robert Windrem (Aug. 29, 2013). "Snowden Impersonated NSA Officials, Sources Say." In: *NBC News*. http://investigations.nbcnews.com/_news/2013/08/29/20234171-snowden-impersonated-nsa-officials-sources-say (cit. on p. 278).

Evans, C. (June 14, 2011). "New Chromium Security Features, June 2011." In: *The Chromium Blog*. http://blog.chromium.org/2011/06/new-chromium-security-features-june.html (cit. on p. 167).

Evans, C., C. Palmer, and R. Sleevi (Apr. 2015). *Public Key Pinning Extension for HTTP*. RFC 7469. http://www.rfc-editor.org/rfc/rfc7469.txt (cit. on p. 159).

Fahl, Sascha, Marian Harbach, Thomas Muders, Lars Baumgärtner, Bernd Freisleben, and Matthew Smith (2012). "Why Eve and Mallory Love Android: An Analysis of Android SSL (In)Security." In: *Proceedings of the 2012 ACM Conference on Computer and Communications Security*. ACM, pp. 50–61. (Cit. on p. 197).

Falliere, Nicolas, Liam O Murchu, and Eric Chien (Feb. 2011). *W32.Stuxnet Dossier*. Symantec Security Response. Version 1.4. http://www.symantec.com/content/en/us/enterprise/media/ security_response/whitepapers/w32_stuxnet_dossier.pdf (cit. on pp. 37, 50, 55, 164, 194, 269).

Farley, R.D. and H.F. Schorreck (Aug. 1982). *Oral History Interview with Dr. Solomon Kullback*. http://www.nsa.gov/public_info/_files/oral_history_interviews/nsa_oh_17_82_kullback.pdf (cit. on p. 87).

Federal Trade Commission (June 24, 2010). *Twitter Settles Charges that it Failed to Protect Consumers' Personal Information; Company Will Establish Independently Audited Information Security Program*. http://www.ftc.gov/opa/2010/06/twitter.shtm (cit. on p. 194).

——— (May 2014). *Data Brokers: A Call for Transparency and Accountability*. http://www.ftc. gov/system/files/documents/reports/data-brokers-call-transparency-accountability-report-federal-trade-commission-may-2014/140527databrokerreport.pdf (cit. on p. 224).

Feilner, Markus (2006). *OpenVPN: Building and Integrating Virtual Private Networks*. Birmingham, UK: Packt Publishing. http://www.openvpn.net (cit. on p. 95).

Felten, Edward W. (Nov. 3, 2009). "Election Day; More Unguarded Voting Machines." In: *Freedom to Tinker (blog)*. https://freedom-to-tinker.com/blog/felten/election-day-more-unguarded-voting-machines/ (cit. on p. 55).

Fenker, S.P. and K.W. Bowyer (Jan. 2011). "Experimental Evidence of a Template Aging Effect in Iris Biometrics." In: *2011 IEEE Workshop on Applications of Computer Vision (WACV)*, pp. 232–239. DOI: 10.1109/WACV.2011.5711508. (Cit. on p. 128).

Ferguson, N., J. Kelsey, S. Lucks, Bruce Schneier, M. Stay, David Wagner, and D. Whiting (2000). "Improved Cryptanalysis of Rijndael." In: *Seventh Fast Software Encryption Workshop*. http://www.schneier.com/paper-rijndael.pdf (cit. on p. 103).

Field, Tom (Dec. 24, 2010). "Marcus Ranum on 2011 Security Outlook." In: *Bank Info Security*. http://www.bankinfosecurity.com/marcus-ranum-on-2011-security-outlook-a-3205/op-1 (cit. on p. 73).

Fillinger, Maximilian Johannes (2013). "Reconstructing the Cryptanalytic Attack behind the Flame Malware." MA thesis. Universiteit van Amsterdam. http://www.illc.uva.nl/Research/ Reports/MoL-2013-23.text.pdf (cit. on pp. 28, 83).

Fine, Glenn A. (Aug. 2003). *A Review of the FBI's Performance in Deterring, Detecting, and Investigating the Espionage Activities of Robert Philip Hanssen*. Unclassified executive summary. http://www.usdoj.gov/oig/special/0308/index.htm (cit. on p. 35).

Finke, Jon (Sept. 1994). "Monitoring Usage of Workstations with a Relational Database." In: *8th System Administration Conference (LISA)*. Usenix. San Diego. http://static.usenix.org/ publications/library/proceedings/lisa94/finke.html (cit. on p. 286).

——— (Oct. 1997a). "Automation of Site Configuration Management." In: *The 11th Systems Administration Conference (LISA)*. Usenix. http://static.usenix.org/publications/library/ proceedings/lisa97/full_papers/18.finke/18.pdf (cit. on p. 274).

————— (Oct. 1997b). "Monitoring Application Use with License Server Logs." In: *The 11th Systems Administration Conference (LISA)*. Usenix. http://static.usenix.org/publications/library/proceedings/lisa97/full_papers/03.finke/03.pdf (cit. on p. 286).

————— (Dec. 2000). "An Improved Approach to Generating Configuration Files from a Database." In: *The 14th Systems Administration Conference (LISA)*. Usenix. New Orleans, pp. 23–38. http://www.rpi.edu/~finkej/Papers/LISA2000-FileGen.pdf (cit. on p. 274).

————— (2003). "Generating Configuration Files: The Directors Cut." In: *The 17th Systems Administration Conference*. Usenix, pp. 105–204. http://static.usenix.org/events/lisa03/tech/finke.html (cit. on p. 274).

FINRA (Jan. 2010). *Guidance on Blogs and Social Networking Web Sites*. Tech. rep. 10-06. Financial Industry Regulatory Authority. http://www.finra.org/Industry/Regulation/Notices/2010/P120779 (cit. on p. 76).

————— (Sept. 2011). *Guide to the Web for Registered Representatives*. Web page. http://www.finra.org/industry/issues/advertising/p006118 (cit. on p. 76).

Flaherty, Mary Pat (Aug. 21, 2008). "Ohio Voting Machines Contained Programming Error That Dropped Votes." In: *The Washington Post*. http://www.freerepublic.com/focus/f-news/2065845/posts (cit. on p. 55).

Florêncio, Dinei and Cormac Herley (2010). "Where Do Security Policies Come From?" In: *Proceedings of the Sixth Symposium on Usable Privacy and Security*, p. 10. http://dl.acm.org/citation.cfm?id=1837124 (cit. on p. 112).

Florêncio, Dinei, Cormac Herley, and Baris Coskun (2007). "Do Strong Web Passwords Accomplish Anything?" In: *Proceedings of HOTSEC '07*. http://www.usenix.org/events/hotsec07/tech/full_papers/florencio/florencio.pdf (cit. on pp. xii, 109).

Ford-Hutchinson, P. (Oct. 2005). *Securing FTP with TLS*. RFC 4217. http://www.rfc-editor.org/rfc/rfc4217.txt (cit. on p. 24).

Forrest, Stephanie and Anil Somayaji (Aug. 2000). "Automated Response Using System-Call Delays." In: *Proceedings of the 9th Usenix Security Symposium*. (Cit. on p. 72).

Frankel, Sheila, P. Hoffman, Angela Orebaugh, and Richard Park (July 2008). *Guide to SSL VPNs*. NIST Special Publication 800-113. http://csrc.nist.gov/publications/nistpubs/800-113/SP800-113.pdf (cit. on p. 95).

Fuller, V. and T. Li (Aug. 2006). *Classless Inter-domain Routing (CIDR): The Internet Address Assignment and Aggregation Plan*. RFC 4632. http://www.rfc-editor.org/rfc/rfc4632.txt (cit. on p. 93).

Gage, Deborah (Feb. 15, 2008). "Virus from China the Gift that Keeps on Giving." In: *SFGate*. http://www.sfgate.com/cgi-bin/article.cgi?f=/c/a/2008/02/14/BU47V0VOII.DTL (cit. on p. 53).

Galbally, Javier, Arun Ross, Marta Gomez-Barrero, Julian Fierrez, and Javier Ortega-Garcia (2013). "Iris Image Reconstruction from Binary Templates: An Efficient Probabilistic Approach Based on Genetic Algorithms." In: *Computer Vision and Image Understanding* 117.10, pp. 1512–1525. http://www.sciencedirect.com/science/article/pii/S1077314213001070 (cit. on p. 126).

Gallagher, Sean (Nov. 21, 2012). "French Fried: US Allegedly Hacked Sarkozy's Office with Flame." In: *Ars Technica*. http://arstechnica.com/security/2012/11/french-fried-us-allegedly-hacked-sarkozys-office-with-flame/ (cit. on p. 18).

Galperin, Eva, Seth Schoen, and Peter Eckersley (Sept. 13, 2011). "A Post Mortem on the Iranian DigiNotar Attack." In: *Deep Links (blog)*. https://www.eff.org/deeplinks/2011/09/post-mortem-iranian-diginotar-attack (cit. on pp. 153, 262).

Ganesan, R. and C. Davies (1994). "A New Attack on Random Pronounceable Password Generators." In: *Proceedings of the 17th NIST-NCSC National Computer Security Conference*. http://fortdodgewebsites.com/docs/ANewAttackonRandomPronounceablePassw.pdf (cit. on p. 122).

Garfinkel, Simson L. (1995). *PGP: Pretty Good Privacy*. Sebastopol, CA: O'Reilly & Associates. (Cit. on p. 167).

Garfinkel, Simson L. and Robert C. Miller (2005). "Johnny 2: A User Test of Key Continuity Management with S/MIME and Outlook Express." In: *SOUPS '05: Proceedings of the 2005 Symposium on Usable Privacy and Security*. Pittsburgh, PA: ACM, pp. 13–24. ISBN: 1-59593-178-3. DOI: http://doi.acm.org/10.1145/1073001.1073003. (Cit. on p. 105).

Garfinkel, Simson L. and A. Shelat (Jan.–Feb. 2003). "Remembrance of Data Passed: A Study of Disk Sanitization Practices." In: *IEEE Security & Privacy* 1.1, pp. 17–27. ISSN: 1540-7993. DOI: 10.1109/MSECP.2003.1176992. (Cit. on p. 92).

Garfinkel, Tal and Mendel Rosenblum (2003). "Virtual Machine Introspection Based Architecture for Intrusion Detection." In: *Proceedings of NDSS '03*. http://www.isoc.org/isoc/conferences/ndss/03/proceedings/papers/13.pdf (cit. on p. 188).

Gentry, Craig (Mar. 2010). "Computing Arbitrary Functions of Encrypted Data." In: *Communications of the ACM* 53.3, pp. 97–105. http://crypto.stanford.edu/craig/easy-fhe.pdf (cit. on p. 313).

Georgiev, Martin, Subodh Iyengar, Suman Jana, Rishita Anubhai, Dan Boneh, and Vitaly Shmatikov (2012). "The Most Dangerous Code in the World: Validating SSL Certificates in Non-browser Software." In: *Proceedings of the 2012 ACM Conference on Computer and Communications Security*. ACM, pp. 38–49. (Cit. on p. 197).

Gerrold, David (1972). *When Harlie Was One*. New York: Ballantine Books. (Cit. on pp. 45, 311).

Gilbert, W. S. and Arthur Sullivan (1875). *Trial by Jury*. London: Chappell & Co. (Cit. on p. 225).

——— (1885). *The Mikado*. New York: W. A. Pond. (Cit. on p. 239).

Goldman, William (1987). *The Princess Bride*. Movie. (Cit. on pp. 12, 379).

Goldstein, Matthew (July 22, 2015). "4 Arrested in Schemes Said to Be Tied to JPMorgan Chase Breach." In: *The New York Times*. http://www.nytimes.com/2015/07/22/business/dealbook/4-arrested-in-schemes-said-to-be-tied-to-jpmorgan-chase-breach.html (cit. on pp. 40, 224).

Golić, Jovan (1997). "Linear Statistical Weakness of Alleged RC4 Keystream Generator." In: *Advances in Cryptology—EUROCRYPT '97*. Ed. by Walter Fumy. Vol. 1233. Lecture Notes in Computer Science. 10.1007/3-540-69053-0_16. Springer Berlin / Heidelberg, pp. 226–238. ISBN: 978-3-540-62975-7. http://dx.doi.org/10.1007/3-540-69053-0_16 (cit. on p. 100).

Goodin, Dan (Sept. 23, 2009). "Texas Instruments Aims Lawyers at Calculator Hackers." In: *The Register*. http://www.theregister.co.uk/2009/09/23/texas_instruments_calculator_hacking/ (cit. on p. 82).

—— (June 13, 2012a). "Attention All Windows Users: Patch Your Systems Now: A Critical IE Vulnerability Microsoft Patched Tuesday Is Under Active Exploit." In: *Ars Technica*. http://arstechnica.com/security/2012/06/windows-users-patch-now/ (cit. on pp. 179, 244).

—— (June 7, 2012b). "Crypto Breakthrough Shows Flame Was Designed by World-Class Scientists." In: *Ars Technica*. http://arstechnica.com/security/2012/06/flame-crypto-breakthrough/ (cit. on pp. 28, 83, 84, 164).

—— (Aug. 16, 2012c). "Mystery Malware Wreaks Havoc on Energy Sector Computers." In: *Ars Technica*. http://arstechnica.com/security/2012/08/shamoon-malware-attack (cit. on p. 310).

—— (Apr. 12, 2013). "Microsoft Tells Windows 7 Users to Uninstall Faulty Security Update." In: *Ars Technica*. http://arstechnica.com/security/2013/04/microsoft-tells-windows-7-users-to-uninstall-faulty-security-update/ (cit. on p. 243).

—— (July 12, 2015a). "Hacking Team Orchestrated Brazen BGP Hack to Hijack IPs it Didn't Own." In: *Ars Technica*. http://arstechnica.com/security/2015/07/hacking-team-orchestrated-brazen-bgp-hack-to-hijack-ips-it-didnt-own/ (cit. on p. 300).

—— (Sept. 9, 2015b). "How Highly Advanced Hackers (Ab)used Satellites to Stay Under the Radar." In: *Ars Technica*. http://arstechnica.com/security/2015/09/how-highly-advanced-hackers-abused-satellites-to-stay-under-the-radar/ (cit. on p. 87).

—— (Sept. 18, 2015c). "In Blunder Threatening Windows Users, D-Link Publishes Code-Signing Key." In: *Ars Technica*. http://arstechnica.com/security/2015/09/in-blunder-threatening-windows-users-d-link-publishes-code-signing-key/ (cit. on p. 165).

—— (Sept. 21, 2015d). "Symantec Employees Fired for Issuing Rogue HTTPS Certificate for Google." In: *Ars Technica*. http://arstechnica.com/security/2015/09/symantec-employees-fired-for-issuing-rogue-https-certificate-for-google/ (cit. on p. 160).

Grampp, Fred T. and Robert H. Morris (Oct. 1984). "Unix Operating System Security." In: *AT&T Bell Laboratories Technical Journal* 63.8, Part 2, pp. 1649–1672. (Cit. on pp. 54, 113, 114, 264).

Green, Matthew (Sept. 18, 2013). "The Many Flaws of Dual_EC_DRBG." In: *A Few Thoughts on Cryptographic Engineering (blog)*. http://blog.cryptographyengineering.com/2013/09/the-many-flaws-of-dualecdrbg.html (cit. on p. 101).

Greenberg, Andy (Aug. 31, 2012). "Oracle's Java Security Woes Mount as Researchers Spot a Bug in Its Critical Bug Fix." In: *Forbes*. http://www.forbes.com/sites/andygreenberg/2012/08/31/oracles-java-security-woes-mount-as-researchers-spot-a-bug-in-its-critical-bug-fix/ (cit. on pp. 240, 243).

—— (Aug. 7, 2014). "Hacker Redirects Traffic from 19 Internet Providers to Steal Bitcoins." In: *Wired: Threat Level*. http://www.wired.com/2014/08/isp-bitcoin-theft/ (cit. on pp. 215, 310).

—— (2015a). "Hackers Can Disable a Sniper Rifle—Or Change Its Target." In: *Wired*. http://www.wired.com/2015/07/hackers-can-disable-sniper-rifleor-change-target/ (cit. on p. 302).

—— (July 21, 2015b). "Hackers Remotely Kill a Jeep on the Highway—With Me in It." In: *Wired*. http://www.wired.com/2015/07/hackers-remotely-kill-jeep-highway/ (cit. on p. 302).

Griffith, Virgil and Markus Jakobsson (2005). "Messin' with Texas: Deriving Mother's Maiden Names Using Public Records." In: *Applied Cryptography and Network Security*. Ed. by John

Ioannidis, Angelos D. Keromytis, and Moti Yung. Vol. 3531. Lecture Notes in Computer Science. Springer Berlin / Heidelberg, pp. 91–103. ISBN: 978-3-540-26223-7. DOI: http://dx.doi.org/10.1007/11496137_7. http://citeseerx.ist.psu.edu/viewdoc/download?doi=10.1.1.147.2471&rep=rep1&type=pdf (cit. on p. 122).

Gueury, Marc and Daniel Veditz (Apr. 27, 2009). "Crash in nsTextFrame::ClearTextRun()." In: *Mozilla Foundation Security Advisory 2009-23*. https://www.mozilla.org/security/announce/2009/mfsa2009-23.html (cit. on p. 241).

Haber, S. and W. S. Stornetta (1991a). "How to Time-Stamp a Digital Document." In: *Advances in Cryptology: Proceedings of CRYPTO '90*. Springer-Verlag, pp. 437–455. (Cit. on p. 162).

——— (1991b). "How to Time-Stamp a Digital Document." In: *Journal of Cryptology* 3.2, pp. 99–112. (Cit. on p. 162).

Hagino, Jun-ichiro "itojun" (Oct. 2003). *IAB Concerns against Permanent Deployment of Edge-Based Port Filtering*. Internet Architecture Board statement. https://www.iab.org/documents/correspondence-reports-documents/docs2003/2003-10-18-edge-filters/ (cit. on p. 253).

Halderman, J. Alex, Brent Waters, and Edward W. Felten (May 2005). "A Convenient Method for Securely Managing Passwords." In: *Proc. 14th Intl. World Wide Web Conference*. http://userweb.cs.utexas.edu/~bwaters/publications/papers/www2005.pdf (cit. on p. 119).

Haller, N. (Feb. 1995). *The S/KEY One-Time Password System*. RFC 1760. http://www.rfc-editor.org/rfc/rfc1760.txt (cit. on p. 129).

Halzack, Sarah (Mar. 11, 2015). "Privacy Advocates Try to Keep 'Creepy,' 'Eavesdropping' Hello Barbie from Hitting Shelves." In: *The Washington Post*. https://www.washingtonpost.com/blogs/the-switch/wp/2015/03/11/privacy-advocates-try-to-keep-creepy-eavesdropping-hello-barbie-from-hitting-shelves/ (cit. on p. 302).

Hamzeh, K., G. Pall, W. Verthein, J. Taarud, W. Little, and G. Zorn (July 1999). *Point-to-Point Tunneling Protocol (PPTP)*. RFC 2637. http://www.rfc-editor.org/rfc/rfc2637.txt (cit. on p. 95).

Handley, Mark, Christian Kreibich, and Vern Paxson (2001). "Network Intrusion Detection: Evasion, Traffic Normalization, and End-to-End Protocol Semantics." In: *Proceedings of the USENIX Security Symposium*, pp. 115–131. http://static.usenix.org/events/sec01/handley.html (cit. on pp. 66, 70).

Hanks, S., T. Li, D. Farinacci, and P. Traina (Oct. 1994). *Generic Routing Encapsulation (GRE)*. RFC 1701. http://www.rfc-editor.org/rfc/rfc1701.txt (cit. on p. 95).

Hansen, Stephen E. and E. Todd Atkins (Sept. 1992). "Centralized System Monitoring with Swatch." In: *Unix Security III Symposium*. Baltimore, MD: USENIX, pp. 105–117. http://static.usenix.org/publications/library/proceedings/sec92/full_papers/hansen.pdf (cit. on p. 287).

——— (Nov. 1993). "Automated System Monitoring and Notification with Swatch." In: *7th System Administration Conference (LISA)*. Usenix. Monterey. http://static.usenix.org/publications/library/proceedings/lisa93/hansen.html (cit. on p. 287).

Hardt, D., ed. (Oct. 2012). *The OAuth 2.0 Authorization Framework*. RFC 6749. http://www.rfc-editor.org/rfc/rfc6749.txt (cit. on p. 138).

Harper, Tom (June 22, 2013). "The Other Hacking Scandal: Suppressed Report Reveals that Law Firms, Telecoms Giants and Insurance Companies Routinely Hire Criminals to Steal Rivals'

Information." In: *The Independent*. http://www.independent.co.uk/news/uk/crime/the-other-hacking-scandal-suppressed-report-reveals-that-law-firms-telecoms-giants-and-insurance-companies-routinely-hire-criminals-to-steal-rivals-information-8669148.html (cit. on pp. 18, 41).

Heath, Brad (Aug. 24, 2015). "Police Secretly Track Cellphones to Solve Routine Crimes." In: *USA Today*. http://www.usatoday.com/story/news/2015/08/23/baltimore-police-stingray-cell-surveillance/31994181/ (cit. on p. 180).

Heath, Laura J. (2005). "An Analysis of the Systemic Security Weaknesses of the U.S. Navy Fleet Broadcasting System, 1967–1974, as Exploited by CWO John Walker." MAS. US Army Command and General Staff College. http://www.fas.org/irp/eprint/heath.pdf (cit. on p. 278).

Heinlein, Robert A. (1966). *The Moon Is a Harsh Mistress*. Putnam. (Cit. on p. 311).

Hoare, C.A.R. (Feb. 1981). "The Emperor's Old Clothes." In: *Communications of the ACM* 24.2, pp. 75–83. http://dl.acm.org/citation.cfm?id=358549.358561 (cit. on p. 208).

Hobbs, Alfred Charles (1857). *Rudimentary Treatise on the Construction of Door Locks*. Ed. by Charles Tomlinson. London: J. Weale. (Cit. on p. 249).

Hoffman, P. and J. Schlyter (Aug. 2012). *The DNS-Based Authentication of Named Entities (DANE) Transport Layer Security (TLS) Protocol: TLSA*. RFC 6698. http://www.rfc-editor.org/rfc/rfc6698.txt (cit. on p. 159).

Hofmeyr, S. A., Anil Somayaji, and Stephanie Forrest (1998). "Intrusion Detection Using Sequences of System Calls." In: *Journal of Computer Security* 6. (Cit. on p. 49).

Hollis, Duncan B (Summer 2011). "An e-SOS for Cyberspace." In: *Harvard International Law Journal* 52.2. http://ssrn.com/abstract=1670330 (cit. on p. 17).

Housley, Russ (Sept. 2004). *A 224-bit One-way Hash Function: SHA-224*. RFC 3874. http://www.rfc-editor.org/rfc/rfc3874.txt (cit. on p. 105).

——— (Sept. 2009). *Cryptographic Message Syntax (CMS)*. RFC 5652. http://www.rfc-editor.org/rfc/rfc5652.txt (cit. on p. 104).

Housley, Russ and Tim Polk (2001). *Planning for PKI: Best Practices Guide for Deploying Public Key Infrastructure*. New York: Wiley. (Cit. on p. 150).

Howard, Michael, Jon Pincus, and Jeannette M. Wing (2005). "Measuring Relative Attack Surfaces." In: *Computer Security in the 21st Century*. Ed. by D.T. Lee, S.P. Shieh, and J.D. Tygar. Springer US, pp. 109–137. ISBN: 978-0-387-24005-3. DOI: 10.1007/0-387-24006-3_8. http://dx.doi.org/10.1007/0-387-24006-3_8 (cit. on p. 228).

Hypponen, Mikko (Nov. 14, 2011). "Malware Signed with a Governmental Signing Key." In: *F-Secure News from the Lab (blog)*. http://www.f-secure.com/weblog/archives/00002269.html (cit. on p. 164).

Intel (1983). *iAPX 286 Programmer's Reference Manual*. Santa Clara, CA: Intel Corporation. http://bitsavers.trailing-edge.com/pdf/intel/80286/210498-001_1983_iAPX_286_Programmers_Reference_1983.pdf (cit. on p. 47).

Internet Initiative Japan, Inc. (Feb. 2012). "Targeted Attacks and Their Handling." In: *Internet Infrastructure Review: Infrastructure Security*. http://www.iij.ad.jp/en/company/development/iir/pdf/iir_vol14_infra_EN.pdf (cit. on p. 164).

Ioannidis, Sotiris and Steven M. Bellovin (June 2001). "Building a Secure Web Browser." In: *Usenix Conference*. https://www.cs.columbia.edu/~smb/papers/sub-browser.pdf (cit. on pp. 59, 201).

Ioannidis, Sotiris, Steven M. Bellovin, and Jonathan Smith (Sept. 2002). "Sub-Operating Systems: A New Approach to Application Security." In: *SIGOPS European Workshop*. https://www.cs. columbia.edu/~smb/papers/subos.pdf (cit. on p. 59).

Israel, Jerome W. (June 2012). "Why the FBI Can't Build a Case Management System." In: *IEEE Computer*. http://www.computer.org/csdl/mags/co/2012/06/mco2012060073.html (cit. on p. 315).

ITU-T (2012). *ITU-T Recommendation X.509—ISO/IEC 9594–8:2005, Information Technology— Open Systems Interconnection—The Directory: Public-Key and Attribute Certificate Frameworks*. http://www.itu.int/itu-t/recommendations/rec.aspx?rec=X.509 (cit. on p. 150).

Jacobs, Andrew and Miguel Helft (Jan. 12, 2010). "Google, Citing Attack, Threatens to Exit China." In: *The New York Times*. http://www.nytimes.com/2010/01/13/world/asia/13beijing. html (cit. on p. 38).

Johnson, Maritza, Steven M. Bellovin, Robert W. Reeder, and Stuart Schechter (Sept. 2009). "Laissez-Faire File Sharing: Access Control Designed for Individuals at the Endpoints." In: *New Security Paradigms Workshop*. https://www.cs.columbia.edu/~smb/papers/nspw-use.pdf (cit. on p. 198).

Johnson, S. C. (1978). *Lint, a C Program Checker*. Tech. rep. 65. Bell Labs. http://citeseerx.ist. psu.edu/viewdoc/summary?doi=10.1.1.56.1841 (cit. on pp. 53, 209).

Jolly, David (Nov. 10, 2011). "Hacker, Cyclist, Executive, Spy." In: *The New York Times (Green blog)*. http://green.blogs.nytimes.com/2011/11/10/hacker-cyclist-executive-spy/ (cit. on p. 41).

Joncheray, Laurent (1995). "A Simple Active Attack Against TCP." In: *Proceedings of the Fifth Usenix Unix Security Symposium*. Salt Lake City, UT. (Cit. on p. 88).

Jones, Douglas W. and Barbara Simons (2012). *Broken Ballots: Will Your Vote Count?* Stanford, CA: Center for the Study of Language and Information. http://brokenballots.com/ (cit. on p. 56).

Josefsson, S. (Oct. 2006). *The Base16, Base32, and Base64 Data Encodings*. RFC 4648. http: //www.rfc-editor.org/rfc/rfc4648.txt (cit. on p. 91).

Josifovski, Vanja, Peter Schwarz, Laura Haas, and Eileen Lin (2002). "Garlic: A New Flavor of Federated Query Processing for DB2." In: *Proceedings of the 2002 ACM SIGMOD International Conference on Management of Data*. SIGMOD '02. Madison, Wisconsin: ACM, pp. 524–532. ISBN: 1-58113-497-5. DOI: 10.1145/564691.564751. http://doi.acm.org/10. 1145/564691.564751 (cit. on pp. 217, 284).

Kahn, David (1967). *The Codebreakers*. New York: Macmillan. (Cit. on pp. 82, 254).

——— (1991). *Seizing the Enigma: The Race to Break the German U-Boat Codes, 1939–1943*. Boston: Houghton Mifflin. (Cit. on p. 249).

Kaliski, B. (Sept. 2000). *PKCS #5: Password-Based Cryptography Specification Version 2.0*. RFC 2898. http://www.rfc-editor.org/rfc/rfc2898.txt (cit. on pp. 127, 133, 140).

Kaminsky, Dan (2008). *It's the End of the Cache as We Know It*. Black Ops. http://kurser.lobner. dk/dDist/DMK_BO2K8.pdf (cit. on p. 215).

Kaufman, Charlie, ed. (Dec. 2005). *Internet Key Exchange (IKEv2) Protocol*. RFC 4306. http: //www.rfc-editor.org/rfc/rfc4306.txt (cit. on p. 95).

Kaufman, Charlie, Radia Perlman, and Mike Speciner (2002). *Network Security: Private Communication in a Public World*. Second. Prentice Hall. (Cit. on p. 256).

Kent, Jonathan (Mar. 31, 2005). "Malaysia Car Thieves Steal Finger." In: *BBC News*. http://news. bbc.co.uk/2/hi/asia-pacific/4396831.stm (cit. on p. 125).

Kent, Stephen T. and Lynette I. Millett, eds. (2003). *Who Goes There? Authentication Through the Lens of Privacy*. National Academies Press. http://www.nap.edu/catalog/10656.html (cit. on p. 125).

Kent, Stephen T. and K. Seo (Dec. 2005). *Security Architecture for the Internet Protocol*. RFC 4301. http://www.rfc-editor.org/rfc/rfc4301.txt (cit. on pp. 95, 104).

Kenyon, Henry (June 30, 2011). "Found Thumb Drives: Another Way Employees are a Security Menace." In: *GCN*. http://gcn.com/articles/2011/06/30/dhs-test-found-thumb-drives-disks-network.aspx (cit. on pp. 55, 269).

Kim, Gene and Eugene H. Spafford (1994a). "Experiences with Tripwire: Using Integrity Checkers for Intrusion Detection." In: *Proceedings of Systems Administration, Networking, and Security III*. http://docs.lib.purdue.edu/cgi/viewcontent.cgi?article=2114&context=cstech (cit. on pp. 71, 188).

——— (Nov. 1994b). "The Design and Implementation of Tripwire: A File System Integrity Checker." In: *Proceedings of the 2nd ACM Conference on Computer and Communications Security*. https://dl.acm.org/citation.cfm?id=191183 (cit. on pp. 71, 188).

——— (1994c). "Writing, Supporting, and Evalutaing Tripwire: A Publically Available Security Tool." In: *Proceedings of the Usenix Unix Applications Development Symposium*. http://www. usenix.org/publications/library/proceedings/appdev94/kim.html (cit. on pp. 71, 188).

Kim, Hyoungshick, John Tang, and Ross Anderson (2012). "Social Authentication: Harder than it Looks." In: *Proceedings of Financial Cryptography and Data Security*. (Cit. on p. 123).

Kivinen, T., B. Swander, A. Huttunen, and V. Volpe (Jan. 2005). *Negotiation of NAT-Traversal in the IKE*. RFC 3947. http://www.rfc-editor.org/rfc/rfc3947.txt (cit. on p. 95).

Knightley, Phillip (Mar. 12, 2010). "The History of the Honey Trap." In: *Foreign Policy*. http: //www.foreignpolicy.com/articles/2010/03/12/the_history_of_the_honey_trap (cit. on p. 254).

Knudsen, Lars, Willi Meier, Bart Preneel, Vincent Rijmen, and Sven Verdoolaege (1998). "Analysis Methods for (Alleged) RC4." In: *Advances in Cryptology—ASIACRYPT'98*. Ed. by Kazuo Ohta and Dingyi Pei. Vol. 1514. Lecture Notes in Computer Science. 10.1007/3-540-49649-1_26. Springer Berlin / Heidelberg, pp. 327–341. ISBN: 978-3-540-65109-3. http://dx.doi.org/ 10.1007/3-540-49649-1_26 (cit. on p. 100).

Koenig, Andrew (May 16, 2008). "Interface Design by Adverse Possession." In: *Dr. Dobbs*. http: //www.drdobbs.com/architecture-and-design/interface-design-by-adverse-possession/ 228701758 (cit. on p. 48).

Kohnfelder, Loren M. (May 1978). "Toward a Practical Public-Key Cryptosystem." MA thesis. Department of Electrical Engineering, Massachusetts Institute of Technology. (Cit. on p. 150).

Kolata, Gina (Feb. 20, 2001). "The Key Vanishes: Scientist Outlines Unbreakable Code." In: *The New York Times*. http://www.nytimes.com/2001/02/20/science/the-key-vanishes-scientist-outlines-unbreakable-code.html (cit. on p. 39).

Kormanik, Beth (Nov. 16, 2011). "3 Accused of Theft Using a Device at A.T.M.'s." In: *The New York Times*. http://www.nytimes.com/2011/11/17/nyregion/chase-atm-fraud-case-indictment-is-unsealed.html (cit. on p. 115).

Koscher, Karl, Alexei Czeskis, Franziska Roesner, Shwetak Patel, Tadayoshi Kohno, Stephen Checkoway, Damon McCoy, Brian Kantor, Danny Anderson, Hovav Shacham, and Stefan Savage (May 2010). "Experimental Security Analysis of a Modern Automobile." In: *Proceedings of the IEEE Symposium on Security and Privacy*. http://www.autosec.org/pubs/cars-oakland2010.pdf (cit. on p. 312).

Kravets, David (July 12, 2011). "Wi-Fi-Hacking Neighbor from Hell Sentenced to 18 Years." In: *Wired: Threat Level*. http://www.wired.com/threatlevel/2011/07/hacking-neighbor-from-hell/ (cit. on p. 83).

Krawczyk, H., M. Bellare, and R. Canetti (Feb. 1997). *HMAC: Keyed-Hashing for Message Authentication*. RFC 2104. http://www.rfc-editor.org/rfc/rfc2104.txt (cit. on p. 140).

Krebs, Brian (Aug. 2, 2007). "New Tool Automates Webmail Account Hijacks." In: *The Washington Post: Security Fix*. https://web.archive.org/web/20081006085441/http://blog.washingtonpost.com/securityfix/2007/08/new_tool_automates_webmail_acc.html (cit. on p. 94).

———— (Aug. 20, 2008). "Web Fraud 2.0: Validating Your Stolen Goods." In: *The Washington Post: Security Fix*. http://voices.washingtonpost.com/securityfix/2008/08/web_fraud_20_try_before_you_bu.html (cit. on p. 32).

———— (Oct. 12, 2009). "E-Banking on a Locked Down (Non-Microsoft) PC." In: *Security Fix (Washington Post blog)*. http://voices.washingtonpost.com/securityfix/2009/10/e-banking_on_a_locked_down_non.html?wprss=securityfix (cit. on p. 118).

———— (Nov. 8, 2011a). "How Much Is Your Identity Worth?" In: *Krebs on Security*. http://krebsonsecurity.com/2011/11/how-much-is-your-identity-worth/ (cit. on p. 33).

———— (Sept. 26, 2011b). "'Right-to-Left Override' Aids Email Attacks." In: *Krebs on Security*. http://krebsonsecurity.com/2011/09/right-to-left-override-aids-email-attacks/ (cit. on p. 9).

———— (June 21, 2012). "A Closer Look: Email-Based Malware Attacks." In: *Krebs on Security*. http://krebsonsecurity.com/2012/06/a-closer-look-recent-email-based-malware-attacks/ (cit. on p. 57).

———— (Feb. 13, 2013). "Zero-Day Flaws in Adobe Reader, Acrobat." In: *Krebs on Security*. http://krebsonsecurity.com/2013/02/zero-day-flaws-in-adobe-reader-acrobat/ (cit. on p. 300).

———— (Feb. 5, 2014). "Target Hackers Broke in Via HVAC Company." In: *Krebs on Security*. http://krebsonsecurity.com/2014/02/target-hackers-broke-in-via-hvac-company/ (cit. on p. 281).

———— (Apr. 15, 2015). "Critical Updates for Windows, Flash, Java." In: *Krebs on Security*. http://krebsonsecurity.com/2015/04/critical-updates-for-windows-flash-java/ (cit. on p. 300).

Kruegel, Christopher and Giovanni Vigna (2003). "Anomaly Detection of Web-based Attacks." In: *Proceedings of the 10th ACM Sonference on Computer and Communications Security*. CCS '03. Washington DC: ACM, pp. 251–261. ISBN: 1-58113-738-9. DOI: 10.1145/948109.948144. http://doi.acm.org/10.1145/948109.948144 (cit. on p. 286).

Lamport, Leslie (Nov. 1981). "Password Authentication with Insecure Communication." In: *Communications of the ACM* 24.11, pp. 770–772. http://dl.acm.org/citation.cfm?id=358797 (cit. on p. 129).

Landau, Susan (2004). "Polynomials in the Nation's Service: Using Algebra to Design the Advanced Encryption Standard." In: *American Mathematical Monthly*, pp. 89–117. (Cit. on p. 103).

——— (2013). "Making Sense from Snowden: What's Significant in the NSA Surveillance Revelations." In: *IEEE Security and Privacy* 11.4, pp. 54–63. ISSN: 1540-7993. DOI: 10.1109/MSP.2013.90. (Cit. on p. 278).

——— (Jan.–Feb. 2014). "Highlights from Making Sense of Snowden, Part II: What's Significant in the NSA Revelations." In: *IEEE Security and Privacy* 12.1, pp. 62–64. http://ieeexplore.ieee.org/xpls/abs_all.jsp?arnumber=6756737 (cit. on p. 278).

Landwehr, Carl E., Alan R. Bull, John P. McDermott, and William S. Choi (Sept. 1994). "A Taxonomy of Computer Program Security Flaws." In: *Computing Surveys* 26.3, pp. 211–254. http://citeseerx.ist.psu.edu/viewdoc/download?doi=10.1.1.85.4150&rep=rep1&type=pdf (cit. on p. 7).

Larus, James R., Thomas Ball, Manuvir Das, Robert DeLine, Manuel Fähndrich, Jon Pincus, Sriram K. Rajamani, and Ramanathan Venkatapathy (May 2004). "Righting Software." In: *IEEE Software* 21.3, pp. 92–100. ISSN: 0740-7459. DOI: 10.1109/MS.2004.1293079. (Cit. on p. 209).

Laurie, B., A. Langley, and E. Kasper (June 2013). *Certificate Transparency*. RFC 6962. http://www.rfc-editor.org/rfc/rfc6962.txt (cit. on p. 160).

Lee, Wenke and Salvatore J. Stolfo (1998). "Data Mining Approaches for Intrusion Detection." In: *7th USENIX Security Symposium*. San Antonio, Texas. http://static.usenix.org/publications/library/proceedings/sec98/lee.html (cit. on p. 50).

Leffall, Jabulani (Oct. 12, 2007). "Are Patches Leading to Exploits?" In: *Redmond*. http://redmondmag.com/articles/2007/10/12/are-patches-leading-to-exploits.aspx (cit. on pp. 240, 243).

Legnitto, Jan (May 25, 2012). "FBI Warns Travelers Abroad: Watch Out for WiFi Crime at Hotel Hotspots." In: *privatei (blog)*. http://www.privatewifi.com/fbi-warns-travelers-abroad-watch-out-for-wifi-crime-at-hotel-hotspots/ (cit. on p. 179).

Lemos, Rob (July 28, 1998). "US Report: Gamers Believe Activision's 'SiN' carries CIH Virus." In: *ZDNet UK*. http://www.zdnet.co.uk/news/security-management/1998/07/28/us-report-gamers-believe-activisions-sin-carries-cih-virus-2068990/ (cit. on p. 59).

Leyden, John (Dec. 10, 2012). "Saudi Aramco: Foreign Hackers Tried to Cork our Gas Output." In: *The Register*. http://www.theregister.co.uk/2012/12/10/saudi_aramco_shamoon_inquest/ (cit. on p. 310).

Li, Wei-Jen, Salvatore J. Stolfo, Angelos Stavrou, Elli Androulaki, and Angelos D. Keromytis (July 2007). "A Study of Malcode-Bearing Documents." In: *Proceedings of 4th GI International Conference on Detection of Intrusions & Malware, and Vulnerability Assessment*. Lucerne, Switzerland. http://sneakers.cs.columbia.edu/ids/publications/Sparse.pdf (cit. on p. 50).

Li, Zhiwei, Warren He, Devdatta Akhawe, and Dawn Song (Aug. 2014). "The Emperor's New Password Manager: Security Analysis of Web-based Password Managers." In: *Proc. 23rd USENIX Security Symposium*. http://devd.me/papers/pwdmgr-usenix14.pdf (cit. on p. 117).

Libicki, Martin C. (2009). *Cyberdeterrence and Cyberwar*. Tech. rep. MG-877. Rand Corporation. http://www.rand.org/pubs/monographs/MG877.html (cit. on p. 29).

Lichtman, Doug and Eric Posner (2006). "Holding Internet Service Providers Accountable." In: *Supreme Court Economic Review* 14, pp. 221–259. http://www.law.uchicago.edu/files/files/217-dgl-eap-isp.pdf (cit. on p. 253).

Limoncelli, Thomas A., Christina J. Hogan, and Strata R. Chalup (2007). *The Practice of System and Network Administration*. Boston: Addison-Wesley. (Cit. on p. 273).

Lindholm, Tim and Frank Yellin (1996). *The Java Virtual Machine*. Reading, MA: Addison-Wesley. (Cit. on p. 23).

Linn, J. (Aug. 1989). *Privacy Enhancement for Internet Electronic Mail: Part I—Message Encipherment and Authentication Procedures*. RFC 1113. http://www.rfc-editor.org/rfc/rfc1113.txt (cit. on p. 91).

Litke, Pat and Joe Stewart (Aug. 7, 2014). "BGP Hijacking for Cryptocurrency Profit." In: *Dell SecureWorks Counter Threat Unit*. http://www.secureworks.com/cyber-threat-intelligence/threats/bgp-hijacking-for-cryptocurrency-profit/ (cit. on pp. 215, 310).

Lochter, M. and J. Merkle (Mar. 2010). *Elliptic Curve Cryptography (ECC) Brainpool Standard Curves and Curve Generation*. RFC 5639. http://www.rfc-editor.org/rfc/rfc5639.txt (cit. on p. 101).

Lowe, Gavin (1996). "Breaking and Fixing the Needham-Schroeder Public-Key Protocol Using FDR." In: *Tools and Algorithms for the Construction and Analysis of Systems (TACAS)*. Vol. 1055. Springer-Verlag, Berlin Germany, pp. 147–166. http://www.intercom.virginia.edu/~evans/crab/lowe96breaking.pdf (cit. on pp. 86, 105).

Lucas, Michael W. (2006). *PGP & GPG: Email for the Practical Paranoid*. San Francisco: No Starch Press. (Cit. on p. 167).

Lynn III, William J. (Sept.–Oct. 2010). "Defending a New Domain." In: *Foreign Affairs* 89.5, pp. 97–108. http://www.foreignaffairs.com/articles/66552/william-j-lynn-iii/defending-a-new-domain (cit. on p. 55).

Lynn, C., Stephen T. Kent, and K. Seo (June 2004). *X.509 Extensions for IP Addresses and AS Identifiers*. RFC 3779. http://www.rfc-editor.org/rfc/rfc3779.txt (cit. on p. 152).

MacAskill, Ewen (June 30, 2013). "New NSA Leaks Show How US is Bugging its European Allies." In: *The Guardian*. http://www.guardian.co.uk/world/2013/jun/30/nsa-leaks-us-bugging-european-allies (cit. on p. 18).

Madejski, Michelle, Maritza Johnson, and Steven M. Bellovin (2012). "A Study of Privacy Setting Errors in an Online Social Network." In: *Proceedings of SESOC 2012*. https://www.cs.columbia.edu/~smb/papers/fb-violations-sesoc.pdf (cit. on p. 197).

Malis, A. and W. Simpson (June 1999). *PPP over SONET/SDH*. RFC 2615. http://www.rfc-editor.org/rfc/rfc2615.txt (cit. on p. 88).

Mandiant (2013). *APT1: Exposing One of China's Cyber Espionage Units*. White paper. http://intelreport.mandiant.com/Mandiant_APT1_Report.pdf (cit. on p. 18).

Markoff, John (Feb. 11, 2011a). "Malware Aimed at Iran Hit Five Sites, Report Says." In: *The New York Times*. http://www.nytimes.com/2011/02/13/science/13stuxnet.html (cit. on p. 37).

——— (Oct. 18, 2011b). "New Malicious Program by Creators of Stuxnet Is Suspected." In: *The New York Times*. http://www.nytimes.com/2011/10/19/technology/stuxnet-computer-worms-creators-may-be-active-again.html (cit. on pp. 28, 37).

——— (Mar. 17, 2011c). "SecurID Company Suffers a Breach of Data Security." In: *The New York Times*. http://www.nytimes.com/2011/03/18/technology/18secure.html (cit. on p. 38).

Markoff, John and Thom Shanker (Aug. 1, 2009). "Halted '03 Iraq Plan Illustrates U.S. Fear of Cyberwar Risk." In: *The New York Times*. http://www.nytimes.com/2009/08/02/us/politics/02cyber.html (cit. on p. 18).

Marlinspike, Moxie and David Hulton (July 29, 2012). "Divide and Conquer: Cracking MS-CHAPv2 with a 100% Success Rate." In: *CloudCracker (blog)*. https://www.cloudcracker.com/blog/2012/07/29/cracking-ms-chap-v2/ (cit. on p. 95).

Martin, David M., Sivaramarkrishnan Rajagopalan, and Aviel D. Rubin (Feb. 1997). "Blocking Java Applets at the Firewall." In: *Proceedings of the Symposium on Network and Distributed System Security*. San Diego, pp. 16–26. (Cit. on p. 23).

Martin, George R. R. (2000). *A Storm of Swords*. New York: Bantam Books. (Cit. on p. xv).

Matsui, M. (1994). "Linear Cryptanalysis Method for DES Cipher." In: *Advances in Cryptology—EUROCRYPT '93*. Ed. by Tor Helleseth. Vol. 765. Lecture Notes in Computer Science. 10.1007/3-540-48285-7_33. Springer Berlin / Heidelberg, pp. 386–397. ISBN: 978-3-540-57600-6. http://dx.doi.org/10.1007/3-540-48285-7_33 (cit. on p. 98).

Matsui, M., J. Nakajima, and S. Moriai (Apr. 2004). *A Description of the Camellia Encryption Algorithm*. RFC 3713. http://www.rfc-editor.org/rfc/rfc3713.txt (cit. on p. 103).

Matsumoto, Tsutomu, Hiroyuki Matsumoto, Koji Yamada, and Satoshi Hoshino (Jan. 2002). "Impact of Artificial 'Gummy' Fingers on Fingerprint Systems." In: *Proceedings of SPIE: Optical Security and Counterfeit Deterrence Techniques IV*. Vol. 4677, pp. 275–289. http://dx.doi.org/10.1117/12.462719 (cit. on p. 125).

Maxwell, Winston and Christopher Wolf (May 23, 2012). *A Global Reality: Governmental Access to Data in the Cloud*. White paper. http://goo.gl/zAmKkO (cit. on p. 193).

Mayer, Alain, Avishai Wool, and E. Ziskind (2000). "Fang: A Firewall Analysis Engine." In: *Proceedings of the IEEE Symposium on Security and Privacy*, pp. 177–187. (Cit. on p. 218).

McGraw, Gary (2006). *Software Security: Building Security In*. Upper Saddle River, NJ: Addison-Wesley. (Cit. on p. 209).

McGraw, Gary and Edward W. Felten (1999). *Securing Java: Getting Down to Business with Mobile Code*. New York: John Wiley & Sons. http://www.securingjava.com (cit. on p. 23).

McGrew, D., K. Igoe, and M. Salter (Feb. 2011). *Fundamental Elliptic Curve Cryptography Algorithms*. RFC 6090. http://www.rfc-editor.org/rfc/rfc6090.txt (cit. on p. 100).

McKenzie, Patrick (June 17, 2010). "Falsehoods Programmers Believe About Names." In: *Kalzumeus (blog)*. http://www.kalzumeus.com/2010/06/17/falsehoods-programmers-believe-about-names/ (cit. on p. 312).

Meserve, Jeanne (Sept. 26, 2007). "Sources: Staged Cyber Attack Reveals Vulnerability in Power Grid." In: *CNN*. http://articles.cnn.com/2007-09-26/us/power.at.risk_1_generator-cyber-attack-electric-infrastructure (cit. on p. 20).

Meyer, R. A. and L. H. Seawright (1970). "A Virtual Machine Time-sharing System." In: *IBM Systems Journal* 9.3, pp. 199–218. ISSN: 0018-8670. DOI: 10.1147/sj.93.0199. (Cit. on pp. 185, 187).

Meyers, Michelle (Aug. 28, 2009). "Accused Mastermind of TJX Hack to Plead Guilty." In: *CNET News*. http://news.cnet.com/8301-1009_3-10320761-83.html (cit. on p. 33).

Michaels, Dave (July 2, 2014). "Hacked Companies Face SEC Scrutiny Over Disclosure, Controls." In: *San Francisco Chronicle*. http://www.sfgate.com/business/article/Hacked-companies-face-SEC-scrutiny-over-5596541.php (cit. on p. 287).

Microsoft (Jan. 15, 2009). *Microsoft Root Certificate Program*. http://technet.microsoft.com/en-us/library/cc751157.aspx (cit. on p. 153).

Miller, Frank (1882). *Telegraphic Code to Insure Privacy and Secrecy in the Transmission of Telegrams*. New York: Charles M. Cornwell. http://books.google.com/books?id=tT9WAAAAYAAJ&pg=PA1#v=onepage&q&f=false (cit. on p. 122).

Miller, S. P., B. Clifford Neuman, Jeffrey I. Schiller, and J. H. Saltzer (Dec. 1987). "Kerberos Authentication and Authorization System." In: *Project Athena Technical Plan*. Section E.2.1. MIT. http://web.mit.edu/Saltzer/www/publications/athenaplan/e.2.1.pdf (cit. on pp. 81, 84).

Mills, Elinor (Aug. 25, 2010). "Bad Flash Drive Caused Worst U.S. Military Breach." In: *CNET News*. http://news.cnet.com/8301-27080_3-20014732-245.html (cit. on p. 269).

Milmo, Cahal (June 30, 2006). "Secrets Revealed of Gay 'Honey Trap' That Made Spy of Vassall." In: *The Independent*. http://www.independent.co.uk/news/uk/this-britain/secrets-revealed-of-gay-honey-trap-that-made-spy-of-vassall-406096.html (cit. on p. 254).

Mitnick, Kevin D., William L. Simon, and Steve Wozniak (2002). *The Art of Deception: Controlling the Human Element of Security*. New York: John Wiley & Sons. (Cit. on p. 254).

Mockapetris, P.V. (Nov. 1987). *Domain Names—Implementation and Specification*. RFC 1035. http://www.rfc-editor.org/rfc/rfc1035.txt (cit. on p. 91).

Moore, David, Vern Paxson, Stefan Savage, Colleen Shannon, Stuart Staniford, and Nicholas Weaver (July–Aug. 2003). "Inside the Slammer Worm." In: *IEEE Security & Privacy* 1.4. http://cseweb.ucsd.edu/~savage/papers/IEEESP03.pdf (cit. on p. 72).

Morris, Robert H. and Ken Thompson (Nov. 1979). "Unix Password Security." In: *Communications of the ACM* 22.11, p. 594. http://dl.acm.org/citation.cfm?id=359172 (cit. on pp. xii, 9, 108, 139, 140).

Morse, Stephen (1982). *The 8086/8088 Primer*. 2nd ed. Indianapolis: Hayden Book Co., Inc. (Cit. on p. 47).

Myers, M., R. Ankney, A. Malpani, S. Galperin, and C. Adams (June 1999). *X.509 Internet Public Key Infrastructure Online Certificate Status Protocol—OCSP*. RFC 2560. http://www.rfc-editor.org/rfc/rfc2560.txt (cit. on p. 161).

Nakashima, Ellen, Greg Miller, and Julie Tate (June 19, 2012). "U.S., Israel Developed Flame Computer Virus to Slow Iranian Nuclear Efforts, Officials Say." In: *The Washington Post*. http://www.washingtonpost.com/world/national-security/us-israel-developed-computer-virus-to-slow-iranian-nuclear-efforts-officials-say/2012/06/19/gJQA6xBPoV_story.html (cit. on p. 38).

Naraine, Ryan (June 13, 2007). "Exploit Wednesday Follows MS Patch Tuesday." In: *ZDnet*. http://www.zdnet.com/blog/security/exploit-wednesday-follows-ms-patch-tuesday/296 (cit. on p. 243).

——— (Feb. 14, 2012). "Nortel Hacking Attack Went Unnoticed for Almost 10 Years." In: *Zero Day (ZDnet blog)*. http://www.zdnet.com/blog/security/nortel-hacking-attack-went-unnoticed-for-almost-10-years/10304 (cit. on p. 166).

Narayanan, Arvind and Vitaly Shmatikov (May 2008). "Robust De-anonymization of Large Sparse Datasets." In: *IEEE Symposium on Security and Privacy*, pp. 111–125. DOI: 10.1109/SP.2008.33. http://www.cs.utexas.edu/~shmat/shmat_oak08netflix.pdf (cit. on p. 314).

National Research Council (2010). *Letter Report for the Committee on Deterring Cyberattacks: Informing Strategies and Developing Options for U.S. Policy*. Washington, DC: National Academies Press. http://www.nap.edu/catalog.php?record_id=12886 (cit. on p. 39).

Needham, R. M. and M. Schroeder (Dec. 1978). "Using Encryption for Authentication in Large Networks of Computers." In: *Communications of the ACM* 21.12, pp. 993–999. http://dl.acm.org/citation.cfm?id=359659 (cit. on p. 86).

——— (Jan. 1987). "Authentication Revisited." In: *Operating Systems Review* 21.1, p. 7. (Cit. on p. 86).

Neuman, B. Clifford, T. Yu, S. Hartman, and K. Raeburn (July 2005). *The Kerberos Network Authentication Service (V5)*. RFC 4120. http://www.rfc-editor.org/rfc/rfc4120.txt (cit. on pp. 81, 84).

Newman, Lesléa (1989). *Heather Has Two Mommies*. Boston: Alyson Wonderland. (Cit. on p. 122).

NIST (July 2013). *Digital Signature Standard (DSS)*. Federal Information Processing Standards Publication 186-4. http://nvlpubs.nist.gov/nistpubs/FIPS/NIST.FIPS.186-4.pdf (cit. on p. 100).

——— (Aug. 2015a). *SHA-3 Standard: Permutation-Based Hash and Extendable-Output Functions*. Draft FIPS Pub 202. http://nvlpubs.nist.gov/nistpubs/FIPS/NIST.FIPS.180-4.pdf (cit. on p. 101).

——— (Oct. 1993). *Automated Password Generator (APG)*. Tech. rep. 181. NIST. http://csrc.nist.gov/publications/fips/fips181/fips181.pdf (cit. on p. 122).

——— (Aug. 2015b). *Secure Hash Standard*. Tech. rep. 180-4. NIST. http://nvlpubs.nist.gov/nistpubs/FIPS/NIST.FIPS.180-4.pdf (cit. on pp. 101, 104).

Niven, Larry (1977). *Ringworld*. New York: Holt, Rinehart and Winston. (Cit. on p. 169).

——— (1985). "The Theory and Practice of Teleportation." In: *All the Myriad Ways*. New York: Del Rey. (Cit. on p. 21).

Niven, Larry and Jerry Pournelle (1993). *The Gripping Hand*. New York: Pocket Books. (Cit. on p. 7).

——— (1994). *The Mote in God's Eye*. Simon and Schuster. (Cit. on p. 149).

Norman, Don (Dec. 11, 2003). "Proper Understanding of the 'Human Factor'." In: *RISKS Digest* 07. (Cit. on p. 256).

Oates, John (July 21, 2010). "Dell Warns on Spyware Infected Server Motherboards: Windows Snoopware Buried in Server Firmware." In: *The Register*. http://www.theregister.co.uk/2010/07/21/dell_server_warning/ (cit. on p. 53).

Office of the National Counterintelligence Executive (Oct. 2011). *Foreign Spies Stealing US Economic Secrets in Cyberspace*. Report to Congress on Foreign Economic Collection and Industrial Espionage, 2009–2011. http : / / www . ncix . gov / publications / reports / fecie_all / Foreign_Economic_Collection_2011.pdf (cit. on pp. 18, 20).

Office of the Privacy Commissioner of Canada (Sept. 25, 2007). *Report of an Investigation into the Security, Collection and Retention of Personal Information*. http://www.priv.gc.ca/cf-dc/2007/TJX_rep_070925_e.cfm (cit. on pp. 82, 120).

Ohm, Paul (2010). "Broken Promises of Privacy: Responding to the Surprising Failure of Anonymization." In: *UCLA Law Review* 57. U of Colorado Law Legal Studies Research Paper No. 9-12, pp. 1701–1777. http://ssrn.com/abstract=1450006 (cit. on p. 314).

Oprea, Alina, Michael K. Reiter, and Ke Yang (2005). "Space-Efficient Block Storage Integrity." In: *Proceedings of NDSS 2005*. http://www.cs.unc.edu/~reiter/papers/2005/NDSS.pdf (cit. on p. 75).

Organick, Elliot (1972). *The Multics System: An Examination of its Structure*. Cambridge, MA: MIT Press. (Cit. on pp. 58, 59).

Orman, H. and P. Hoffman (Apr. 2004). *Determining Strengths for Public Keys Used for Exchanging Symmetric Keys*. RFC 3766. http://www.rfc-editor.org/rfc/rfc3766.txt (cit. on p. 100).

Owens, William A., Kenneth W. Dam, and Herbert S. Lin, eds. (2009). *Technology, Policy, Law, and Ethics Regarding U.S. Acquisition and Use of Cyberattack Capabilities*. Washington, DC: National Academies Press. http://www.nap.edu/catalog.php?record_id=12651 (cit. on p. 40).

Pappas, Vasilis (2014). "Defending against Return-Oriented Programming." PhD thesis. Columbia University. (Cit. on p. 206).

Parker, Donn (1976). *Crime by Computer*. New York: Scribner. (Cit. on p. 32).

Paul, Ryan (Dec. 1, 2011). "Wikileaks Docs Reveal that Governments Use Malware for Surveillance." In: *Ars Technica*. http://arstechnica.com/business/news/2011/12/wikileaks-docs-reveal-that-governments-use-malware-for-surveillance.ars (cit. on p. 39).

Pauli, Darren (July 23, 2014). "Attackers Raid SWISS BANKS with DNS and Malware Bombs." In: *The Register*. http://www.theregister.co.uk/2014/07/23/ruskie_vxers_change_dns_nuke_malware_in_swiss_bank_raids/ (cit. on p. 123).

——— (Aug. 10, 2015). "HTC Caught Storing Fingerprints AS WORLD-READABLE CLEARTEXT." In: *The Register*. http://www.theregister.co.uk/2015/08/10/htc_caught_storing_fingerprints_as_worldreadable_cleartext/ (cit. on p. 124).

Paxson, Vern (1998). "Bro: A System for Detecting Network Intruders in Real-Time." In: *Proceedings of the Seventh USENIX Security Symposium*, pp. 31–51. (Cit. on p. 71).

——— (1999). "Bro: A System for Detecting Network Intruders in Real-time." In: *Computer Networks (Amsterdam, Netherlands: 1999)* 31.23–24, pp. 2435–2463. (Cit. on p. 71).

Pear, Robert (May 26, 2015). "Tech Rivalries Impede Digital Medical Record Sharing." In: *The New York Times*. http://www.nytimes.com/2015/05/27/us/electronic-medical-record-sharing-is-hurt-by-business-rivalries.html (cit. on p. 294).

Perlroth, Nicole (Feb. 10, 2012). "Traveling Light in a Time of Digital Thievery." In: *The New York Times*. http://www.nytimes.com/2012/02/11/technology/electronic-security-a-worry-in-an-age-of-digital-espionage.html (cit. on pp. 174, 271).

———— (July 21, 2014). "A Tough Corporate Job Asks One Question: Can You Hack It?" In: *The New York Times*. http://www.nytimes.com/2014/07/21/business/a-tough-corporate-job-asks-one-question-can-you-hack-it.html (cit. on p. 281).

Perlroth, Nicole and Matthew Goldstein (Sept. 13, 2014). "After Breach, JPMorgan Still Seeks to Determine Extent of Attack." In: *The New York Times*. http://www.nytimes.com/2014/09/13/technology/after-breach-jpmorgan-still-seeks-to-determine-extent-of-attack.html (cit. on p. 40).

Perlroth, Nicole, Jeff Larson, and Scott Shane (Sept. 6, 2013). "N.S.A. Able to Foil Basic Safeguards of Privacy on Web." In: *The New York Times*. http://www.nytimes.com/2013/09/06/us/nsa-foils-much-internet-encryption.html (cit. on p. 101).

Perrow, Charles (1999). *Normal Accidents: Living with High-Risk Technologies*. Princeton, NJ: Princeton University Press. (Cit. on p. 157).

Poe, Robert (May 17, 2006). "The Ultimate Net Monitoring Tool." In: *Wired*. http://www.wired.com/science/discoveries/news/2006/05/70914 (cit. on p. 71).

Postel, J. (Sept. 1981). *Transmission Control Protocol*. RFC 793. http://www.rfc-editor.org/rfc/rfc793.txt (cit. on p. 88).

Postel, J. and J. Reynolds (Oct. 1985). *File Transfer Protocol*. RFC 959. http://www.rfc-editor.org/rfc/rfc959.txt (cit. on p. 23).

Potter, Shaya, Steven M. Bellovin, and Jason Nieh (Nov. 2009). "Two Person Control Administration: Preventing Administration Faults through Duplication." In: *LISA '09*. http://www.usenix.org/events/lisa09/tech/full_papers/potter.pdf (cit. on p. 277).

Poulsen, Kevin (Aug. 19, 2003). "Slammer Worm Crashed Ohio Nuke Plant Network." In: *SecurityFocus*. http://www.securityfocus.com/news/6767 (cit. on p. 54).

Poulsen, Kevin and Kim Zetter (June 10, 2010). "'I Can't Believe What I'm Confessing to You': The Wikileaks Chats." In: *Wired: Threat Level*. http://www.wired.com/2010/06/wikileaks-chat/ (cit. on p. 73).

Powers, Thomas (Dec. 3, 2000). "Computer Security; The Whiz Kid vs. the Old Boys." In: *The New York Times Magazine*. http://www.nytimes.com/2000/12/03/magazine/computer-security-the-whiz-kid-vs-the-old-boys.html (cit. on pp. 248, 250).

Prevelakis, Vassilis and Diomidis Spinellis (July 2007). "The Athens Affair." In: *IEEE Spectrum* 44.7, pp. 26–33. http://spectrum.ieee.org/telecom/security/the-athens-affair/0 (cit. on p. 235).

Ramachandran, Anirudh and Nick Feamster (2006). "Understanding the Network-level Behavior of Spammers." In: *ACM SIGCOMM Computer Communication Review* 36.4, pp. 291–302. (Cit. on p. 213).

Ramsdell, B. and S. Turner (Jan. 2010). *Secure/Multipurpose Internet Mail Extensions (S/MIME) Version 3.2 Message Specification*. RFC 5751. http://www.rfc-editor.org/rfc/rfc5751.txt (cit. on p. 104).

Rawnsley, Adam (July 1, 2013). "Espionage? Moi?" In: *Foreign Policy*. http://www.foreignpolicy.com/articles/2013/07/01/espionage_moi_france (cit. on p. 39).

Raymond, Eric Steven (2000). *The Cathedral and the Bazaar*. Version 3.0. http://www.catb.org/~esr/writings/cathedral-bazaar/cathedral-bazaar/index.html (cit. on p. 235).

[Redacted] (1996). "Out of Control." In: *Cryptologic Quarterly* 15, Special Edition. Originally classified SECRET. There is another, and differently redacted, version at http://www.nsa.gov/

public_info/_files/cryptologic_quarterly/Out_of_Control.pdf. http://www.gwu.edu/~nsarchiv/ NSAEBB/NSAEBB424/docs/Cyber-009.pdf (cit. on p. 277).

Reed, Thomas (2004). *At the Abyss: An Insider's History of the Cold War*. New York: Presidio Press. (Cit. on pp. 17, 18, 311).

Reeder, Robert W., Patrick Gage Kelley, Aleecia M. McDonald, and Lorrie Faith Cranor (2008). "A User Study of the Expandable Grid Applied to P3P Privacy Policy Visualization." In: *WPES '08: Proceedings of the 7th ACM Workshop on Privacy in the Electronic Society*. Alexandria, VA: ACM, pp. 45–54. ISBN: 978-1-60558-289-4. http://doi.acm.org/10.1145/1456403.1456413 (cit. on p. 197).

Reeder, Robert W., E Kowalczyk, and Adam Shostack (2011). *Helping Engineers Design NEAT Security Warnings*. Pittsburgh, PA. http://download.microsoft.com/download/2/C/A/2CAB7 DDD-94DF-4E7B-A980-973AFA5CB0D0/NEATandSPRUCEatMicrosoft-final.docx (cit. on p. 264).

Reeder, Robert W. and Roy A. Maxion (2005). "User Interface Dependability through Goal-Error Prevention." In: *International Conference on Dependable Systems and Networks*, pp. 60–69. (Cit. on pp. 197, 257).

Rekhter, Y., B. Moskowitz, D. Karrenberg, G. J. de Groot, and E. Lear (Feb. 1996). *Address Allocation for Private Internets*. RFC 1918. http://www.rfc-editor.org/rfc/rfc1918.txt (cit. on pp. 285, 301).

Rescorla, Eric K. (Sept. 23, 2011). "Security Impact of the Rizzo/Duong CBC 'BEAST' Attack." In: *Educated Guesswork (blog)*. http://www.educatedguesswork.org/2011/09/security_impact_of_the_rizzodu.html (cit. on p. 83).

Rescorla, Eric K. and IAB (June 2005). *Writing Protocol Models*. RFC 4101. http://www.rfc-editor.org/rfc/rfc4101.txt (cit. on p. 226).

Rescorla, Eric K. and N. Modadugu (Apr. 2006). *Datagram Transport Layer Security*. RFC 4347. http://www.rfc-editor.org/rfc/rfc4347.txt (cit. on p. 88).

Richmond, Riva (Apr. 2, 2011). "The RSA Hack: How They Did It." In: *The New York Times (Bits blog)*. http://bits.blogs.nytimes.com/2011/04/02/the-rsa-hack-how-they-did-it/ (cit. on pp. 38, 248).

Rifkin, Glenn (Feb. 8, 2011). "Ken Olsen, Who Built DEC Into a Power, Dies at 84." In: *The New York Times*, A24. http://www.nytimes.com/2011/02/08/technology/business-computing/08olsen.html (cit. on p. 8).

Riley, Michael (Dec. 20, 2011). "Stolen Credit Cards Go for $3.50 at Amazon-like Online Bazaar." In: *Businessweek*. http://www.businessweek.com/news/2011-12-20/stolen-credit-cards-go-for-3-50-at-amazon-like-online-bazaar.html (cit. on p. 32).

Riley, Michael, Ben Elgin, Dune Lawrence, and Carol Matlack (Mar. 13, 2014). "Missed Alarms and 40 Million Stolen Credit Card Numbers: How Target Blew It." In: *Businessweek*. http://www.businessweek.com/articles/2014-03-13/target-missed-alarms-in-epic-hack-of-credit-card-data (cit. on pp. 214, 222).

Ristic, Ivan (Nov. 2010). *Internet SSL Survey 2010*. http://media.blackhat.com/bh-ad-10/Ristic/BlackHat-AD-2010-Ristic-Qualys-SSL-Survey-HTTP-Rating-Guide-slides.pdf (cit. on p. 262).

Ritchie, Dennis M. and Ken Thompson (July 1974). "The UNIX Time-Sharing System." In: *Commun. ACM* 17.7, pp. 365–375. ISSN: 0001-0782. DOI: 10.1145/361011.361061. http://doi.acm.org/10.1145/361011.361061 (cit. on p. 47).

Rivner, Uri (Apr. 1, 2011). "Anatomy of an Attack." In: *Speaking of Security (blog)*. http://blogs.rsa.com/rivner/anatomy-of-an-attack/ (cit. on pp. 38, 248).

Roberts, Paul (June 5, 2003). "Sobig: Spam, Virus, or Both?" In: *Computer World*. http://www.computerworld.com/s/article/81825/Sobig_Spam_virus_or_both_ (cit. on p. 28).

Roesch, Martin (1999). "Snort—Lightweight Intrusion Detection for Networks." In: *LISA '99: 13th Systems Administration Conference*. http://static.usenix.org/publications/library/proceedings/lisa99/full_papers/roesch/roesch.pdf (cit. on p. 71).

Roizenblatt, Roberto, Paulo Schor, Fabio Dante, Jaime Roizenblatt, and Rubens Belfort Jr. (2004). "Iris Recognition as a Biometric Method After Cataract Surgery." In: *Biomedical Engineering Online* 3.2. DOI: http://dx.doi.org/10.1186/1475-925X-3-2. http://www.biomedical-engineering-online.com/content/3/1/2 (cit. on p. 128).

Rosenblatt, Seth (Apr. 28, 2014). "Stop Using Microsoft's IE Browser Until Bug is Fixed, US and UK warn." In: *CNET*. http://www.cnet.com/news/stop-using-ie-until-bug-is-fixed-says-us/ (cit. on p. 244).

Ross, Blake, Collin Jackson, Nick Miyake, Dan Boneh, and John C. Mitchell (2005). "Stronger Password Authentication Using Browser Extensions." In: *Proc. 14th USENIX Security Symposium*. https://www.usenix.org/legacy/events/sec05/tech/full_papers/ross/ross_html/ (cit. on p. 119).

Rouf, Ishtiaq, Rob Miller, Hossen Mustafa, Travis Taylor, Sangho Oh, Wenyuan Xu, Marco Gruteser, Wade Trappe, and Ivan Seskar (2010). "Security and Privacy Vulnerabilities of In-Car Wireless Networks: A Tire Pressure Monitoring System Case Study." In: *Proceedings of the Usenix Security Conference*. http://www.usenix.org/event/sec10/tech/full_papers/Rouf.pdf (cit. on p. 54).

Rubin, Aviel D. (2006). *Brave New Ballot*. http://www.bravenewballot.org/. New York: Random House. (Cit. on p. 56).

Sagan, Carl (1985). *Contact*. New York: Simon and Schuster. (Cit. on p. 241).

Saletan, William (July 18, 2011). "Springtime for Twitter: Is the Internet Driving the Revolutions of the Arab Spring?" In: *Slate*. http://www.slate.com/articles/technology/future_tense/2011/07/springtime_for_twitter.html (cit. on p. 310).

Sanger, David E. (June 1, 2012). "Obama Order Sped Up Wave of Cyberattacks against Iran." In: *The New York Times*. http://www.nytimes.com/2012/06/01/world/middleeast/obama-ordered-wave-of-cyberattacks-against-iran.html (cit. on p. 28).

Sanger, David E., David Barboza, and Nicole Perlroth (Feb. 19, 2013). "Chinese Army Unit Is Seen as Tied to Hacking against U.S." In: *The New York Times*. https://www.nytimes.com/2013/02/19/technology/chinas-army-is-seen-as-tied-to-hacking-against-us.html?pagewanted=all (cit. on p. 18).

Santesson, S., Russ Housley, S. Bajaj, and L. Rosenthol (May 2011). *Internet X.509 Public Key Infrastructure – Certificate Image*. RFC 6170. http://www.rfc-editor.org/rfc/rfc6170.txt (cit. on p. 150).

Santesson, S., Russ Housley, and T. Freeman (Feb. 2004). *Internet X.509 Public Key Infrastructure: Logotypes in X.509 Certificates*. RFC 3709. http://www.rfc-editor.org/rfc/rfc3709.txt (cit. on p. 150).

Scarfone, Karen and Peter Mell (Feb. 2007). *Guide to Intrusion Detection and Prevention Systems (IDPS)*. Tech. rep. National Institute of Standards and Technology (NIST). http://csrc.nist.gov/publications/nistpubs/800-94/SP800-94.pdf (cit. on p. 72).

Schiffman, Allan M. (July 2, 2007). "Instant Immortality." In: *Marginal Guesswork*. http://marginalguesswork.blogspot.com/2004/07/instant-immortality.html (cit. on p. xii).

Schneider, Fred B., ed. (1999). *Trust in Cyberspace*. National Academy Press. http://www.nap.edu/openbook.php?record_id=6161 (cit. on pp. 31, 208).

Schneier, Bruce (July 15, 2000). "Security Risks of Unicode." In: *Crypto-Gram Newsletter*. http://www.schneier.com/crypto-gram-0007.html#9 (cit. on p. 9).

——— (Feb. 16, 2005). "Unicode URL Hack." In: *Schneier on Security (blog)*. http://www.schneier.com/blog/archives/2005/02/unicode_url_hac_1.html (cit. on p. 9).

——— (Mar. 20, 2008). "Inside the Twisted Mind of the Security Professional." In: *Wired*. http://www.wired.com/politics/security/commentary/securitymatters/2008/03/securitymatters_0320 (cit. on p. 15).

——— (Sept. 13, 2013). "New NSA Leak Shows MITM Attacks against Major Internet Services." In: *Schneier on Security (blog)*. https://www.schneier.com/blog/archives/2013/09/new_nsa_leak_sh.html (cit. on p. 153).

——— (Apr. 9, 2014). "Heartbleed." In: *Schneier on Security (blog)*. https://www.schneier.com/blog/archives/2014/04/heartbleed.html (cit. on pp. 182, 298).

Schneier, Bruce and Mudge (1999). "Cryptanalysis of Microsoft's PPTP Authentication Extensions (MS-CHAPv2)." In: *CQRE '99*. Springer-Verlag, pp. 192–203. http://www.schneier.com/paper-pptpv2.html (cit. on p. 95).

Scholl, Matthew, Kevin Stine, Joan Hash, Pauline Bowen, Arnold Johnson, Carla Dancy Smith, and Daniel I. Steinberg (Oct. 2008). *An Introductory Resource Guide for Implementing the Health Insurance Portability and Accountability Act (HIPAA) Security Rule*. NIST Special Publication 800-66 Revision 1. National Institute of Standards and Technology. http://csrc.nist.gov/publications/nistpubs/800-66-Rev1/SP-800-66-Revision1.pdf (cit. on p. 295).

Schreier, Jason (Apr. 25, 2011). "Sony Scrambles After 'External Intrusion' Takes Down PlayStation Network." In: *Wired: Game Life*. http://www.wired.com/gamelife/2011/04/psn-down/ (cit. on p. 121).

Schwartz, Matthew J. (July 13, 2011). "Zeus Banking Trojan Hits Android Phones." In: *Information Week*. http://www.informationweek.com/news/security/mobile/231001685 (cit. on p. 136).

——— (July 16, 2012). "One Secret That Stops Hackers: Girlfriends." In: *Information Week*. http://www.informationweek.com/news/security/management/240003767 (cit. on p. 34).

Schwartz, Nelson D. (June 26, 2012). "F.B.I. Says 24 Are Arrested in Credit Card Theft Plan." In: *The New York Times*. http://www.nytimes.com/2012/06/27/business/fbi-says-24-people-are-arrested-in-credit-card-theft.html (cit. on p. 34).

Seltzer, Larry (June 12, 2015). "Even with a VPN, Open Wi-Fi Exposes Users." In: *Ars Technica*. http://arstechnica.com/security/2015/06/even-with-a-vpn-open-wi-fi-exposes-users/ (cit. on p. 173).

Shacham, Hovav (2007). "The Geometry of Innocent Flesh on the Bone: Return-Into-libc without Function Calls (on the x86)." In: *Proceedings of the 14th ACM Conference on Computer and Communications Security (CCS)*. (Cit. on p. 206).

Shacham, Hovav, Matthew Page, Ben Pfaff, Eu-Jin Goh, N. Modadugu, and Dan Boneh (2004). "On the Effectiveness of Address-space Randomization." In: *Proceedings of the 11th ACM Conference on Computer and Communications Security*. CCS '04. Washington DC: ACM, pp. 298–307. ISBN: 1-58113-961-6. DOI: 10.1145/1030083.1030124. http://doi.acm.org/10.1145/1030083.1030124 (cit. on p. 313).

Shakespeare, William (1596). *The Merchant of Venice*. http://www.gutenberg.org/ebooks/1515 (cit. on p. 288).

—— (1603). *Hamlet*. http://www.gutenberg.org/ebooks/1524 (cit. on p. 242).

Shannon, Claude E. (July 1948). "A Mathematical Theory of Communication." In: *Bell System Technical Journal* 27.3,4, pp. 379–423, 623–656. (Cit. on p. 145).

—— (1951). "Prediction and Entropy in Printed English." In: *Bell System Technical Journal* 30.1, pp. 50–64. (Cit. on p. 145).

Shannon, Colleen and David Moore (July 2004). "The Spread of the Witty Worm." In: *IEEE Security & Privacy* 2.4, pp. 46–50. ISSN: 1540-7993. DOI: 10.1109/MSP.2004.59. (Cit. on p. 70).

Sheffer, Y., R. Holz, and P. Saint-Andre (Feb. 2015). *Summarizing Known Attacks on Transport Layer Security (TLS) and Datagram TLS (DTLS)*. RFC 7457. http://www.rfc-editor.org/rfc/rfc7457.txt (cit. on p. 83).

Shirey, R. (Aug. 2007). *Internet Security Glossary, Version 2*. RFC 4949. http://www.rfc-editor.org/rfc/rfc4949.txt (cit. on p. 150).

Shor, Peter W. (1994). "Algorithms for Quantum Computation: Discrete Logarithms and Factoring." In: *Proc. 35th Annual Symposium on Foundations of Computer Science*. IEEE Computer Society, pp. 124–134. http://www.csee.wvu.edu/~xinl/library/papers/comp/shor_focs1994.pdf (cit. on p. 105).

Shostack, Adam (2014). *Threat Modeling: Designing for Security*. Indianapolis: Wiley. http://threatmodelingbook.com/ (cit. on pp. 226, 228).

Simske, Steven J., Jason S. Aronoff, Margaret M. Sturgill, and Galia Golodetz (Sept. 2008). "Security Printing Deterrents: A Comparison of Thermal Ink Jet, Dry Electrophotographic, and Liquid Electrophotographic Printing." In: *Journal of Imaging Science and Technology* 52.5. http://jist.imaging.org/resource/1/jimte6/v52/i5/p050201_s1?bypassSSO=1 (cit. on p. 16).

Singel, Ryan (June 20, 2011). "Dropbox Left User Accounts Unlocked for 4 Hours Sunday." In: *Wired: Threat Level*. http://www.wired.com/threatlevel/2011/06/dropbox/ (cit. on p. 196).

Singer, Abe, Warren Anderson, and Rik Farrow (Aug. 2013). "Rethinking Password Policies." In: *;login:* 38.4. https://www.usenix.org/sites/default/files/rethinking_password_policies_unabridged.pdf (cit. on p. 108).

Skype (July 23, 2012). *Survey Finds Nearly Half of Consumers Fail to Upgrade Software Regularly and One Quarter of Consumers Don't Know Why to Update Software*. Press release.

http://about.skype.com/press/2012/07/survey_finds_nearly_half_fail_to_upgrade.html (cit. on p. 271).

Smedinghoff, Thomas J. and Ruth Hill Bro (Spring 1999). "Moving with Change: Electronic Signature Legislation as a Vehicle for Advancing E-Commerce." In: *The John Marshall Journal of Computer & Information Law* 17.3. A version of this article may be found at http://library.findlaw.com/1999/Jan/1/241481.html, pp. 723–768. (Cit. on p. 165).

Smetters, D. K. and Nathan Good (2009). "How Users Use Access Control." In: *Proceedings of the 5th Symposium on Usable Privacy and Security (SOUPS '09)*, 15:1–15:12. http://dl.acm.org/citation.cfm?id=1572552 (cit. on p. 197).

Smith, E. E. "Doc" (1950a). *First Lensman*. Reading, PA: Fantasy Press. (Cit. on p. 124).

——— (1950b). *Galactic Patrol*. Reading, PA: Fantasy Press. (Cit. on p. 31).

——— (1953). *Second Stage Lensman*. Reading, PA: Fantasy Press. (Cit. on pp. 15, 70).

——— (1954). *Children of the Lens*. Reading, PA: Fantasy Press. (Cit. on p. 309).

Smith, George (Mar. 10, 2003). "Iraqi Cyberwar: An Ageless Joke." In: *SecurityFocus*. http://www.securityfocus.com/columnists/147 (cit. on p. 311).

Snider, L. Britt and Daniel S. Seikaly (Feb. 2000). *CIA Inspector General Report of Investigation: Improper Handling of Classified Information by John M. Deutch*. 1998-0028-IG. Central Intelligence Agency Inspector General. https://www.cia.gov/library/reports/general-reports-1/deutch.pdf (cit. on pp. 248, 250).

Soghoian, Christopher (Oct. 2007). "Insecure Flight: Broken Boarding Passes and Ineffective Terrorist Watch Lists." In: *First IFIP WG 11.6 Working Conference on Policies & Research in Identity Management (IDMAN 07)*. http://papers.ssrn.com/sol3/papers.cfm?abstract_id=1001675 (cit. on p. 16).

Song, Yingbo, Michael Locasto, Angelos Stavrou, Angelos D. Keromytis, and Salvatore J. Stolfo (2010). "On the Infeasibility of Modeling Polymorphic Shellcode." In: *Machine Learning* 81 (2). 10.1007/s10994-009-5143-5, pp. 179–205. ISSN: 0885-6125. http://ids.cs.columbia.edu/sites/default/files/polymorph-mlj.pdf (cit. on p. 49).

Sontag, Sherry and Christopher Drew (1998). *Blind Man's Bluff: The Untold Story of American Submarine Espionage*. New York: Public Affairs. (Cit. on p. 300).

Spafford, Eugene H. (Jan. 1989). "The Internet Worm Program: An Analysis." In: *Computer Communication Review* 19.1, pp. 17–57. http://dl.acm.org/authorize.cfm?key=729660 (cit. on p. 46).

——— (Apr. 19, 2006). "Security Myths and Passwords." In: *CERIAS Blog*. http://www.cerias.purdue.edu/site/blog/post/password-change-myths/ (cit. on p. 114).

Springer, John (Dec. 28, 2010). "Is Snooping in your Spouse's E-mail a Crime?" In: *MSNBC*. http://today.msnbc.msn.com/id/40820892/ns/today-today_tech/t/snooping-your-spouses-e-mail-crime/ (cit. on p. 123).

Srisuresh, P. and K. Egevang (Jan. 2001). *Traditional IP Network Address Translator (Traditional NAT)*. RFC 3022. http://www.rfc-editor.org/rfc/rfc3022.txt (cit. on pp. 67, 95).

Srivatsan, Shreyas, Maritza Johnson, and Steven M. Bellovin (July 2010). *Simple-VPN: Simple IPsec Configuration*. Tech. rep. CUCS-020-10. Department of Computer Science, Columbia University. https://mice.cs.columbia.edu/getTechreport.php?techreportID=1433 (cit. on pp. 95, 156).

Staniford, Stuart, Vern Paxson, and Nicholas Weaver (Aug. 2002). "How to Own the Internet in Your Spare Time." In: *Proceedings of the 11th Usenix Security Symposium*. http://www.icir.org/vern/papers/cdc-usenix-sec02/ (cit. on p. 48).

Steiner, Jennifer, B. Clifford Neuman, and Jeffrey I. Schiller (1988). "Kerberos: An Authentication Service for Open Network Systems." In: *Proc. Winter USENIX Conference*. Dallas, TX, pp. 191–202. http://www.cse.nd.edu/~dthain/courses/cse598z/fall2004/papers/kerberos.pdf (cit. on pp. 81, 84).

Stevens, Gina (Apr. 12, 2012). *Data Security Breach Notification Laws*. CRS Report for Congress R42475. Congressional Research Service. http://fas.org/sgp/crs/misc/R42475.pdf (cit. on p. 287).

Stoll, Cliff (May 1988). "Stalking the Wily Hacker." In: *Communications of the ACM* 31.5, pp. 484–497. DOI: 10.1145/42411.42412. http://doi.acm.org/10.1145/42411.42412 (cit. on pp. 28, 32, 66, 74, 288, 311).

——— (1989). *The Cuckoo's Egg: Tracking a Spy Through the Maze of Computer Espionage*. New York: Doubleday. (Cit. on pp. 28, 32, 66, 74, 311).

Strobel, Daehyun (July 13, 2007). *IMSI Catcher*. Unpublished seminar paper. http://www.emsec.rub.de/media/crypto/attachments/files/2011/04/imsi_catcher.pdf (cit. on p. 180).

Stross, Charles (2004). *The Atrocity Archives*. Urbana, IL: Golden Gryphon Press. (Cit. on pp. 181, 267, 279, 379, 380).

——— (2006). *The Jennifer Morgue*. Urbana, IL: Golden Gryphon Press. (Cit. on pp. 92, 229, 379, 380).

——— (2012). *The Apocalypse Codex*. New York: Ace Books. (Cit. on pp. 61, 178, 379).

——— (2015). *The Annihilation Score*. New York: Ace Books. (Cit. on pp. 71, 379).

Stross, Randall (Dec. 8, 2012). "Billion-Dollar Flop: Air Force Stumbles on Software Plan." In: *The New York Times*. https://www.nytimes.com/2012/12/09/technology/air-force-stumbles-over-software-modernization-project.html (cit. on p. 315).

Stubblefield, Adam, John Ioannidis, and Aviel D. Rubin (Feb. 2002). "Using the Fluhrer, Mantin, and Shamir Attack to Break WEP." In: *Proceedings of the 2002 Network and Distributed Systems Security Symposium*. San Diego, CA, pp. 17–22. http://www.isoc.org/isoc/conferences/ndss/02/papers/stubbl.pdf (cit. on pp. 175, 177).

——— (May 2004). "A Key Recovery Attack on the 802.11b Wired Equivalent Privacy Protocol (WEP)." In: *ACM Transactions on Information and System Security*. http://avirubin.com/wep.pdf (cit. on p. 175).

Sullivan, Bob (June 9, 2005). "Israel Espionage Case Points to New Net Threat." In: *MSNBC*. http://www.msnbc.msn.com/id/8145520/ns/technology_and_science-security/t/israel-espionage-case-points-new-net-threat/ (cit. on pp. 18, 41).

Tao, Ping, Algis Rudys, Andrew Ladd, and Dan S. Wallach (Sept. 2003). "Wireless LAN Location Sensing for Security Applications." In: *ACM Workshop on Wireless Security (WiSe 2003)*. San Diego, CA. http://www.cs.rice.edu/~dwallach/pub/wise2003.html (cit. on p. 175).

Tatlow, Didi Kirsten (June 26, 2013). "U.S. Is a 'Hacker Empire,' Says Chinese Military Analyst." In: *I.H.T Rendezvous (blog)*. http://rendezvous.blogs.nytimes.com/2013/06/26/u-s-is-a-hacker-empire-says-chinese-military-analyst/ (cit. on p. 18).

Taylor, T., D. Paterson, J. Glanfield, C. Gates, S. Brooks, and J. McHugh (Mar. 2009). "FloVis: Flow Visualization System." In: *Cybersecurity Applications and Technology Conference for Homeland Security (CATCH)*, pp. 186–198. DOI: 10.1109/CATCH.2009.18. (Cit. on p. 52).

Thornburgh, Nathan (Aug. 25, 2005). "Inside the Chinese Hack Attack." In: *Time*. http://www.time.com/time/nation/article/0,8599,1098371,00.html (cit. on p. 28).

Timberg, Craig (Sept. 6, 2013). "Google Encrypts Data Amid Backlash against NSA Spying." In: *The Washington Post*. http://www.washingtonpost.com/business/technology/google-encrypts-data-amid-backlash-against-nsa-spying/2013/09/06/9acc3c20-1722-11e3-a2ec-b47e45e6f8ef_story.html (cit. on p. 220).

Tolkien, J. R. R. (1954). *The Lord of the Rings*. London: Allen & Unwin. (Cit. on p. 261).

Townsley, W., A. Valencia, A. Rubens, G. Pall, G. Zorn, and B. Palter (Aug. 1999). *Layer Two Tunneling Protocol "L2TP"*. RFC 2661. http://www.rfc-editor.org/rfc/rfc2661.txt (cit. on p. 95).

Toxen, Bob (May 2014). "The NSA and Snowden: Securing the All-seeing Eye." In: *Commun. ACM* 57.5, pp. 44–51. ISSN: 0001-0782. DOI: 10.1145/2594502. http://doi.acm.org/10.1145/2594502 (cit. on p. 286).

Trimmer, John D. (Oct. 10, 1980). "The Present Situation in Quantum Mechanics: A Translation of Schrödinger's 'Cat Paradox' Paper." In: *Proceedings of the American Philosophical Society* 124.5, pp. 323–338. http://www.jstor.org/stable/pdfplus/986572.pdf (cit. on pp. 189, 241).

UPI (June 4, 2012). "Unit 8200 and Israel's High-Tech Whiz Kids." In: *UPI.com*. http://www.upi.com/Business_News/Security-Industry/2012/06/04/Unit-8200-and-Israels-high-tech-whiz-kids/UPI-43661338833765/ (cit. on p. 18).

Valdes, Alfonso and Keith Skinner (2001). "Probabilistic Alert Correlation." In: *Proceedings of the 4th International Conference on Recent Advances in Intrusion Detection*. Berlin, Heidelberg: Springer. http://www.cc.gatech.edu/~wenke/ids-readings/Valdes_Alert_Correlation.pdf (cit. on p. 50).

Valentino-DeVries, Jennifer (Sept. 21, 2011). "'Stingray' Phone Tracker Fuels Constitutional Clash." In: *The Wall Street Journal*. http://online.wsj.com/article/SB10001424053111904194604576583112723197574.html. (Cit. on p. 180).

Valentino-DeVries, Jennifer and Jeremy Singer-Vine (Dec. 7, 2012). "They Know What You're Shopping For." In: *The Wall Street Journal*. http://www.wsj.com/articles/SB10001424127887324784404578143144132736214 (cit. on p. 314).

Vanhoef, Mathy and Frank Piessens (Aug. 2015). "All Your Biases Belong to Us: Breaking RC4 in WPA-TKIP and TLS." In: *24th USENIX Security Symposium (USENIX Security 15)*. Washington, DC: USENIX Association. https://www.usenix.org/conference/usenixsecurity15/technical-sessions/presentation/vanhoef (cit. on pp. 100, 176, 299, 300).

Verini, James (Nov. 10, 2010). "The Great Cyberheist." In: *The New York Times Magazine*. http://www.nytimes.com/2010/11/14/magazine/14Hacker-t.html (cit. on p. 33).

Vervier, Pierre-Antoine, Olivier Thonnard, and Marc Dacier (Feb. 2015). "Mind Your Blocks: On the Stealthiness of Malicious BGP Hijacks." In: *Proceedings of NDSS '15*. http://www.internetsociety.org/doc/mind-your-blocks-stealthiness-malicious-bgp-hijacks (cit. on p. 215).

Visa (2008). *Card Acceptance and Chargeback Management Guidelines for Visa Merchants.* http://www.uaf.edu/business/forms/cardacceptanceguide.pdf (cit. on p. 252).

Vixie, P. (Aug. 1999). *Extension Mechanisms for DNS (EDNS0).* RFC 2671. http://www.rfc-editor.org/rfc/rfc2671.txt (cit. on p. 91).

Volz, Dustin (July 14, 2015). "How Much Damage Can Hackers Do with a Million Fingerprints from the OPM Data Breach?" In: *Government Executive.* http://www.govexec.com/pay-benefits/2015/07/how-much-damage-can-hackers-do-million-fingerprints-opm-data-breach/117760/ (cit. on p. 127).

Wagner, David and Bruce Schneier (Nov. 1996). "Analysis of the SSL 3.0 Protocol." In: *Proceedings of the Second USENIX Workshop on Electronic Commerce*, pp. 29–40. http://www.cs.berkeley.edu/~daw/papers/ssl3.0.ps (cit. on p. 82).

Wallach, Dan S. (Oct. 2011). Private communication. (Cit. on p. 175).

Wang, Helen J., Chris Grier, Alex Moshchuk, Samuel T. King, Piali Choudhury, and Herman Venter (2009). "The Multi-Principal OS Construction of the Gazelle Web Browser." In: *Proc. USENIX Security Symposium.* http://static.usenix.org/events/sec09/tech/full_papers/wang.pdf (cit. on p. 201).

Wang, Xiaoyun, Dengguo Feng, Xuejia Lai, and Hongbo Yu (2004). *Collisions for Hash Functions MD4, MD5, HAVAL-128 and RIPEMD.* Cryptology ePrint Archive, Report 2004/199. http://eprint.iacr.org/2004/199 (cit. on p. 161).

Ward, Mark (Oct. 31, 2005). "Warcraft Game Maker in Spying Row." In: *BBC News.* http://news.bbc.co.uk/2/hi/technology/4385050.stm (cit. on p. 283).

Weil, Nancy (Apr. 8, 1999). "Some Aptivas Shipped with CIH Virus." In: *CNN.* http://articles.cnn.com/1999-04-08/tech/9904_08_aptivirus.idg_1_aptiva-pcs-cih-ibm-representatives (cit. on p. 53).

Weinrib, A. and J. Postel (Oct. 1996). *IRTF Research Group Guidelines and Procedures.* RFC 2014. http://www.rfc-editor.org/rfc/rfc2014.txt (cit. on p. 104).

Weir, Matt, Sudhir Aggarwal, Michael Collins, and Henry Stern (2010). "Testing Metrics for Password Creation Policies by Attacking Large Sets of Revealed Passwords." In: *Proceedings of the 17th ACM Conference on Computer and Communications Security.* CCS '10. Chicago: ACM, pp. 162–175. ISBN: 978-1-4503-0245-6. http://doi.acm.org/10.1145/1866307.1866327 (cit. on p. 108).

Weiss, Debra Cassens (Oct. 20, 2010). "Chief Justice Roberts Admits He Doesn't Read the Computer Fine Print." In: *ABA Journal.* http://www.abajournal.com/news/article/chief_justice_roberts_admits_he_doesnt_read_the_computer_fine_print/ (cit. on pp. 173, 232).

White House (Apr. 15, 2011). *National Strategy for Trusted Identities in Cyberspace.* http://www.whitehouse.gov/sites/default/files/rss_viewer/NSTICstrategy_041511.pdf (cit. on p. 139).

Whitney, Lance (Feb. 28, 2013). "China Blames U.S. for Most Cyberattacks against Military Web Sites." In: *CNET News.* http://news.cnet.com/8301-1009_3-57571811-83/china-blames-u.s-for-most-cyberattacks-against-military-web-sites/ (cit. on p. 18).

Whittaker, Zack (Aug. 5, 2015). "Hackers Can Remotely Steal Fingerprints from Android Phones." In: *ZDnet.* http://www.zdnet.com/article/hackers-can-remotely-steal-fingerprints-from-android-phones/ (cit. on p. 125).

Whitten, Alma and J.D. Tygar (1999). "Why Johnny Can't Encrypt: A Usability Evaluation of PGP 5.0." In: *Proceedings of Usenix Security Symposium.* http://db.usenix.org/publications/library/proceedings/sec99/whitten.html (cit. on p. 105).

Williams, Christopher (July 1, 2010). "Two Infosec Blunders that Betrayed the Russian Spy Ring." In: *The Register.* http://www.theregister.co.uk/2010/07/01/spy_ring_blunders/ (cit. on pp. 115, 175).

——— (Feb. 16, 2011). "Israeli Security Chief Celebrates Stuxnet Cyber Attack." In: *The Telegraph.* http://www.telegraph.co.uk/technology/news/8326274/Israeli-security-chief-celebrates-Stuxnet-cyber-attack.html (cit. on p. 37).

Willis, Connie (1997). *To Say Nothing of the Dog.* New York: Bantam Books. (Cit. on p. 293).

Wilson, Charles, R. Austin Hicklin, Harold Korves, Bradford Ulery, Melissa Zoepfl, Mike Bone, Patrick Grother, Ross Micheals, Steve Otto, and Craig Watson (June 2004). *Fingerprint Vendor Technology Evaluation 2003: Summary of Results and Analysis Report.* Tech. rep. 7123. National Institute of Standards and Technology. http://www.nist.gov/itl/iad/ig/fpvte03.cfm (cit. on p. 125).

Wise, David (2002). *Spy: The Inside Story of How the FBI's Robert Hanssen Betrayed America.* Random House. (Cit. on p. 35).

Wondracek, Gilbert, Thorsten Holz, Christian Platzer, Engin Kirda, and Christopher Kruegel (2010). "Is the Internet for Porn? An Insight into the Online Adult Industry." In: *Proceedings of the Workshop on the Economics of the Information Society.* http://iseclab.org/papers/weis2010.pdf (cit. on pp. 93, 254, 272, 283).

Wood, Paul, ed. (Apr. 2012). *Internet Security Threat Report: 2011 Trends.* Vol. 17. Mountain View, CA: Symantec. http://www.symantec.com/content/en/us/enterprise/other_resources/b-istr_main_report_2011_21239364.en-us.pdf (cit. on p. 272).

Wood, Roy (Oct. 5, 2012). "Self-Driving Cars." In: *Wired: Geek Dad.* http://archive.wired.com/geekdad/2012/10/self-driving-cars/ (cit. on p. 312).

Wright, Peter (1987). *Spycatcher: The Candid Autobiography of a Senior Intelligence Officer.* New York: Viking. (Cit. on p. 82).

Wulf, William A. and Anita K. Jones (2009). "Reflections on Cybersecurity." In: *Science* 326.5955, pp. 943–944. DOI: 10.1126/science.1181643. http://www.sciencemag.org/cgi/reprint/326/5955/943.pdf (cit. on pp. 78, 312).

Wuokko, D.R. (Apr. 2, 2003). *Worm Virus Infection.* Email to Nuclear Regulatory Commission. http://pbadupws.nrc.gov/docs/ML0310/ML031040567.pdf (cit. on p. 54).

Wylie, Philip and Edwin Balmer (1934). *After Worlds Collide.* New York: Frederick A. Stokes Company. (Cit. on p. 315).

Yadron, Danny (Aug. 5, 2014). "Executives Rethink Merits of Going Public with Data Breaches." In: *The Wall Street Journal.* http://online.wsj.com/articles/a-contrarian-view-on-data-breaches-1407194237 (cit. on pp. 166, 287).

Ylönen, Tatu (July 1996). "SSH–Secure Login Connections over the Internet." In: *Proceedings of the Sixth Usenix Unix Security Symposium,* pp. 37–42. http://www.usenix.org/publications/library/proceedings/sec96/ylonen.html (cit. on p. 88).

Zetter, Kim (Sept. 18, 2008). "Palin E-Mail Hacker Says It Was Easy." In: *Wired: Threat Level.* http://www.wired.com/threatlevel/2008/09/palin-e-mail-ha/ (cit. on p. 123).

—— (Sept. 30, 2009a). "New Malware Re-Writes Online Bank Statements to Cover Fraud." In: *Wired: Threat Level*. http://www.wired.com/threatlevel/2009/09/rogue-bank-statements/ (cit. on p. 120).

—— (July 14, 2009b). "Researcher: Middle East Blackberry Update Spies on Users." In: *Wired: Threat Level*. http://www.wired.com/threatlevel/2009/07/blackberry-spies/ (cit. on p. 271).

—— (June 18, 2009c). "TJX Hacker Was Awash in Cash; His Penniless Coder Faces Prison." In: *Wired: Threat Level*. http://www.wired.com/threatlevel/2009/06/watt (cit. on p. 34).

—— (Nov. 12, 2010). "Sarah Palin E-mail Hacker Sentenced to 1 Year in Custody." In: *Wired: Threat Level*. http://www.wired.com/threatlevel/2010/11/palin-hacker-sentenced/ (cit. on p. xiii).

—— (Dec. 18, 2011). "Forensic Expert: Manning's Computer Had 10K Cables, Downloading Scripts." In: *Wired: Threat Level*. http://www.wired.com/threatlevel/2011/12/cables-scripts-manning/ (cit. on p. 73).

—— (May 28, 2012). "Meet 'Flame,' The Massive Spy Malware Infiltrating Iranian Computers." In: *Wired: Threat Level*. http://www.wired.com/threatlevel/2012/05/flame/ (cit. on pp. 50, 83).

—— (2014). *Countdown to Zero Day: Stuxnet and the Launch of the World's First Digital Weapon*. New York: Crown Publishers. (Cit. on pp. 18, 20, 28, 37, 38, 50, 83, 84, 164, 194).

—— (July 9, 2015). "The Massive OPM Hack Actually Hit 21 Million People." In: *Wired*. http://www.wired.com/2015/07/massive-opm-hack-actually-affected-25-million/ (cit. on p. 254).

Zhang, Yinqian, Fabian Monrose, and Michael K. Reiter (2010). "The Security of Modern Password Expiration: An Algorithmic Framework and Empirical Analysis." In: *Proceedings of the 17th ACM Conference on Computer and Communications Security*. CCS '10. Chicago: ACM, pp. 176–186. ISBN: 978-1-4503-0245-6. DOI: http://doi.acm.org/10.1145/1866307.1866328. http://www.cs.unc.edu/~reiter/papers/2010/CCS.pdf (cit. on p. 114).

Zhao, Hang and Steven M. Bellovin (July 2009). *Source Prefix Filtering in ROFL*. Tech. rep. CUCS-033-09. Department of Computer Science, Columbia University. https://mice.cs.columbia.edu/getTechreport.php?techreportID=613 (cit. on p. 94).

Zhao, Hang, Chi-Kin Chau, and Steven M. Bellovin (Sept. 2008). "ROFL: Routing as the Firewall Layer." In: *New Security Paradigms Workshop*. A version is available as Technical Report CUCS-026-08. https://mice.cs.columbia.edu/getTechreport.php?techreportID=541 (cit. on p. 94).

Zimmermann, Philip (1995). *The Official PGP User's Guide*. Cambridge, MA: MIT Press. (Cit. on p. 167).

Ziobro, Paul and Joann S. Lublin (May 28, 2014). "ISS's View on Target Directors Is a Signal on Cybersecurity." In: *The Wall Street Journal*. http://online.wsj.com/articles/iss-calls-for-an-overhaul-of-target-board-after-data-breach-1401285278 (cit. on p. 287).

Ziobro, Paul and Danny Yadron (Jan. 2014). "Target Now Says 70 Million People Hit in Data Breach." In: *The Wall Street Journal*. http://online.wsj.com/news/articles/SB10001424052702303754404579312232546392464 (cit. on p. 287).

Zittrain, Jonathan, Kendra Albert, and Lawrence Lessig (June 12, 2014). "Perma: Scoping and addressing the problem of link and reference rot in legal citations." In: *Legal Information Man-*

agement 14.02, pp. 88–99. http://journals.cambridge.org/action/displayAbstract?fromPage=online&aid=9282809&fileId=S1472669614000255 (cit. on p. xv).

Zwienenberg, Righard (June 22, 2012). "ACAD/Medre.A—10000's of AutoCAD Files Leaked in Suspected Industrial Espionage." In: *ESET Threat Blog*. http://blog.eset.com/2012/06/21/acadmedre-10000s-of-autocad-files-leaked-in-suspected-industrial-espionage (cit. on p. 48).

Index

Credits

Page 12. Quotation. William Goldman (1987). *The Princess Bride*. Movie.

Page 24. Cartoon. Randall Munroe. *Xkcd*. https://xkcd.com/327/.

Page 56. Cartoon. Randall Munroe. *Xkcd*. https://xkcd.com/463/.

Page 61. Quotation. Charles Stross (2012). *The Apocalypse Codex*. New York: Ace Books.

Page 71. Quotation. Charles Stross (2015). *The Annihilation Score*. New York: Ace Books.

Page 92. Quotation. Charles Stross (2006). *The Jennifer Morgue*. Urbana, IL: Golden Gryphon Press.

Page 110. Cartoon. Randall Munroe. *Xkcd*. https://xkcd.com/936/.

Page 119. Cartoon. © Bizarro- © 2011 McNelly. Distributed by King Features Syndicate, Inc. World Rights Reserved. http://bizarro.com/comics/november-3-2011/.

Page 129. Photograph. Alexander Klink (2008). https://commons.wikimedia.org/wiki/File:RSA_SecurID_Token_Old.jpg. Used under a Creative Commons Attribution Unported license.

Page 136. Photograph. Erastus Dow Palmer (American, Pompey, New York 1817–1904. Albany, New York), *Indian Girl, or The Dawn of Christianity* 1853–56; carved 1855–56, Marble 60 x 19 3/4 x 22 1/4 in. (152.4 x 50.2 x 56.5 cm). The Metropolitan Museum of Art, Bequest of Hamilton Fish, 1894 (94.9.2)/The Metropolitan Museum of Art/Art Resource, NY. http://www.metmuseum.org/toah/works-of-art/94.9.2.

Page 176. Cartoon. Bill Holbrook (2005). *Kevin and Kell*. http://www.kevinandkell.com/2005/kk0611.html

Page 178. Quotation. Charles Stross (2012). *The Apocalypse Codex*. New York: Ace Books.

Page 180. Quotation. Charles Stross (2004). *The Atrocity Archives*. Urbana, IL: Golden Gryphon Press.

Page 205. Quotation. Arthur C. Clarke (1953). *Childhood's End*. New York: Ballantine Books. Reprinted by permission of the author's estate and the author's agents Scovil Galen Ghosh Literary Agency, Inc.

Page 192. Section 10.4. Derived from Steven M. Bellovin (May–June 2011a). "Clouds from Both Sides." In: *IEEE Security & Privacy* 9.3. ISSN: 1540-7993. http://dx.doi.org/10.1109/MSP.2011.48, © IEEE.

Page 229. Quotation. Charles Stross (2006). *The Jennifer Morgue*. Urbana, IL: Golden Gryphon Press.

Page 267. Quotation. Charles Stross (2004). *The Atrocity Archives*. Urbana, IL: Golden Gryphon Press.

Page 268. Cartoon. Randall Munroe. *Xkcd*. https://xkcd.com/705/

Page 273. Diagram. Bruno Oliveira (2012). Google+ post. https://plus.google.com/102451193315916178828/posts/MGxauXypb1Y

Page 279. Quotation. Charles Stross (2004). *The Atrocity Archives*. Urbana, IL: Golden Gryphon Press.

Colophon

This book was typeset by the author using LaTeX, many packages from *Comprehensive TeX Archive Network (CTAN)*, and a host of custom macros and environments.

The cover picture, taken on Barrientos Island, is called "Penguin Insecurity." The Gentoo penguin on the right is trying to steal a pebble from the other penguin's nest. (The PBS show *Nature* noted in the episode "Penguin Post Office" that "all penguins have criminal tendencies.")

(Penguin photos by the author.)